1985 COOKBOC

Mrs. Wayne (Linda) Za

Mrs. Fernand (Joan) Falg

Mrs. Hardee (Betty Jo) Brian, *2nd Vice-Chairman*

Mrs. Richard (Kathleen) Watkins, *3rd Vice-Chairman*

Mrs. Eugene (Edwina) Harper, *Secretary-Treasurer*

1990 COOKBOOK COMMITTEE

Mrs. Wayne (Linda) Zaunbrecher, *Chairman*

Mrs. Fernand (Joan) Falgoust, *1st Vice-Chairman*

Mrs. Hardee (Betty Jo) Brian, *2nd Vice-Chairman*

Mrs. Ronald (Cheryl) Gonsoulin, *3rd Vice-Chairman*

Mrs. Eugene (Edwina) Harper, *Secretary-Treasurer*

1992 COOKBOOK COMMITTEE

Mrs. Hardee (Betty Jo) Brian, *Chairman*

Mrs. Fernand (Joan) Falgoust, *1st Vice-Chairman*

Miss Cindy Moore, *2nd Vice-Chairman*

Mrs. Glen (Mindy) Hetzel, *3rd Vice-Chairman*

Mrs. Evelyn Bieber, *Secretary-Treasurer*

1995 COOKBOOK COMMITTEE

Mrs. Glen (Mindy) Hetzel, *Chairman*

Mrs. Evelyn Bieber, *1st Vice-Chairman*

Miss Cindy Moore, *2nd Vice-Chairman*

Mrs. George (Denise) Hymel, *3rd Vice-Chairman*

Mrs. Daniel (Genevieve) Lyons, *Secretary-Treasurer*

FOREWORD

The common denominator of homes everywhere is the preparation of food. Some of our most prized possessions are the old tried-and-true recipes handed down from generation to generation.

In the fast pace of today, we believe the home is still the foundation of our society, and we believe it is our responsibility to create memories for our children. Often the only time for a busy family to be together is at the evening meal. Some of our fondest recollections are those of the family enjoying food and conversation around a bountifully laden table.

This is what we want *Food à la Louisiane* to reflect—love for our families, pride in our homes, and the fun and enjoyment of entertaining friends.

The contents of this book are the mealtime experiences of not only the families of our members, but also our special friends. To both we are truly grateful. The recipes are not all originals, but they do represent family favorites.

We are proud to offer you a collection of our best memories in *Foods à la Louisiane.*

Farm Bureau is a free, independent, nongovernmental, voluntary organization of farm and ranch families united for the purpose of analyzing their problems and formulating action to achieve educational improvement, economic opportunity, and social advancement, thereby promoting the growth of our country and the quality of our national life.

The Louisiana Farm Bureau is the largest farm organization in the state. Its specific aims include:

1. The furtherance of democratic processes of home rule and individual freedom and rights.

2. The provision of a two-way channel for the promotion of broader understanding of political, economic, and specifically, agricultural issues and techniques.

3. The attainment of higher net income for the farmer and the general improvement of his standard of living.

4. The enlargement of opportunity for youth.

5. The provision of opportunity for the development of farm and civic leadership.

Louisiana cooking, like all regional cuisine, is a reflection of the variety of predisposed opinion expressed in lifestyle. The South Louisiana Cajun's *joie de vivre* sets wine on his midday table alongside the Tabasco; and until recently, each Friday the outline of a fish bespoke his somber side. North of Alexandria and north of "the Lake" as well, the Sunday dinner best epitomized the Protestant's culinary expertise: chicken and dumplings was almost *de rigueur*, but the desserts ranged to three and four — pecan pie, chess pie, a white layer cake with perhaps a caramel icing, banana pudding — and on Thanksgiving and at Christmas, ambrosia. From Shreveport to Monroe to Lake

Providence down into Tensas Parish and across into the Felicianas, ambrosia left its aftertaste of 'tis the season. And an orange in the Christmas stocking, north or south, meant an orange *was* in season.

"In season," "out of season." In a day when our supermarkets bulge with vegetables and fruits practically year-round, we forget how much those two phrases once defined the limits of regional cuisine. To our forebears what was "fresh" was very fresh . . . or unobtainable. Such limitation did not defeat them; rather, it inspired a culinary inventiveness. Indeed, Creole and Cajun cooking as it has come down to us exists because of the limitations climate and terrain imposed upon the harvest. It is a cuisine rooted in ingenious substitution, in "making do." That spirit of thrift and of savoring what did appear in brief abundance, harvest by harvest, is surprisingly apparent in both the recipes of the Protestant north and the Catholic south, reminding us that Louisianians of an earlier day experienced the qualm of scarcity, too, and by resourcefulness mastered much of it. By hand. "From scratch." Without a quibble.

Louisiana cooking state-wide as expressed in these recipes tells us what we have been and if we wish, can remain. In the contrast of two diverse cultures, north and south, are hidden strengths of character whose recognition can delight. The North Louisianian is not less dismayed by how to peel a crawfish than is his South Louisiana cousin when confronted by a pickled peach. Dismay, but then delight. We teach each other. In that tolerance which comes from the commingling of the Protestant and Catholic cultures *in the kitchen* is a lesson for other lands—a small one perhaps, but one not to be dismissed. The courtesy which can lead one from dismay into delight has always been indicative of American good will. Giving out a recipe's a courtesy. Remember that when you try these.

Our thanks to
David Williams
Donaldsonville

Special Thanks To:
Mrs. Cody Ray
Louisiana Tourist Development Commission
Greater New Orleans Tourist and Convention Commission

TABLE OF CONTENTS

A Little
Something Extra

Louisiana State Flag

ACADIAN DYED EGGS

Eggs
Egg piercer or needle
Clover or small fern leaves

Stockings
Dry brown outer skin of onions
Cold water

Gently punch a tiny hole in large end of eggs; let eggs drain. Dampen egg shells with water, and press clover or fern leaves face down on shell. Cut stockings in pieces large enough to cover eggs. While holding leaves in place, stretch and wrap a stocking piece around each egg; twist lightly and tie securely with a thread or string.

Place eggs and onion skins in cold water in a large pan; gradually heat to boiling. Reduce to low heat and simmer 30 minutes. Remove eggs; let cool.

Cut stocking from eggs; remove leaves. Eggs will be rosy brown with a pattern of clover or fern leaves.

Louisiana Farm Bureau Women's Committee

BORDELAISE-CHICKEN

2 to 3 pounds chicken
Salt and pepper
½ cup margarine
6 toes garlic, peeled and
   minced

1 cup water
½ cup chopped fresh parsley
2½ pounds potatoes, peeled
Vegetable oil

Cut chicken into pieces; sprinkle with salt and pepper, as desired.

Melt margarine over low heat in a 10-inch skillet; add garlic, and sauté until tender. Add chicken pieces to skillet; cook over medium heat until browned. Add water and parsley to skillet. Cover and reduce heat; simmer 20 minutes or until chicken is tender, stirring frequently.

Cut potatoes as desired for French fries. Deep fry potatoes in hot vegetable oil (375°) until done. Drain on absorbent paper towels.

Place French fries on serving platter; top with chicken pieces. Spoon pan drippings over chicken. Yield: 6 to 8 servings.

Note: For convenience, use 1 (2.5 pound) package frozen French fries instead of potatoes.

Mrs. Grace Graugnard
St. James Parish (St. James)

BOUDIN

1 large hoghead
2 pounds mixed variety meats
(hearts, kidneys, etc.)
3 medium onions, quartered
2 cups chopped green onion
tops

20 sprigs fresh parsley
3 pounds lean pork
2 pounds pork liver
2 gallons cooked rice
Salt and pepper to taste

Boil hog's head until tender; let cool. Remove meat from bones. Grind hoghead meat, heart, kidney, onions, and parsley in a meat grinder. Combine all ingredients, adding salt and pepper, as desired; mix well. Stuff meat mixture into sausage casing. Boil for 5 minutes or until meat is done.

Mrs. George Elliot
Vermilion Parish (Gueydan)

STUFFED CHAUDIN

Water
Soda
Vinegar
1 medium-size chaudin (hog's
stomach)
4 pounds ground pork

1 medium onion, chopped
½ cup chopped green onion
4 sprigs fresh parsley
3 cloves garlic, minced
Salt and pepper
1 cup vegetable oil

Combine water, soda, and vinegar in a large bowl to make a solution; set aside.

Remove fat from chaudin; soak in soda solution for 1 hour. Remove from solution, and scrape outer surface well with a knife. Rinse chaudin in water and vinegar until thoroughly cleaned of all debris; pat dry with absorbent paper then set aside.

Combine ground pork, onion, parsley, and garlic in a large bowl; add salt and pepper as desired. Using a spoon, stuff meat mixture into chaudin. Close cavity, secure with toothpicks; truss.

Heat oil in a large Dutch oven; add chaudin and cook until well browned on all sides. Once browned, remove chaudin from pan; discard all but 2 tablespoons vegetable oil. Return chaudin to pan; add enough water to cover. Bring to a boil; reduce heat and let simmer until chaudin is tender and water boils down to form a gravy. Slice chaudin, and serve warm with gravy.

Note: In some areas of Louisiana the Chaudin is called Ponce.

Mrs. George Elliot
Vermilion Parish (Gueydan)

CHERRY BOUNCE

2 quarts wild cherries, cleaned
    and stemmed
Bourbon

2 cups sugar
2 cups water

Place cherries in a gallon jar with a tight-fitting lid; add enough bourbon to cover cherries. Cover jar loosely; let stand 1 month at room temperature.

Combine sugar and water in a large saucepan; bring to a boil. Boil 5 minutes to form a syrup. Remove from heat; let cool.

Strain cherries, reserving juice. Combine 1 cup cherry juice and ¾ cup cooled syrup; store in a liqueur decanter or a covered jar for 6 to 8 weeks before serving. Yield: about 1 pint.

Mrs. Eddie Schexnaydre (Doris)
Terrebonne Parish (Shriever)

CAJUN COFFEE

For each cup coffee:
1 cup water

2 tablespoons ground dark roast
    coffee

Boil water; drip water through coffee in top of a French drip coffee pot, 1 tablespoon at a time, until all water has been used. To reheat coffee, place pot in a pan of boiling water, never over direct heat. Yield: one cup.

Note: True Cajun coffee must be made in a French drip coffee pot. This pot must be kept hot while water is dripping through by placing it in a pan of boiling water.

Louisiana Farm Bureau Women's Committee

CAFE AU LAIT (COFFEE WITH HOT MILK)

Freshly brewed dark strong
    coffee

Milk

Heat coffee and milk in separate pots until hot; pour equal amounts of coffee and milk into each coffee cup. Serve with sugar, if desired.

Note: Equal amounts of coffee and milk may be heated together in a pot until hot, then served with just one pouring.

Louisiana Farm Bureau Women's Committee

CREOLE PRALINES

2 cups sugar
1 cup firmly packed brown
  sugar
½ cup butter

1 cup milk
2 tablespoons corn syrup
4 cups pecan halves

Combine first 5 ingredients in a 3-quart saucepan; bring to a boil; cook, stirring constantly, until mixture reaches 225 degrees or about 20 minutes after boiling starts. Add pecans; cook, stirring constantly, until mixture reaches soft ball stage (236°). Remove from heat; beat well, and drop by tablespoonfuls onto waxed paper. Let stand until firm. Store in an airtight container. Yield: about 18.

Mrs. James Parkerson (Joyce)
Ouachita Parish (Monroe)

COOSH-COOSH

2 cups corn meal (yellow or
  white)
1½ teaspoons salt

1½ cups water
1 tablespoon bacon grease
  or butter

Combine corn meal and salt in a medium bowl. Sprinkle 1 cup water over meal, and mix lightly with a fork.

Melt grease or butter over low heat in a heavy cast iron pot. When grease is hot, add corn meal mixture and cover. Cook over low heat, stirring frequently, for 15 minutes.

Sprinkle remaining ½ cup water over corn meal mixture in skillet to dampen. Cover; cook over low heat, stirring frequently for 15 to 30 minutes or until thickened, but moist.

Serve corn meal mixture as a cereal, or top each serving with pure cane syrup, and serve with milk. Yield: 2 servings.

Mrs. Robella Langlinais
Vermilion Parish (Erath)

COOSH-COOSH A LA MICROWAVE

3 cups corn meal
1½ teaspoons salt

1⅔ cups water
2 tablespoons vegetable oil

Combine corn meal, salt, water, and oil in a 2-quart round glass casserole. Cover; microwave on HIGH for 5 minutes. Stir well, then microwave, covered, on HIGH for 6 minutes. Stir well.

Serve Coosh-Coosh with milk as cereal, or topped with syrup. Yield: 3 to 4 servings.

Note: Sugar may be added, if desired.

Mrs. Larry Langlinais (Anna)
Vermilion Parish (Erath)

COURTBOUILLON (KOO-BEE-YON)

3 stalks celery, chopped
1 large bunch green onions, chopped
1 bunch fresh parsley, washed, drained and chopped
1 large green pepper, chopped
2 cloves garlic, minced
5 pounds fresh Blue catfish
Salt
Pepper

Red pepper
3 tablespoons vegetable oil
2 tablespoons all-purpose flour, divided
1½ cups tomato sauce, divided
¼ cup water
2 lemon slices
1 large bay leaf
¼ teaspoon whole thyme leaves

Combine vegetables; divide in half, and set aside.

Cut fish into large pieces; generously sprinkle each piece with salt, pepper, and crushed red pepper. Set aside.

Put oil in a large cast iron pot; top with half of fish pieces. Place half of vegetable mixture over fish; top with 1 tablespoon flour, then ¾ cup tomato sauce. Repeat layers with remaining fish pieces, vegetables, flour, and tomato sauce. Add remaining ingredients.

Cover and cook over low heat for 1 hour or until fish flakes easily when tested with a fork. Shake pot frequently to keep fish from sticking to the bottom (stirring will break up the fish). Add additional seasonings before serving, if desired. Yield: 6 servings.

Mrs. Charlotte Castille
Lafayette Parish (Lafayette)

CORN SOUP WITH SHRIMP

½ cup vegetable oil
1 cup all-purpose flour
1 large onion, chopped
1 stalk celery, chopped
½ green pepper, chopped
1 clove garlic, minced
1 gallon hot water
1 16-ounce can whole
  tomatoes, undrained
1 8-ounce can tomato sauce

1 24-ounce package frozen whole
  kernel corn
1 16-ounce can cream-style corn
1 tablespoon salt
½ teaspoon pepper
¼ teaspoon red pepper
2 pounds raw shrimp, peeled and
  deveined
6 sprigs fresh parsley

Combine oil and flour in a heavy pot over medium heat; cook, stirring constantly, until roux is the color of a copper penny (about 20 to 30 minutes). Add onion, celery, green pepper, and garlic to roux; cook, stirring constantly until vegetables are tender.

Gradually add hot water to roux, in small amounts first, blending well after each addition; add tomatoes, tomato sauce, corn, and seasonings. Bring to a boil. Reduce heat; simmer, stirring occasionally, for 1 hour.

Add shrimp and parsley to soup. Bring to a boil; simmer 10 minutes. Serve soup with corn bread or hot buttered French bread. Yield: 12 servings.

Mrs. Fernand Falgoust (Joan)
St. James Parish (St. James)

CREOLE SHRIMP SAUCE

2 teaspoons creole mustard
½ cup vegetable oil
1 cup tarragon-flavored vinegar
2 teaspoons commercial
  horseradish
1 teaspoon ground mace

½ teaspoon sugar
½ teaspoon salt
¼ teaspoon celery salt
⅛ teaspoon paprika
¼ teaspoon pepper
6 small shallots, chopped

Place mustard in a small mixing bowl; gradually add oil, beating constantly with a fork after each addition until oil is blended. Add vinegar, ½ teaspoon at a time, beating constantly until blended. Add remaining ingredients, except shallots, blending well. Put sauce in a jar with a tight-fitting lid; chill. Add shallots just before serving with cooked shrimp. Keeps well for 1 week. Yield: 1½ cups.

Charlotte Castille
Lafayette Parish (Lafayette)

13

SAUCE PIQUANTE-BASIC RECIPE

½ cup roux
2 large onions, chopped
2 green peppers, chopped
4 stalks celery, chopped
2 cloves garlic, minced
3 8-ounce cans tomato sauce

2 cups water
Salt to taste
Louisiana hot sauce to taste
Fresh shrimp, poultry, or beef
2 tablespoons vegetable oil
Hot cooked rice

Combine roux, onion, peppers, celery, and garlic in a heavy Dutch oven; sauté until tender. Add tomato sauce, water, salt, and hot sauce; heat to boiling. Reduce heat and simmer 1 hour, stirring frequently. Add more water, if necessary to prevent sticking.

Brown seafood or meat in oil; add to sauce mixture. Simmer 20 minutes longer if seafood was added (simmer 45 minutes if poultry or beef was used). Water may be added if sauce is too thick. Serve sauce over hot cooked rice. Yield: about 1 quart.

Louisiana Farm Bureau Women's Committee

CREOLE HOT PEPPER SAUCE

5 quarts vinegar
5 quarts hot red peppers,
   washed
3 pounds onion, peeled and
   quartered
3 whole garlic buds, peeled and
   chopped

½ cup sugar
½ cup salt
2 tablespoons pepper
1½ tablespoons lemon juice
   (optional)

Combine 4 quarts vinegar, peppers, onions, and garlic in a large Dutch oven; bring to a boil. Cook over low heat until vegetables are tender, about 1 hour. Drain vegetables, reserving liquid. Place vegetables in blender; blend until chopped. Press vegetables through a rice strainer and discard seeds.

Combine puréed vegetables, reserved vegetable liquid, and remaining ingredients in a large Dutch oven. Cook until thickened over medium heat. Let mixture simmer 30 minutes.

Quickly pour into sterilized jars, leaving ⅛-inch headspace. Cover at once with metal lids and screw metal band tight. Process in boiling water bath for 10 minutes.

Mrs. Floyd Zaunbrecher
Vermilion Parish (Gueydan)

CRAWFISH DIP

½ cup butter
1 large onion, ground
3 jalapeño peppers, seeded and ground
1 small green pepper, seeded and ground
2 pounds raw crawfish, peeled and ground

3 10¾-ounce cans cream of mushroom soup, undiluted
Salt
Pepper
Garlic powder
Red pepper
Chopped parsley (optional)

Melt butter over low heat in a 10-inch skillet; add onion and peppers. Sauté vegetables until tender, about 5 minutes. Add ground crawfish; cook 7 minutes over low heat, stirring frequently. Stir in mushroom soup; add seasonings, as desired. Remove from heat; garnish with parsley, if desired. Serve warm with buttery round crackers. Yield: 36 servings.

Note: Ground crabmeat or shrimp may be substituted for crawfish, if desired.

Mrs. Happy Broussard (Alice)
Iberia Parish (New Iberia)

JAMBALAYA-BASIC RECIPE

½ cup vegetable oil or drippings
2 medium onions, chopped
2 stalks celery, chopped
1 cup fresh parsley, chopped
1 medium green pepper, seeded and chopped
½ cup chopped green onion tops
Water

2½ teaspoons salt
1 teaspoon garlic powder
Red pepper to taste
Pepper to taste
Browning agent or 2 teaspoons Kitchen Bouquet
2 pounds peeled raw shrimp
4 cups uncooked long grain rice

Heat oil over low heat in a heavy 6-quart Dutch oven until warmed. Add vegetables; sauté until lightly browned. Add enough water to cover vegetables; add seasonings and browning agent. Bring to a boil; add shrimp. Cook over medium heat for 10 minutes. Stir in rice; cook 10 minutes. Cover and cook until rice is tender, stirring occasionally. Yield: 10 to 12 servings.

BROWNING AGENT:
1 tablespoon sugar

1 cup cold water

Brown sugar in a heavy saucepan over low heat, stirring constantly. Remove from heat; slowly add water, stirring until sugar is dissolved. Yield: 1 cup.

Louisiana Farm Bureau Women's Committee

GRILLADES

½ cup vegetable oil
4 stalks celery, finely chopped
2 large onions, finely chopped
2 thin beef slices or veal
  rounds, cut into strips
3 cups water
2 cups fresh or canned
  mushrooms, sliced

2 green peppers, seeded and cut
  into strips
½ cup finely chopped shallots
⅓ cup chopped fresh parsley
Salt to taste
Pepper to taste
Hot cooked rice

Heat oil in a heavy 10-inch skillet until warmed; add celery and onion, sautéing until tender (about 5 minutes). Add meat; cook until browned over medium heat.

Reduce heat and add 1 cup water; cook gently several minutes. Add remaining 2 cups water, mushrooms, green peppers, and shallots; cover. Cook over medium heat until meat is tender. Add parsley and seasonings to taste; cook 2 minutes longer. Serve warm over hot cooked rice. Yield: 3 to 4 servings.

Mrs. F. A. Graugnard, Jr. (Mary Ann)
West St. James Parish (St. James)

GUMBO (BASIC RECIPE)

1 cup roux
1 large onion, chopped
3 pounds poultry or fresh
  seafood
Water
Salt to taste

Pepper to taste
Red pepper to taste
2 tablespoons chopped green onion
  tops
1 tablespoon minced fresh parsley

Heat prepared roux over low heat in a large deep gumbo pot until warm. Add onion and meat to roux and sauté until onion is tender (3 to 5 minutes). Add enough water to cover 2 inches above meat; stir in salt, pepper and red pepper to taste. Bring to a boil; reduce heat and simmer 1 to 1½ hours, stirring frequently. Add chopped green onion and parsley; cook 10 minutes longer. Extra water may be added if gumbo cooks down too much before serving time. Yield: 12 servings.

Note: When poultry is used, let gumbo cook until it is tender. If using fresh seafood, cooking time is not as long.

Louisiana Farm Bureau Women's Committee

ROUX

¼ cup lard
¼ cup all-purpose flour

2 large onions, finely chopped
Fresh chopped parsley

Melt lard in a heavy cast iron pot over medium heat; add flour, stirring constantly. Cook over medium heat, stirring constantly, until roux is light brown. Add onions; cook until onions are brown, stirring constantly. Add parsley, as desired; stir well. Roux is done when it is the color of a copper penny. Yield: ½ cup.

Mrs. Eddie Schexnaydre (Doris)
Terrebonne Parish (Schriever)

BAKED ROUX

1 quart vegetable oil

2 quarts all-purpose flour

Combine oil and flour in a heavy pot; stir well. Bake at 400 degrees for 1½ to 2 hours, stirring every 15 minutes, until roux is the color of a copper penny. Remove from oven and let cool. Store roux in jars with tight-fitting lids in refrigerator. Yield: 3 quarts.

Louisiana Farm Bureau Women's Committee

FAT FREE ROUX

1 cup all-purpose flour

Method 1:
Place flour in a cast iron skillet. Bake at 400 degrees, stirring occasionally, until dark brown. Yield: 1 cup.

Method 2:
Place flour in a cast iron skillet; cook over medium heat, stirring constantly, until flour is dark brown. Yield: 1 cup.

Method 3:
Place flour in a glass casserole. Microwave on HIGH for 2 minutes; stir well. Repeat microwaving flour at 2 minute intervals, stirring well, until flour is dark brown. Yield: 1 cup.

Louisiana Farm Bureau Women's Committee

MICROWAVE ROUX

1 cup vegetable oil   1 cup all-purpose flour

Combine oil and flour in a 4-cup glass measuring cup; microwave on HIGH for 6 minutes. Stir well. Microwave on HIGH for 30 seconds to 1 minute or until roux is dark brown. Yield: 2 cups.

Louisiana Farm Bureau Women's Committee

FILÉ

Gather sassafras leaves in August (preferably during a full moon). Pick leaves off branches; put leaves in a clean pillow case, filling only half full. Hang pillow case outside to dry, but not in direct sunlight. Let dry until leaves are very brittle.

Grind leaves (only a dry day) with a meat grinder. Grind twice. Place ½ cup ground leaves in a sifter; tap lightly (do not sift) to form a powder. Discard all coarse sticks and branches. Repeat with remaining ground leaves. Work slowly-never rush tapping process. Store filé in clean jars with tight-fitting lids.

Mrs. Richard Watkins (Kathleen)
Jefferson Davis Parish (Iowa)

CREOLE SEASONING MIX

⅔ cup salt   1 tablespoon chili powder
2 tablespoons red pepper   2 teaspoons garlic powder

Combine all ingredients in a small bowl; store in an air-tight container. Use as seasoning for meats, poultry, and fish. Yield: about 1 cup.

Mrs. John R. Denison
Calsasieu Parish (Iowa)

COOKING RICE

METHOD I

3 quarts water
Salt
1 tablespoon vegetable oil

1 tablespoon vinegar
1 cup uncooked long grain rice

Bring salted water to a boil in a 4-quart saucepan; add oil and vinegar. Slowly add rice, stirring constantly. Heat to boiling; reduce heat and simmer 18 minutes. Drain rice in a colander and rinse with cold water. Place rice filled colander over boiling water and cover. Steam until rice is warm. (Rice may be kept warm this way for a while). Yield: 4 to 6 servings.

METHOD II

1½ cups water
1 teaspoon salt

½ teaspoon vegetable oil
1 cup uncooked long grain rice

Combine all ingredients in a 1-quart saucepan; heat to boiling, stirring occasionally. Reduce heat to low and cover. Cook 30 minutes or until all water is absorbed. Yield: 4 to 6 servings.

Louisiana Farm Bureau Women's Committee

RED BEANS AND RICE

1 pound dried red beans
1 ham bone
1 large onion, chopped
1 cup chopped green onions
  (tops and bottoms)
¼ cup chopped green pepper
¼ cup chopped fresh parsley

¼ cup butter
2 bay leaves
Salt
Cayenne pepper
½ pound cooked ham or sliced
  cooked sausage
Hot cooked rice

Wash and sort beans; cover beans with water and bring to a boil. Let beans boil several minutes. Remove from heat; cover, and let soak overnight.

Heat bean mixture to boiling; add remaining ingredients, except ham and rice. Cover and simmer 2 hours or until beans are tender. Add more water during cooking, if necessary. Add ham or sausage to beans, if desired. Remove bay leaves before serving. Serve over hot cooked rice. Yield: 4 to 6 servings.

Louisiana Farm Bureau Women's Committee

CREOLE RED BEANS AND RICE

1 pound dried red beans	1 bay leaf
Water	Salt
Ham bone or ham pieces	Hot sauce (optional)
1 medium onion, chopped	Hot cooked rice
1 stalk celery, chopped	Smoked link sausage

Sort and wash beans. Place beans in a large Dutch oven; cover with water. Add ham bone, onion, celery, and bay leaf. Cover; bring to a boil. Reduce heat and simmer 2 hours or until beans are tender, stirring occasionally.

Add salt and hot sauce to taste. Serve over hot cooked rice and smoked sausage links. Yield: 8 to 10 servings.

Mrs. B. F. Lemoine, Jr. (Grace)
Avoyelles Parish (Hamburg)

CAJUN COUNTRY'S DIRTY RICE DRESSING

Steamed Rice:

1½ cups long grain rice	1 teaspoon vegetable oil
3 cups water	Salt to taste

Combine all ingredients in a 3-quart saucepan; heat to boiling. Reduce heat; let simmer until water has been absorbed. Cover; simmer 30 more minutes or until tender. Yield: 3 cups.

Dressing:

¼ cup vegetable oil	1 cup chopped celery
1 pound finely ground chicken livers and gizzards	2 to 3 sprigs fresh parsley, chopped
1 onion, chopped	Salt and pepper to taste
1 large green pepper, seeded and chopped	1½ cups water

Heat oil until warm in a large Dutch oven; add meat and cook until browned. Drain meat, and return to skillet. Add onion, pepper, celery, and parsley to skillet; add salt and pepper to taste. Stir in water; heat to boiling. Reduce heat and simmer 20 minutes. Add steamed rice; heat until warmed. Yield: Serves 6 to 8.

Mrs. Bernard Bordelon (Marie)
Avoyelles Parish (Moreauville)

DIRTY RICE

2 pounds chicken
1 cup chicken giblets
2 cups uncooked long grain rice
Water
2 tablespoons vegetable oil
1 pound lean ground beef
1 cup chopped onion
¾ cup chopped celery
¾ cup chopped green pepper
1 cup chicken stock
1 cup chicken livers
1½ cups water
¼ cup chopped fresh parsley
¼ cup chopped green onions
Salt
Cayenne pepper

Boil chicken until tender, about 1 hour. Let chicken cool to touch; debone and chop. Reserve 1 quart chicken stock; set aside.

Remove all muscle from giblets; cook giblets for 15 minutes in a pressure cooker. Let cool to touch; debone and chop giblets; set aside.

Place rice in salted water and boil for 18 minutes; drain rice in colander.

Heat oil until warm in a 4-quart Dutch oven; add giblets and ground beef; cook meat over medium heat until browned. Add vegetables; sauté until tender, about 10 minutes. Add chicken stock; simmer 30 minutes. Reduce heat to low; add liver. Cover and cook on low heat for 15 minutes. Add chicken and 1½ cups water; cook 20 minutes longer. Stir in parsley and green onion; cook 5 minutes. Add rice, salt, and cayenne pepper; serve warm. Yield: 16 servings.

Mrs. Carol Aucoin
St. James Parish (Vacherie)

TOOT'S DIRTY RICE

½ pound chicken gizzards
¾ teaspoon salt
⅛ teaspoon pepper
Water
1 tablespoon vegetable oil
1 bunch green onions, chopped
4 stalks celery, chopped

1 medium onion, chopped
1 medium green pepper, seeded
  and chopped
1 pound ground beef
4 chicken livers
4 cups cooked rice
Salt and pepper to taste

Combine gizzards, salt, pepper, and enough water to cover ingredients in a saucepan; heat to boiling. Cook until gizzards are tender. Drain, reserving liquid. Let gizzards cool to touch.

Heat oil in a 10-inch skillet; add vegetables and sauté until tender. Crumble ground beef into skillet; cook over medium heat until browned. Drain ground beef mixture on absorbent paper, and reserve pan drippings.

Place livers in pan drippings; fry over medium heat until browned. Remove livers and drain.

Grind gizzards and livers; return to skillet with ground meat mixture and reserved liquid from boiling gizzards. Heat mixture to boiling; reduce heat and simmer 45 minutes to 1 hour. Remove from heat; stir in rice, and add seasonings to taste. Yield: 10 to 12 servings.

Connie Granger
Beauregard Parish (DeRidder)

PAIN ORDINAIRE (FRENCH BREAD)

1 envelope dry yeast
¼ cup warm water (105° to
   115°)
1¾ cups warm water (105° to
   115°)

1½ teaspoons salt
5 cups all-purpose flour
Milk

Combine yeast and ¼ cup warm water; let stand 5 minutes.

Add remaining water and salt to yeast mixture; stir in flour until well combined.

Turn dough out onto a floured surface; knead 8 to 10 minutes or until dough is smooth and elastic. Place dough in a lightly greased bowl. Cover and let rise in a warm place (85°), free from drafts until doubled in bulk (about 2 hours).

Punch dough down; cover and let rise until doubled in bulk. Punch dough down; turn out onto a floured surface and knead gently.

Shape dough into 2 long loaves; place each loaf on a greased baking sheet. Cover and let rise in a warm place (85°), free from drafts, until doubled in bulk. Cut diagonal slits along top of each loaf; brush tops with a small amount of milk. Bake at 400 degrees for 50 minutes or until golden brown. Let cool on wire racks. Yield: 2 loaves.

Note: A pan of boiling water placed in the bottom of the oven during bread baking will produce a heavier crust.

Louisiana Farm Bureau Women's Committee

"PO-BOYS"

1 small loaf French bread
Mayonnaise or salad dressing
Butter
Hot mustard
Ketchup

Ham slices
Cheese slices
Tomato slices
Onion slices
Lettuce

Slice loaf lengthwise; spread each half with mayo. ... utter, mustard, ketchup, or hot sauce, as desired. Add ham slices, cheese, tomatoes, and sliced onion; top with lettuce. Yield: 1 sandwich.

Variations:
Barbecued meat, roast beef, fried seafood, meat loaf, salami, bologna, pastrami, chicken salad, and corned beef are excellent for fillings!

Louisiana Farm Bureau Women's Committee

Lagniappe

PIG'S EARS (CAJUN DOUGHNUTS)

6 cups all-purpose flour
1 tablespoon plus 1 teaspoon
  baking powder
1 teaspoon soda
1 cup sugar

3 eggs, beaten
3 tablespoons shortening
1 cup milk
1 tablespoon vanilla extract

Combine flour, baking powder, and soda; set aside.

Combine sugar, eggs, and shortening in a medium mixing bowl, creaming until light. Add dry ingredients and milk, alternately, mixing well between additions. Add vanilla.

Turn dough out onto a floured surface and knead gently several times. Roll dough out to ½-inch thickness; cut dough into shape of pig's ears. Put 2 slits in each dough piece (the slits allow dough to brown on both sides).

Fry dough in deep fat fryer in hot oil (350°) until golden brown. Drain on absorbent paper. Yield: 30 to 35 doughnuts.

Note: In North Louisiana these doughnuts are rolled in a cinnamon-sugar mixture while hot.

Mrs. D. M. Herbert (Edna)
Evangeline Parish (Ville Platte)

GATEAU DE SIROP (SYRUP CAKE)

⅓ cup sugar
½ cup shortening
2 eggs
1 cup pure cane syrup
¾ cup milk

2½ cups all-purpose flour
1½ teaspoons ground cinnamon
1 teaspoon soda
1 teaspoon ground ginger
½ teaspoon salt

Preheat oven to 350 degrees.

Combine sugar and shortening in a medium mixing bowl, creaming well. Add eggs; mix well. Add syrup and milk; mix until smooth. Add dry ingredients; mix until well blended. Pour batter into a well-greased and floured 10-inch tube pan. Bake at 350 degrees for 30 to 35 minutes or until done. Yield: one 10-inch cake.

Louisiana Farm Bureau Women's Committee

NATCHITOCHES MEAT PIES

Filling:
1½ pounds ground beef
1½ pounds ground pork
1 cup chopped green onions
  (tops and bottoms)
1 tablespoon salt
1 teaspoon coarsely ground pepper
1 teaspoon coarsely ground red
  pepper
½ teaspoon cayenne pepper
⅓ cup all-purpose flour

Combine first seven ingredients in a large Dutch oven; cook over medium heat until meat is browned. Sift ⅓ cup flour into Dutch oven and stir well to combine with meat mixture. Remove from heat; let cool slightly. Drain meat mixture in colander; set aside.

Pastry:
2 cups self-rising flour, sifted
⅓ cup shortening
¾ cup milk
1 egg, beaten

Sift flour into a medium bowl; cut in shortening until mixture resembles coarse crumbs. Add milk and egg; stir with a fork until ingredients are moistened. Shape dough into a ball; divide into 3 parts.

Roll ⅓ of dough out on a lightly floured surface to ⅛-inch thickness; cut dough into 5 ½-inch circles, using a saucer as a cutting guide. Place dough circles on a lightly greased baking sheet. Repeat rolling and cutting procedure with remaining dough.

Place a heaping tablespoon of meat filling on one side of each pastry round. Moisten edges of rounds with a small amount of water. Fold pastry over to cover filling; seal edges using a fork dipped in water. Prick pastry gently with a fork. Deep fry in hot oil (350°) until golden brown. Drain on absorbent paper; serve warm. Yield: 26 to 28 pies.

Note: Freeze uncooked pies in plastic freezer bags; no need to thaw before frying. Also, dough may be cut with a biscuit cutter and filled with 1 teaspoon filling to make cocktail meat pies.

Mrs. Charles E. Cloutier
Natchitoches Parish (Natchitoches)

HOGSHEAD CHEESE

1 hog's head
4 hog's feet
3 pounds lean pork
2 cups chopped onions
½ green pepper, seeded and
  chopped

Water
Salt and pepper to taste
1 envelope unflavored gelatin
¼ cup water
½ cup chopped green onion tops
½ cup chopped fresh parsley

Cut hog's head into 4 pieces; remove brains, ears, eyes and tissue. Combine head pieces, hog's feet, pork, 2 cups onion, and green pepper in a large Dutch oven; add enough water to cover all ingredients. Bring to a boil; reduce heat and simmer until meat falls off bones and is tender.

Remove meat from pot and chop or grind, as desired. Cook remaining broth down to about 2 quarts or less. Strain broth; set aside.

Combine gelatin and ¼ cup water; let stand 5 minutes to soften.

Combine meat, reserved broth, gelatin mixture, and seasonings to taste in Dutch oven; cook over medium heat for 15 minutes. Add remaining ingredients; remove from heat.

Pour mixture into soup bowls to mold. Place bowls in refrigerator until cheese is set.

Allen J. Brouillette
Avoyelles Parish (Marksville)

COOKING WITH SOYBEANS

- Soybeans have been called the meat of the field.

- Soybeans are rich in minerals, B vitamins, lecthin, and protein.

- Soybeans absorb herbs and spices slowly; cinnamon, basil, oregano, rosemary, chili powder, cumin, and dill complement soybean flavor.

- Make soybean recipes ahead to let seasonings penetrate and complement the bean.

- Add ½ teaspoon soda to basic soybean recipe, if desired, to prevent gastric disturbance.

- Cooked soybeans freeze well.

Mrs. Richard Watkins (Kathleen)
Jefferson Davis Parish (Iowa)

SWEET POTATO PUDDING CASSEROLE

6 to 8 sweet potatoes
½ cup butter
¼ cup evaporated milk
2 eggs

½ to 1 cup sugar
1 teaspoon ground cinnamon
Marshmallows

Preheat oven to 325 degrees.

Boil potatoes until fork tender; drain and let cool to touch. Peel potatoes.

Combine potatoes, butter, milk, eggs, sugar, and cinnamon in a large mixing bowl; beat until well combined. Add additional milk if mixture is too thick.

Place potato mixture in a lightly greased 3-quart baking dish; top with marshmallows, as desired. Bake at 325 degrees for 25 minutes or until hot and bubbly. Yield: 8 to 10 servings.

Mrs. Fernand Falgoust (Joan)
St. James Parish (St. James)

POTATO SALAD

10 new potatoes, washed
6 hard cooked eggs
Chopped shallots
Chopped celery
½ green pepper, chopped
2 tablespoons diced pimiento
Chopped sweet pickle
Salt and pepper to taste

½ cup mayonnaise
1 tablespoon French mustard
1 teaspoon vinegar
½ teaspoon sugar
Green pepper rings (optional)
Sliced pimiento-stuffed olives
  (optional)
Paprika (optional)

Boil new potatoes in water until tender. Drain; let cool to touch. Dice unpeeled potatoes, and place in a large bowl. Add shallots, celery, green pepper, pimiento, and sweet pickle to taste. Season as desired with salt and pepper.

Combine mayonnaise, mustard, vinegar, and sugar; add to potato mixture, stirring well to coat evenly. Cover and chill. Garnish with green pepper rings, pimiento-stuffed olive slices or paprika, if desired. Yield: 10 to 12 servings.

Note: Seasoning potatoes while they are still warm will add flavor to the salad.

Louisiana Farm Bureau Women's Committee

OLD FASHIONED POTATO STEW

½ cup corn oil
½ cup all-purpose flour
1½ cups fresh shrimp, peeled and deveined
1 medium onion, minced
2 cloves garlic, minced
1 teaspoon salt
⅛ teaspoon red pepper
⅛ teaspoon pepper
6 large new potatoes, peeled and diced

½ cup chopped green onion
½ cup chopped celery
1 tablespoon finely chopped fresh parsley
3 cups hot water
1 small tomato, peeled and diced
1 tablespoon butter or margarine
Hot cooked rice

Combine oil and flour in a heavy pot over medium heat; cook, stirring constantly, until roux is the color of a copper penny (about 20 to 30 minutes).

Add shrimp, onion, and garlic; sauté for 3 minutes on medium heat. Add seasonings and reduce heat; cook 10 minutes, stirring frequently. Add potatoes, green onion, celery, and parsley; cook 10 minutes, stirring frequently.

Gradually add water and tomatoes; heat to boiling. Reduce heat; simmer 1 hour, stirring frequently. Add butter to stew and cover; remove from heat. Serve over hot cooked rice. Yield: 10 to 12 servings.

Note: Ham or smoked sausage may be substituted for fresh shrimp, if desired.

Mrs. James Graugnard, Sr.
West St. James Parish (St. James)

HOW TO COOK GRITS

5 cups water
2 tablespoons butter
1 teaspoon salt

1 cup white hominy grits
Butter (optional)

Heat water to boiling in a 1½-quart saucepan; add butter and salt. Gradually add grits, stirring constantly to prevent lumping. Cover; reduce heat to low and cook 30 minutes, stirring frequently. Serve warm with additional butter, if desired. Yield: 6 to 8 servings.

Louisiana Farm Bureau Women's Committee

Appetizers and Beverages

Louisiana State Capitol Building

ARTICHOKE DIP

1 14-ounce jar marinated
artichoke hearts
1 cup mayonnaise
1 package Good Seasons Italian
seasoning mix (dry)

Salt
Pepper

Drain artichoke hearts and cut them with scissors (try not to mash them). Add mayonnaise, Good Seasons mix, and salt and pepper to taste. Chill. Serve with crisp vegetables.

Mrs. Gerald Klein (Pat)
Allen Parish (Oberlin)

Mrs. Anita Joyner
Tangipahoa Parish (Hammond)

STUFFED ARTICHOKES

4 large artichokes
2 cans seasoned bread crumbs
1 pint olive oil

2 tablespoons minced garlic
8 ounces Parmesan cheese, grated
2 lemon slices

Wash artichokes well; clip off points ½ inch. Mix all other ingredients well until bread crumbs are wet. Spoon filling on each leaf; put each artichoke into foil with 1 tablespoon water. Put a lemon slice on top, if desired. Wrap each artichoke tightly in foil; place in pan with water to halfway cover artichokes. Cook 1 hour and 15 minutes over medium heat. Artichoke is done when a leaf can be easily pulled from heart.

Mrs. Sandra Sotile
Ascension Parish (Donaldsonville)

AVOCADO DIP

1 ripe avocado
1 3-ounce package cream
cheese, softened
Mayonnaise (to obtain desired
consistency)

1 tablespoon lemon juice
⅛ teaspoon onion salt
⅛ teaspoon garlic salt
Salt and pepper to taste

Cream avocado and cream cheese in bowl. Add mayonnaise to desired smoothness. Add lemon juice, onion salt and garlic salt. Add salt and pepper to taste. Serve with favorite chips.

Mrs. Anita Joyner
Tangipahoa Parish (Hammond)

ARTICHOKE BALLS

1 8-ounce can artichoke hearts,
  drained and chopped
2½ cups Progresso Italian
  bread crumbs
3 tablespoons grated Italian
  cheese

2 eggs, beaten
2 tablespoons Plaignol olive oil,
  warmed
1 teaspoon garlic salt
1 teaspoon garlic powder

Combine artichokes, 1 cup bread crumbs, 2 tablespoons cheese, and eggs. Blend in warmed olive oil, garlic salt and garlic powder; shape into small bite-size balls. Roll in remaining 1½ cups bread crumbs and 1 tablespoon Italian cheese. Chill before serving. Yield: 3 dozen.

Mrs. George Viator (Shara)
Iberia Parish (New Iberia)

BEEF BOLOGNA

2 pounds ground beef
2 tablespoons Morton's
  Tenderquick Salt
1 cup water

1½ teaspoons liquid smoke
½ teaspoon onion powder
½ teaspoon garlic powder

Mix all ingredients well with hands; roll into 3 logs. Wrap in cellophane wrap and refrigerate overnight. Preheat oven to 375 degrees. Unwrap bologna rolls and place on a wire rack on a cookie sheet. Bake 45 to 60 minutes. Turn over once during baking time. *Store well in refrigerator or freezer.*

Mrs. Marvin Spangler (Inez)
Ouachita Parish (West Monroe)

MOCK BOURSIN AU POIVRE

8 ounces cream cheese,
  softened
1 clove garlic, crushed
1 teaspoon caraway seed

1 teaspoon basil
1 teaspoon dill weed
1 teaspoon chopped chives
Lemon pepper

Combine first 6 ingredients; pat into round flat shape. Roll on all sides in lemon pepper. Chill. Make up a few days ahead. Serve with assorted crackers. Tastes like French Boursin Au Poivre. *This spread gets instant raves.* Yield: 1 small ball.

Mrs. Ada Lee
West Carroll Parish (Oak Grove)

CARAMEL CORN

2 cups brown sugar	1 teaspoon vanilla extract
½ cup Karo corn syrup	½ teaspoon soda
1 cup margarine	6 quarts freshly popped popcorn
½ teaspoon salt	

Boil sugar, Karo, margarine and salt for 5 minutes. Add vanilla and soda. Mix with popcorn; place in a shallow casserole. Bake 1 hour at 250 degrees, stirring occasionally. When you take out of oven, keep stirring until slightly cooled to prevent sticking to pan.

Mrs. Charles Staples (Bobbie)
Ouachita Parish (Calhoun)

CHEESE BALL

2 12-ounce packages sharp Cheddar cheese	8 shakes Tabasco
1 12-ounce package mild Cheddar cheese	12 shakes Worcestershire sauce
	30 shakes garlic powder
1 tablespoon prepared horseradish	¼ cup paprika
	1 cup pecans

Shred cheese; combine with next 5 ingredients, mixing well. Roll into a ball. Roll ball in paprika and pecans to cover outside.

Mrs. JoBaya Foreman
Beauregard Parish (DeRidder)

 CHEESE CRISPS

½ pound sharp Cheddar cheese, shredded	½ teaspoon salt
½ cup butter, softened	Dash of crushed red pepper
1¼ cups sifted all-purpose flour	3 drops Tabasco
1 teaspoon Lea & Perrin Worcestershire sauce	1 cup pecans, finely chopped

Preheat oven to 375 degrees. Cream cheese and butter; add flour, Worcestershire sauce, salt, red pepper, Tabasco and pecans, mixing well. This makes a stiff dough. Divide into small rolls and chill. Slice very thin. Bake on an ungreased cookie sheet for 10 minutes.

Mrs. John Smith (Thelma)
St. James Parish (St. James)

CHEESE LOGS

1 8-ounce package Velveeta
  cheese
1 3-ounce package cream
  cheese, softened

1 teaspoon garlic salt
¼ cup chopped pecans
Paprika or chopped pecans (to
  cover logs)

Combine first 3 ingredients. Mix thoroughly. Roll in paprika or pecans, as desired; chill overnight.

Mrs. Rosalie Melaneon
St. Martin Parish (St. Martinville)

AUNT VILLA'S CHEESE ROLL

1 roll smoked cheese
1 pound Wisconsin cheese,
  grated
2 3-ounce packages
  Philadelphia cream cheese
1 teaspoon Tabasco
1 teaspoon Lea & Perrin
  Worcestershire sauce

½ teaspoon ground red pepper
1 cup finely chopped pecans
2 teaspoons grated onion
2 teaspoons garlic powder
Dash of salt
Chili powder (to cover roll)

Let all cheese come to room temperature. Combine all ingredients, except chili powder; mix until smooth. Divide into four parts; shape into small rolls. Roll cheese mixture in chili powder. Wrap in Saran Wrap and put in refrigerator. *Good on Ritz crackers. Large quantities may be frozen until ready to use. This is my aunt's recipe and it has been in our family for over twenty-five years.*

Mrs. Don Odom (Brenda)
Claiborne Parish (Homer)

GARLIC CHEESE ROLL

8 ounces American cheese,
  grated
½ cup chopped pecans

¼ teaspoon garlic powder
8 ounces cream cheese
Chili powder

Let cheeses stand at room temperature. Mix all ingredients together, except chili powder. Form into two small rolls and roll in chili powder. Chill; slice and serve on assorted crackers.

Mrs. H. E. Tull, Jr. (Renee)
Ouachita Parish (West Monroe)

CHEESE SNACKS

2 cups grated sharp Cheddar
  cheese
1 cup margarine
2 cups all-purpose flour

2 cups Rice Krispies cereal
¼ teaspoon ground red pepper
¼ teaspoon garlic salt
¼ teaspoon onion salt

Preheat oven to 350 degrees. Let cheese soften with margarine. Combine cheese, margarine, flour, Rice Krispies, red pepper, garlic salt and onion salt; mix well. Roll dough in little balls and press onto a cookie sheet or roll into a log. Chill; slice and place on a cookie sheet. Bake at 350 degrees for 15 minutes.

Mrs. Marvin Spangler (Inez)
Ouachita Parish (West Monroe)

CHEESE STRAWS

½ cup margarine
2 cups self-rising flour
½ teaspoon cayenne pepper

1 teaspoon salt
1 pound New York sharp Cheddar
  cheese, shredded

Cream margarine. Sift all dry ingredients together. Add sifted mixture to margarine. Stir well. Add cheese. Roll out on wax paper with rolling pin. Cut into 4 x ½-inch strips with knife. Bake on ungreased cookie sheet at 400 degrees for 10 minutes. Delicious with dips or to eat as snacks. Store in an airtight container. Will keep for a month.

Mrs. Lucille Booth
St. Tammany Parish (Falsom)

SAUSAGE CHEESE BALLS

1 pound hot bulk sausage
1 10-ounce package sharp
  Cheddar cheese, shredded

3 cups Bisquick baking mix

Cook sausage until browned; drain. Add cheese to sausage; stir until melted. Remove from heat; add baking mix, blending well. Roll into 1-inch balls. Place on cookie sheet; bake at 350 degrees until light brown. Serve hot.

Note: To freeze, place on cookie sheet. When frozen, place in plastic bag; bake as needed. Do not thaw before baking. Yield: about 150 balls.

Mrs. Randall F. Bracy (Regina)
Tangipahoa Parish (Amite)

CRAB DIP

1 8-ounce package Philadelphia
cream cheese, softened
1 cup mayonnaise or salad
dressing

1 tablespoon Worcestershire sauce
1 large onion, minced
1 6½-ounce can crabmeat, drained

Mix all ingredients. Cover; chill overnight.

Mrs. Doug Moore (Liz)
Ouachita Parish (Monroe)

CRABMEAT DIP

½ cup butter
1 onion, finely chopped
1 8-ounce package Philadelphia
cream cheese, cut into
chunks
1 3-ounce package Philadelphia
cream cheese, cut into
chunks

1 pound lump crabmeat
Dash of Tabasco
¼ teaspoon garlic powder
Dash of crushed red pepper

In a 2-quart pot melt butter over low heat; add onions and cook until wilted. Add cheese, crabmeat, and seasonings, stirring well. Serve in fondue to keep warm. Serve with corn chips or Doritos.

Mrs. James Graugnard, Jr. (Carolyn)
West St. James Parish (St. James)

CRAB NUGGETS

2 6½-ounce cans crabmeat
2 3-ounce packages cream
cheese, softened
1 tablespoon lemon juice

2 teaspoons prepared horseradish
¼ teaspoon hot pepper sauce
1 cup fresh chopped parsley

Drain and flake crabmeat; combine with cheese, mixing well. Add seasonings; mix well. Shape into small balls and roll in parsley. Chill. Yields approximately 40 hors d'oeuvres.

Mrs. Eddie Schexnaydre (Doris)
Terrebonne Parish (Schriever)

LOUISIANA SHRIMP AND CRAB DIP

½ cup margarine or butter
¼ cup minced parsley (dried or fresh)
½ cup chopped green onion tops
1 10-ounce can cream of mushroom soup, undiluted

2 4-ounce cans shrimp, drained and mashed
1 4½-ounce can crabmeat, drained
1 tablespoon Worcestershire sauce
1 teaspoon salt
½ teaspoon pepper
Dash of Tabasco sauce

Melt butter in a two-quart saucepan; add onion and parsley. Sauté vegetables until wilted; add soup, shrimp, crabmeat, Worcestershire sauce, salt, pepper and Tabasco. Heat to boiling; reduce heat and simmer for 30 minutes. Add more seasonings if desired. Serve in a chafing dish with chips.

Note: May be served in small individual pastry shells.

Mrs. Kathleen Watkins
Jeff Davis Parish (Iowa)

CRABMEAT DIP

½ cup melted butter
1 bunch green onions, chopped
1 bell pepper, seeded and chopped
1 cup diced celery
1 10-ounce can cream of mushroom soup

1 pound lump crabmeat
2 6-ounce cans water chestnuts, drained and sliced
Salt to taste
Black or red pepper to taste

Sauté onions, peppers, and celery in butter. Stir in cream of mushroom soup. Add crabmeat and water chestnuts. Cook 20 minutes over low heat. Serve in chafing dish with Melba toast or crackers.

Note: Must be served warm to be good.

Mrs. Randall F. Bracy (Regina)
Tangipahoa Parish (Amite)

HOT CRAWFISH DIP

¼ cup butter
1 medium onion, chopped
2 bunches shallots, minced
½ green pepper, chopped
1 or 2 stalks celery, minced
2 10-ounce cans cream of
  mushroom soup
1 pound peeled crawfish tails,
  chopped (not too small)
Red pepper to taste
Minced garlic (optional)
1 whole pimiento, chopped

Melt butter in saucepan. Add onion, shallots, green pepper, and celery. Cook over low heat until soft. Add soup; heat through. Add crawfish, red pepper, and garlic, if desired. Heat for 20 minutes or until crawfish are cooked. Add pimiento just before removing from heat. Serve with favorite crackers or chips. Serves 10.

Note: You may substitute crawfish with 1 pound shrimp, 1 pound lump crabmeat or 3 dozen oysters, if desired.

Mrs. R. Ernest Girouard, Jr.
Vermilion Parish (Kaplan)

DIET DIP

1 16-ounce carton commercial
  cottage cheese
1 envelope onion soup mix
1 tablespoon lemon juice
Dash of hot sauce

Mix all ingredients in electric blender. Cover; chill for several hours. Serve with a tray of assorted fresh vegetables such as: cauliflower, broccoli, cucumbers, tender yellow squash slices, celery and carrot sticks and/or radishes.

Mrs. Doug Moore (Liz)
Ouachita Parish (Monroe)

SHRIMP DIP

1 6½-ounce can shrimp,
  drained
1 8-ounce package cream
  cheese, softened
1 medium onion, chopped
Dash of Worcestershire sauce
3 tablespoons mayonnaise

Blend together all ingredients with mixer. Chill; serve with assorted crackers. Yield: about 2 cups.

Mrs. Wista White
Ouachita Parish (Monroe)

SHRIMP DIP

1 quart fresh shrimp, peeled and deveined
1 tablespoon lemon juice
1 tablespoon salt or more if desired
1 tablespoon black or red pepper
1 quart boiling water
1 8-ounce package Philadelphia cream cheese, softened
1 8-ounce carton commercial sour cream
½ cup green onion tops, finely chopped
Tabasco sauce to taste

Put peeled shrimp, lemon juice, salt and pepper in saucepan with boiling water; boil until tender (about 12 minutes at a rolling boil). Grind shrimp in a meat grinder or food processor. Combine shrimp with cream cheese and sour cream; add green onion and Tabasco. Chill. Serve with Ritz crackers or any assortment of crackers. Also can be served with short, crisp celery sticks.

Mrs. Dorothy McCown
Jeff Davis Parish (Welsh)

SHRIMP SPREAD

½ cup butter, softened
1 8-ounce package cream cheese, softened
¼ cup mayonnaise
1 small onion, grated
Salt, pepper and garlic salt to taste
2 6¼-ounce cans deveined shrimp, drained and chopped
Juice of 1 lemon

Combine butter, cream cheese, mayonnaise, onion, salt, pepper and garlic salt in a small mixing bowl; mix well. Fold shrimp into cheese mixture. Stir in lemon juice. Serve with crackers.

Note: This appetizer is "dee-vine" and it freezes well.

Mrs. Louis D. Curet (Jean)
East Baton Rouge Parish (Baton Rouge)

DADDY RED'S PICKLED EGGS

24 hard-cooked eggs, peeled
  and chilled
3 tablespoons salt
1 12-ounce jar jalapeño
  peppers, undrained and sliced
6 bay leaves

2 onions, sliced or quartered
2 teaspoons pickling spice
1 quart white vinegar
1 quart water
1 gallon glass wide mouth jar

Boil eggs, peel and chill. Put eggs in a 1-gallon wide mouth jar, sprinkle salt over them. Drain juice from jalapeño peppers and pour over eggs. Add bay leaves, onions, and pickling spice. Heat vinegar and water to boiling; pour over eggs. Put lid on jar. The longer the eggs sit the better, but you may start eating them in twenty-four hours.

Note: Daddy Red is a neighbor of ours and these are the best pickled eggs I have ever eaten. A jar of these are usually found on my counter top.

Mrs. Don Odom (Brenda)
Claiborne Parish (Homer)

ROSY PICKLED EGGS

1 cup juice from pickled beets
1 cup vinegar
4 cups water
1 clove garlic
1 medium bay leaf

2 teaspoons mixed pickling spice
½ teaspoon salt
12 hard-cooked eggs
1 small onion, sliced and separated
  in rings

Place beet juice, vinegar, and water in large bowl; add garlic, bay leaf, pickling spice, and salt, and mix well. Add eggs and onion rings; cover and refrigerate for several days. Makes 1 dozen pickled eggs.

Mrs. Pam Accardo
Ouachita Parish (Monroe)

SAUSAGE AND CHEESE BISCUITS

2 cups Pioneer Biscuit Mix
1 pound bulk sausage

10 ounces sharp Cheddar cheese,
  shredded

In large bowl combine biscuit mix, sausage and grated cheese. Mix well. Shape into 1-inch balls; place on ungreased cookie sheet. Bake at 350 degrees for 15 minutes or until brown.

Mrs. Rick Caldwell (Jeanie)
Ouachita Parish (West Monroe)

MUSHROOM CHEESE APPETIZERS

2 cups Bisquick baking mix
½ cup cold water
½ pound bulk pork sausage
½ cup finely chopped green
  onion
¾ cup mayonnaise or salad
  dressing

35 medium mushrooms (about 1
  pound)
2 cups shredded Cheddar cheese
Paprika as needed

Preheat oven to 350 degrees. Grease oblong pan (13 x 9 x 2). Combine baking mix and water; mix until soft dough forms, beating vigorously, about 20 strokes. Press dough in bottom of greased pan with floured hands. Cook and stir sausage in skillet until brown. Drain; mix sausage, onions and mayonnaise. Remove stems from mushrooms. Finely chop stems and stir into sausage mixture. Fill mushroom caps with sausage mixture. Place mushrooms in rows on dough in pan. Sprinkle with cheese and paprika. Cover pan loosely with aluminum foil. Bake at 350 degrees for 20 minutes; remove foil. Bake until cheese is bubbly, about 5 to 10 minutes. Let stand 15 minutes. Cut into pieces—makes 35 appetizers.

Mrs. Henry Hess (Peggy)
Avoyelles Parish (Moreauville)

MARINATED MUSHROOMS

¼ cup red wine vinegar
1 teaspoon pepper
2 teaspoons salt
¼ teaspoon garlic powder
1 dash Tabasco
2 teaspoons sweet basil leaves

3 green onion tops, chopped
2 teaspoons dried parsley flakes
6 tablespoons olive oil
1 pound can whole mushrooms or
  4 4-ounce jars whole
  mushrooms, drained

In a large jar, combine vinegar, pepper, salt, garlic powder, Tabasco and sweet basil. Cover the jar; shake until salt is dissolved. Add onion tops, parsley, olive oil and mushrooms. Once again, shake well and let stand for 4 hours at room temperature. During the 4-hour period, shake occasionally, then refrigerate overnight.

Mrs. Larry Langlinais (Anna)
Vermilion Parish (Erath)

MARINATED MUSHROOMS

2 4-ounce cans of mushrooms, drained
2/3 cup tarragon-flavored vinegar
1/2 cup vegetable oil
1 clove garlic

Crushed red pepper
1 onion, cut in rings
1 green pepper, cut in rings
Salt to taste

Mix all ingredients in medium sized bowl; cover. Let marinate in refrigerator overnight.

Mrs Jackie Theriot (Sue)
St. Martin Parish (St. Martinville)

PICKLED MUSHROOMS

2 packages Good Seasons Italian dressing mix
1/4 cup shredded green onions
1 tablespoon parsley flakes
1 tablespoon Worcestershire sauce
8 dashes Tabasco

2 bottles wine vinegar
1/2 cup tarragon-flavored vinegar
3 8-ounce jars or cans of medium mushrooms, drained
3 2½-ounce jars medium mushrooms, drained

Combine first 7 ingredients. Pour over mushrooms and mix well. Marinate overnight or at least 6 hours. Will last for several weeks in the refrigerator if tightly covered. Serves 30.

Mrs. John Smith (Thelma)
St. James Parish (St. James)

SOYBEAN SANDWICH SPREAD

2 cups mashed soybeans
2¼ tablespoons mayonnaise or salad dressing
2 tablespoons sweet pickle relish

2¼ tablespoons minced green onions (optional)
1/4 teaspoon salt

Combine all ingredients; mix well. Chill for 3 or 4 hours. Spread on bread slices.

Note: Excellent after school snack for youngsters. Serves 6 to 8.

Mrs. Kathleen Watkins
Jeff Davis Parish (Iowa)

HOT PEPPER SANDWICHES

1 loaf French bread, sliced in half crosswise

1 jar Cheez Whiz with jalapeño peppers

1 pound ground beef

3 large jalapeño peppers, chopped (may be omitted if too hot)

1 15-ounce can tomato sauce

1½ teaspoons oregano leaves

Salt to taste

1 4-ounce can chopped mushrooms, drained

¾ cup chopped onions

¼ cup salad oil

5 ounces grated Parmesan or shredded Mozzarella cheese

Preheat oven to 325 degrees. Cover cookie sheet with foil. Spread Cheez Whiz on bread halves; place on cookie sheet. Brown ground beef in a skillet; pour off excess fat. Add peppers if desired. Add ½ can tomato sauce; heat to boiling. Simmer 5 minutes. Add oregano and salt to taste. Cook 2 minutes longer. Spread meat mixture on bread halves (each). Top with mushrooms and onions. Spoon enough of remaining tomato sauce over onion layer. Drizzle oil on top to prevent drying out. Top with cheese. Bake at 325 degrees for 20 minutes.

Mrs. Donna Bolton Jenkins
East Baton Rouge Parish (Baton Rouge)

OPEN FACED HAMBURGERS

½ pound ground beef

2 tablespoons milk

2 teaspoons prepared mustard

2 tablespoons chopped onion

1 tablespoon catsup

Salt and pepper to taste

4 slices bread, toasted

¼ cup prepared mustard (to spread on bread)

Mix together ground meat, milk, mustard, onion, catsup, salt, and pepper. Set aside. Toast 4 slices of bread on 1 side; cut bread in triangles. Spread the untoasted side with mustard. Spread meat mixture on the bread. Bake at 400 degrees for 15 minutes or until meat is brown. Yield: 16 triangles. Note: Appropriate for small parties or gatherings.

Mrs. Alvin Klein (Margie)
Allen Parish (Oberlin)

PARTY SANDWICHES

1 8-ounce package Philadelphia
   cream cheese, softened
1 3-ounce package Philadelphia
   cream cheese, softened
3 tablespoons mayonnaise
Cake coloring (any color)
Celery salt to taste

1 loaf bread from bakery, sliced
   lengthwise, (colored if desired)
1 4-ounce jar small stuffed olives
1 medium green pepper, sliced in
   thin strips
1 3-ounce jar pimiento, sliced thin

Mix cream cheese, mayonnaise, cake coloring, and celery salt thoroughly. Spread mixture on bread evenly. Place 4 olives at one end of bread; alternate strips of green pepper and pimiento to the end of the bread. Beginning with olives, roll as tightly as possible. Wrap in wax paper. Store in refrigerator overnight. Slice with bread knife just before serving. Makes approximately 4 dozen sandwiches. Special kind of bread must be used for success. *This recipe has been made lots of times by us with a friend, Evelyn Kitchens. There are no short cuts if you want a perfect sandwich. This is a must for entertaining. DO NOT FREEZE. DO NOT USE A BLENDER.*

Mrs. Roy Anderson (Catherine)
Mrs. Doug Moore (Liz)
Ouachita Parish (Monroe)

PARTY SHRIMP MOLD

1 pound raw peeled shrimp
1 10½-ounce can tomato soup,
   undiluted
1 8-ounce package Philadelphia
   cream cheese
1 tablespoon onion juice
2 envelopes Knox gelatin

½ cup cold water
½ cup mayonnaise
½ cup chopped pimento-stuffed
   olives
Salt to taste
1 tablespoon Worcestershire sauce
½ cup chopped celery

Boil shrimp until done in lemon juice and onion-seasoned water. Drain; chop shrimp. Heat soup in double boiler; add cheese and onion juice, stirring to blend. While cheese is heating, mix gelatin and cold water. When heated mixture is smooth, add gelatin mixture stirring well; cool. Stir in shrimp, and remaining ingredients. Turn into wet mold or mold greased with mayonnaise. Chill until set (about 2 hours).

Note: This may be frozen, if desired.

Louisiana Farm Bureau Women's Committee

COCKTAIL MEATBALLS

1½ pounds ground beef
½ cup dry bread or cracker
  crumbs
⅓ cup minced onions
¼ cup milk
1 egg
1 tablespoon minced parsley

1 teaspoon salt
1 teaspoon pepper
1 teaspoon Worcestershire sauce
¼ cup shortening
1 12-ounce jar chili sauce
1 10-ounce jar grape jelly

Mix ground beef, bread crumbs, onion, milk, and egg; add parsley, salt, pepper and Worcestershire sauce. Shape meat mixture into 1-inch balls. Melt shortening in a skillet; brown meatballs in skillet until done. Remove meatballs from skillet and pour off fat. Heat chili sauce and jelly in skillet over low heat, stirring constantly until jelly is melted. Add meatballs and stir until they are well coated with sauce. Simmer uncovered 30 minutes. Makes 5 dozen.

Mrs. Rick Caldwell (Jeanie)
Ouachita Parish (West Monroe)

PIGS IN A BLANKET

8 all-beef weiners
1 can crescent dinner rolls

Cheddar cheese strips
Jalapeño pepper (slices)

Slice raw weiners lengthwise. Fill opening with cheese and slices of pepper. Roll each weiner up in a separated crescent roll; place on greased cookie sheet. Bake at 350 degrees for 20 minutes or until golden brown. Serves 8.

Mrs. Laurie Ann Hart
Ouachita Parish (Monroe)

SAUSAGE AND BEER

2 to 3 pounds smoked sausage
1 32-ounce bottle catsup

1 12-ounce can beer (any kind)

Cut smoked sausage into ½ inch rounds. Brown sausage in a skillet over medium high heat. Drain off excess fat. In crock pot mix catsup and beer; add sausage. Cook for 8 hours on low heat (or 4 hours on high).

Note: this may be cooked on top of stove or in oven. Just taste for tenderness and goodness of flavor desired.

Mrs. Rick Caldwell (Jeanie)
Ouachita Parish (West Monroe)

SOY CRISPIES

½ cup vegetable oil
½ cup margarine
1½ cups sugar
2 eggs, well beaten
1 cup soy flour
1 teaspoon soda

¼ teaspoon salt
1 tablespoon cream of tartar
1 teaspoon almond extract
⅓ cup sugar
1½ teaspoons ground cinnamon

Combine oil and margarine, creaming until smooth. Add sugar; cream well. Add eggs; mix well. Combine flour, soda, salt, and cream of tartar; add to creamed mixture in small amounts, beating thoroughly. Add almond extract; blend well. Chill 1 hour or until dough is easy to handle. Shape dough into small balls. Roll balls in mixture of sugar and cinnamon. Place coated balls on greased cookie sheet. Bake at 375 degrees for 10 to 12 minutes or until golden brown. Yield: 10 dozen bite-size cookies.

Note: This recipe has been sent out by the L.S.U. Cooperative Extension Service Department.

Mrs. Kathleen Watkins
Jeff Davis Parish (Iowa)

PARTY PIZZAS

1 4½-ounce can chopped ripe
olives, drained
2 cups shredded sharp Cheddar
cheese
1 cup mayonnaise

1 teaspoon basil leaves
½ teaspoon oregano leaves
2 tablespoons chopped onion
2 loaves party rye bread rounds

Mix olives, cheese, mayonnaise, basil, oregano, and onion. Spread one teaspoon of mixture on each slice of bread. Toast under a 400 degree broiler for 5 to 10 minutes. *These may be spread and placed in an airtight container, layered with wax paper and stored ahead for a party.*

Variation for spread:
1 pound hot sausage or ground
beef with salt
1 pound American processed
cheese

1 teaspoon basil leaves
½ teaspoon oregano leaves

Combine all ingredients; spread on bread, toast, and store as directed.

Mrs. Marvin Spangler (Inez)
Ouachita Parish (West Monroe)

JEAN'S SWEDISH MEATBALLS AND GRAVY

Meatballs:

1 green pepper
4 medium onions
8 cloves garlic, minced
1 slice stale bread
2 envelopes Lipton's dry onion
　soup mix

1 teaspoon thyme leaves
¼ cup chopped fresh parsley
½ teaspoon white pepper
4 beaten eggs
3 pounds extra lean ground beef

Preheat oven to 350 degrees. Grind green pepper, onion, garlic and stale bread; add soup mix, thyme, parsley, white pepper and eggs. Add ground beef; mix well. Shape meat mixture into balls; place on cookie sheets. Bake at 350 degrees for 15 to 20 minutes. Yield: about 13 dozen.

Gravy:

2 envelopes Lipton's dry onion
　soup mix
2 15-ounce cans beef gravy

2 15-ounce cans tomato sauce
4 cloves garlic, chopped
1 teaspoon sweet basil leaves

Combine soup mix, beef gravy, tomato sauce, garlic and basil in a saucepan. Simmer for 20 minutes. Add meatballs and simmer 20 to 30 minutes longer.

Mrs. Louis D. Curet
Baton Rouge Parish (Baton Rouge)

SUGARED PECANS

3 cups sugar
6 tablespoons margarine

1 cup Pet evaporated milk
3 to 4 cups pecan halves

Mix sugar, margarine, and milk into pot. Cook until mixture reaches soft ball stage (234°) and forms a ball in a cup of cold water. Remove from heat. Add pecans. Stir until all pecans are well coated. Pour onto waxed paper. Separate pecans into individual pieces, using 2 tablespoons.

Mrs. Doug Moore (Liz)
Ouachita Parish (Monroe)

BUCKHORN CHRISTMAS PECANS

1¼ cups sugar
2 tablespoons light corn syrup
Pinch of cream of tartar

Juice of 1 orange
Grated rind of 1 orange
2 cups pecan halves

Mix all of above ingredients, except pecans. Using a heavy boiler, cook over low heat until mixture reaches soft ball stage (234°) (when dropped into a small bowl of cold water). Remove from heat; beat until mixture starts to thicken. Add pecans; stir until well coated. Drop onto waxed paper. When thoroughly cool, separate and store.

Note: These keep well and are very tasty to have around at Christmas.

Mrs. Laurie Ann Hart
Ouachita Parish (Monroe)

SWEDISH MEATBALLS I

Meatballs:
2 small onions
2 small green peppers, cut into
  chunks
1 stalk celery
4 pounds ground chuck
1 package dry onion soup mix
1 10¾-ounce can cream of
  mushroom soup, undiluted
3 eggs, beaten

½ cup all-purpose flour
3 cups dry bread crumbs
Worcestershire sauce to taste
Parsley flakes, about 1 or 2
  tablespoons
Tabasco to taste
Garlic powder to taste
Salt to taste

Chop onions, green pepper, and celery in electric blender. Combine chopped vegetables, ground chuck, onion soup, mushroom soup, eggs, flour, bread crumbs, Worcestershire sauce, parsley flakes, Tabasco, garlic powder, and salt; mix well. Form into balls and put on cookie sheet. Bake at 350 degrees for 25 minutes or until done.

Sauce:
1 quart barbecue sauce
1 10¾ ounce can golden
  cream of mushroom soup

Pinch of parsley flakes
Worcestershire sauce to taste
Lemon juice to taste

Combine all ingredients in a Dutch oven; heat to boiling. Add meatballs; heat through. Serve warm.

Mrs. Wayne Jennings (Kaye)
Ouachita Parish (Monroe)

SWEDISH MEATBALLS II

Meatballs:

4 pounds ground beef
4 eggs, beaten

1 12-ounce can Italian-style bread crumbs

Combine all ingredients; season to taste; roll into meatballs with wet hands. Place on greased cookie sheet; bake at 425 degrees for 10 minutes, or until done.

Sauce:

¼ cup olive oil
¾ cup chopped onion
1 garlic clove, crushed
1 cup honey
1 cup catsup
1 cup red wine vinegar

½ cup Worcestershire sauce
1 tablespoon dry mustard
1½ teaspoons salt
1 teaspoon oregano leaves
1 teaspoon pepper
½ teaspoon thyme leaves

Heat oil in a 10-inch skillet; add onion and garlic. Cook over medium heat until tender. Add remaining ingredients, stirring well. Heat to boiling; cook five minutes. (This sauce is better if it is made the day before and allowed to marinate without meatballs.) Add meatballs to sauce when ready to heat and serve.

Mrs. Joan Falgoust
St. James Parish (St. James)

SWEDISH MEATBALLS III

1½ pounds ground chuck
2 slices bread, crumbled
Pepper to taste
Salt to taste
A-1 sauce to taste
1 egg, beaten
½ teaspoon onion powder
  (more if desired)

½ teaspoon garlic powder (more if desired)
1 cup commercial barbecue sauce
Dash of Worcestershire sauce
1 10¾-ounce can cream of mushroom soup, undiluted
⅓ cup milk

Combine all ingredients in a large bowl, except soup, milk, and ½ cup of barbecue sauce; shape into small meatballs. Fry meatballs in a little bit of hot grease until brown. Add soup, milk and remaining ½ cup barbecue sauce. Cook on low heat for 20-30 minutes.

Note: This can be served over rice or used for parties as appetizers on toothpicks.

Mrs. Roy Martin Anderson (Linda Sue)
Ouachita Parish (Monroe)

PARTY BEEF BALLS

Meatballs:

2 pounds ground beef
2 eggs
1 cup milk
2 cups seasoned bread crumbs
Dried onions to taste

2 teaspoons black pepper
2 teaspoons Accent
2 teaspoons soy sauce
½ teaspoon red pepper

Crumble ground beef into a large bowl; add remaining ingredients. Mix well. Roll into very small balls, (about the size of a marble). Freeze on cookie sheets. When frozen, store in plastic bags, place in the freezer. When you are ready to serve, remove from the freezer and place on cookie sheet. Bake at 400 degrees until brown, about 15 minutes. Serve with sweet and sour sauce with toothpicks.

Sweet and Sour Sauce:

1 cup tomato juice
¼ cup white vinegar
2 tablespoons brown sugar
1 teaspoon cornstarch
1 teaspoon salt
1 teaspoon minced onion (or to taste)
1 teaspoon oil

1 teaspoon dry mustard
½ teaspoon garlic powder
¼ teaspoon crushed red pepper
1 or 2 beef bouillon cubes
1 cup pineapple juice
1 cup grapefruit juice
1 or 2 bottles chili sauce (optional)

Combine all ingredients in a large saucepan, stirring well. Bring to a boil over medium heat; reduce heat and simmer 30 minutes stirring constantly until thick. Cool; store in a covered container. Freeze or chill in refrigerator. Stir and reheat before serving.

Note: You may pour over party beef balls or serve the sauce as a dip. You may also store meatballs and sauce in the freezer.

Mrs. Thelma Fletcher
Franklin Parish (Winnsboro)

TANGY DOGS

3 pounds hot dogs, cut into
  bite-size pieces
1 cup firmly packed light brown
  sugar

1 cup bourbon whiskey
1 cup commercial chili sauce

Place hot dogs in a 2-quart casserole. Mix together brown sugar, bourbon, and chili sauce; pour over hot dogs. Bake, covered, at 325 degrees for 3 hours. Serve hot in chafing dish.

Note: Can be made ahead; it freezes well.

Mrs. John Smith (Thelma)
St. James Parish (St. James)

AMARETTO FREEZE (AFTER DINNER DRINK)

½ gallon vanilla ice cream
⅔ cup Amaretto liqueur

½ cup Triple Sec liqueur
½ cup Creme de Cacao liqueur

Using food processor with steel blade, or electric blender, combine all ingredients; blend until smooth. Freeze for 1 hour. Serves 4 to 6.

Mrs. George Viator (Shara)
Iberia Parish (New Iberia)

EGG NOG

6 eggs, separated
¼ cup brandy
½ pint whipping cream,
  whipped

6 tablespoons sugar
Ground nutmeg

Beat egg whites in small mixing bowl until stiff; set aside. Beat egg yolks thoroughly; add sugar one tablespoon at a time, beating well after each addition. Slowly add brandy to egg yolk mixture; beat well. Gently fold whipped cream into egg yolk mixture. Fold in beaten egg whites. Serve immediately with nutmeg.

Note: This egg nog recipe may be doubled; it must be served immediately after mixing.

Mrs. Patrick J. Quinn (Mary Kathryn)
Concordia Parish (Monterey)

EGG NOG

6 eggs, separated
¾ cup sugar, divided
1 quart milk
¼ teaspoon salt
1 15-ounce can evaporated milk
Ground nutmeg (optional)

Beat egg whites with half of the sugar until stiff peaks form; set aside. Beat egg yolks with remaining sugar until thick and lemon-colored. Heat 1 quart milk on low heat until scalded. Remove from heat; add salt and evaporated milk. Let cool. Fold egg yolks into cooled mixture, then fold in beaten egg whites. Chill; sprinkle with nutmeg and serve. Serves 8.

Mrs. R. Ernest Girouard, Jr.
Vermilion Parish (Kaplan

HOT EGG NOG

10 quarts (2½ gallons) milk
1 pint half-and-half cream
2 vanilla beans or one 2-ounce
    bottle vanilla extract
27 eggs, separated
3 to 3½ cups sugar
½ cup cornstarch
2 whole nutmegs, grated

Heat milk in a very large pot, on low heat until it reaches 60 degrees on a candy thermometer (a little above scalding temperature). Add 2 vanilla beans; heat milk to scalding. Beat egg yolks in mixer, gradually adding sugar and cornstarch. Gradually add about 2 cups hot milk slowly to beaten egg yolks, stirring constantly. Add egg mixture to remaining hot milk, stirring constantly; cook on low heat until egg nog slightly thickens (20 to 30 minutes). If not using vanilla beans, add the vanilla now. Remove from heat. Beat egg whites until stiff peaks form; to serve, fold beaten whites into the hot mixture. Grate nutmeg over top. Stir gently; serve hot in large silver punch bowl. Serves 30 cups.

Note: You may have a decanter of bourbon whiskey nearby, for those who desire it; add 1 ounce of whiskey to each cup. This egg nog is excellent served cold the next day.

Mrs. John Smith (Thelma)
West St. James Parish (St. James)

HOLIDAY EGG NOG

5 eggs, separated
1/3 cup sugar, divided
1 quart milk
2 quarts vanilla ice cream
  (softened)

Ground cinnamon and ground
  nutmeg to taste
Bourbon to taste (about 1/3 cup)
1/4 cup sugar

Beat egg yolks and 2 tablespoons sugar until light and fluffy. Stir in milk, softened ice cream, spices, and bourbon. Beat egg whites with remaining sugar until they peak. Spread meringue over mixture; sprinkle with additional spices. Chill several hours or overnight. Yield: about one gallon.

Mrs. Bernard Bordelon (Marie)
Avoyelles Parish (Moreauville)

SLUSH PUNCH

4 cups boiling water
6 cups sugar
3 3-ounce packages orange
  gelatin
1 3-ounce package lemon
  gelatin

2 6-ounce cans frozen lemonade
1 6-ounce can frozen orange juice
2 46-ounce cans pineapple juice
2 tablespoons almond extract
1 gallon water

Combine boiling water, sugar, gelatins, and frozen juices; stir well to dissolve. Add remaining ingredients to mixture. Pour in large mouth containers and freeze. Thaw 4 hours before serving. Stir to distribute ice crystals. Makes 2 gallons.

Mrs. Randall F. Bracy (Regina)
Tangipahoa Parish (Amite)

RUSSIAN TEA

3 quarts water
1 teaspoon whole cloves
1 teaspoon cinnamon
4 teaspoons orange Pekoe tea

1 cup sugar
Juice of 4 oranges
Juice of 3 lemons

Bring water to a boil; add cloves and cinnamon in separate cheesecloth bags. Cover; let simmer 5 minutes. Remove spices; add orange tea. Remove from heat; let stand three minutes, then remove tea. Add sugar to hot liquid. Add juice of oranges and lemons. Serve hot. Serves 20.

Mrs. John Smith (Thelma)
St. James Parish (St. James)

SHERRY FREEZE

1 bottle New York State dry
  sherry
1 tablespoon lemon juice

2 cups frozen apple juice
Sprigs of fresh mint

Combine first 3 ingredients, stirring well; freeze. To serve, put in blender; frappé until smooth. Garnish with mint.

Louisiana Farm Bureau Women's Committee

BEST BREWED TEA

1 quart water
1 quart size tea bag
1 quart ice cubes

1 cup sugar
1 teaspoon lemon juice

Bring water to a boil; turn off heat and put tea bag into boiling water. Allow to brew 15-20 minutes. Pour brewed tea over ice cubes which have been placed in a 2-quart pitcher. Add sugar and lemon juice to taste. Serves 10.

Mrs. Gary Bordelon (Melanie)
Avoyelles Parish (Moreauville)

CHAMPAGNE PUNCH

4½ cups sugar
2 cups lemon juice, warmed
1 large can crushed pineapple,
  undrained

2 quarts soda water, chilled
1 fifth Sauterne wine, chilled
1 fifth orange wine, chilled
1 fifth Champagne, chilled

Dissolve sugar completely in heated lemon juice; add pineapple. To serve, mix together soda water, wines and pineapple mixture. You may add a few ice cubes to keep punch chilled. Serves 40 to 50.

Louisiana Farm Bureau Women's Committee

SPICED TEA

1 14-ounce or 16-ounce jar of
  Tang
3 cups Lipton tea with lemon

3 cups sugar
2 teaspoons ground cinnamon
1 teaspoon ground cloves

Combine all ingredients; mix well. Store in an airtight container. To serve, use 2 or 3 teaspoons in a cup of hot water.

Mrs. Allen Bares (Lynn)
Vermilion Parish (Erath)

Gumbos,
Soups, and Sauces

Louisiana Governor's Mansion

CHICKEN ANDOUILLE GUMBO

1 cup all-purpose flour
1 cup shortening
1 cup chopped onions
1 cup chopped celery
1 cup chopped green pepper
1 clove garlic, chopped
Salt, pepper and cayenne to
 taste

1 hen, cut into pieces and seasoned
1 gallon water
1 pound andouille sausage, fried
 and drained
½ cup chopped parsley
Filé powder to taste

Make a roux by slowly browning the flour in the fat. This is a slow process and must be carefully watched and stirred constantly. When golden brown, add the onion, celery, garlic, and green pepper. Cook on low heat until the vegetables separate from the fat. Meanwhile, brown the cut-up chicken in some extra fat, using enough to sear the chicken. Add the chicken to the brown roux mixture; cook for a few minutes, stirring occasionally. Meanwhile, carefully pour out fat in which chicken has browned, leaving only the brown drippings at the bottom. Add water to brown drippings and bring to a boil; pour over the chicken, adding enough extra boiling water to render the meat tender and to give the gumbo the desired consistency. Cook on low heat for several hours. Add the cooked andouille during the last hour of cooking. Stir in parsley 15 minutes before done. To serve, gradually add filé until the desired flavor has been obtained.

Louisiana Farm Bureau Women's Committee

CHICKEN OKRA GUMBO

¼ cup butter or other fat
1 cup diced celery
½ cup diced green pepper
1 clove garlic, minced
1 cup chopped onion
2 cups cut okra
1 pound tomatoes, peeled and
 chopped

2 quarts hot water
1 2 to 3-pound chicken, cut into
 pieces
3 bay leaves
½ teaspoon cayenne pepper
1 teaspoon Worcestershire sauce

Melt butter in a large Dutch oven; add celery, pepper, garlic, onion and okra. Cook 5 minutes. Add tomatoes and water; heat to boiling. Simmer 10 minutes. Add chicken meat, bay leaves, cayenne and Worcestershire sauce. Simmer 40 minutes. Salt to taste. Serve hot with cooked rice. Note: Filé may be used if you like.

Mrs. Zoe Ray
Madison Parish (Tallulah)

CHICKEN AND SHRIMP GUMBO

1 4 to 5 pound hen
½ cup chopped celery
1 medium onion, chopped
1 medium green pepper,
  chopped
1½ pounds okra, cut into
  pieces
3 tablespoons bacon fat
1 teaspoon garlic salt
3 bay leaves
2 15-ounce cans tomatoes,
  undrained

1 6-ounce can tomato paste
1 tablespoon salt
1 teaspoon pepper
2 tablespoons Worcestershire sauce
1 tablespoon sugar
1 tablespoon paprika
½ tablespoon thyme
2 to 3 pounds raw shrimp, peeled
  and deveined
1 bunch green onions, chopped
Parsley leaves, if desired

Boil hen; debone chicken and save broth (2 to 3 quarts will be needed). Heat bacon fat in a large Dutch oven; add celery, onions, green pepper and okra, sautéing until tender. Add broth, garlic salt, bay leaves, tomatoes, tomato paste, salt, pepper, Worcestershire, sugar, paprika, and thyme. Simmer 3 hours. Add chicken and shrimp and simmer for an additional 30 minutes. Green onion and parsley leaves may be added if desired. Serve over rice, if desired.

Louisiana Farm Bureau Women's Committee

OKRA, SHRIMP, CRAB GUMBO

2 cups raw shrimp, peeled,
  deveined
1 teaspoon Tony's creole
  seasoning
1 cup vegetable oil
1 cup all-purpose flour
2 medium onions, chopped
½ cup chopped bell pepper

½ cup chopped green onion tops
6 cloves garlic, chopped
4 cups cut okra
1 teaspoon Tony's creole seasoning
4 quarts boiling water
12 boiled and cleaned crabs
1 tablespoon butter or margarine

Combine shrimp and creole seasoning; set aside. In a 10-quart soup pot, make a roux with oil and flour over medium-high heat, stirring until golden brown. Add shrimp, onion, celery, pepper, onion, and garlic; cook for 20 minutes. Add okra and creole seasoning; cook 20 minutes, stirring occasionally. Add boiling water and crabs; cook on medium heat for about ¾ hour, stirring often. Turn heat off; add butter and cover pot until ready for use. Serve with rice or hot garlic bread. Serves 16.

Mrs. James Graugnard, Sr. (Bertha)
West St. James Parish (St. James)

OLD FASHIONED OKRA GUMBO

2 tablespoons shortening
1 2½ pound broiler-fryer, cut up
2 pounds fresh okra
2 large onions, chopped
1 large green pepper, seeded and chopped

1 stalk celery, chopped
1 8-ounce can tomato sauce
1 pound smoked sausage, sliced ½-inch thick
Water
Salt and pepper to taste

Melt shortening in skillet; add chicken and fry until browned. Remove chicken, and fry okra, onion, bell pepper, and celery in drippings, until okra is tender. Combine all ingredients in 5-quart aluminum pot. Cook over low heat for 2 hours or until chicken is tender, but not falling off the bone. *NEVER use a black iron pot to fry or cook okra.*

Variations: Shrimp, crab, crawfish or any combination may be substituted. *Seafood should not be browned. Add to okra gumbo about 1 hour before serving.*

Mrs. Dewey Couvillon (Anne)
Avoyelles Parish (Hamburg)

SHRIMP GUMBO

2 pounds raw shrimp, peeled and deveined
2 tablespoons vegetable oil
2 tablespoons all-purpose flour
2 onions, chopped
1 green pepper, chopped
1 cup chopped celery
1 tablespoon melted butter
1 tablespoon filé powder

½ teaspoon garlic salt
½ teaspoon crushed red pepper
4 bay leaves
¼ teaspoon Tabasco sauce
2 tablespoons Lea & Perrins Worcestershire sauce
3 8-ounce cans tomato sauce
2 quarts water

Make a dark roux of flour and oil in a large Dutch oven. Sauté onion, peppers, and celery in butter. Combine vegetables and remaining ingredients in Dutch oven; bring to a boil; simmer for 2 hours. Serve over cooked rice.

Mrs. Allen Weeks (Cindy)
Ouachita Parish (West Monroe)

SEAFOOD GUMBO

2 cups all-purpose flour
1½ cups vegetable oil
1 medium onion, chopped
2 quarts water
Liquid from drained oysters

3 pounds cleaned shrimp
2 dozen cleaned crabs
1 quart drained oysters
2 teaspoons filé powder
Hot cooked rice

Brown flour in oil until golden brown. Add chopped onion and continue cooking about 3 minutes until onions are soft. Add 2 quarts of water and liquid from oysters. Boil until onions are tender. Add shrimp, crabs, and salt and pepper to taste. Boil 20 minutes; add oysters and enough water to make the amount of gumbo liquid you would like to have. Cook until oysters are curled, about 10 minutes. Add filé and serve over hot rice in a deep bowl.

Mrs. Marian Hargrave
Vermilion Parish (Gueydan)

DUCK GUMBO

Small amount of vegetable oil
1 onion, chopped
1 green pepper, chopped
4 to 5 stalks celery, chopped
2 tablespoons all-purpose flour
2 6-ounce cans tomato paste
2 quarts water

Salt, garlic salt, pepper, cayenne red
   pepper to taste
2 cups sliced okra
2 or 3 wild ducks, cooked and
   deboned
Steamed rice

Sauté onion, bell pepper and celery in small amount of heated oil; remove vegetables. Make a roux with oil and flour. Add water, tomato paste, sautéed vegetables and seasonings. Simmer 30 minutes. Add duck and okra. Simmer 15 minutes longer. Serve over steamed long grain rice.

Mrs. Marvin Spangler (Inez)
Ouachita Parish (West Monroe)

EASY CHILI

1½ pounds ground beef
1 chopped onion
1 chopped green pepper
1 clove garlic, minced
2 6-ounce cans Hunt's tomato
    paste

1 cup water
3 1-pound cans red beans
2 tablespoons chili powder
2 teaspoons salt

Brown beef, onion, green pepper and garlic in a large Dutch oven; add remaining ingredients. Heat to boiling; reduce heat and simmer all ingredients for 30 minutes.

Mrs. Marie Harper
Tangipahoa Parish (Hammond)

FRENCH ONION SOUP

3 large onions, thinly sliced
½ cup butter
1 quart seasoned chicken broth
1 quart hot water

6 slices toasted French bread
2 dashes Worcestershire sauce
Salt and pepper to taste
Sliced Mozzarella cheese

Melt butter over low heat in a 3-quart Dutch oven; sauté onions in butter until wilted and soft. Add broth, water, Worcestershire sauce, salt, and pepper; simmer about 1 hour. Place toast on top of soup; cover with slice of Mozzarella cheese. Place pot in oven and broil until cheese is melted, about 3 to 5 minutes.

Microwave Variation:
Melt butter in a 3-quart casserole for 1 minute on HIGH temperature; add onions and cover. Microwave on HIGH for 10 minutes. Add broth, water, and seasonings; microwave on HIGH for 15 minutes. Add toast and cheese slices; microwave on HIGH for 1 to 2 minutes or until cheese is melted.

Mrs. Grace Graugnard
St. James Parish (St. James)

MAQUECHOU A'LA AVOYELLES (CORN SOUP)

4 chicken bouillon cubes
3 quarts boiling water
2 large onions, chopped
2 medium bell peppers,
  chopped
Salt, pepper and garlic powder
  to taste

1 2½-pound soup bone
1 16-ounce can whole tomatoes,
  mashed and undrained
1 cup Ragu spaghetti sauce
1 quart fresh or frozen corn

Dissolve bouillon cubes in water; add onion, green pepper, salt, pepper, garlic powder and meat. Simmer until tender, about 45 minutes. Add tomatoes and spaghetti sauce; heat gently. Cook corn separately until tender; add to soup. Simmer soup about 15 minutes. Serve with homemade bread, if desired. Serves 6.

Mrs. Allen Brouillette (Joann)
Avoyelles Parish (Marksville)

POTATO SOUP BONNE FEMME

4 green onions bottoms or
  leeks, thinly sliced
2 onions, thinly sliced
5 tablespoons butter, divided
7 cups chicken stock (or beef
  stock)

4 medium sized potatoes
Salt to taste
Freshly ground pepper
1 tablespoon chopped parsley

Slice thinly the white part of green onion and the onion. Melt 3 tablespoons butter in a large saucepan. Add onions; cook over low heat until tender. Add stock, salt, and freshly ground pepper; bring to a boil. Cover; reduce heat and simmer. Peel potatoes and thinly slice; add to soup. Cover and let simmer until potatoes are very tender. Adjust seasonings, if needed. Just before serving, remove soup from the heat and stir in remaining 2 tablespoons of butter. Continue stirring until potatoes are well-blended. Add 1 tablespoon of chopped parsley. Serve with crusty French bread, or croutons, if desired. Serves 8.

Mrs. Leonard Gauthier (Motsy)
Avoyelles Parish (Moreauville)

MOMMA TWO'S POTATO SOUP

6 medium white potatoes, sliced
½ cup chopped onions
Water

1 or 2 teaspoons salt
Pepper to taste
½ cup butter
1 cup milk

Put potatoes and onions in heavy pot; cover with cold water. Add salt and pepper. Bring to a boil; reduce heat and simmer until potatoes flake and water is cooked down. Remove from heat; add butter. Mash potato mixture until slightly lumpy; add milk, stirring well. Simmer 3 minutes. Serves 4.

Mrs. JoBaya Foreman
Beauregard Parish (DeRidder)

CABBAGE SOUP

¼ cup butter
2 large onions, chopped
2 tablespoons all-purpose flour
4 pounds cabbage, shredded
4 cups water
2 cups canned whole tomatoes

2 teaspoons salt
½ teaspoon pepper
2 tablespoons sugar
2 tablespoons lemon juice
1 teaspoon caraway seed

Melt butter in large saucepan or Dutch oven. Add onions; sauté until tender. Stir in flour, blending well. Add cabbage, mixing well. Slowly add water, stirring constantly, and bring to a boil. Stir in tomatoes, salt, pepper, sugar, lemon juice, and caraway seed; simmer on low heat for at least 1 hour. Serves 12.

Note: This is even better the next day.

Mrs. Randall Bracy (Regina)
Tangipahoa Parish (Amite)

SPLIT PEA SOUP

1 package dry green split peas
¼ cup vegetable oil
½ pound bacon, cut in tiny
  strips
2 large onions
¼ cup chopped celery

2 cloves garlic
½ pound ham, cut in pieces
3 cups water
1 quart chicken broth
1 carrot, peeled and sliced
Salt and pepper to taste

Wash split peas and drain. Heat oil in a Dutch oven; add bacon. Fry until grease is out; add onions, celery, garlic and ham. Fry until vegetables are wilted. Add drained split peas, water, and chicken broth. Cook over low heat 1 to 1½ hours or until peas are completely dissolved. Add carrot 30 minutes before soup is done. If soup is too thick, add a little more water. Salt and pepper to taste.

Mrs. Grace Graugnard
St. James Parish (St. James)

OLD FASHIONED VEGETABLE SOUP

4 pounds soup meat with bone
1 large onion, chopped
2 stalks celery, chopped
½ head cabbage, shredded
1 15-ounce can whole tomatoes
1 8-ounce can tomato sauce
4 carrots, sliced
4 potatoes, cubed
1 turnip, cubed (when available)

1 4-ounce can green peas, drained
1 4-ounce can string beans, drained
1 4-ounce can butterbeans, drained
1 4-ounce can whole kernel corn,
  drained
1 7-ounce package vermicelli
  noodles
½ cup chopped parsley
Salt and pepper

Put soup meat in cold water; boil one hour. Add onion, celery, cabbage, tomatoes and tomato sauce. Heat to boiling; simmer 2 hours. About 45 minutes before done, add all vegetables and seasonings; cook 30 minutes. Add vermicelli and parsley; cook 15 minutes longer.

Variation: Omit vermicelli and add 1 cup wilted okra.

Louisiana Farm Bureau Women's Committee

BAR-B-Q SAUCE

18 large onions, peeled and
   quartered
2 pods garlic
1½ stalks celery, chopped
3 large green peppers, diced

3 quarts oil
3 small bottles Worcestershire
   sauce
1 9-ounce jar prepared mustard
1 6-ounce can tomato paste

Grind onions, garlic, celery, and green pepper; set aside. Heat oil in large Dutch oven. Add ground vegetables; cook until wilted, about ½ hour. Add Worcestershire sauce, mustard and tomato paste; cook on low heat 2 to 3 hours. Remove from heat; cool completely. Sauce may be stored in pints and placed in freezer.

Note: A deep pot is best for this recipe because of the splattering.

Mrs. Ulysse Gonsouldin Jr.
Iberia Parish (New Iberia)

BAR-B-Q SAUCE

15 ounces catsup
7 to 8 ounces (1 cup)
   Worcestershire sauce
1 cup vinegar

Juice of 1 lemon
1 tablespoon pepper
1 teaspoon sugar
¼ cup vegetable oil

Mix all together in a large saucepan; cook on low heat for 30 minutes. Yields 1 quart.

Note: This recipe can be used in preparing beef, pork, poultry, and wild game.

Mrs. Doug Moore (Liz)
Ouachita Parish (Monroe)

BAR-B-QUE SAUCE

1 bunch celery
3 pounds onions
1 clove garlic
1 15-ounce bottle ketchup
2 cups vegetable oil

2 cups water
2 8-ounce cans tomato paste
1 8-ounce can tomato sauce
2 tablespoons prepared mustard
1 tablespoon sugar

Grind celery, onions and garlic. Combine all ingredients in a large saucepan; bring to a boil. Reduce heat, and simmer for 1½ hours.

Mrs. Floyd Zaunbrecher (Cene Mae)
Vermilion Parish (Gueydan)

JIFFY BARBECUE SAUCE

¼ cup vegetable oil	3 tablespoons sugar
¾ cup chopped onion	3 tablespoons Worcestershire sauce
¾ cup catsup	2 tablespoons prepared mustard
¾ cup water	2 teaspoons salt
¼ cup lemon juice	½ teaspoon pepper

Heat oil in a skillet; add onions and sauté until soft. Add remaining ingredients; simmer for about 30 minutes.

Note: Can be used with any type of meat or poultry when barbecuing or baking. Especially delicious when used with cooked smoked sausage.

Mrs. Ronald Scioneaux (Hazel)
St. James Parish (Vacherie)

BARBEQUE SAUCE

1 8-ounce can tomato sauce	3 cups vegetable oil
10 medium onions, blended fine	Dash of salt
6 32-ounce bottles catsup, more or less	Crushed red pepper (optional)

Mix all ingredients in large pot; cook on low heat for about 2 hours. Yield: approximately 3 gallons.

Note: The finer the onions are blended the smoother the sauce.

Mrs. Anthony Hornsby (Jeannette)
Allen Parish (Oberlin)

JEZEBEL SAUCE

1 18-ounce jar pineapple preserves	1 5-ounce jar dry mustard
1 18-ounce jar apple jelly	5 tablespoons prepared horseradish
	1 tablespoon cracked black pepper

Mix all ingredients in electric mixer. Store indefinitely in refrigerator. Tangy and delicious with ham or as a dip for cocktail sausages, ham chunks or pork bits. May serve over softened cream cheese with crackers, if desired.

Mrs. Kaye Jennings　　　　　　　　　*Mrs. Codie Ray*
Ouachita Parish (Monroe)　　　　*Madison Parish (Tallulah)*

SEAFOOD COCKTAIL SAUCE

1 tablespoon lemon juice
½ teaspoon Mexene chili
  powder
1 tablespoon Worcestershire
  sauce

1 tablespoon prepared horseradish
½ teaspoon salt
½ cup catsup

Blend lemon juice and chili powder. Add Worcestershire, horseradish, salt and catsup. Chill and serve with any seafood. Yield: about ¾ cup.

Mrs. Marvin Spangler (Inez)
Ouachita Parish (West Monroe)

REMOULADE SAUCE

¼ cup lemon juice
¼ cup vinegar
  (tarragon-flavored vinegar is
  best, if available)
¼ cup prepared mustard
¼ cup horseradish
2 teaspoons salt

½ teaspoon pepper
2 teaspoons paprika
2 tablespoons catsup
1 cup vegetable oil
½ cup finely chopped celery
½ cup minced shallots

Combine lemon juice, vinegar, mustard, horseradish, salt, black pepper, paprika, dash red pepper, and catsup. Gradually add oil, stir with fork or beater to blend well. Add chopped celery and onions. Yield: 2 cups.

Note: Use tarragon-flavored vinegar for a better taste.

Louisiana Farm Bureau Women's Committee

TARTAR SAUCE

1 cup mayonnaise (always
  pronounced my-o-nez in
  French Louisiana)

1 large dill pickle, cut in chunks
1 medium-sized onion, quartered

Mix all ingredients in a food processor or blender; chill. Serve with your favorite seafood.

Louisiana Farm Bureau Women's Committee

RONNIE'S SMOKED TURKEY BASTING SAUCE

1 cup butter-flavored oil
½ cup margarine
2 bottles garlic juice
2 bottles onion juice

3 tablespoons salt
1 tablespoon red pepper
1 tablespoon pepper

Mix all ingredients in a saucepan; simmer for 20 to 30 minutes over low heat. Using a large syringe and needle, inject basting sauce into a 12 to 16 pound turkey at various points until all sauce is used. Place turkey in smoker and cook until done. For a delicious smoked turkey, try this sauce!!

Mrs. Ronald R. Anderson
East Feliciana Parish (Ethel)

CHEESE SAUCE FOR VEGETABLES

2 tablespoons butter or
  margarine
2 tablespoons all-purpose flour

1½ cups milk
4-5 slices process American cheese

Melt butter in a saucepan over medium heat; add flour, blending well to form a paste. Gradually add milk, stirring constantly, until mixture thickens. Remove from heat, add cheese and stir until blended. Pour over parboiled cauliflower, broccoli, cabbage or potatoes; bake at 350 degrees for 15 minutes. Make ahead and keep in refrigerator to bake the next day. Easy microwave recipe.

Mrs. Martin Cancienne (Sally)
Assumption Parish (Belle Rose)

HOLLANDAISE SAUCE

4 egg yolks
1 to 2 tablespoons lemon juice
1 cup butter, melted

¼ teaspoon salt
Dash of pepper

In top of a double boiler, beat egg yolks slightly; stir in lemon juice. Place over hot, but not boiling, water (Don't allow water in bottom pan to touch top pan). Add the butter gradually, stirring constantly, with wooden spoon. Stir in salt and pepper; continue cooking slowly, stirring constantly until mixture thickens. Yield: 1 cup.

Louisiana Farm Bureau Women's Committee

Salads and
Salad Dressings

Cochon De Lait

AMBROSIA

1 fresh coconut
1 dozen sweet Louisiana
   oranges, peeled and
   sectioned

1 cup sugar
Powdered sugar

Remove outer casing from coconut; grate, then set aside.

Place a layer of orange sections in the bottom of a large glass salad bowl; sprinkle with a portion of sugar. Top with a layer of coconut. Repeat layering until all ingredients are used, ending with coconut. Sprinkle ambrosia with powdered sugar, as desired. Chill at least 2 hours before serving. Yield: 10 to 12 servings. This is a famous Creole dessert.

Mrs. Allen Bares (Lynn)
Vermilion Parish (Erath)

FROZEN AMBROSIA SALAD

1 3¾-ounce package instant
   banana pudding mix
2 cups milk
1 8-ounce package cream
   cheese, softened
1 cup sour cream
1 8-ounce carton Cool Whip,
   thawed
1 30-ounce can fruit cocktail,
   drained

1 20-ounce can crushed pineapple,
   drained
1 8-ounce jar cherries, drained
1 cup miniature marshmallows
1 cup chopped pecans
¼ cup flaked coconut
¼ cup raisins

Prepare pudding according to package directions, using 2 cups milk; set aside. Combine cream cheese and sour cream in a medium mixing bowl; beat until creamy. Fold in pudding and Cool Whip; add remaining ingredients, stirring gently. Place fruit mixture in a large container or loafpan, or place in individual molds; Freeze until set. Remove salad from freezer ½ hour before serving. *This salad can be made up to 1 month in advance of serving time.*

Elise Castille
St. Martin Parish (Breaux Bridge)

FROZEN FRUIT SALAD

1 8-ounce carton frozen
  whipped topping, thawed
1 8-ounce carton commercial
  sour cream
1 16-ounce bottle maraschino
  cherries, drained and chopped

1 15¼-ounce can crushed
  pineapple, drained
5 bananas, mashed
1 cup chopped pecans

Combine all ingredients in a large bowl; stir well. Spoon mixture into a 10 x 6 x 1¾-inch glass dish or pan; cover. Freeze until firm. Remove salad from freezer 30 minutes before serving. Cut into squares, as desired. Yield: 8 servings.

Mrs. Alvin Klein (Margie)
Allen Parish (Oberlin)

FRUIT SALAD

1 29-ounce can sliced peaches
1 20-ounce can pineapple
1 12-ounce package cream
  cheese, softened
1 small package miniature
  marshmallows

1 7-ounce package flaked coconut
1 5-ounce package walnuts,
  chopped or ½ cup chopped
  pecans

Drain fruit, reserving about ⅛ of liquid. Cut fruit into bite-size pieces. Set aside. Beat cream cheese until fluffy in a large mixing bowl; add fruit, reserved liquid, and remaining ingredients, stirring well. Chill until serving time. Yield: 4 to 6 servings.

Anita Joyner
Tangipahoa Parish (Hammond)

FIVE CUP FRUIT SALAD

1 cup fresh orange sections
1 cup miniature marshmallows
1 cup flaked coconut

1 cup pecans, chopped
1 cup sour cream

Combine all ingredients; cover and chill several hours before serving. Yield: 4 to 6 servings.

Mrs. Ronald Scioneaux
St. James Parish (Vacherie)

FLUFFY FRUIT SALAD

1 8-ounce carton Cool Whip, thawed
1 8-ounce carton sour cream
¼ cup powdered sugar
1 16-ounce can fruit cocktail, drained

1 11-ounce can mandarin orange sections, drained
1 small can crushed pineapple, drained

Combine Cool Whip, sour cream, and powdered sugar in a medium bowl; fold in fruit. Chill until serving time. Yield: 4 to 6 servings.

Note: This salad can be made ahead and kept refrigerated for several days.

Mrs. James F. Harvey (Martha)
East Feliciana Parish (Jackson)

FRUIT CASSEROLE

1 1-pound 13-ounce can peach halves, drained
1 1-pound 13-ounce can pear halves, drained
1 1-pound 13-ounce can apricot halves, drained

1 1-pound 13-ounce can pineapple chunks, drained
1 16-ounce can cherry pie filling
½ cup Morgan David wine
¼ cup firmly packed brown sugar

Combine first 4 ingredients in a 3-quart glass casserole. Combine remaining ingredients; pour over fruit. Bake at 350 degrees for 1 hour and 30 minutes or until hot and bubbly. Yield: 12 servings. *This casserole freezes well.*

Mrs. Don Odom (Brenda)
Claiborne Parish (Homer)

PINEAPPLE PECAN SALAD

1 10-ounce can pineapple chunks
1 8-ounce package cream cheese, softened

½ cup miniature marshmallows
½ cup chopped pecans
Lettuce leaves

Drain pineapple, reserving 2 tablespoons juice. Set chunks aside. Combine cream cheese and reserved pineapple juice; mix well. Add pineapple chunks, marshmallows, and pecans, stirring well. Chill. Serve on lettuce leaves. Yield: 4 servings.

Mrs. Charles Waguespack (Lisa)
Ascension Parish (Donaldsonville)

JEAN'S CANTALOUPE SALAD

1 envelope unflavored gelatin
½ cup cold water
1 3-ounce box lemon Jello
1 3-ounce box orange Jello
2 cups boiling water
1 cantaloupe

½ cup mayonnaise
2 tablespoons vinegar
1 can apricot nectar
Chopped pecans (optional)
Drained crushed pineapple
   (optional)

Combine unflavored gelatin and cold water; let stand 5 minutes. Dissolve Jello in boiling water; add softened unflavored gelatin and stir until dissolved. Set aside. Slice cantaloupe in half; scoop out small balls. Peel remaining cantaloupe and mash or purée in a blender. Combine mashed cantaloupe, mayonnaise and vinegar in a large bowl; add gelatin mixture and apricot nectar. Chill until mixture is slightly thickened. When mixture is slightly thickened, gently fold in cantaloupe balls, and chopped pecans and crushed pineapple, if desired. Place gelatin in a ring mold or into individual salad molds. Chill until set. Yield: 6 to 8 servings.

Mrs. Louis D. Curet
East Baton Rouge Parish (Baton Rouge)

BUTTERFLY SALAD

1 egg
2 tablespoons sugar
1 tablespoon all-purpose flour
1 15-ounce can crushed
   pineapple, drained
1 16-ounce jar Royal Ann
   cherries

Juice of 1 lemon
2 tablespoons butter
2 cups miniature marshmallows
1 cup chopped pecans
1 pint whipping cream, whipped

Beat egg until broken up in a medium mixing bowl; stir in sugar, flour, pineapple, cherries, and lemon juice. Place mixture in a medium saucepan; cook over medium heat, stirring constantly, until thickened. Remove from heat; add butter. Let cool. Gently fold marshmallows, pecans, and whipped cream into cooled fruit mixture. Cover and let chill overnight. Yield: 4 to 6 servings.

Mrs. Marvin Spangler (Inez)
Ouachita Parish (West Monroe)

PINK PERFECTION SALAD

1 16-ounce can whole berry
   cranberry sauce
4 bananas, diced
1 cup canned crushed
   pineapple, drained

½ cup sugar
1 8-ounce carton Cool Whip,
   thawed
Lettuce leaves
Mayonnaise

Combine first 4 ingredients in a medium bowl; gently fold in Cool Whip. Spoon mixture into paper cup cake liners in muffin tins; freeze until set. To serve, remove paper liner and place on lettuce leaf with a dollop of mayonnaise. Yield: 20 large or 30 small salads. After salads are frozen, remove from muffin tins and store in plastic containers.

Mrs. U. M. Youngblood
Caldwell Parish (Columbia)

MILLION DOLLAR SALAD

1 16-ounce can crushed
   pineapple, drained
1 large package miniature
   marshmallows
1 cup chopped pecans

1 8-ounce package cream cheese,
   softened
2 tablespoons sugar
1 cup whipping cream, whipped
1 tablespoon mayonnaise

Combine first 3 ingredients; set aside. Beat cream cheese and sugar until fluffy in a medium mixing bowl; add pineapple mixture, stirring well. Gently fold whipped cream and mayonnaise into fruit mixture. Chill before serving. *This salad will keep well for several days in the refrigerator.*

Marie Harper
Tangipahoa Parish (Hammond)

CONGEALED PISTACHIO SALAD

1 16-ounce can fruit cocktail,
   drained
1 15-ounce can crushed
   pineapple
1 8-ounce carton Cool Whip,
   thawed

1 3¾-ounce package instant
   pistachio pudding mix
1 cup miniature marshmallows
1 cup chopped pecans

Combine all ingredients in a large bowl; chill 1 hour before serving. Yield: 4 to 6 servings.

Mrs. H. E. Baird (Tena)
Ouachita Parish (Monroe)

GREEN GELATIN MOLD

1 8-ounce package cream
   cheese, softened
1 6-ounce package lime Jello
1 cup finely chopped celery

1 cup miniature marshmallows
1 envelope Dream Whip instant
   topping mix

Combine cream cheese and Jello in a medium saucepan; cook over low heat, stirring constantly, until gelatin is dissolved. Add celery and marshmallows; cook over low heat only until marshmallows are melted. Remove from heat; let cool. Prepare Dream Whip according to package directions. Fold Dream Whip into cooled gelatin mixture; chill for 2 hours. Beat gelatin mixture until fluffy; pour into desired mold and chill until set. Yield: 6 servings.

Mrs. Wista White
Ouachita Parish (Monroe)

ORANGE SALAD

1 6-ounce package or 2
   3¾-ounce packages orange
   Jello
2 cups hot water
1 20-ounce can crushed
   pineapple, drained
1 11-ounce can mandarin
   oranges, drained

1 6-ounce can frozen orange juice
   concentrate, thawed
1 3¾-ounce package instant lemon
   pudding mix
1 cup milk
1 cup whipping cream, whipped

Combine gelatin and hot water; stir until dissolved. Add pineapple, oranges, and orange juice concentrate to gelatin mixture; stir well. Pour into a 13 x 9 x 2-inch dish; chill until set.

Combine pudding mix and milk; beat with electric mixer until thickened. Fold whipped cream into pudding mixture; spread over congealed orange mixture. Chill until serving time. Yield: 10 to 12 servings. *2 cups thawed Cool Whip may be used in place of whipped cream, if desired.*

Mrs. Ronald R. Anderson
E. Feliciana Parish (Ethel)

ORANGE GELATIN SALAD

2 cups boiling water
1 6-ounce package orange Jello
¼ cup sugar
1½ cups cold water
1 16-ounce can crushed
   pineapple, undrained

2 oranges, peeled and sectioned
1 envelope Dream Whip or 1
   8-ounce carton Cool Whip,
   thawed

Combine boiling water, gelatin, and sugar; stir until gelatin is dissolved. Add cold water, stirring well. Chill until mixture is slightly thickened. Prepare Dream Whip according to package directions; set aside. Gently add pineapple and juice, orange sections, and Dream Whip to cooled mixture. Pour gelatin into a mold; chill until set. Yield: 4 to 6 servings.

Mrs. Sam Womack
East Baton Rouge Parish (Baton Rouge)

ORANGE JELLO SALAD I

1 15-ounce can crushed
   pineapple, undrained
½ cup sugar
1 6-ounce package orange Jello
2 cups cold water

1 8-ounce carton Cool Whip,
   thawed
2 cups shredded Longhorn cheese
½ cup chopped pecans

Combine pineapple and sugar in a medium saucepan; bring to a boil over medium heat. Reduce heat to low; add Jello, stirring until well dissolved. Remove from heat; add cold water, stirring well. Place gelatin mixture in the freezer for 30 minutes or until it is slightly thickened. Gently add remaining ingredients to slightly thickened gelatin mixture. Pour mixture into mold or bowl, as desired; chill until set. Yield: 6 to 8 servings.

Mrs. H. E. Baird (Tena)
Ouachita Parish (Monroe)

ORANGE JELLO SALAD II

1 3¾-ounce package orange
Jello
1 8-ounce carton commercial
cottage cheese
1 12-ounce can crushed
pineapple

1 10-ounce can mandarin oranges
1 4-ounce carton Cool Whip,
thawed

Combine dry Jello and cottage cheese in a large bowl; stir well. Add fruit; mix well. Gently fold Cool Whip into gelatin mixture. Chill before serving. Yield: 4 to 6 servings. *Chopped pecans and flaked coconut may be added, if desired.*

Mrs. Donald Johnson (Brenda)
Ouachita Parish (Monroe)

STRAWBERRY-NUT SALAD

1 6-ounce package strawberry
Jello
1 cup boiling water
3 bananas, mashed
2 10-ounce packages frozen
sliced strawberries, thawed

1 5-ounce can crushed pineapple,
undrained
1 cup chopped nuts
1 16-ounce carton commercial sour
cream

Combine Jello and boiling water in a medium bowl; stir until gelatin is dissolved. Add bananas, strawberries, pineapple, and nuts; stir well. Pour half of gelatin mixture into a 12 x 8 x 2-inch pan; chill until set. Let remaining gelatin mixture stand at room temperature.

Spread sour cream over congealed gelatin mixture; pour remaining gelatin mixture over top. Chill until serving time. Yield: 12 servings.

Mrs. Henry Zeringue (Kathleen)
St. James Parish (St. James)

STRAWBERRY CONGEALED SALAD

1 6-ounce package strawberry Jello
2 cups boiling water
1 13½-ounce can crushed pineapple, undrained
2 10-ounce packages frozen sliced strawberries, thawed
2 bananas, sliced
½ cup chopped pecans (optional)
1 8-ounce carton sour cream

Combine Jello and boiling water in a large bowl; stir until gelatin is dissolved. Add pineapple, strawberries, and bananas; stir well. Add pecans, if desired. Pour half of gelatin mixture into a 13 x 9 x 2-inch dish; chill until set. Let remaining gelatin mixture stand at room temperature. Spread sour cream over congealed gelatin mixture; pour remaining gelatin mixture over top. Chill until serving time. Cut into about 20 squares to serve. Yield: 20 servings.

Mrs. Yvonne Waguespack
Terrebonne Parish (Gray)

RED AND WHITE DELIGHT

1 3-ounce package strawberry gelatin
1 cup boiling water
1 10-ounce package frozen strawberries, thawed
1 banana, mashed
1 small can crushed pineapple, drained
1 cup chopped nuts (optional)
1 16-ounce carton commercial sour cream

Combine gelatin and boiling water in a large bowl; stir until gelatin is dissolved. Add strawberries, banana, and pineapple; stir well. Add nuts, if desired. Pour half of gelatin mixture into an 8-inch square pan; chill until set. Let remaining gelatin mixture stand at room temperature. Spread sour cream over congealed gelatin mixture; pour remaining gelatin mixture over top to achieve a ribbon effect. Chill until serving time. Yield: 6 servings.

Helen Moreland
Concordia Parish (Monterey)

LOW CALORIE SALAD

1 5-ounce can crushed
  pineapple
1 3¾-ounce package
  strawberry gelatin

1½ cups cottage cheese
4 ounces Cool Whip

Combine crushed pineapple with juice, and gelatin in a saucepan; cook over low heat, stirring occasionally, until gelatin is dissolved. Remove from heat; let cool. Gently fold cottage cheese and Cool Whip into cooled gelatin mixture. Pour into individual molds or dish as desired. Chill until set. Yield: 4 servings.

Note: Any other flavor of gelatin may be used.

Mrs. Roy Anderson (Catherine)
Ouachita Parish (Monroe)

JELLIED PINEAPPLE AND CARROT SALAD

1 large can crushed pineapple
1 3-ounce package
  lemon-flavored gelatin
1 cup boiling water
1 tablespoon vinegar or lemon
  juice

½ teaspoon salt
1 cup grated carrots
Lettuce leaves
Mayonnaise

Drain pineapple, reserving 1 cup liquid. Set aside 1 cup pineapple. Combine gelatin and boiling water; stir until dissolved. Add reserved pineapple juice, vinegar, and salt. Chill until slightly thickened. Gently fold 1 cup crushed pineapple and carrots into thickened gelatin mixture; pour into 6 individual molds. Chill until set. Unmold salad, and serve on lettuce leaves with a dollop of mayonnaise. Yield: 6 servings.

Mrs. Eddie Schexnaydre (Doris)
Terrebonne Parish (Schriever)

HEAVENLY DIVINITY SALAD

1 8-ounce carton Cool Whip,
  thawed
1 14-ounce can sweetened
  condensed milk

1 21-ounce cherry pie filling
1 15-ounce can crushed pineapple,
  drained
1 cup chopped pecans

Place Cool Whip in a large bowl and stir well to fluffy up; fold in remaining ingredients. Chill at least 2 hours before serving. Serve on lettuce leaves, if desired. Yield: 4 servings.

Anita Joiner
Tangipahoa Parish (Hammond)

CRAWFISH MOLD

2 envelopes unflavored gelatin
1 cup water
1 10¾-ounce can tomato soup,
  undiluted
1 8-ounce package cream
  cheese, softened
2 pounds boiled crawfish,
  peeled and chopped

½ cup chopped celery
2 tablespoons chopped shallots
½ cup mayonnaise
Tabasco to taste (about ½ jar per
  recipe)

Combine gelatin and water; let stand 5 minutes. Combine soup and cream cheese in a large saucepan; cook over medium heat, stirring constantly, until mixture reaches boiling point. Remove from heat; add softened gelatin, stirring until dissolved. Cool; beat lightly with mixer to remove lumps of cheese. Add remaining ingredients to cooled gelatin mixture. Pour into a mold which has been sprayed with Pam; chill for 1½ to 2 hours or until set. Unmold and serve on a platter with Escort crackers. Yield: 8 servings.

Kitty Martin
St. James Parish (Paulina)

RICE BOX SALAD

1 pound fresh shrimp, cooked,
  peeled, and deveined
1 cup cooked rice, chilled
1 8-ounce can mandarin
  oranges, drained
12 pitted ripe olives, sliced
12 cherry tomatoes, halved
3 green onions, minced
3 canned water chestnuts, thinly
  sliced

1 cucumber, peeled and sliced
1 teaspoon salt
¼ teaspoon pepper or red pepper
2 cups mayonnaise
½ cup commercial sour cream
1 hard-cooked egg yolk, mashed
Juice of 1 lemon

Combine first 10 ingredients in a large salad bowl. Combine remaining ingredients in a medium bowl, stirring well to mix. Stir mayonnaise mixture into shrimp mixture, coating all ingredients well. Chill before serving. Yield: 6 servings.

Mrs. Patricia Pousson
Jeff Davis Parish (Welsh)

SHRIMP MOLD

2 envelopes unflavored gelatin
¼ cup cold water
1 10¾-ounce can tomato soup, undiluted
3 3-ounce packages cream cheese, softened

2 cups cooked, peeled shrimp
1 cup mayonnaise
¾ cup finely diced celery
¼ cup finely chopped green onions
Tabasco to taste

Combine gelatin and water; let stand 5 minutes. Heat soup to boiling in a medium saucepan; add cream cheese, stirring until dissolved. Remove from heat; add gelatin mixture, shrimp, mayonnaise, celery, onions, and hot sauce to taste. Pour into a lightly-greased mold; chill until set (about 24 hours). Unmold salad onto a platter; serve with crackers. Yield: 6 to 8 servings. Cooked chicken, ham or beef may be substituted for shrimp, if desired. Also, Lea and Perrins sauce may be added to taste, if desired.

Mrs. Randall Bracy (Regina)
Tangipahoa Parish (Amite)

SHRIMP SALAD

2 pounds seasoned boiled shrimp, peeled, and deveined
3 hard-cooked eggs, grated
2 stalks celery, finely chopped
½ cup mayonnaise
1 teaspoon prepared mustard
½ teaspoon salt

¼ teaspoon pepper
Tomatoes, cut into wedges (optional)
Avocados, cut in half
Olives
1 hard-cooked egg, quartered

Combine first 7 ingredients in a medium bowl; chill. Spoon shrimp salad into tomato wedges or avocado halves to serve. Top each serving with an olive and a quarter of remaining hard-cooked egg. Yield: 4 servings.

Joan Falgoust
St. James Parish (St. James)

CRABMEAT SALAD

1 14-ounce package frozen
  crabmeat, thawed and drained
1 cup chopped celery
¼ cup chopped green onions

¼ cup French dressing
1 teaspoon grated onion
¼ teaspoon garlic salt
1 cup mayonnaise

Combine all ingredients, except mayonnaise, in a medium bowl; chill several hours. Stir in mayonnaise, serve as a sandwich filling or as a salad on a lettuce leaf.

Marie Harper
Tangipahoa Parish (Hammond)

BEET SALAD

1 head lettuce
4 large fresh beets
¼ teaspoon salt

1 8-ounce bottle Wishbone Salad
  Dressing

Wash and core lettuce; pat lettuce dry and place in refrigerator to crisp. Wash beets; cook beets in boiling water until tender. Drain and let cool. Remove skin from beets and cut into ¼-inch cubes. Sprinkle beets with salt. Arrange beet cubes on lettuce leaves; top with salad dressing, as desired. Yield: 4 servings.

Mrs. Kerry Burns (Nancy)
Webster Parish (Minden)

WILTED LETTUCE SALAD

3 slices bacon
2 large heads lettuce
4 green onions, chopped

1 tablespoon vinegar
Salt and pepper to taste
2 hard-cooked eggs, sliced

Fry bacon until crisp in a skillet; drain bacon and reserve pan drippings. Let bacon cool to touch; crumble into pieces. Tear lettuce into bite-size pieces in a heatproof bowl; add onion and crumbled bacon. Combine hot bacon drippings and vinegar; pour over lettuce. Add salt and pepper to taste. Toss well, and garnish with hard cooked egg slices. Yield: 8 servings.

Donna Thompson
Concordia Parish (Monterey)

MARINATED BEAN AND PEA SALAD

Salad:

1 15-ounce can French-cut
   green beans, drained
1 15-ounce can green peas,
   drained
1 15-ounce can kidney beans,
   drained
1 15-ounce can wax beans,
   drained
1 15-ounce can bean sprouts,
   drained

1 3-ounce jar pimiento strips,
   drained
1 to 2 jars artichoke hearts, drained
   and cut into halves
1 cup chopped celery
1 green pepper, sliced
1 purple onion, thinly sliced
½ cup carrot strips
Sliced fresh mushrooms (optional)

Combine all ingredients in a large bowl; stir well.

Marinade:

1 8-ounce bottle Italian salad
   dressing
1 cup sugar
1¼ cups vinegar

½ cup vegetable oil
1 tablespoon salt
Pepper to taste

Combine all ingredients; stir well. Add marinade to salad mixture, stirring well. Cover and refrigerate overnight, stirring twice. Store covered in the refrigerator for up to 1 week. Yield: 10 to 12 servings.

Wynnde Farmer
Beauregard Parish (Dry Creek)

THREE BEAN SALAD

1 15-ounce can green beans,
   drained
1 15-ounce can yellow wax
   beans, drained
1 15-ounce can kidney beans,
   drained

3 medium onions, thinly sliced
½ cup sugar
¾ cup vegetable oil
¾ cup vinegar
½ teaspoon salt

Combine all ingredients in a large bowl; cover. Marinate for 24 hours in the refrigerator. Serve with a slotted spoon. Yield: 4 to 6 servings.

Mrs. Doug Moore (Liz)
Ouachita Parish (Monroe)

MARINATED CARROT SALAD

5 cups drained canned carrots
(about 3 cans)
1 medium-sized onion, thinly
sliced and separated into
rings
1 medium-sized green pepper,
seeded and sliced into rings
½ cup sugar

½ cup vinegar
¼ cup vegetable oil
1 teaspoon salt
1 teaspoon pepper
1 teaspoon dry mustard
1 teaspoon Worcestershire sauce
1 10¾-ounce can tomato soup,
undiluted

Combine vegetables in a large heatproof bowl or casserole; set aside. Combine remaining ingredients, except soup, in a saucepan; cook over medium heat until boiling. Add soup, stirring well; cook until hot. Pour soup mixture over vegetables. Cover and marinate in refrigerator overnight. Yield: 8 servings.

Mrs. Clifton Lofton (Helen)
Oberlin Parish (Allen)

MARINATED CARROTS

2 pounds carrots, peeled and
sliced
1 large onion thinly sliced and
separated into rings
1 medium-sized green pepper,
seeded and sliced into rings
1 10¾-ounce can tomato soup,
undiluted

¾ cup sugar
¾ cup vinegar
½ cup vegetable oil
1 teaspoon prepared mustard
1 teaspoon Worcestershire sauce

Cook carrots in boiling water until crisp tender. Drain, and let carrots cool to touch. Alternate layers of carrot slices, onion rings and green pepper rings in a deep casserole until all are used. Combine remaining ingredients in a medium bowl, stirring well. Pour soup mixture over vegetables; cover. Marinate in refrigerator overnight. Store in refrigerator for several weeks. Yield: 8 to 10 servings.

Connie Granger
Beauregard Parish (DeRidder)

MOLDED CABBAGE SALAD

1 3¾-ounce package lime
   gelatin
1 cup hot water
1 cup cabbage, finely chopped
1 9-ounce can crushed
   pineapple, drained

½ cup coarsely chopped nuts
¾ cup mayonnaise
1 5.3-ounce can evaporated milk,
   chilled well

Combine gelatin and hot water; stir until gelatin is dissolved. Add cabbage, pineapple, and nuts to gelatin mixture. Fold in mayonnaise; chill until slightly thickened.

Beat chilled milk until stiff with an electric mixer. Fold whipped milk into slightly thickened gelatin mixture. Pour into a lightly greased mold; chill until set. Yield: 4 to 6 servings.

Dottie Schoendorf
St. Tammany Parish (Folsom)

SPINACH SALAD AND DRESSING

Dressing:
1 cup vegetable oil
5 tablespoons red wine vinegar
¼ cup commercial sour cream
2 tablespoons sugar
1½ teaspoons salt

¼ teaspoon dry mustard
¼ teaspoon pepper
2 teaspoons chopped fresh parsley
2 cloves garlic, crushed

Combine all ingredients in container of electric blender; blend well. Chill. Store covered in refrigerator for 2 weeks. Yield: 1½ cups.

Salad:
4 bunches fresh spinach,
   washed
½ pound fresh mushrooms,
   sliced
1 8-ounce can water chestnuts,
   drained and sliced

8 slices bacon, cooked, drained,
   and crumbled
4 hard cooked eggs, sliced

Tear spinach into bite-size pieces and place in a salad bowl; add mushrooms, water chestnuts, bacon, and eggs. Add dressing at serving time; toss well. Yield: 16 servings.

Joan Falgoust
St. James Parish (St. James)

Salads

LAYERED SALAD I

1 small head lettuce, torn into bite-size pieces
1 bunch fresh spinach, torn into bite-size pieces
1 17-ounce can tiny peas, drained or 1 10-ounce package frozen green peas, thawed
1 can water chestnuts, drained and sliced
½ cup thinly sliced onion
½ pound bacon, cooked, drained, and crumbled
4 hard-cooked eggs, sliced
Salt
Pepper
1 cup mayonnaise
1 8-ounce carton commercial sour cream
1 cup grated Parmesan cheese
2 tablespoons sugar

Place lettuce and spinach in the bottom of a large salad bowl. Top with peas, water chestnuts, onion, crumbled bacon and two sliced hard cooked eggs. Sprinkle with salt, then pepper, as desired. Combine mayonnaise and sour cream, stirring well. Spread mayonnaise mixture over salad to seal tightly. Sprinkle with cheese, then sugar. Garnish with remaining 2 hard cooked egg slices. Cover, chill 8 hours or overnight. Yield: 10 to 12 servings.

Karen Logan
Caddo Parish (Gilliam)

LAYERED SALAD II

1 small head lettuce
½ cup chopped celery
½ cup chopped green onion
1 small green pepper, seeded and chopped
1 10-ounce package frozen green peas, thawed
1 8-ounce carton commercial sour cream
1 cup mayonnaise
1 cup grated Parmesan cheese or shredded Cheddar cheese
4 slices bacon, cooked, drained, and crumbled

Tear lettuce into bite-size pieces and place in the bottom of a large salad bowl or deep casserole; layer next 4 ingredients over lettuce. Spread sour cream over pea layer; top with mayonnaise, spreading well to seal edges of salad tightly. Sprinkle with cheese, as desired; top with bacon. Cover; refrigerate overnight. Toss well to serve. Yield: 12 servings. This salad remains crisp for 3 to 4 days when the seal of sour cream and mayonnaise is not broken.

Mrs. Randall F. Bracy (Regina)
Tangipahoa Parish (Amite)

SEVEN LAYER SALAD I

½ cup chopped purple onion
Sugar
1 head lettuce, shredded
½ cup chopped green pepper
¾ cup chopped celery
1 17-ounce can English peas, drained

2 cups mayonnaise
3 hard-cooked eggs, sliced
12 slices bacon, cooked, drained, and crumbled
¾ cup grated Parmesan cheese

Combine onion and a small amount of sugar; set aside. Place lettuce in the bottom of a 3-quart casserole or a large salad bowl; top with sweetened onion. Layer with green pepper, celery, and peas. Spread mayonnaise over top of salad to seal tightly. Place egg slices over mayonnaise, then sprinkle with cheese. Top with bacon; cover. Chill overnight. Toss well to serve. Yield: 10 to 12 servings.

Mrs. James Parkerson (Joyce)
Ouachita Parish (Monroe)

SEVEN LAYER SALAD II

1 head lettuce, washed and well dried
1 large purple onion, chopped
2 cups chopped celery
1 large green pepper, thinly sliced into rings

1 28-ounce can English peas, drained
2 cups mayonnaise
2 cups shredded Cheddar cheese
12 slices bacon, cooked, drained, and crumbled

Tear lettuce into bite-size pieces and place in the bottom of a large glass salad bowl. Top with onion, then celery, pepper rings, and peas. Spread mayonnaise over top of salad to seal tightly. Sprinkle with cheese. Cover with plastic wrap; refrigerate overnight. To serve, top with bacon, then toss well. Yield: 18 servings. Two teaspoons sugar may be added to mayonnaise before spreading over salad, if desired.

Lavon G. Pruitt
Webster Parish (Minden)

SEVEN LAYER SALAD III

1 head lettuce, washed
1 bunch fresh spinach, washed
2 bunches green onions,
  chopped
1 10-ounce package frozen
  green peas, thawed
¾ pound bacon, cooked,
  drained, and crumbled
8 hard-cooked eggs, sliced
1 cup mayonnaise
1 cup commercial sour cream
1 package Hidden Valley Ranch
  Dressing (Original Flavor)

Tear lettuce and spinach into bite-size pieces and place in the bottom of a large sealable container or salad bowl. Layer next 4 ingredients over salad green mixture.

Combine remaining ingredients in a medium bowl; spread dressing over salad to seal tightly. Refrigerate overnight. Toss well to serve. Yield: 20 servings.

Mrs. Charles Waguespack
Ascension Parish (Donaldsonville)

SPRING PARTY SALAD

Salad:
1 10-ounce package frozen
  broccoli spears
1 10-ounce package frozen
  artichoke hearts
1 10-ounce package frozen
  baby lima beans
1 10-ounce package frozen
  asparagus
1 10-ounce package French-style
  green beans

Cook all vegetables half the time directed on packages. Drain vegetables well; chop broccoli and artichoke hearts into bite-sized pieces. Combine all vegetables in a large bowl.

Dressing:
1 cup mayonnaise
¾ cup chopped fresh parsley
½ cup half-and-half
¼ cup chopped onion
2 teaspoons lemon juice
2 teaspoons garlic-flavored vinegar
2 teaspoons anchovy paste
  (optional)

Combine all ingredients in container of electric blender; blend well. Pour dressing over vegetables; toss well. Cover; marinate 24 hours in the refrigerator, stirring occasionally. Yield: 8 to 10 servings.

Mrs. Melba McIntosh
W. Carroll Parish (Pioneer)

TWENTY-FOUR HOUR SALAD

Salad:
1 16-ounce can French-style
  green beans, drained
1 16-ounce can English peas,
  drained
1 cup chopped celery

1 3-ounce can pimiento, drained
  and chopped
1 onion, chopped
½ large green pepper, chopped

Combine all ingredients in a large bowl.

Dressing:
1¼ cups sugar
1 cup vinegar

½ cup vegetable oil
¼ cup water

Combine all ingredients, stirring well. Pour dressing over mixed vegetables; toss well to coat. Cover; marinate for 24 hours in the refrigerator. Yield: 8 servings. *Wine vinegar may be substituted for vinegar, if desired.*

Mrs. Perry Fisher (Bert)
Ouachita Parish (Monroe)

MARINATED VEGETABLE SALAD

1 16-ounce can whole kernel
  corn, drained
1 16-ounce can sliced carrots,
  drained
1 17-ounce can cut green
  beans, drained
1 medium onion, thinly sliced
  and separated into rings

1 green pepper, seeded and sliced
1 stalk celery, sliced diagonally
¾ cup sugar
½ cup vegetable oil
½ cup cider vinegar
1 tablespoon celery seed or
  poppy seeds
1 teaspoon salt

Combine first 6 ingredients in a large bowl with a tight-fitting lid; stir well. Combine remaining ingredients; pour over vegetable mixture; stir well. Cover; chill for at least 12 hours before serving. Yield: 6 servings. *This salad will keep well for several days in the refrigerator.*

Mrs. Wayne Zaunbrecher (Linda)
Vermilion Parish (Gueydan)

POLYNESIAN SALAD

¾ cup vinegar
1 cup sugar
1 teaspoon salt
1 12-ounce can French-style
green beans, drained
1 12-ounce can small English
peas, drained

1 12-ounce can mixed Chinese
vegetables, drained
1 6-ounce can water chestnuts,
drained and chopped
1½ cups chopped celery
3 purple onions, thinly sliced and
separated into rings

Heat vinegar until warm over low heat; remove from heat and add sugar and salt. Stir vinegar until sugar and salt are dissolved. Set aside. Combine vegetables in a bowl; add vinegar mixture, stirring well. Cover; marinate overnight. Drain and serve. Yield: 4 to 6 servings. This salad remains crisp for 3 weeks in the refrigerator.

Alice Faye Hart
Ouachita Parish (Monroe)

GOLDEN RICE SALAD

1½ cups long grain rice
3 cups chicken broth
¼ cup vegetable oil
2 tablespoons vinegar
2 tablespoons prepared
mustard
1½ teaspoons salt
⅛ teaspoon pepper
1½ cups diced celery
1 cup pitted ripe olives, diced

4 green onions, minced
2 hard-cooked eggs, diced
½ cup mayonnaise
¼ cup chopped dill pickles
¼ cup diced pimiento
Lettuce leaves
Sliced hard-cooked eggs, (optional)
Ripe olives (optional)
Pimiento strips (optional)

Cook rice in 3 cups chicken broth until done. Meanwhile, combine oil, vinegar, mustard, salt, and pepper; pour over hot cooked rice, tossing well to coat. Set rice aside to cool. Add next seven ingredients to cooled rice; toss well. Chill thoroughly. Serve rice salad on lettuce leaves; garnish with hard-cooked egg slices, ripe olives, or pimiento strips as desired. Yield: 8 to 10 servings.

Mrs. James R. Frieson (Billie)
Calcasieu Parish (Lake Charles)

RICE SALAD

3 cups cold cooked rice
4 hard-cooked eggs, chopped
½ cup finely chopped onion
½ cup finely chopped sweet
   pickle
¼ cup finely chopped celery

¼ cup finely chopped
   pimiento-stuffed olives
1 teaspoon salt
1 teaspoon prepared mustard
½ teaspoon pepper
1 cup mayonnaise

Combine all ingredients in a large bowl; chill, if desired, or serve at room temperature. Serve on lettuce leaves; garnish with fresh parsley and olive slices, if desired. Yield: 6 to 7 servings.

Mrs. Wayne Zaubrecher (Linda)
Vermilion Parish (Gueydan)

RICE SALAD

3 cups hot cooked rice
½ cup chopped shallots or
   onions
½ cup chopped celery
3 hard-cooked eggs, chopped
⅓ cup Creamy Cucumber
   dressing
⅓ cup sweet pickle relish

¼ cup chopped green pepper
¼ cup chopped fresh parsley
¼ cup chopped pimiento
Salt and pepper to taste
Green pepper strips (optional)
Pimiento strips (optional)
Paprika (optional)

Combine first 9 ingredients in a large bowl; add salt and pepper to taste. Pack rice salad into a bowl; chill. To serve, invert bowl onto a serving platter. Garnish with green pepper strips and pimiento strips, if desired. Sprinkle with paprika. Yield: 8 servings. *Mixing all ingredients while rice is hot adds flavor to this salad. It may also be garnished with chopped cucumber, if desired.*

Louisiana Farm Bureau Women's Committee

OVERNIGHT LETTUCE SALAD

1 head lettuce
1 head cauliflower, separated
   into flowerets
1 onion, thinly sliced and
   separated into rings
1 pound bacon, fried, drained,
   and crumbled

⅓ cup grated Parmesan cheese
¼ cup sugar
1 to 2 cups mayonnaise or salad
   dressing

Tear lettuce into bite-size pieces and place in a large salad bowl. Top with cauliflower, onion rings, and then bacon; sprinkle with cheese, then sugar. Spread mayonnaise over top of salad to seal tightly. Cover and refrigerate overnight. Toss well to serve. Yield: 8 servings. *Green pepper rings, carrot slices, or canned green peas may be added to this salad if desired.*

Mrs. Mansel S. Slaughter (Pearl)
East Baton Rouge Parish (Baker)

PEA SALAD

1 8-ounce package cream
   cheese, softened
3 to 4 tablespoons mayonnaise
4 hard-cooked eggs, chopped

1 16-ounce can sweet green peas,
   drained
Salt and pepper to taste

Combine cream cheese and mayonnaise in a medium bowl; mix well. Add chopped eggs, stirring well. Gently fold peas into cheese mixture; add salt and pepper to taste. Chill before serving. Serve with tomatoes, green peppers, or salad, if desired. Yield: 6 servings. Add chopped ham to pea salad to make this a hearty main dish salad. Extra sweet peas and hard-cooked eggs may be added for large gatherings.

Mrs. Ricky Monceaux (Tina)
Allen Parish (Oberlin)

WATERGATE SALAD

1 3¾-ounce package pistachio pudding and pie filling mix
1 medium can crushed pineapple, undrained
1 12-ounce carton Cool Whip, thawed
2 cups miniature marshmallows
½ cup chopped nuts
1 small jar maraschino cherries, drained (optional)

Combine pudding mix and crushed pineapple with juice in a medium bowl; stir well. Gently fold Cool Whip, marshmallows, and nuts into pudding mixture. Add cherries, if desired. Pour into a casserole or mold; chill until set. Yield: 4 to 6 servings.

Mrs. Dorothy Scheondorf
St. Tammany Parish (Folsom)

CRUNCHY SPINACH SALAD DRESSING

8 to 10 slices bacon
¼ cup chopped onion
1 tablespoon brown sugar
1 tablespoon vinegar
1 teaspoon dry mustard
1 teaspoon salt
½ teaspoon pepper
Fresh spinach, washed and torn into pieces

Fry bacon until done in a skillet; remove bacon and drain, reserving pan drippings. Let bacon cool to touch, then crumble. Set bacon aside. Sauté onions in pan drippings until clear. Add sugar, vinegar, mustard, salt, and pepper to onion mixture. Heat to boiling over medium heat, stirring frequently. Remove from heat.

Place spinach in a salad bowl; pour hot dressing over spinach. Toss well. Sprinkle with bacon. Yield: 6 to 8 servings.

Mrs. Melba McIntosh
W. Carroll Parish (Pioneer)

SPECIAL SALAD DRESSING

½ cup grated Parmesan cheese
2 teaspoons salt
2 teaspoons dry mustard
1 teaspoon white pepper
1 teaspoon garlic powder
1 teaspoon celery salt
1 teaspoon paprika

2 eggs, well beaten
1 quart vegetable oil
Juice of 2 lemons
¼ cup wine vinegar
½ cup finely chopped anchovies
2 teaspoons Worcestershire sauce

Combine first 7 ingredients in a large bowl. Add eggs, mix thoroughly with an electric mixer. Add oil, lemon juice, vinegar, anchovies, and Worcestershire sauce, beating constantly at medium speed of mixer. Beat until thick and creamy. Yield: 5 cups.

Mrs. Louis D. Curet
East Baton Rouge Parish (Baton Rouge)

BLENDER MAYONNAISE

2 eggs
¼ cup lemon juice
1 teaspoon salt

1 teaspoon prepared mustard
2 cups vegetable oil

Combine eggs, lemon juice, salt, mustard, and ½ cup oil in the container of an electric blender; blend 5 seconds. Gradually add remaining oil, blending on low speed; blend until all oil is added and mixture is thick and creamy. Yield: 2 cups.

Mrs. H. G. Hardee, Jr. (Sue)
Vermilion Parish (Gueydan)

MOCK ROQUEFORT SALAD DRESSING

2 cups mayonnaise
1 cup buttermilk
2 green onions, chopped
1 teaspoon garlic salt
½ to 1 teaspoon salt

1 teaspoon dried onion flakes
1 teaspoon Accent
½ teaspoon dried parsley flakes
½ teaspoon pepper

Combine all ingredients in container of electric blender; blend well. Chill. Yield: about 3¼ cups.

Mrs. Marvin Spangler (Inez)
Ouachita Parish (West Monroe)

Seafood

Louisiana Brown Pelican

CRABMEAT

Sweet, fresh crabmeat is so versatile that its use is only limited by the creativity of the cook. "Crabbing" is a great past time for adults and children alike. Almost everyone knows a place not far from home where crabs can be caught. The only necessity is a string and some leftovers for bait. Crab shells stuffed with deviled crab meat are the universal favorite. Crabmeat is also used in cocktails, salads, soups, jambalaya, gumbo, elegant main dishes and a wide variety of casseroles.

CRABMEAT IMPERIAL

1 green pepper, chopped
1 tablespoon prepared mustard
1 tablespoon salt
½ teaspoon pepper

2 eggs, beaten
1 cup mayonnaise
3 pounds lump crabmeat

Preheat oven to 350 degrees. In a large mixing bowl, thoroughly mix green pepper, mustard, salt, egg, mayonnaise and pepper. Add crabmeat. Mix with fingers so lumps are broken. Pour into casserole. Bake at 350 degrees for 15 minutes or until bubbly.

Note: Sliced mushrooms and onion may be added, if desired.

Mrs. Wayne Petticrow (Betty)
Calcasieu Parish (Iowa)

CRABMEAT MORNAY

½ cup butter
4 to 6 green onions, chopped
½ cup finely chopped fresh
  parsley
2 tablespoons all-purpose flour
1 pint half-and-half

½ pound Swiss cheese, shredded
1 tablespoon cooking sherry
Red pepper to taste
Salt to taste
1 pound white crabmeat

Melt butter in a heavy saucepan over low heat; add onions and parsley. Sauté until tender. Blend in flour, stirring constantly, until well combined. Gradually stir in cream and cheese, stirring well until cheese is melted and mixture is thickened. Add remaining ingredients; heat through. Serve as a dip with Melba toast, or over rice as a main dish.

Mrs. Codie Ray
Madison Parish (Tallulah)

CRABMEAT AU GRATIN

1 cup chopped onion
1 stalk celery, chopped
½ cup butter, melted
2 tablespoons chopped green
  onion
½ cup all-purpose flour
1 13-ounce can Pet evaporated
  milk

1 teaspoon salt
1 tablespoon fresh minced parsley
½ teaspoon cayenne red pepper
½ teaspoon pepper
2 egg yolks, slightly beaten
1 pound fresh crabmeat
½ pound shredded process
  American cheese

Preheat oven to 375 degrees. Sauté onions and celery in butter over low heat. Add green onions and fry slightly. Blend in flour, stirring well. Gradually add milk, and seasonings, stirring constantly. Cook until thickened; remove from heat. Gradually add beaten egg yolks, stirring constantly. Cook on low heat 5 minutes or until thickened. Remove from heat; gradually fold in crabmeat. Pour mixture into a greased 1½-quart casserole; top with cheese. Bake at 375 degrees for 20 minutes. Yield: 4 servings.

Grace Graugnard
St. James Parish (St. James)

CRABMEAT CASSEROLE

½ cup chopped onions
⅔ cup chopped green peppers
1 clove garlic, minced
1 cup chopped celery
½ cup margarine, melted
1 pound crabmeat (fresh or
  canned)
¼ cup diced pimiento
4 slices bread, moistened and
  torn into pieces

2 cups cooked rice
½ cup water
1 10¾-ounce can cream of
  mushroom soup, undiluted
Seasonings to taste
Butter
Dry breadcrumbs

Preheat oven to 375 degrees. In a medium saucepan, sauté onions, green peppers, garlic and celery in margarine until tender. Add crabmeat and pimiento; heat until hot. Stir in bread, cooked rice, water and soup. Cook 5 minutes over low heat; season to taste. Place in a large lightly greased casserole; dot with butter and breadcrumbs. Bake at 375 degrees for 45 minutes.

Evelina Smith
Beauregard Parish (DeRidder)

CRAB CASSEROLE

2 tablespoons butter
2 tablespoons all-purpose flour
½ cup milk
½ cup whipping cream
¼ teaspoon ground nutmeg
¼ teaspoon dry mustard
Salt to taste

Pepper to taste
1 teaspoon instant onion flakes
2 egg yolks
Hot sauce
3 cups crabmeat
Shredded Cheddar cheese

Preheat oven to 350 degrees. In a heavy saucepan make cream sauce with butter and flour, over low heat, heating milk and cream before adding to saucepan. Stir constantly until smooth. Remove from heat and stir in nutmeg, mustard, salt, pepper and onion. Beat egg yolks lightly with a dash of hot sauce and gradually add to sauce. Cook over low heat, stirring constantly until thickened. Remove from heat; fold in crabmeat. Pour into buttered casserole and sprinkle with cheese. Bake at 350 degrees until hot and cheese is melted, about 15 minutes.

Anita Joyner
Tangipahoa Parish (Hammond)

ALMOND-TOPPED CRAB QUICHE

1 9-inch baked pie shell
1 cup (¼ pound) shredded
  Swiss cheese
½ pound fresh crabmeat
2 green onions, sliced
3 eggs

1 cup half-and-half
½ teaspoon salt
½ teaspoon grated lemon rind
Dash of dry mustard
Dash of pepper
¼ cup sliced almonds

Preheat oven to 325 degrees. Sprinkle cheese in pastry shell. Remove and discard cartilage from crabmeat. Place crabmeat on top of cheese; sprinkle with green onions. Beat eggs until foamy; stir in half-and-half, salt, lemon rind, dry mustard and pepper. Pour into pastry shell, and sprinkle with almonds. Bake for 1 hour or until set. Let stand 10 minutes before serving. Yield: One 9-inch quiche.

Elsie Castille
St. Martin Parish (Breaux Bridge)

FRIED HARD SHELL CRABS

2 dozen fresh crabs
2 tablespoons salt
2 tablespoons black pepper
1 tablespoon red cayenne
  pepper
3 tablespoons prepared
  mustard

1 tablespoon Worcestershire sauce
1 tablespoon garlic powder
1 lemon
2 large onions, sliced
Zatarain's Chicken Fry
Vegetable oil

Scald 2 dozen crabs. Remove hull, feelers, lungs, etc. Place crabs in a large covered bowl and season with salt, pepper, red pepper, mustard, Worcestershire sauce and garlic powder. Squeeze juice of 1 lemon over crabs; add onions and mix well. Cover and chill for 3 to 4 hours. Remove crabs and roll in Zatarain's Chicken Fry. Fry in deep fat for 5 to 7 minutes. Drain on paper towels.

Note: Seasonings may be adjusted to taste. Crabs are even more tasty if marinated overnight.

Mrs. Roger Rousseau (Gert)
St. James Parish (St. James)

STUFFED CRABS

½ cup margarine
1½ cups finely chopped onions
¾ cup finely chopped celery
½ cup finely chopped shallots
2 pounds fresh lump crabmeat
  (5 cups)
3 slices bread, soaked in water,
  squeezed

1 cup water
½ teaspoon red cayenne pepper
¼ teaspoon pepper
1½ teaspoons salt
1 teaspoon garlic powder
8 clean crab shells or ramekins
1 lemon
Plain dry bread crumbs

Preheat oven to 350 degrees. Melt butter in a 4-quart saucepan over low heat; add onions, celery and shallots. Sauté until tender. Add crabmeat, bread, water, and seasonings; cook for 20 minutes on low heat, stirring constantly. Pile mixture into shells; squeeze lemon juice over crabs. Sprinkle with bread-crumbs; bake at 350 degrees for 20 minutes.

Note: This stuffing may be used to stuff shrimp or flounder.

Mrs. Roger Rousseau (Gert)
St. James Parish (St. James)

CRAWFISH

This is crawfish country. The little mud bug is growing in importance as fast as his home area. He is more than a fast growing new industry or a gourmet's delight. He is a way of life. He is festivals, family gatherings, restaurant hospitality, and food that is a little different. But most of all, he is demanding that the nation take notice—like the nation must take notice of the promising area he calls home. This is crawfish country!! We are proud of the country; we are proud of the crawfish. The species of crawfish native to Louisiana was known in early times to the Indians living on the lowlands skirting Louisiana's Gulf Coast, and were an important source of protein to such tribes as the Houmas, who inhabited what is now Terrebonne Parish.

Not long after the founding of New Orleans, French gourmets, ever on the alert for new taste treats, discovered this same crawfish to be a delectable delicacy for the table. Crawfish bisque became a favorite dish in the homes of the early Acadians. Like gumbo, it was fashioned lovingly with ingredients available almost at the doorstep; bay leaf, onions, garlic and thyme. The succulent tail meat of the crawfish was minced with the spicy condiments, stuffed back into the scrubbed heads and simmered into an unmatched delicacy. Down by the bayou, when the first signs of spring make their appearance—when the willows start to turn green, the most speculated subject among the good Cajun folks is whether there is enough water in the swamp to produce a good crop of crawfish. If so, then everybody is happy, but if the water is low, then the faces are long, long, and not even a State visit from a King can dispel the gloom.

CRAWFISH ÉTOUFFEE

¼ cup margarine or butter	1 pound crawfish tails
1 cup finely chopped onions	2 teaspoons cornstarch
2½ cups water	½ cup water
½ cup chopped green onion tops	Chopped parsley or parsley flakes
	Steamed rice

Melt margarine in a Dutch oven over low heat. Add onions; cook until clear. Add 2 cups water and bring to a boil. Add crawfish tails and green onion; cook over low heat for 5 minutes, stirring occasionally. Add seasoning to taste. Dissolve cornstarch in ½ cup water; pour into gravy. Allow to simmer for 15 minutes, stirring occasionally. Remove from heat; sprinkle with parsley. Stir; let set for a few minutes. Serve over steaming rice.

Note: Shrimp may be substituted for crawfish, if desired.

Pat Cain
St. Landry Parish (Opelousas)

CRAWFISH AND RICE FIESTA

2 tablespoons vegetable oil
2 tablespoons all-purpose flour
1 large onion, chopped
1/3 teaspoon garlic juice
1/4 cup chopped green pepper
1 cup chopped canned Rotel
  tomatoes
1 cup water
Red cayenne pepper to taste
1 teaspoon salt

1 teaspoon Accent
2 cups crawfish
1 10¾-ounce can cream of
  mushroom soup, undiluted
1/4 cup chopped green onion tops
2 tablespoons chopped parsley
3 cups cooked rice
Lemon wedges (optional)
Parsley (optional)

In an electric skillet, combine oil and flour. Set skillet to 325 degrees and lightly brown cooking oil and flour, stirring frequently. When brown, add onion, garlic juice, green pepper, tomatoes, water, and seasonings. Heat to boiling; simmer for 5 minutes, stirring occasionally. Add crawfish, cream of mushroom soup, onion tops and parsley to skillet. Cook 5 minutes, stirring occasionally. Add cooked rice; stir well, and remove from heat. Serve hot; garnish with lemon wedges and parsley, if desired.

Mrs. Melanie Gonsoulin
Iberia Parish (New Iberia)

CRAWFISH QUICHE (MICROWAVE OVEN RECIPE)

3 tablespoons margarine
1/2 cup finely chopped green
  onion
1 cup finely chopped onion
1 9-inch baked pastry shell
1/2 pound chopped, peeled
  crawfish tails

1 cup shredded Swiss cheese
3 eggs
1 cup evaporated milk
1 teaspoon salt
1/4 teaspoon cayenne pepper

In a 4-cup glass measure, place margarine and onions; microwave at HIGH for 5 to 7 minutes, stirring once, until tender. Line the bottom of the baked pastry shell with crawfish, sautéed onions and cheese; set aside. In a 4-cup glass measure, beat eggs, milk, and salt until well combined. Pour egg mixture over crawfish and cheese mixture; sprinkle with cayenne pepper. Microwave at MEDIUM-LOW (50%) power for 16 to 18 minutes, turning pan 2 or 3 times during cooking until knife inserted near center comes out clean. Let stand 5 minutes. Serve as a main dish or appetizer.

Mrs. George Viator (Shara)
Iberia Parish (New Iberia)

CRAWFISH PIES AND PIE CRUST RECIPE

Crust:

2¾ cups flour
1½ teaspoons salt
1 cup Crisco

1 egg
Water

In a large mixing bowl, sift together flour and salt. Cut in shortening with fork or pastry blender until mixture resembles crumbs. Beat egg well; add enough water to egg to make ¼ cup liquid. Add egg mixture to flour mixture; mix well. Roll dough out on lightly floured board to make 4 double pie crusts. Set aside.

Filling:

1 cup ground celery
1 cup ground green pepper
1 package frozen chopped
  onions
¼ cup vegetable oil
2 tablespoons crawfish fat
4 cups water
2 pounds peeled raw crawfish
1 heaping tablespoon prepared
  roux

2 tablespoons chopped green
  onions
2 tablespoons minced parsley
Salt to taste
Pepper to taste
Garlic powder to taste
Cornstarch (optional)
Water (optional)

Preheat oven to 350 degrees. Combine celery, peppers, and onion in a large pot. Add oil, crawfish fat, and water. Cook over medium heat until tender. Add crawfish, roux, green onions, parsley, salt, pepper and garlic powder. Cook for 20 minutes. If not thick enough, add enough cornstarch mixed in a small amount of water to thicken. Pour into unbaked pie shell. Cover with top pie crust. Make 4 slits in top of crust. Bake at 350 degrees until brown. Yield: 4 pies.

Mrs. Gilbert McCroskey (Granny)
Iberia Parish (New Iberia)

BOILED CRAWFISH

20 pounds fresh live crawfish
1½ boxes salt (approximately)
Water
1 diced and seeded lemon

3 pounds diced onions
4 ounces liquid crab boil
1½ ounces red pepper
2 clusters garlic

Place 20 pounds of live crawfish in a large tub. Add ⅓ box of salt and enough water to cover crawfish. Let set for 30 minutes. Drain well. In a large pot, have enough water to cover crawfish. Add other ingredients, except crawfish. Bring to boil. Boil for 10 minutes. Add crawfish; let boil for 7 minutes. Remove from heat, allowing crawfish to soak for 15 minutes. Serve.

Note: Corn on the cob and potatoes may be boiled with crawfish and taste delicious when these seasonings are absorbed. Allow 5 pounds of crawfish per person.

Louisiana Farm Bureau Women's Committee

CRAWFISH BISQUE

40-50 pounds fresh live crawfish	1 cup shallots
Water	4 slices stale French bread
Soda	4 eggs, slightly beaten
2 green peppers	1 tablespoon garlic powder
7 stalks celery	Salt to taste
1 cup fresh parsley	Red pepper to taste
3 large onions, quartered	Pepper to taste
	Flour

Scald live crawfish. Peel and save tails, fat and at least 300 large heads. Clean heads by soaking outside shell in water. Clean off eyes, feelers, etc. Keep the point. Soak and clean heads again. Soak overnight in water and soda solution. Grind cleaned crawfish tails, peppers, celery, parsley, onions, shallots, and bread. Add eggs and seasonings. Stuff drained crawfish heads with meat mixture. Coat the meat with flour. Fry the outsides to a golden brown in vegetable oil.

Roux:	½ cup chopped green pepper.
2 cups all-purpose flour	4 quarts boiling water, divided
2 cups vegetable oil	Salt, pepper, and red cayenne pepper to taste
Crawfish fat	½ cup chopped parsley
1 large onion, chopped	
1 cup shallots, chopped	

Brown flour and oil to peanut butter color over low heat. Add crawfish fat, onion, shallots, and pepper. Cook over low heat until grease rises. Add 2 quarts boiling water, stirring constantly until roux is dissolved. In a large Dutch oven place browned stuffed heads. Cover with remaining 2 quarts boiling water or until heads are completely covered. Add dissolved roux. Bring to a boil; reduce heat and simmer. Taste after 15 minutes; season to taste with salt, red pepper, and pepper. Simmer for 1 hour or until desired thickness. Add parsley 10 minutes before serving. Stir occasionally.

Mrs. Fernand Falgoust (Joan)
St. James Parish (St. James)

CRAWFISH JAMBALAYA IN RICE COOKER

1 10½-ounce can Beef Broth
  (bouillon)
1 medium whole onion, chopped
1 medium bell pepper, chopped
1 Jalapeno pepper, chopped
1 can mushrooms, drain and chop
  4 ounce

1 stick oleo or butter, melted
1 pound clean crawfish tails, chop if
  crawfish are large
2½ cups raw rice, rice cooker
  measure cup
1 8-ounce can tomato sauce

Wash raw rice and drain. Place all ingredients in Hitachi Rice Cooker with drained rice. *Do not* add any water. Taste for seasoning. Add salt and red pepper if needed. Put rice cooker on cook cycle. After cook cycle is completed, keep on warm cycle for at least ½ hour. Serve with garlic bread and green salad for a complete meal.

Must be cooked in 8 or 10 cup Rice Cooker. *Do not* attempt to double recipe as cooker will not complete cooking cycle due to extra weight of ingredients.

Note: This recipe may be used in the microwave using cooking time for rice.

Mrs. Bobby (Norma Jean) Miller
St. Landry Parish (Eunice)

CRAWFISH STEW

3 tablespoons fat or shortening
2 small onions, chopped
½ green pepper, chopped
2 stalks celery, chopped
½ clove garlic, minced
2 tablespoons all-purpose flour
½ cup tomato sauce

¼ teaspoon hot pepper sauce
1 tablespoon Worcestershire sauce
Salt and pepper to taste
Cayenne pepper to taste
1½ cups water
2 pounds peeled crawfish tails
Hot cooked rice

In an iron pot, heat fat until melted. Add onion, green pepper, celery, garlic; sauté until clear. Add flour, stirring well to blend. Gradually add tomato sauce, seasonings, water, and crawfish tails. Simmer on low heat for 30 minutes. Serve over hot rice. Serves 8.

Mrs. Hardee Brian (Betty Jo)
East Baton Rouge Parish (Zachary)

CRAWFISH BOULETS

1 pound peeled crawfish tails
1 chopped onion
1 chopped green pepper
3 tablespoons chopped green
   onion
3 tablespoons chopped parsley
1 tablespoon chopped celery

1 tablespoon paprika
2 eggs, lightly beaten
1 cup soft breadcrumbs
Salt to taste
Pepper to taste
Flour
Vegetable oil

Chop crawfish tails into small pieces. Finely chop vegetables (do not grind). Combine this mixture with eggs, paprika, bread crumbs and seasoning. If too dry, add water. If too soft, add more breadcrumbs. Form into balls; 1½ to 2-inch balls; roll in flour. Fry in hot oil until golden brown.

Mrs. Herman Deshotel
Allen Parish (Oberlin)

RICE AND OYSTER DRESSING

3 cups cooked rice
Thyme leaves to taste
Sage leaves to taste
Salt to taste
Pepper to taste
Small bunches of young
   shallots, chopped

1 to 2 stalks chopped celery
½ cup minced parsley
2 small green peppers, chopped
Melted butter
1 pint oysters, undrained
2 cups chopped cooked giblets with
   liquid

Preheat oven to 325 degrees. Season rice with thyme, sage, salt and pepper. Sauté shallots, celery, parsley and peppers in butter on low heat until soft and yellowed. Add rice mixture, stirring well. Oysters may be added whole or cut into pieces. Add giblets. Add liquid from oysters and giblets as needed. Stuff fowl with mixture. Bake any remainder in a covered dish at 325 degrees for 40 minutes.

Note: As you can see, dirty rice and rice dressing are very similar in character. Actually dirty rice can be used as a dressing and rice dressing can be served in a separate serving dish from the bird, so there is great overlap. Each cook has her own preference of what she wants to call the mixture and what she wants to put into it, and there is a great variation. Perhaps you would like to make up your own version.

Louisiana Farm Bureau Women's Committee

OYSTERS BIENVILLE

2 tablespoons melted butter
2 tablespoons flour
2 cups chopped green onions
1 cup oyster, shrimp or fish
   stock
½ cup chopped, drained
   mushrooms
1 tablespoon minced parsley

¾ cup dry white wine
2 egg yolks
½ pound chopped, boiled shrimp
Salt to taste
Pepper to taste
3 dozen fresh oysters
Grated Parmesan cheese
Dry breadcrumbs

Preheat oven to 350 degrees. Blend butter and flour in a medium saucepan over low heat. Add green onions and cook until wilted. Add 1 cup desired stock. Add mushrooms, parsley, and wine; simmer until tender. Beat egg yolks until thickened; add slowly to heated mixture. Cook over low heat, stirring constantly, until thickened. Add shrimp, and season to taste with salt and pepper. Arrange oysters on individual shells or in ramekins. Pour shrimp mixture over oysters, and top generously with Parmesan cheese and breadcrumbs. Bake at 350 degrees until brown on top.

Louisiana Farm Bureau Women's Committee

DEVILED OYSTERS

1 cup butter or margarine
1 cup milk
1 pint oysters, undrained
2 medium onions, chopped
2 cups toast crumbs
3 chopped hard-cooked eggs
½ cup chopped green onion
   tops

½ cup chopped green pepper
¼ cup chopped fresh parsley
1 tablespoon Worcestershire sauce
1 teaspoon salt
¼ teaspoon red cayenne pepper
¼ teaspoon pepper

Preheat oven to 350 degrees. In a heavy saucepan, scald milk. Add butter and oysters; cook until oysters begin to curl. Remove from heat. Add remaining ingredients, stirring well. Put into a greased 13 x 9 x 2-inch pan or individual shells. Bake at 350 degrees for 20 to 30 minutes. Serves 6.

Note: 2 cups Ritz crackers may be used instead of toast crumbs, if desired.

Mrs. Ida Mae Watkins
Jeff Davis Parish (Lake Arthur)

OYSTERS ROCKEFELLER

Medium white sauce:
½ cup butter   Milk
Flour

Filling:
2 to 3 packages frozen spinach
1 small stalk celery   Red pepper to taste
Chopped parsley   Salt to taste
Chopped green onion tops   ⅓ cup seasoned dry breadcrumbs
½ cup plain soft breadcrumbs   1 ounce absinthe liqueur
Minced garlic to taste   ½ teaspoon anise seed or anise
Dash of Tabasco sauce   extract
Dash of Worcestershire sauce   ½ cup melted butter
Pepper to taste   3 to 4 dozen oysters
                                Buttered breadcrumbs

Prepare medium white sauce using 1 stick butter and adding flour and milk to thicken. Set aside. Boil the spinach and drain well. Combine spinach, celery, parsley, onion, and white sauce; stir well. Add soft breadcrumbs, garlic, Tabasco, Worcestershire sauce, pepper and salt to taste. Toss lightly. Add seasoned crumbs, absinthe, anise seed and butter. Prepare oysters by draining them well and drying. Place in shallow pan under broiler for a few minutes to remove excess liquid. When dry, remove and place 2 or 3 oysters in small shell until you have used all oysters, or you may place all of them in one large greased casserole. Top each oyster with spinach sauce; cover with buttered crumbs and broil until brown.

Note: Small foil cups are good to use for individual servings. Be sure the oysters are well drained.

Louisiana Farm Bureau Women's Committee

DEEP FRIED FROG LEGS

Frog legs   1 cup all-purpose flour
Vinegar   ½ cup milk
Sliced onions   ¼ teaspoon cayenne pepper
Minced garlic, to taste   1 teaspoon salt
1 egg, beaten

Marinate clean frog legs in vinegar seasoned with onions and garlic for at least 3 hours. Prepare batter by mixing remaining ingredients. Drain frog legs well and dip in batter. Fry in deep fat at 375 degrees until golden brown.

Louisiana Farm Bureau Women's Committee

FISH COURTBOUILLION

5 pounds catfish steaks
Salt to taste
Red cayenne pepper to taste
¼ cup vegetable oil
4 heaping tablespoons
  all-purpose flour

1 cup chopped green onion tops
¼ cup chopped parsley
¼ cup minced garlic
Hot cooked rice (optional)

Season fish steaks with salt and pepper. Pour oil in large pot; place fish in single layer on oil. Start cooking on high temperature until fish bubbles. Immediately reduce heat to low. Sprinkle flour, onion, parsley, and garlic over fish. Cover; let simmer slowly for 45 minutes. Do not stir. Shake the pot occasionally to keep fish from sticking. Fish should make its own gravy. If necessary, add a little water. Serve fish over hot, fluffy rice, if desired.

Note: The pronunciation of the name is koo-bee-on.

Mrs. Mary Paul
Jeff Davis Parish (Welsh)

BAKED REDFISH (UNSTUFFED)

½ cup vegetable oil
½ cup all-purpose flour
4 cloves garlic, chopped
1 small chopped green pepper,
  chopped
2 chopped green onions
1 onion, chopped
1 10½-ounce can Rotel
  tomatoes

1 15-ounce can whole tomatoes
1 6-ounce can tomato paste
Water
Salt to taste
Pepper to taste
Large red fish or snapper
Chopped parsley
Lemon slices
Hot cooked rice

Prepare roux with oil and flour. When brown, add garlic, green pepper and onions. Cook until tender. Add tomatoes, tomato paste and enough water to make a medium thick gravy. Season well. Cook on low heat for about an hour, adding more water when needed. Preheat oven to 325 degrees. Wash and dry fish. Season liberally inside and out with salt and pepper. Place in roasting pan; pour gravy over fish. Bake uncovered at 325 degrees for 45 minutes, basting frequently. This should not overcook and is done when meat is tender and flaky when tested with a fork. Carefully remove fish to warmed platter. Sprinkle top with chopped parsley. Garnish with lemon slices. Serve gravy over rice.

Louisiana Farm Bureau Woman's Committee

BAKED RED SNAPPER

Seafood

Stuffing:

6 green onions, chopped
2 stalks celery, chopped
2 tablespoons chopped parsley
¼ cup melted butter
1 cup toasted breadcrumbs
Boiling water

½ teaspoon whole thyme leaves
½ teaspoon whole basil leaves
Salt to taste
Pepper to taste
1 cup crabmeat
¼ cup white wine

Preheat oven to 350 degrees. In a saucepan over low heat sauté vegetables in butter until tender. Remove from heat. Moisten breadcrumbs with a little boiling water; add to sautéed vegetables. Add seasonings, crabmeat and wine to crumb mixture.

Filling:

Cleaned whole red snapper
Butter
Salt and pepper

Water
Chopped onion

Place cleaned fish in a baking dish. Head is usually left on. Rub outside of fish with butter. Season with salt and pepper. Stuff fish with filling mixture. Fasten cavity closed. Pour a little water around it in the dish with some butter and chopped onions. Bake for 30 minutes. Baste occasionally with water and more white wine, adding as needed. Save juices.

Sauce:

1 teaspoon lemon juice
1 teaspoon all-purpose flour
¼ cup melted butter
1 egg, beaten
Salt to taste

Pepper to taste
Basil to taste
Bay leaf to taste
½ teaspoon sugar

Mix juices from baked fish with lemon juice, flour, butter, egg, salt and pepper. Add more water if necessary; add basil, bay leaf and ½ teaspoon sugar. Pour sauce over fish and bake at 275 degrees for 30 minutes.

Note: More wine may be added along with mushrooms and shrimp if desired. If shrimp is added, simmer until shrimp are done about 10-15 minutes.

Louisiana Farm Bureau Women's Committee

SALMON PATTIES

1 pound can salmon
²⁄₃ cup seasoned dry
　breadcrumbs or ²⁄₃ cup
　cracker crumbs
1½ tablespoons instant minced
　onion

2 tablespoons chopped green
　onions
1 egg, slightly beaten
²⁄₃ cup evaporated milk
3 tablespoons melted butter
Vegetable oil

Remove skin and bones from salmon. In a large mixing bowl, flake salmon with a fork. Add breadcrumbs, minced onion, green onions, beaten egg, milk and butter. Mix well. Shape into patties. Fry in deep fat until brown.

Mrs. Thelma Smith
St. James Parish (St. James)

SEAFOOD CASSEROLE

1 cup chopped celery
1 cup chopped green pepper
1 cup chopped onions
½ cup margarine, melted
1 cup milk
2 10¾-ounce cans cream
　of mushroom soup,
　undiluted

2 4½-ounce cans shrimp or 1
　pound fresh boiled and peeled
　shrimp
2 6½-ounce cans crabmeat or 1
　pound fresh crabmeat
3 cups cooked rice
Pepper to taste
1 cup soft breadcrumbs

Preheat oven to 375 degrees. Sauté celery, green pepper and onions in margarine. Add milk, mushroom soup, shrimp and crabmeat; stir well. Add cooked rice and pepper. Remove from heat; pour in a greased casserole. Top with breadcrumbs. Bake at 375 degrees for 40 minutes.

Note: Do not add rice until you are ready to bake since rice will swell.

Mrs. Larry Langlinais (Anna)
Vermilion Parish (Erath)

SEAFOOD CASSEROLE

4 slices bread
1 cup milk
½ pound lump crabmeat
½ pound cooked, cleaned
 shrimp
4 hard-cooked eggs, chopped

1 small onion, chopped
½ to 1 cup mayonnaise (as
 desired)
2 tablespoons Worcestershire sauce
Salt to taste
Pepper to taste

Soak bread in milk; tear into small pieces. Combine all ingredients thoroughly. Pour into a greased casserole; top with buttered breadcrumbs. Bake at 350 degrees for 30 minutes. Serves 6.

Elsie Castille
St. Martin Parish (Breaux Bridge)

EGGPLANT AND SEAFOOD CASSEROLE

4 large eggplants, cubed
1 large onion, chopped
1 green pepper, chopped
¼ cup vegetable oil
1 cup seasoned dry
 breadcrumbs
½ teaspoon whole basil leaves
½ teaspoon whole thyme leaves

Salt to taste
Pepper to taste
1 cup lump crabmeat
1 pound cleaned crawfish, fat
 reserved
Additional seasoned breadcrumbs
Butter
Paprika

Preheat oven to 350 degrees. In a heavy saucepan boil eggplant cubes until tender. Drain well, preferably overnight. Sauté onion and green pepper in oil. Add cooked eggplant. Gradually add seasoned breadcrumbs as eggplant continues to draw water. Add basil, thyme, salt and pepper to eggplant. Add 1 cup crabmeat and 1 pound cleaned crawfish with fat; mix well. Spoon into greased casserole; sift additional breadcrumbs over top. Dot with butter and dust with paprika. Bake at 350 degrees until bubbly and hot.

Louisiana Farm Bureau Women's Committee

SHRIMP

The Louisiana shrimp shares international fame with his cousin, the crawfish, but each creates his own unique flavor. On any early morning during the months of May through August, the muffled chug-chug of a trawler may be heard in the shallow bays heading out to the Gulf of Mexico. It could be May's white shrimp or August's brown shrimp the fisherman is intent on bringing home tons of; the tasty delicacies for summer shrimp boils, gumbo and spicy stews. Although the shrimp and crawfish each has its own unique flavor and texture, shrimp may be substituted for crawfish in any recipe.

SHRIMP AND BEEF JAMBALAYA

3 tablespoons vegetable oil
2 large green peppers, chopped
1 cup chopped onion
1 clove garlic, crushed
(optional)
1 pound lean ground beef
1 16-ounce can stewed
tomatoes
1 8-ounce can tomato sauce

½ teaspoon chili powder
¼ teaspoon paprika
½ teaspoon Worcestershire sauce
Few drops Tabasco sauce
Salt to taste
Pepper to taste
1 pound package frozen shrimp,
thawed
2 cups cooked rice

Heat oil in heavy skillet or Dutch oven, sauté green pepeprs, onions and garlic in oil until soft, but not browned. Add ground beef and cook until brown. Drain off excess fat. Add remaining ingredients, except shrimp and rice. Cover; heat to boiling. Simmer on low for 20 minutes. Add shrimp and rice; simmer until thoroughly heated.

Note: I find that the best way to drain off all excess fat is by pouring meat in a colander. Also freshly boiled shrimp is just as successful to use as frozen shrimp.

Mrs. Doug Moore (Liz)
Ouachita Parish (Monroe)

SHRIMP CURRY

⅓ cup butter
½ cup chopped onions
¼ cup chopped green pepper
2 cloves garlic, minced
2 cups commercial sour cream
2 teaspoons lemon juice
2 teaspoons curry powder

¼ teaspoon salt
Dash of chili powder
Dash of pepper
3 cups cooked, peeled, deveined
shrimp
Hot cooked rice

Melt butter on low heat in heavy saucepan. Add onions, green pepper, and garlic; sauté until tender, but not browned. Stir in sour cream, lemon juice and seasonings. Add shrimp. Cook over low heat, stirring constantly, until hot. Serve over rice with condiments. Serves 6.

Condiments:
Flaked coconut
Chopped peanuts

Raisins
Chutney

Note: Sauce is traditionally thin.

Mary Jo Harrell
Ouachita Parish (West Monroe)

SHRIMP CANTONESE OVER RICE

1 pound peeled, deveined raw
  shrimp
2 tablespoons melted margarine
  or butter
1 cup diagonally sliced celery
1 cup sliced onions
2 16-ounce cans mixed Chinese
  vegetables, drained and rinsed

¼ teaspoon pepper
¼ cup soy sauce
1¼ cups chicken broth
2 tablespoons cornstarch
3 cups rice, cooked

On low heat, sauté shrimp in melted butter in a large skillet until shrimp turns pink. Add celery and onions; cook for 3 minutes, stirring occasionally. Add Chinese vegetables; cover. Cook for one minute. Blend pepper, soy sauce, chicken broth, and cornstarch; stir into shrimp-vegetable mixture. Cook approximately 3 minutes, stirring constantly until sauce is thickened. Serve over hot cooked rice.

Mrs. Larry Langlinais (Anna)
Vermilion Parish (Erath)

SHRIMP GRAND CHENIERE

5 pounds medium-sized raw
  shrimp
2 cups melted butter
1 16-ounce bottle Wishbone
  Italian dressing

Juice of 2 lemons
6 tablespoons pepper

Preheat oven to 400 degrees. Place raw shrimp in a deep baking pan. Melt butter in a saucepan. Remove from heat; add dressing, lemon juice and pepper. Mix thoroughly. Pour sauce over shrimp. Bake at 400 degrees for 45 minutes, stirring gently every 10 minutes. Serves 8-10.

Note: Individual place settings should include small bowl for sauce and dampened hand towel. French bread is delicious dipped in this sauce.

Mrs. Jimmy Lee Sloan (Pam)
Caddo Parish (Dixie)

SHRIMP CREOLE I

2 tablespoons butter
½ teaspoon paprika
1 cup chopped onions
1 cup chopped green pepper
½ clove garlic, chopped

1 pint stewed tomatoes
Salt to taste
Pepper to taste
1 cup peeled and deveined raw
  shrimp

Melt butter in a skillet over low heat; add paprika and stir thoroughly. Add onion, green pepper, and garlic; simmer on low heat until tender. Add tomatoes, salt and pepper. Boil 5 minutes. Add shrimp; boil 10 minutes. Serve hot over fluffy rice. Serves 6.

Mrs. Eddie Schexnaydre (Doris)
Terrebonne Parish (Schriever)

SHRIMP CREOLE II

¼ cup prepared roux
2 diced onions
½ medium-sized green pepper
2 8-ounce cans tomato sauce
2 tablespoons brown sugar
1 tablespoon salt

1 teaspoon pepper
¼ teaspoon garlic powder
½ gallon fresh, peeled and deveined
  shrimp
1 cup chopped green onion tops
Hot cooked fluffy rice

Prepare roux by referring to the section on "How to Make a Roux". Add onions and green pepper to hot roux in a Dutch oven; cook until tender. Add tomato sauce, brown sugar, salt, pepper and garlic powder. Cook on medium heat for 30 minutes. Add shrimp; cook for 20 minutes. Before serving, add chopped green onion tops. Serve over hot fluffy rice.

Mrs. Lorraine Watkins
Jeff Davis Parish (Welsh)

BEER BATTER FOR SHRIMP

1 12-ounce can beer
1½ cups all-purpose flour
1 tablespoon salt

1 tablespoon paprika
Red pepper to taste

Combine all ingredients in a large mixing bowl and beat with a wire whisk until frothy. Batter may be used immediately or stored in refrigerator for several days. Use wire whisk freely to assure smoothness and uniformity of batter.

Note: If batter is too thin add a little extra flour.

Louisiana Farm Bureau Woman's Committee

RICE AND SHRIMP CASSEROLE

1 pound cleaned and cooked
  shrimp
½ cup chopped onions
½ cup chopped green peppers
¼ cup vegetable oil
2 cups tomato sauce

2 cups cooked rice
¼ teaspoon salt
¼ teaspoon pepper
¼ teaspoon red pepper (optional)
Corn Flake crumbs
Green pepper rings

Preheat oven to 350 degrees. Sauté onions and green pepper in oil in a large skillet. Add tomato sauce, cooked rice, salt, pepper, and red pepper, if desired. Cut shrimp into bite-size pieces and stir into mixture. Simmer 2 minutes. Pour into 1-quart greased casserole; top with crumbs. Bake at 350 degrees for 20 minutes. Garnish with green pepper rings and 4 whole shrimp.

Note: This casserole tastes like shrimp étouffe and is easy to make and serve. It also freezes well.

Mrs. Cathie Miller
Jeff Davis Parish (Lacassine)

MIRLITON STUFFED WITH SHRIMP

6 medium mirlitons
¼ cup margarine or vegetable
  oil
2 cups raw small or medium
  shrimp, peeled and deveined
1 cup finely chopped onions
2 slices bread, soaked in water
  and squeezed dry

1 bunch shallots, chopped
3 tablespoons chopped parsley
1½ teaspoons salt
¼ teaspoon pepper
Dash of red pepper
Buttered breadcrumbs

Preheat oven to 350 degrees. Wash mirlitons, and cut in half lengthwise. Place in a pot of boiling water sufficient to cover. Cover and boil for 25 to 30 minutes or until tender. Drain; allow to cool until mirliton can be handled. Rub a shallow baking dish with margarine. Scoop pulp out of mirliton shells into a colander. Allow to drain for about 5 minutes. Melt margarine in a skillet over low heat; add shrimp and continue to cook for another 5 minutes. Add mirliton pulp, bread, shallots, parsley, salt, and pepper. Cook, stirring well for 10 minutes or longer if needed to reduce liquid left from mirliton. Spoon into reserved mirliton shells. Top with buttered crumbs. Bake at 350 degrees for 20 minutes.

Note: 1 pound ground beef may be substituted for shrimp. Soft breadcrumbs may be substituted for bread slices, if desired.

Mrs. Charles Gravois
West St. James Parish (Vacherie)

BARBEQUED SHRIMP

1 pound peeled and deveined
  raw shrimp
Salt to taste
Pepper to taste
2 teaspoons lemon juice

½ cup melted butter
2 teaspoons olive oil
1 teaspoon Worcestershire sauce
Pinch of garlic powder
1 teaspoon Tabasco sauce

Preheat oven to 350 degrees. Arrange shrimp in single layer in a pyrex baking dish. Add salt and pepper to taste. Combine remaining ingredients, stirring well. Pour mixture over shrimp. Bake at 350 degrees for 25 to 30 minutes. Shrimp will turn pink when done. Serves 2.

Note: Serve with plenty of French bread.

Anita Joyner
Tangipahoa Parish (Hammond)

SHRIMP JAMBALAYA

1 tablespoon all-purpose flour
3 tablespoons lard, melted
3 large onions, chopped
2 pounds fresh cleaned shrimp
Salt to taste

Pepper to taste
1 pound uncooked long grain rice
3 cups water
1 small bunch fresh parsley
Finely chopped green onion tops

Brown flour in lard over low heat; add onions, and make a roux. Add shrimp and seasonings; cook a few minutes. Wash rice; add 3 cups water to rice. Pour rice in shrimp; add remaining ingredients. Cover; cook slowly on low heat until rice is done. Do not stir after adding rice.

Note: If dried shrimp are used, pour boiling water over them and let stand one hour before using.

Mrs. Eddie Schexnaydre (Doris)
Terrebonne Parish (Schriever)

SHRIMP QUICHE

¾ cup Kraft mayonnaise
3 tablespoons flour
3 beaten eggs
¾ cup milk
2 cups seasoned, cooked
    shrimp

1 12-ounce package Swiss cheese,
    diced
⅔ ounce sliced green onions
1 10-inch unbaked pie shell

Preheat oven to 350 degrees. Combine mayonnaise, flour, eggs, and milk; mix thoroughly. Stir in cooked shrimp, cheese and green onions. Pour into unbaked pie shell. Bake 1 hour and 15 minutes or until set.

Note: Crabmeat may be added, if desired.

Mrs. John Smith (Thelma)
St. James Parish (St. James)

SHRIMP STEW

2 tablespoons vegetable oil
2 tablespoons all-purpose flour
2 medium onions, chopped
2 cloves garlic, minced
1 tablespoon dried parsley
    flakes
1 pound raw shrimp, peeled

1 to 2 cups water
Salt to taste
Pepper to taste
Cayenne pepper to taste
Garlic salt to taste
Onion salt to taste
Hot cooked rice

Make a dark roux with oil and flour in a large pan. Add onions, garlic, parsley and shrimp. Brown for 10 minutes, stirring frequently. Add water and seasonings; stir constantly. Simmer on low for 45 minutes to 1 hour. Serve over rice.

Louisiana Farm Bureau Women's Committee

FRIED SHRIMP

Fresh peeled and deveined large
    shrimp
Salt
Red pepper
Pepper

All-purpose flour
1 egg, well beaten
Dry breadcrumbs
Oil (peanut oil is best)

Large shrimp may be butterflied. Season cleaned shrimp with the desired amount of salt, red pepper and pepper. Dredge shrimp in flour. Dip in beaten egg and roll in bread crumbs. Deep fat fry at 375 degrees until golden brown.

Note: Overcooking toughens shrimp.

Louisiana Farm Bureau Woman's Committee

SHRIMP VICTORIA

1 pound shrimp
1 small onion, finely chopped
¼ cup butter or margarine, melted
1 6-ounce can mushrooms, drained

1 tablespoon all-purpose flour
¼ teaspoon salt
Cayenne pepper to taste
1 cup sour cream
Hot cooked rice

Peel and clean shrimp. Sauté shrimp and onion in butter on low heat for 10 minutes or until shrimp are tender. Add mushrooms; cook 5 minutes. Sprinkle in flour, salt and pepper; blend well. Stir in sour cream. Cook gently for 10 minutes, not allowing mixture to boil. Serve over rice.

Mrs. Alden Horton (Susan)
Vermilion Parish (Gueydan)

TUNA OR CHICKEN CASSEROLE

1 8-ounce package wide noodles
Water
3 chicken bouillon cubes
½ cup chopped onion
½ cup chopped green pepper
½ cup chopped celery
2 tablespoons chopped fresh parsley or 1 tablespoon dry parsley
2 tablespoons melted butter
1 10-ounce can white tuna, drained

1 10¾-ounce can cream of mushroom soup, undiluted
1 3-ounce jar pimientos, drained and diced
1 4-ounce jar sliced mushrooms, drained
Salt to taste
Pepper to taste
Dash of Tabasco sauce
2 grated hard-cooked eggs
1 cup cubed Cheddar cheese
1 cup shredded Cheddar cheese

Cook noodles with water and chicken bouillon cubes according to package directions; drain and set aside. Sauté onion, green pepper, celery, and parsley in butter until tender, but not brown. Add tuna; cook slowly for 5 minutes. Remove from heat; add soup, pimiento, mushrooms, salt, pepper, and Tabasco. Mix well. Stir in eggs and cubed cheese. Layer tuna mixture and noodles in casserole dish. Top with shredded cheese. Bake at 350 degrees for 20 minutes or until cheese melts.

Note: Chicken may be used in place of tuna using 3 large breasts and cooking noodles in broth from chicken.

Mrs. Perry Fisher (Bert)
Ouachita Parish (Monroe)

TUNA CASSEROLE

1 box macaroni & cheese
  dinner
1 10¾-ounce can cream of
  mushroom soup, undiluted

1 6½-ounce can tuna, drained
1 small can mushroom, drained
Shredded Cheddar cheese

Preheat oven to 350 degrees. Prepare macaroni and cheese according to package directions. Add soup, tuna, and mushrooms to cooked macaroni; mix well. Place mixture in a greased 1¾-quart casserole; top with lots of shredded cheese. Bake at 350 degrees until cheese melts.

Note: This casserole may be microwaved until cheese melts, if desired.

Anita Joiner
Tangipahoa Parish (Hammond)

TURTLE SAUCE PIQUANTE

1 cup vegetable oil
1½ cups all-purpose flour
1 large onion, chopped
1 large green pepper, chopped
4 stalks celery, chopped
1 12-ounce can tomato paste

1 14-ounce can whole tomatoes
4 cups water
10 pounds diced turtle meat
Salt to taste
Pepper to taste
Hot cooked rice

Brown flour in hot oil on low heat until golden brown; add onion, green pepper and celery. Cook for 5 minutes, until tender. Add tomatoes, tomato paste and water; heat to boiling. Reduce heat and simmer 1 hour. Add turtle meat, salt, and pepper (this should be highly peppered). Continue cooking for 1½ to 2 hours on low heat until turtle meat is tender. Serve over hot rice.

Marian Hargrave
Vermilion Parish (Gueydan)

Wild Game

Mardi Gras - New Orleans

ARMADILLO SAUCE PIQUANT

Marinade:

¼ cup salad oil
1 cup vinegar
1 quart water

1 sliced onion
1 tablespoon salt

Combine all ingredients, stirring well.

6 pounds armadillo meat

Prepare armadillo by cleaning and cutting into serving pieces. Marinate for 24 hours. Remove from solution and allow to drain for 30 minutes before cooking.

Sauce:

3 pieces smoked sausage
½ cup salad oil
3 large onions, finely chopped
Finely chopped green onion
  tops
1 large green pepper, chopped
2 cloves garlic, finely chopped
4 celery stalks, chopped
1 4-ounce can
  mushroom-flavored steak
  sauce

¼ cup pick-a-peppa sauce
Salt to taste
Pepper to taste
1 tablespoon MSG
2 tablespoons Worcestershire sauce
2 cups water
1 8-ounce can mushrooms, drained
1 cup cooking wine
1 bunch parsley, chopped
1 lemon, sliced
Hot cooked rice

In a heavy black iron pot, brown sausage and armadillo in hot oil, permitting meat to stick to bottom of pot just a little for extra flavor. Remove armadillo from pot and set aside leaving sausage in pot. Add onions, green pepper, garlic, and celery; stir continuously, cooking until tender. Add steak sauce, pick-a-peppa sauce, salt, pepper, MSG, and Worcestershire sauce; mix well. Add armadillo and water. Heat to boiling; reduce heat and simmer for 10 minutes. Reduce to low heat and cover with tight lid. Cook until tender. (Do not stir but take pot by handle and half-spin from left to right every 10 minutes). Add mushrooms and wine; blend gently with a spoon. Sprinkle with parsley and lay thin lemon slices on top. Simmer uncovered for 15 minutes. Serve over rice.

Note: Clear stew meat may be substituted for armadillo, if desired.

Liz Moore
Ouachita Parish (Monroe)

GLAZED DUCK

6 pound duck
Salt to taste
Pepper to taste
¼ cup melted butter
1 cup dry vermouth
2 tablespoons sugar
1½ tablespoons vinegar
1 cup chicken stock

Juice of 3 oranges
Grated orange rind (a small
    amount)
Juice of 1 lemon
3 tablespoons curaçao
2 tablespoons cornstarch
Orange slices
Fresh parsley

Preheat oven to 400 degrees. Dress and clean duck. Rub duck with salt and pepper. In a heavy pan brown duck well in melted butter. Place duck in roasting pan; bake at 400 degrees for 20 minutes. Reduce heat to 350 degrees and bake 1 hour in a covered baking dish. Baste duck frequently with vermouth. In a small saucepan, melt sugar, stirring constantly. Add vinegar and caramelize over low heat. Remove duck from oven. Drain off fat. Add chicken stock to roasting pan. Add the juice of oranges, a little grated orange rind, juice of lemon and curaçao. Blend in cornstarch and the caramelized sugar mixture. Bake at 350 degrees for 10 minutes. Return duck to baking pan. Spoon sauce over duck slowly. Bake at 350 degrees while continuing to baste with sauce until duck is glazed. Garnish with orange slices and parsley.

Louisiana Farm Bureau Women's Committee

POT ROASTED WILD DUCK

4 wild ducks, picked and
    cleaned
Red pepper
Poultry seasoning
Seasoned salt
Garlic powder
Pepper

Paprika
1 apple, sliced
1 medium onion, quartered
4 pieces celery
Bacon drippings
1 cup chopped onions
½ cup water (if necessary)

Season ducks inside and out with red pepper, poultry seasoning, seasoned salt, garlic powder, pepper, and paprika. In each duck cavity place ¼ of apple slices, ¼ onion and 1 piece of celery. Cover bottom of Dutch oven with bacon drippings ⅛-inch deep. Brown backs of ducks in hot drippings; turn and brown breast. Cover; reduce to low heat. Cook 1 hour and 15 minutes. Add chopped onions, and cook 1 hour and 15 minutes. If necessary, add ½ cup water about 30 minutes before done.

Note: 2 cups cubed potatoes may be added 15 minutes before ducks are done, if desired.

JoAnn Irvine
Beauregard Parish (DeRidder)

POT ROASTED DUCK

2 ducks
1 onion, quartered
1 green pepper, sliced
2 stalks celery, halved
4 slices bacon, cut into pieces

Salt to taste
Red pepper to taste
Boiling water
1 cup chopped onion

Stuff ducks with onion, green pepper, celery, and bacon. Season thoroughly with salt and red pepper. Place ducks in Dutch oven. Cover with boiling water. Boil 2 to 3 hours, keeping water level over ducks until they are tender. When ducks are tender, let water boil down to make a brown gravy. Add 1 cup chopped onion to gravy and allow to cook until onions are wilted. Do not cover pot at any time. Serve hot.

Note: This recipe is a variation of Nelson Lejeune's Pot Roasted Duck.

Mrs. Wayne Zaunbrecher (Linda)
Vermilion Parish (Gueydan)

CREOLE DUCK

5 ducks, cut for frying
2 square inches sliced cooked ham, diced
5 chopped onions
2½ tablespoons fat
5 whole cloves
2½ teaspoons chopped parsley

2½ teaspoons chopped celery
2½-3 glasses claret wine (2½ cups)
2½ glasses water (2½ cups)
2 teaspoons chopped green pepper
1 8-ounce large can mushrooms, drained

Preheat oven to 200 degrees. Fry ducks in fat, browning on both sides. Place ducks in roaster; add remaining ingredients. Cover and bake at 200 degrees for 3 to 4 hours. Slightly thicken gravy, and serve warm.

Edna Margaret Federick
E. Carroll Parish (Lake Providence)

SQUIRREL MULLIGAN

3 squirrels, dressed
2 onions, chopped
1 green pepper, chopped
2 Irish potatoes, diced
4 tablespoons chili pepper

Salt to taste
Pepper to taste
Dash of Louisiana Hot Sauce
¼ cup celery
1 cup cooked rice

Stew squirrels in water until tender. Remove from bones. Place meat back into broth. Bring to boil; add remaining ingredients, except rice. Cook 45 minutes or until vegetables are tender. Add rice and serve.

Mrs. Liz Moore
Ouachita Parish (Monroe)

DADDY'S BAKED DUCK

3 ducks (preferably Mallards)
6 slices bacon
Salt to taste
Pepper to taste
1 10¾-ounce can cream of
  mushroom soup, undiluted

¼ cup water
1 large chopped onion
2 4-ounce cans sliced mushrooms,
  drained
Hot cooked rice

Preheat oven to 425 degrees. Season ducks with salt and pepper; place in a roaster pan. Place 2 slices bacon on each duck. Bake at 425 degrees for 20 minutes. Cover; reduce heat to 300 degrees. Cook 1-1½ hours or until tender. Cook duck and debone. Reserve stock. Skim 2 tablespoons oil from duck stock; heat in a skillet until hot. Sauté onion in hot oil until tender. Add remaining stock and cream of mushroom soup. Add ¼ cup water to soup can; add water and mushrooms to mixture. Simmer for 20 minutes. Add sliced deboned duck to mixture; simmer 30 minutes. Serve over hot, fluffy rice.

Mrs. Kathleen Watkins
Jeff Davis Parish (Iowa)

RABBIT SAUCE PIQUANT

3 rabbits, skinned and cut into
  pieces
Fat or shortening
1 6-ounce can tomato paste
3 cloves garlic, chopped
3 large onions, chopped
2 10-ounce cans Rotel
  tomatoes and peppers

3 hot green peppers
2½ tablespoons salt
1 cup cooking sherry
1 cup parsley, chopped
1½ cups chopped green onion tops
Hot cooked rice

Brown rabbit in melted fat. Remove and set aside. Add tomato paste to fat in skillet; cook 5 minutes. Add garlic and onion; stir until onion is transparent. Add tomatoes, peppers, salt, sherry, parsley, and onion tops; mix thoroughly. Add rabbit to mixture. Cover and cook slowly for 2 hours. Serve with rice.

Codie Ray
Madison Parish (Tallulah)

SMOTHERED RABBIT

1 rabbit, dressed
5 cloves garlic, minced
Salt to taste
Red pepper to taste
5 tablespoons oil
2 large onions, chopped

1 cup water
1 4-ounce can mushrooms
2 teaspoons browning gravy
Browning sauce
Hot cooked rice

Cut rabbit into serving pieces. Dry with paper towels. Slit each piece of meat and stuff with minced garlic; sprinkle with salt and pepper. Brown rabbit in hot oil in a heavy pot. Remove rabbit, and sauté onions in same oil. Add rabbit, water and mushrooms. Cover and cook on medium heat until tender, adding water as necessary. Add browning sauce and serve over rice.

Mrs. Herman Falgoust (Eloise)
St. James Parish (St. James)

RAB'S RABBIT FRICASSE

2 medium rabbits, skinned and
  cut up
3 cups all-purpose flour
1 cup vegetable oil
1 large yellow onion, diced
1 clove garlic, diced
1 large green pepper, diced

1 quart water
Salt to taste
Pepper to taste
½ cup chopped parsley
½ cup chopped green onion tops
3 cups hot cooked rice

Dip rabbits in flour; brown in hot oil in a Dutch oven. Remove rabbits; add onions, garlic, and green peppers in hot oil. Place rabbits back into pot, and add water. Allow rabbits to cook until tender. Continue to stir to prevent sticking. Gravy should be thick. Ten minutes before serving, add parsley and green onions. Serve over rice.

Ken Rabalais
Livingston Parish (Denham Springs)

MARINATED VENISON SHISH-KEBABS

2 pounds cubed, boneless
  venison
Salt to taste
Pepper to taste
Garlic powder to taste
1 8-ounce bottle Wishbone
  Italian Dressing

Onions, cubed
Green pepper
1 pound smoked sausage, sliced
  ½-inch thick

Season venison with salt, pepper and garlic powder. Place in a large bowl. Pour Italian dressing over meat; toss to mix. Cover and chill for 24 to 48 hours. Alternate venison, onions, green pepper, and smoked sausage on a skewer. Cook over hot coals until done.

Mrs. Jackie Theriot (Sue)
St. Martin Parish (St. Martinville)

VENISON ROAST

1 4 to 5 pound venison roast
Italian dressing
2 large onions, chopped
3 celery stalks, chopped
1 medium green pepper,
  chopped
2 cloves garlic, finely chopped

3 whole cloves
1 bay leaf
2 chicken bouillon cubes
Tony's Seasoning to taste
Water
Hot cooked Louisiana rice

Wash and dry venison roast. Marinate in Italian dressing overnight. Place meat in crock pot. Add chopped onions, celery, green pepper, garlic, cloves, bay leaf, bouillon cubes and Tony's seasoning. Add enough water to cover roast. Cook on high for 4 hours. Reduce to low setting for 4 to 6 hours. Bones will break away and meat will be very tender. Serve over cooked Louisiana rice.

Mrs. Jude Plauche (Margaret)
Avoyelles Parish (Hamburg)

FRIED VENISON STEAKS

Venison steaks
Meat tenderizer

All-purpose flour
Shortening

Pound steaks well with meat tenderizer. Coat with flour and fry in pan with shortening until browned or deep fry, if preferred.

Mrs. B. F. Lemoine, Jr. (Grace)
Avoyelles Parish (Hamburg)

VENISON POT ROAST

1 medium venison rump roast
Salt to taste
Pepper to taste
1 clove garlic
2 tablespoons vegetable oil

2 tablespoons all-purpose flour
½ cup water
3 tablespoons tomato paste
1 large onion

The day before cooking, season venison thoroughly with salt and pepper. Stuff meat with garlic and refrigerate overnight. Brown venison in hot oil. Remove roast; add flour and water, stirring constantly, to make a light brown roux. Add tomato paste and cook for 1 minute. Add onion and return roast to Dutch oven. Cover; cook slowly for 5 hours or until tender.

Note: Be sure to cook on top of stove.

Ken Rabalais
Livingston Parish (Denham Springs)

SMOTHERED QUAIL

Salt to taste
Pepper to taste
6 quail
6 tablespoons melted butter

3 tablespoons all-purpose flour
2 cups chicken broth
½ cup water
Hot cooked rice

Preheat oven to 350 degrees. Brown quail in a heavy skillet in butter. Remove quail to a baking dish. Stir in flour and slowly add chicken broth and water. Cook until thickened; blend well. Pour sauce over quail. Cover baking dish and bake at 350 degrees for 1 hour or until tender. Serve over hot cooked rice.

Note: This recipe was given to me by a special friend who suffered a severe heart attack and started raising quail for added income. He is a very fine Christian man whom God has spared, Cotton Kitchens.

Mrs. Doug Moore (Liz)
Ouachita Parish (Monroe)

Main Dishes

For a Louisiana Lad

BRACUUOLINI

Gravy:

½ cup olive or vegetable oil
1 medium onion, chopped
3 cloves garlic, minced
¼ cup chopped celery
¼ cup minced parsley

2 6-ounce cans tomato paste
1 8-ounce can tomato sauce
1 teaspoon salt
1 teaspoon pepper
1 quart water (more if needed)

Fry first 5 ingredients together until lightly browned in a large skillet. Add tomato paste and tomato sauce; fry slowly, stirring often, over low heat until sauce starts to separate. Add salt and pepper; add water a little at a time and continue to stir. (Reserve some of the water to be added later when stuffed steak is placed in the gravy.) Bring gravy to a boil; reduce heat to low and cover; simmer while preparing steaks and stuffing.

Meat:

2 medium size light beef round
  steaks, ½-inch thick

Trim fat from steaks, remove bone; Sprinkle steaks with tenderizer; pound meat to ¼-inch thickness.

Stuffing:

1 cup soft breadcrumbs
2 medium onions, chopped
3 cloves garlic, minced
1 cup chopped celery
¼ cup chopped parsley
¼ cup green pepper, diced
2 hard-cooked eggs, diced

1 teaspoon salt
¼ teaspoon pepper
¼ cup grated Parmesan or Romano
  cheese
1 dash dried thyme leaves
1 cup vegetable oil or olive oil

Combine all ingredients, except oil, in large bowl; add oil, ¼ cup at a time, stirring well until mixture holds together. Spread half of stuffing over each steak, and roll like a jelly roll; tie steaks securely with heavy string. Fry steaks in ¼ cup oil over medium heat until well browned; add to prepared gravy and cook 2½ to 3 hours, adding some of reserved water as needed to keep the steaks covered with gravy. Remove steaks 1 hour before serving so they can become compact; continue simmering gravy to thicken. Reheat before serving; remove string from meat and slice. Serve with pasta. Serves 4 to 6.

Mrs. Sandra Sotile
Ascension Parish (Donaldsonville)

BEEF A LA BOURGUIGNON

3 pounds lean beef, cut into
cubes
1½ cups teriyaki sauce
1 cup onion, chopped
1 large green pepper, chopped
½ cup butter
1 clove garlic, crushed
3 tablespoons brandy
12 small white onions, peeled
1 pound fresh mushrooms,
sliced

3 tablespoons all-purpose flour
2 tablespoons tomato paste
1¾ cups burgundy wine
1 cup sherry
1 10½-ounce can beef bouillon,
condensed
⅛ teaspoon pepper
1 bay leaf
Hot cooked rice or noodles
(optional)

Marinate beef in teriyaki sauce at least 3 hours with chopped onion, bell pepper and crushed garlic. Heat ¼ cup butter over low heat in a large skillet or Dutch oven. Brown beef, onion and beef pepper, about ½ at a time, adding more butter when needed. Return all beef, onion, and bell pepper to skillet. Heat the brandy and ignite and pour over beef. When flame goes out, remove beef and set aside. Add 3 tablespoons butter to skillet, add onions and cook, covered, over low heat about 20 minutes. Add mushrooms and cook about 3 minutes while stirring. Remove onions and mushrooms. Stir in flour and tomato paste until well blended. Stir in burgundy, sherry, and bouillon. Preheat oven to 350 degrees. Bring wine mixture to boiling while stirring, remove from heat. Add beef, peppers, onion, mushrooms, pepper and bay leaf and mix well. Bake, tightly covered and stir occasionally until beef is tender (about 1½ to 2 hours). Serve over rice or noodles. Serves 6 to 8.

Gene Adcock
East Baton Rouge Parish (Baton Rouge)

BURGUNDY BEEF

2 pounds beef, cubed
2 10¾-ounce cans mushroom
soup, undiluted
2 tablespoons Worcestershire
sauce

3 tablespoons burgundy wine
2 1¾-ounce packages dry onion
soup mix

Layer in roaster or casserole dish in order given and bake slowly for several hours at 300 degrees or until meat is tender. Serve over chow mein noodles or rice. Serves 4.

Mrs. Lavonne Ater
Concordia Parish (Ferriday)

BRUCCIALUNA

2 thinly sliced round steaks, seasoned with salt and pepper

Stuffing:

1 pound ground meat (Pork gives a nice flavor)
1 cup dry breadcrumbs
2 tablespoons grated Parmesan cheese

¼ cup finely chopped green onions
2 eggs
½ cup vegetable or olive oil

Mix first 5 ingredients for stuffing; place half of stuffing on each round steak. Roll up steaks jellyroll style; wrap rolls with heavy thread to hold in place. In large heavy pot that may also be used to make sauce, brown the meat rolls in ½ cup oil. (If olive oil is used, keep heat very low). Remove meat, reserving pan drippings.

Sauce:

½ cup chopped celery
¼ cup chopped green onions
1 small green pepper, chopped
2 6-ounce cans tomato paste

2 8-ounce cans tomato sauce
Garlic (optional)
1 tablespoon sugar

Sauté the celery, onions and peppers in pan drippings. Add other ingredients; stir and replace rolls in sauce. Simmer 3 to 4 hours. Serve sauce over spaghetti or macaroni. Serves 8 to 10 people.

Note: Rolls can be cooked in microwave to prepare faster. Remove thread and slice rolls in ¾-inch slices.

Esther P. Schexnayder
Pointe Coupee Parish (Ventress)

BEEF MUSHROOM LOAF

¾ cup milk
1½ cups soft breadcrumbs
2 pounds ground beef
½ teaspoon salt
⅛ teaspoon pepper

1 4-ounce can mushrooms
¼ cup catsup
1 12-ounce package soup mix
2 eggs, beaten

Preheat oven to 300 degrees. Pour milk over breadcrumbs; add beef, salt, pepper, mushrooms, and liquid, catsup, soup mix and eggs. Mix thoroughly. Put into a 9 x 5-inch loaf pan. Bake at 300 degrees for 1 hour and 30 minutes until done. Yield: 8 to 12 servings.

Mrs. Lavonne Ater
Concordia Parish (Ferriday)

BARBECUED BEEF BRISKET

2 3-pound briskets or 1
  5-pound brisket
2 teaspoons salt
¼ teaspoon pepper

½ teaspoon garlic powder
½ teaspoon paprika
¼ cup Liquid Smoke

Sauce:
4 cups water
6 beef bouillon cubes
¼ cup Liquid Smoke
1 cup catsup
¼ cup prepared mustard

3 tablespoons brown sugar
2 tablespoons Worcestershire sauce
1 teaspoon garlic powder
4 dashes of Tabasco

The night before cooking, rub salt, pepper, garlic powder, paprika and Liquid Smoke into the brisket; cover and chill overnight. When ready to cook, place brisket in large roasting pan. Roast uncovered (no water) for one hour in 350 degree oven. Pour off excess fat. While the brisket is roasting, prepare sauce by mixing thoroughly the sauce ingredients. After pouring off fat from brisket, pour sauce over meat and continue baking at 350 degrees, basting a few times, about one hour or until fork tender.

Mrs. H. G. Hardee, Jr. (Sue
Vermilion Parish (Gueydan)

SAVORY ROAST IN MUSHROOM GRAVY

1 medium size beef round roast
Meat tenderizer
Salt
Pepper
1 1⅜-ounce package dry onion
  soup mix

1 10¾-ounce can cream of
  mushroom soup
1½ cups water

Spray Corning Ware roasting dish with Pam. Sprinkle meat with tenderizer, salt, and pepper; place in roasting pan. Top with onion soup mix. In a separate bowl, combine mushroom soup and water, stirring well. Pour soup over roast; cover with a lid. Bake at 300 degrees for at least 3 hours. Even better if cooked 5 to 6 hours. Makes its own gravy and it is really delicious and tender.

Note: This is my Grandmother Travis' electric skillet recipe.

Mrs. Wista White
Ouachita Parish (Monroe)

BEEF MARINADE WITH VEGETABLES

3 or 4 pounds round, chuck, or
sirloin steak
1 package Italian salad dressing
mix, prepared
2 tablespoons dried minced
onion
¼ teaspoon dried minced garlic

Salt and pepper to taste
½ to 1 cup water
4 whole tomatoes, peeled
2 green peppers, quartered
2 onions, quartered
½ cup chopped green onion tops
¼ cup chopped fresh parsley

Cut steak into thin strips. In a large bowl combine steak, prepared salad dressing, minced onion, garlic, salt, and pepper; cover tightly. Let steak marinate in the refrigerator overnight. When ready to cook, drain steak from marinade and reserve liquid for sauce. Place steak in cold skillet (use 11 or 12-inch, heavy, covered skillet); brown meat well over high heat, until a brown coating remains on the bottom and sides of the skillet. Reduce heat to medium. Add ½ to 1 cup water to the reserved marinade; pour over meat and start scraping and stirring the brown coating from the sides and bottom of the pan. You may need a little more water to accomplish this. Gently add the tomatoes, green pepper, onion, and parsley. Cover and simmer about 15 minutes or until vegetables are slightly wilted, but firm. Serve over fluffy white rice.

Note: You may omit the vegetables and serve only the meat and gravy. Serves 4 to 6 people.

Mrs. Allen Bares (Lynn)
Vermilion Parish (Erath)

BEEF BURGUNDY

6 slices bacon
3 pounds beef cubes
⅓ cup all-purpose flour
1 10¾-ounce can tomato soup
1 10½-ounce can beef broth
1 cup burgundy or dry red wine
2 large garlic cloves, minced

2 medium bay leaves
½ teaspoon salt
⅛ teaspoon pepper
½ pound carrots, quartered
1½ pounds small white onions
5 or 6 potatoes, halved

Preheat oven to 350 degrees. In a large skillet cook bacon; remove and crumble, reserving pan drippings. Dust beef with flour; brown in bacon drippings. Place cooked beef in a 1-quart casserole. Stir soups into pan drippings in skillet; add wine, garlic, seasonings, and bacon. Cook until hot over medium heat; pour over beef. Cover; bake at 350 degrees for 1 hour. Add carrots, onions, potatoes; bake 1 hour longer. Uncover, and bake 15 minutes to thicken. Serves 8.

Mrs. Lavonne Ater
Concordia Parish (Ferriday)

CABBAGE ROLLS

2 heads cabbage
1 pound ground beef or lean
  pork
1 cup chopped onion
Water
1 cup cooked rice
1 cup seasoned dry
  breadcrumbs

¼ cup chopped fresh parsley
1 clove garlic, crushed
¼ teaspoon thyme leaves
4 teaspoons sage leaves
Salt and lemon pepper
2 eggs, beaten

Parboil large leaves of cabbage for a few minutes until pliable; drain and set aside. Brown meat in a little oil. Remove meat; brown onion in pan drippings. Remove onions; drain off excess oil. Add enough water to make a light brown gravy; cook until done. Pour gravy out and reserve. Put meat, rice, bread-crumbs, and all seasonings in pan; mix thoroughly while heating through on medium heat. Turn off heat; add eggs, and mix again. Place correct amount of stuffing in center of each cabbage leaf. Fold in sides of leaf, roll up tightly and place in large pot. If they are packed tight and fill the pot, they will usually not need to be secured with a toothpick. Heat in reserved brown gravy over medium heat until done. Tomato sauce may be added, if desired.

Note: These are excellent if served with a dollop of sour cream on each.

Louisiana Farm Bureau Women's Committee

CABBAGE ROLLS

½ pound ground beef
½ pound ground pork
½ cup long grain rice,
  uncooked
½ medium-size green pepper,
  chopped

1 small onion, chopped
1 can Rotel tomatoes or stewed
  tomatoes
1 large cabbage, separated into
  leaves

Mix first 5 ingredients; set aside. Steam cabbage leaves in pot of hot water; drain and let cool. Roll meat mixture in soft cabbage leaves and place in deep casserole. Pour 1 can Rotel or stewed tomatoes over rolls; cover. Bake at 350 degrees for 1½ hours.

Mrs. Floyd Zaunbrecher
Vermilion Parish (Gueydan)

COWBOY STEW

1 pound ground beef
½ cup chopped green pepper
  (less, if desired)
1 medium onion, chopped
1 tablespoon chili powder
1 teaspoon salt
1 teaspoon pepper

1 large potato, cut in small pieces
1 16-ounce can whole tomatoes
1 8-ounce can tomato sauce
1 12-ounce can whole kernel corn,
  drained
1 15-ounce can kidney beans,
  drained

Brown meat and drain. Combine meat and next 8 ingredients; cook until potatoes are done. Add whole kernel corn and kidney beans. Simmer for 15 minutes. Serve hot.

Mrs. Leroy Travis (Twink)
Ouachita Parish (Monroe)

CORN STEW

Sauce:
⅓ cup chopped onion
⅓ cup chopped green pepper
1 clove garlic, crushed
1 tablespoon butter, melted
1 16-ounce can whole kernel
  corn, drained

1 28-ounce can whole tomatoes
⅔ cup tomato sauce
2 teaspoons Worcestershire sauce
2 teaspoons sugar
½ teaspoon salt
⅛ teaspoon pepper

In large saucepan or Dutch oven sauté onion, green pepper and crushed garlic in butter until tender, about 5 minutes. Add remaining sauce ingredients; stir to combine. Set aside.

Meatballs:
¾ pound ground beef
½ cup quick or old fashioned
  oats, uncooked
½ teaspoon salt

Dash of pepper
⅓ cup tomato sauce
1 egg, beaten

Combine all ingredients; mix thoroughly. Shape to form 24 one-inch balls. In large skillet in small amount of shortening, brown meatballs on all sides. Drain. Add meatballs to sauce. Bring mixture to boil; reduce heat. Cover and simmer 25 to 30 minutes, stirring occasionally. Serves 6 to 8.

Mrs. Randall F. Bracy (Regina)
Tangipahoa Parish (Amite)

DINNER IN A DISH

1 pound ground beef
1 onion, chopped
¼ cup vegetable oil
Dash of chili powder
Salt

1 tablespoon all-purpose flour
2 6-ounce cans tomato paste
1 15-ounce can cream style corn
¼ pound 4-ounces Velveeta cheese

Brown meat and onions in oil; cook until done. Blend in flour, salt, chili powder, stirring well. Add tomato paste, corn and cheese; stir well. Cook until heated through. Serve over noodles, rice, biscuits, or toast. Serves 8.

Wenonah Lafferty
Caldwell Parish (Columbia)

STEAK DISH

1 pound round steak
3 tablespoons vegetable oil
1 6-ounce can mushrooms, drained
1 1⅜-ounce package dry onion soup mix

⅓ cup water
1 cup commercial sour cream
3 tablespoons all-purpose flour
Hot cooked rice

Cut steak into strips, ¼-inch wide. Brown meat in hot oil. Add mushrooms, onion soup, and water to steak; bring to a boil. Combine sour cream and flour; add to steak. Cook over low heat until mixture thickens and meat is tender. Serve over hot cooked rice or noodles.

Marie Harper
Tangipahoa Parish (Hammond)

MAE'S CASSEROLE

1 pound ground beef
1 cup chopped green pepper
1 cup chopped celery
1 10¾-ounce can cream of mushroom soup, undiluted

1 cup uncooked long grain rice
1 10½-ounce can onion soup (with beef stock)
Salt, pepper and red pepper to taste

In pot, brown meat until done; drain fat. Put the browned meat in large pyrex dish. Add the remaining ingredients. Season with salt, black and red pepper. Cover; bake at 350 degrees for about 1 hour or until done.

Anna Belle Davis
Pointe Coupee Parish (New Roads)

DEVILED STEAK STRIPS

1½ pounds round steak
¼ cup all-purpose flour
¼ cup chopped onion
1 clove garlic, minced
3 tablespoons melted
   shortening
1½ cups water, divided

1½ cups tomato sauce
1 tablespoon vinegar
1 teaspoon prepared horseradish
1 teaspoon prepared mustard
¾ teaspoon salt
¼ teaspoon pepper

Trim excess fat from meat. Cut meat into thin strips, about 2 inches long; coat with flour. In skillet, brown meat, onion, and garlic in shortening. Stir in 1 cup water, tomato sauce, vinegar, horseradish, mustard, salt, and pepper. Cover and simmer for 1 hour or until meat is tender, stirring occasionally. Stir in ½ cup water; scrap browned bits from bottom of pan; heat through.

Mrs. Lavonne Ater
Concordia Parish (Ferriday)

FIVE HUNDRED DEGREE ROAST

1 eye-of-round roast
Adolf's meat tenderizer

Garlic purée
Freshly ground pepper

Preheat oven to 500 degrees. Season meat with meat tenderizer and put garlic purée on top; sprinkle with ground pepper. Place meat on a rack in a roasting pan. Bake at 500 degrees for 5 minutes per pound. Turn oven off; leave meat in oven 2 hours; meat will be perfectly pink in center and delicious.

Mrs. John Whitley (Helen)
East Baton Rouge Parish (Baton Rouge)

GROUND BEEF CASSEROLE

1 cup washed and drained long
   grain rice, uncooked
1 10¾-ounce can cream of
   chicken soup, undiluted
1 10½-ounce can onion soup,
   undiluted
1 pound ground beef

1 teaspoon Kitchen Bouquet
⅓ cup chopped green pepper
⅓ cup chopped fresh parsley
⅓ cup chopped celery
⅓ cup chopped onion
Salt to taste

Preheat oven to 350 degrees. In large bowl mix all ingredients well. Place a 3-quart casserole dish that has been sprayed with Pam. Bake at 350 degrees for 1½ hours.

Mrs. Ronald Scioneaux
St. James Parish (Vacherie)

LOUISIANA HASH

1 green pepper, chopped
2 onions, chopped
2 tablespoons vegetable oil
2 pounds ground beef
½ cup uncooked long grain rice
1 15-ounce can whole tomatoes

1 teaspoon chili powder
2 teaspoons salt
¼ teaspoon pepper
Dash Lea & Perrins Worcestershire
  sauce

Cook onions and green pepper for a few minutes in skillet with oil. Add meat to skillet and brown. Drain meat; combine with other ingredients. Place mixture into a 14 x 11-inch casserole; bake at 350 degrees about 1 hour, or until all moisture is absorbed.

Note: Louisiana Hash is traditionally served on Christmas Eve.

Marilyn Taylor
Ouachita Parish (Monroe)

LOUISIANA RICE HASH

1 pound ground beef
1 medium onion, diced
2 tablespoons melted butter
2 tablespoons green pepper,
  chopped
2 tablespoons chopped green
  onion tops

2 tablespoons chopped fresh
  parsley
1 cup uncooked long grain rice
1 teaspoon salt
2 teaspoons chili powder
1 teaspoon pepper
2 cups tomatoes

Brown meat and onions in butter in a skillet; add remaining ingredients. Place in a 1½-quart casserole; bake at 350 degrees for 1 hour.

Mrs. Elmo Smith (Clara)
Allen Parish (Oberlin)

LOUISIANA HASH

1 pound ground beef
3 large onions, sliced
1 large green pepper, chopped
1 16-ounce can whole tomatoes

½ cup uncooked long grain rice
2 teaspoons salt
1 to 2 teaspoons chili powder
⅛ teaspoon pepper

Brown meat, onions and peppers in a skillet. Drain fat; stir in remaining ingredients. Pour in a 2-quart casserole; cover. Bake at 350 degrees for 1 hour.

Mrs. Allen Weeks (Cindy)
Ouachita Parish (West Monroe)

CREOLE RICE DRESSING

1½ cups long grain rice,
  uncooked
1¼ pounds ground beef
1 cup dried minced onions
1 green pepper, diced
1 10¾-ounce can cream
  mushroom soup, undiluted
1 10¾-ounce can cream of
  chicken soup, undiluted

1 10½-ounce can onion soup
½ cup water
Chopped green onion tops
2 tablespoons minced fresh parsley
½ tablespoon ground red pepper

Mix all ingredients in an iron pot. Cover; bake at 375 degrees for 1½ hours.

Pat Cain
St. Landry Parish (Opelousas)

RICE CASSEROLE

6 tablespoons margarine
1 cup chopped onion
1 cup chopped celery
2 cloves minced garlic
2 pounds ground beef
1 4-ounce can sliced
  mushrooms
1 cup shredded Cheddar cheese
1 cup medium white sauce

1 4-ounce can pimiento, drained
  and chopped
2 cups cooked rice
⅓ cup chopped fresh parsley
1 cup chopped green onions
2 tablespoons hot sauce
1 teaspoon pepper
1 teaspoon salt
Soft breadcrumbs

In a large, deep skillet, melt margarine; add onion, celery, and garlic, sautéing until clear and tender. Remove from pan; brown in pan drippings. After meat is brown, add the onion mixture, mushrooms, cheese, white sauce, pimiento, rice, parsley, green onion, hot sauce, pepper and salt. Heat thoroughly on low heat. Place into a 3-quart deep casserole dish; sprinkle with breadcrumbs, as desired. Bake at 350 degrees for 30 minutes.

Note: Shrimp, crawfish, or crab meat may be used in place of ground beef. White sauce is a basic cornstarch recipe.

Mrs. Wayne Zaunbrecher (Linda)
Vermilion Parish (Gueydan)

MACARONI AND BEEF

1½ pounds ground beef
1 medium onion, chopped
1 16-ounce can whole
  tomatoes, chopped

1 8-ounce can tomato sauce
1 teaspoon salt
½ teaspoon pepper
2 cups uncooked macaroni noodles

In skillet, brown beef and onion. Drain off excess fat. Add cut up pieces of tomatoes, tomato sauce, salt and pepper. Simmer over low heat for 30 minutes. Cook macaroni according to package directions; drain. Combine cooked macaroni and beef into large serving bowl.

Mrs. Allen Weeks (Cindy)
Ouachita Parish (West Monroe)

CHILLIGETTI CASSEROLE

1 pound ground beef
1 large onion
1 teaspoon salt
1 15-ounce can hot chili beans

1½ cups uncooked spaghetti
  noodles
3 cups tomato juice

Preheat oven to 350 degrees. Combine first 3 ingredients; brown in skillet. Arrange meat mixture in 2½-quart casserole with beans, tomato juice, and spaghetti. Bake at 350 degrees for 1 hour.

Mrs. Lavonne Ater
Concordia Parish (Ferriday)

OLD FASHIONED SPAGHETTI

1 pound ground beef or pork
3 cups water
1 8-ounce can tomato sauce
1 6-ounce can tomato paste
Dash of salt
Dash of pepper

1 tablespoon sugar
1 medium onion, chopped
1 6-ounce can sliced mushrooms,
  drained
1 12-ounce package short vermicelli
  noodles

Brown ground meat in large skillet; drain excess fat. Add 3 cups water, tomato sauce, tomato paste, salt, pepper and sugar; heat to boiling. Reduce heat to low; add onion and mushrooms. Simmer for 1½ hours. Cook noodles according to package directions. Drain. Stir into meat sauce 15 minutes before meat is done. Serves 6.

Mrs. Gary Bordelon (Melanie)
Avoyelles Parish (Moreauville)

HANNAH JANE'S SPAGHETTI

2 pounds ground beef
2 pounds ground pork
2 large onions, chopped
1 large green pepper, chopped
5 stalks celery, chopped
1½ to 2 cups soft breadcrumbs

2 eggs, beaten
2 teaspoons basil leaves
2 tablespoons salt
4 cloves garlic, minced
All-purpose flour

Mix first 10 ingredients in a large bowl. Shape into large balls at least 2 inches in diameter. Roll meatballs in flour; brown in oil until done.

Sauce:
4 6-ounce cans tomato paste
1 cup vegetable oil

¼ cup sugar
3 quarts water

Brown ingredients for sauce over low heat for 2 hours. This can be done while you are in the kitchen doing other things. Stir about every 10 minutes. After it is browned to look like a roux (a deep golden brown), add 3 quarts water and start it simmering. Add the meatballs, simmer for about 3 hours. Remove cover for the last hour to thicken the gravy. Serve on spaghetti. Serves 16 to 20 people.

Mrs. L. E. Hardee, Jr. (Hannah Jane)
Vermilion Parish (Kaplan)

MEZETTI

2 tablespoons shortening
1 pound ground beef
¼ cup chopped green pepper
1 cup chopped onion
1 tablespoon chili powder
1 5-ounce package noodles

1 cup water
1 10¾-ounce can cream of
   mushroom soup
1 10¾-ounce can tomato soup
1 cup shredded Cheddar cheese

Heat shortening to 200 degrees, using an electric skillet. Add meat, green pepper, and onion; cook at 350 degrees until brown. Add chili powder and garlic salt. Sprinkle noodles over top and add water. Mix together the tomato soup and mushroom soup; pour over meat mixture. Cover and cook until boiling. Turn heat to 220 degrees and cook for 30 minutes. Sprinkle shredded cheese over top of mixture; and cook for another 5 minutes.

Note: This is an easy, fast dish for those days when you can't put too much time in the kitchen.

Mrs. Dorothy McCown
Jeff Davis Parish (Welsh)

LOUISIANA LASAGNA

1½ pounds ground beef
1 tablespoon vegetable oil
1 onion, chopped
1 clove garlic, minced
2 tablespoons chopped fresh
  parsley
1½ cups water
2 6-ounce cans tomato paste
2 bay leaves
1¼ teaspoons salt

½ teaspoon pepper
¾ teaspoon oregano leaves
¼ cup butter
3 tablespoons all-purpose flour
2 cups milk
½ cup grated Parmesan cheese
2 egg yolks, beaten
1 8-ounce package Lasagna
  noodles

Brown meat in oil until done; add onions, garlic, parsley. Cook 5 minutes. Add water, tomato paste, bay leaves, 1 teaspoon salt, pepper and oregano to skillet; cover and simmer 45 minutes, stirring occasionally. Meanwhile, in saucepan, melt butter over low heat; stir in flour, blending well. Cook until thickened and bubbly. Remove from heat; gradually add the milk, stirring constantly. Cook until thickened. Stir in cheese, egg yolks, and remaining ¼ teaspoon salt; cook 2 minutes. Cook noodles according to package directions. Lay noodles in shallow pan. Pour meat sauce over noodles, then cheese sauce. Bake at 325 degrees, uncovered, for 20 to 25 minutes or until bubbly. Yield: 6 to 8 servings.

Mrs. Rick Caldwell (Jeanie)
Ouachita Parish (Monroe)

SHORTCUT LASAGNA

1 tablespoon olive or vegetable
  oil
1½ pounds ground chuck
1 28-ounce can whole tomatoes
1 8-ounce can tomato sauce
2 envelopes spaghetti sauce
  mix
2 12-ounce cans V-8 juice

1 12-ounce package Lasagna
  noodles
1 12-ounce carton cottage cheese
1 8-ounce package Mozzarella
  cheese, shredded
¼ cup grated Parmesan cheese
Chopped fresh parsley

Heat oil in large skillet; add meat, and cook until done. Stir in tomatoes, tomato sauce, sauce mix, and V-8 juice; bring to a boil. Lower heat; simmer 15 minutes. Cover the bottom of a greased 13 x 9 x 2-inch baking dish with a thin layer of meat sauce; add a layer each of uncooked noodles, cottage cheese and Mozzarella cheese. Repeat layers until all ingredients are used, ending with the meat sauce. Cover casserole tightly with heavy aluminum foil. Set on a jelly roll pan. Bake at 350 degrees for 1 hour. Remove from oven, let stand 15 minutes. Sprinkle with Parmesan cheese and chopped parsley. Cut into squares to serve. Serves 12.

Mrs. Henry G. Hardee, Jr. (Sue)
Vermilion Parish (Gueydan)

ENCHILADA CASSEROLE

1½ pounds ground beef
1 small onion, chopped
3 tablespoons vegetable oil
1 10-ounce can mild enchilada
  sauce
1 4-ounce can peeled chili
  peppers, chopped
1 10¾-ounce can cream of
  chicken soup

1 10¾-ounce can cream of
  mushroom soup
1 cup milk
1 package 6-inch tortillas
1 6-ounce can pitted olives, drained
  and sliced (optional)
1 to 2 cups shredded sharp
  Cheddar cheese

Preheat oven to 350 degrees. Brown meat and onion in hot oil in skillet (Do not season). Drain meat. Mix enchilada sauce, chili peppers, chicken soup, mushroom soup, milk and olives. Alternate layers of meat mixture, tortillas, and sauce in 13 x 9-inch glass casserole or pan. Sprinkle with cheese. Cover with aluminum foil; bake at 350 degrees for 1 hour. Uncover, and bake 10 minutes longer.

Shirley Wood
West Carroll Parish (Pioneer)

TORTILLA PIE

1 green pepper, chopped
1 onion, chopped
2 pounds ground beef
2 10¾-ounce cans mushroom
  soup, undiluted
1 10-ounce can Old El Paso
  enchilada sauce

1 4-ounce can chopped hot green
  chilies, drained
1 9-ounce package tortillas
1 pound (4 cups) shredded
  Cheddar cheese
Chili powder to taste
Garlic salt to taste

Sauté pepper and onion until soft over low heat; add meat, and cook until done. Add soup, sauce and chilies; heat thoroughly. Line a casserole with tortillas. Add a layer of meat sauce, cheese, then more tortillas. Repeat layering until ingredients are used. Chill for 24 hours in refrigerator. Bake at 350 degrees for 45 minutes.

Note: May be frozen before cooking.

Joan Falgoust
St. James Parish (St. James)

TACOS

Meat filling:

1 pound ground meat
1 medium onion, chopped
1 tomato, chopped or ½ cup
  canned tomato sauce
1 teaspoon Lawry's Seasoned
  Salt
1 garlic clove, minced

1 tablespoon chili powder
Dash of hot sauce
¼ teaspoon oregano leaves
10 taco shells, heated
Chopped tomatoes
Shredded lettuce
Shredded Cheddar cheese

Brown ground meat until done; drain fat. Add next 7 ingredients; cook, uncovered, about 10 minutes, stirring occasionally. Place meat filling in each taco shell; top with lettuce, tomatoes, and cheese. Yield: 10 tacos.

Mrs. B. F. Lemoine, Jr. (Grace)
Avoyelles Parish (Hamburg)

OVEN STEW

2 pounds stew meat
2 tablespoons bacon fat
1 1⅜-ounce package dry onion
  soup mix

1 10¾-ounce can cream of
  mushroom soup, undiluted
1 cup water

Preheat oven to 300 degrees. Brown stew meat in bacon fat. Drain meat and add to rest of ingredients. Bake at 300 degrees for 3 hours.

Mrs. Allen Weeks (Cindy)
Ouachita Parish (West Monroe)

SWEET AND SOUR MEAT LOAF

1 15-ounce can tomato sauce
½ cup firmly packed light
  brown sugar
¼ cup vinegar
1 teaspoon prepared mustard
2 pounds ground lean beef

½ pound ground pork
2 eggs, slightly beaten
¼ cup minced onions
½ cup soft breadcrumbs
1 tablespoon salt
¼ teaspoon pepper

Preheat oven to 350 degrees. Mix tomato sauce, sugar, vinegar and mustard in a medium bowl. In a separate bowl, combine the remaining ingredients; add 1 cup tomato sauce mixture. Pack meat into a 1½-quart oval casserole dish. Pour ¼ cup of the sauce mixture over the top. Bake at 350 degrees for one hour. The remaining sauce may be heated and served with the meat loaf.

Mrs. James Parkerson (Joyce)
Ouachita Parish (Monroe)

MEAT LOAF

1½ pounds ground beef
1 egg, beaten
1 cup soft breadcrumbs
1 medium onion, chopped

1¼ teaspoons salt
¼ teaspoon pepper
½ cup tomato sauce

Preheat oven to 350 degrees. Lightly mix together all ingredients and form into a loaf. Place in a greased shallow pan; bake at 350 degrees approximately 1 hour.

Meat sauce:
½ cup tomato sauce
2 tablespoons vinegar
2 tablespoons prepared
    mustard

1 cup water
2 tablespoons brown sugar

Mix sauce ingredients together; pour over meat loaf after baking ½ hour. Continue baking 1½ hours longer, basting occasionally.

Mrs. Sam Womack
East Baton Rouge Parish (Zachary)

MEAT STUFFED PEPPERS

4 large green peppers
2 medium onions, chopped
½ cup vegetable oil
1-1½ pounds ground beef
½ cup chopped celery
1 clove garlic, minced

2 slices sted bread, crumbled
½ cup ch   ed parsley
½ packag   wn gravy mix
½ cup wate
Salt to taste
Soft breadcrum

Preheat oven to 425 degrees. Split peppers in half, remov eeds and scald. Cook onions until golden brown in a small amount of oil.   ground meat, celery, garlic and cook till meat is brown. Drain oil; add toaste   read, brown gravy mix and water, salt, parsley. Fill peppers with meat mix e. Sprinkle peppers with breadcrumbs; and bake at 425 degrees for 25 to 3(inutes or until peppers are soft. Serves 4.

Mrs. Eddie Schexnaydre (Doris)
Terrebonne Parish (Schriever)

MOCK FILET

1½ pounds ground beef
2 cups cooked rice
1 cup minced onion
1 clove garlic, crushed
2 tablespoons Worcestershire sauce

1½ teaspoons salt
¼ teaspoon pepper
1 10¾-ounce can mushroom soup, undiluted
8 strips bacon

Combine meat, rice, onion, garlic, Worcestershire sauce, salt, pepper and mushroom soup. Divide into 8 patties; wrap bacon around each and fasten with toothpicks. Place on an ungreased pan; bake at 450 degrees for 25 minutes.

Mrs. Marvin Spangler
Ouachita Parish (West Monroe)

MOCK VEAL CUTLET

1 pound coarsely ground beef
1 teaspoon salt
¼ teaspoon pepper
1 teaspoon chili powder

1 tablespoon Worcestershire sauce
1 small onion, minced
2 eggs, beaten
Cracker crumbs

Mix ground beef, salt, pepper, chili powder, Worcestershire sauce and onion in mixing bowl. Cover; let chill in refrigerator for 1 hour. Form meat into club steak size pieces; place back in the refrigerator for overnight. Dip cutlets in beaten eggs, and then in bread crumbs, coating well on both sides. Fry in deep fat on medium heat until golden brown. These may be frozen and cooked when needed.

Mrs. Sally Marshall
Jeff Davis Parish (Jennings)

PORCUPINE BALLS

1½ pounds ground beef
½ cup uncooked long-grain rice
2 tablespoons chopped onion
1 teaspoon salt

⅛ teaspoon pepper
vegetable oil
1 10¾-ounce can tomato soup
1 soup can water

Combine meat, rice, onion, salt and pepper. Shape into medium size balls (about 18). Brown meatballs in hot oil. Combine tomato soup and water in a deep skillet; heat to boiling. Add meatballs. Cover and cook slowly for 1 hour. Yield: 8 to 10 servings.

Mrs. Kerry Burns (Nancy)
Webster Parish (Minden)

MOUSSAKA

3 medium eggplants, peeled
   and cut into ⅜-inch slices
Salted water
All-purpose flour
½ cup vegetable oil
¼ cup olive oil
¼ cup butter
2 large onions, finely chopped

2 pounds ground beef
3 tablespoons tomato paste
½ cup dry red wine
½ cup chopped fresh parsley
¼ teaspoon ground cinnamon
Salt and pepper to taste
1 cup soft breadcrumbs
1 cup grated Parmesan cheese

Soak eggplant slices in salted water for 20 minutes. Drain eggplant; dry on paper towels. Coat eggplant with flour. Preheat oven to 400 degrees. Cover large baking sheets with foil and grease with oil. Place eggplant slices on baking sheets, turning to coat well with oil. Bake at 400 degrees about 15-20 minutes; turn off oven, and let eggplant stand in oven another 30 minutes. Heat olive oil and butter in heavy skillet; sauté onions in butter until tender. Add ground beef and cook 10 minutes. Combine tomato paste, wine, parsley, cinnamon, salt and pepper and stir into meat; simmer and stir until all liquid has been absorbed. Remove from heat. Grease a 16 x 11 x 2-inch casserole dish; sprinkle bottom of casserole with bread crumbs, just enough to coat bottom of casserole. Arrange alternate layers of eggplant and meat sauce in casserole, sprinkling each layer with Parmesan cheese and bread crumbs to within 1-inch of casserole top.

Cream sauce:
¼ cup butter
¼ cup all-purpose flour
2 cups milk
4 eggs, beaten

Ground nutmeg to taste
2 teaspoons lemon juice
1 8-ounce carton cottage cheese

Melt butter in skillet; stir in flour and cook 1 minute over low heat. Add milk, stirring constantly, and cook until thickened. Cool slightly, add beaten eggs, nutmeg, cottage cheese and lemon juice. Taste and adjust seasoning. Pour cream sauce over casserole; bake at 350 degrees for 45 minutes. Cool slightly before cutting into squares. Serves 8-10. Freezes well.

Mrs. W. P. Fuller (Judy)
Allen Parish (Kinder)

CAJUN CHOW MEIN

2 tablespoons shortening
1½ pounds ground beef
½ cup diced celery
½ cup diced green pepper
½ cup diced onion
1 4-ounce can mushrooms,
  undrained

1 1-pound can whole tomatoes
1 cup uncooked minute rice
¾ cup water
1 tablespoon Worcestershire sauce
¼ teaspoon hot sauce
1 tablespoon salt
1½ teaspoons pepper

Melt shortening in a skillet; brown meat in shortening. Add onions, celery, green pepper; cook until vegetables are tender (wilted looking). Stir in mushrooms, tomatoes, rice, water and seasonings. Reduce heat to low and cook for 30 to 35 minutes or until rice is tender. Serves 6.

Note: Electric skillet may be used; if so, brown meat at 350 degrees and reduce to 250 degrees to cook.

Mrs. Donald Johnson (Brenda)
Ouachita Parish (Monroe)

CHICKEN FRIED STEAK

2 pounds round steak,
  tenderized
Seasoned salt and pepper
2 eggs

½ cup milk
All-purpose flour
Vegetable oil

Trim all fat and gristle from meat. Cut meat into pieces about the size of your hand. Season with salt and pepper on both sides. Beat eggs and milk together lightly. Dip steak in flour, then in eggs, then in flour again. For thicker crust, repeat procedure. Heat oil, ¼ inch deep, to about 400 degrees in electric skillet or to very hot in a skillet. Place steaks in hot oil, then turn heat to low. Cook 15 to 20 minutes on first side, or until golden brown. Turn without puncturing crust, and cook 10 minutes on second side. Drain on paper towel and keep warm in oven while making gravy.

Note: This is a favorite of my teenage children. Serves 6 to 8.

Mrs. Richard Hebert (Marca)
Evangeline Parish (Ville Platte)

HARD DAYS SUPPER

2 pounds ground beef
1 cup chopped onion
⅔ cup chopped green pepper
2 or 3 teaspoons chili powder
2 teaspoons salt
½ teaspoon thyme leaves
¼ teaspoon pepper
2 6-ounce cans tomato paste

½ cup catsup
2 cups water
2 teaspoons Worcestershire sauce
Dash Tabasco sauce
1 medium bag regular size corn
  chips
2 cups shredded Cheddar cheese

In a large skillet brown beef; add onion and green pepper, cooking until tender. Add chili powder, salt, thyme, pepper, tomato paste, catsup, water, Worcestershire sauce, and Tabasco sauce. Simmer 1 hour stirring occasionally. Serve on corn chips; top with cheese. Serves 6.

Mrs. Donald Johnson (Brenda)
Ouachita Parish (Monroe)

KITCHEN CREW HAMBURGER PIE

1 cup Bisquick baking mix
¼ cup milk
1 pound ground beef
½ cup chopped onion
½ teaspoon salt

¼ teaspoon pepper
1 tablespoon Worcestershire sauce
2 eggs
1 cup shredded Cheddar cheese

Preheat oven to 375 degrees. Stir Bisquick mix and milk together to make a soft dough. Smooth dough into a ball on floured, cloth-covered board. Knead 5 times. Roll dough 2 inches larger than inverted 9-inch pie pan. Ease into pan and flute edge. Cook meat and onions until done. Combine meat, salt, pepper, and Worcestershire sauce; spoon into pie crust. Beat eggs slightly; mix in cheese. Pour egg mixture over meat in pastry. Cover edge with aluminum foil (prevents browning too fast). Bake at 375 degrees for 30 minutes. Uncover last 5 minutes.

Connie Granger
Beauregard Parish (DeRidder)

BEEF CASSEROLE

1 pound ground beef
⅓ cup chopped green pepper
½ cup chopped onions
1 cup chopped celery
1 cup uncooked long grain rice

1 11½-ounce can vegetable soup
2 teaspoons salt
¼ teaspoon black pepper or red
   pepper if preferred
¼ teaspoon Tabasco sauce

Brown beef in a large skillet. Add green pepper, onions, celery to uncooked rice. Cook until golden brown. Prepare the vegetable soup according to directions given on the can. Add salt, pepper and Tabasco sauce to the soup; heat to boiling, stirring well. Combine meat and soup into a 2-quart casserole. Cover and bake 25 minutes at 350 degrees. Makes 6 servings.

Note: 1 3-ounce can chow mein noodles may be sprinkled over the top of casserole before serving, if desired.

Mrs. Ruby Davis
Jeff Davis Parish (Jennings)

HAMBURGER CASSEROLE

1 medium onion, chopped
½ green pepper, chopped
2 tablespoons butter, melted
1 pound ground beef or ground
   chuck
1 teaspoon salt
¼ teaspoon garlic powder

1 16-ounce package frozen mixed
   vegetables
3 hard-cooked eggs
1 10¾-ounce can cream of
   mushroom soup
2 cups soft breadcrumbs
1 cup shredded Cheddar cheese

Sauté onions and peppers in butter. Add meat, salt and garlic; cook until meat is done. Cook mixed vegetables according to directions on package. Layer vegetables, meat, and sliced eggs in a casserole. Dilute soup and pour over top of layers. Sprinkle breadcrumbs and cheese over the top. Bake at 350 degrees for 20 minutes or until bubbly.

Mrs. Doug Moore (Liz)
Ouachita Parish (Monroe)

✳ SLOPPY JOE CASSEROLE

1 or 2 cups uncooked shell
   macaroni
1 pound ground beef
1 envelope Sloppy Joe
   seasoning mix

1 8-ounce can tomato sauce
1¼ cups water
1 6-ounce can tomato paste
2 cups cottage cheese
½ cup shredded Cheddar cheese

Preheat oven to 350 degrees. Cook macaroni and drain. Brown beef; add seasoning mix, tomato sauce and 1¼ cups water and tomato paste. In 2½-quart casserole dish, layer half macaroni, half cottage cheese and half meat sauce, then layer again. Top with Cheddar cheese; bake at 350 degrees, uncovered, for 40 to 50 minutes.

Note: This can be frozen.

Mrs. Leroy Travis (Twink)
Ouachita Parish (Monroe)

CHICKEN AND ASPARAGUS

6 chicken breasts

2 15-ounce cans green tip
   asparagus, drained

Boil chicken in seasoned water until tender. Remove from bone and tear into pieces. In a 9 x 13-inch casserole dish, put a layer of asparagus. Cover with chicken pieces.

Sauce:
1 medium onion, chopped
1 8-ounce can mushrooms,
   drained
½ cup butter or margarine,
   melted
2 10¾-ounce cans mushroom
   or cream of chicken soup,
   undiluted
¾ large can evaporated milk

½ pound (8 ounces) sharp cheese,
   shredded
¼ teaspoon Tabasco
2 teaspoons soy sauce
1 teaspoon salt
½ teaspoon pepper
1 teaspoon Accent
2 tablespoons chopped pimiento
½ cup chopped almonds

Sauté onions and mushrooms in margarine; add soup, milk, cheese, Tabasco, soy sauce, salt, pepper, Accent and pimiento. Simmer mixture until cheese melts, stirring constantly. Pour sauce over the chicken and asparagus; top with chopped almonds. Bake at 350 degrees for 30 minutes or until bubbly.

Mrs. A. M. Youngblood (Carrie)
Caldwell Parish (Columbia)

CHICKEN A'LA KING

1 6-ounce can sliced
  mushrooms, drained (reserve
  ¼ cup liquid)
½ cup finely chopped green
  pepper
½ cup butter or margarine,
  melted
½ cup all-purpose flour

1 teaspoon salt
¼ teaspoon pepper
2 cups half-and-half
1¾ cups chicken broth
2 cups cubed chicken or turkey
½ cup chopped pimiento
Toast cups or toasted bread

In large skillet, cook and stir mushrooms and green pepper in butter for 5 minutes. Blend in flour, salt and pepper. Cook over low heat, stirring constantly, until mixture is bubbly. Remove from heat. Stir in cream, broth and remaining mushroom liquid. Heat to boiling, stirring constantly. Boil and stir 1 minute. Stir in chicken and pimiento; heat thoroughly. Serve in toast cups or on toasted bread slices. Yield: 8 servings.

Evelina Smith
Beauregard Parish (DeRidder)

CHINESE CHICKEN

8 or 10 chicken breast halves
6 tablespoons butter or
  margarine
3 cups chicken broth
2 cups sliced celery
2 cups chopped green string
  beans
1 cup drained sliced water
  chestnuts
1 cup drained bamboo shoots

¼ cup soy sauce
2 teaspoons salt
1 teaspoon sugar
1 teaspoon pepper
2 teaspoons monosodium
  glutamate
2 tablespoons cornstarch
Water
Slivered almonds (optional)

Skin and debone chicken. Cut chicken into bite-size pieces; cook in butter in a large frying pan until done. Add chicken broth, celery, beans, water chestnuts, bamboo shoots, soy sauce, salt, sugar, pepper, and monosodium glutamate; cook for 5 to 10 minutes. Add cornstarch, which has been mixed with a little water to make a paste. Cook over medium heat until thickened. Serve over hot cooked rice. Sprinkle slivered almonds on top of each serving. Serves 8 to 10.

Note: This freezes well. Just thaw and heat.

Mrs. Melba McIntosh
West Carroll Parish (Pioneer)

CHICKEN-BROCCOLI CASSEROLE

1 2 to 3-pound chicken
2 10-ounce packages frozen
chopped broccoli
1 10¾-ounce can cream of
mushroom soup, undiluted

2 tablespoons mayonnaise
½ cup water
6 slices process American cheese

Boil chicken and debone; place in lightly greased baking pan or casserole dish. Cook broccoli according to package directions; drain. Place broccoli in pan over chicken. Dilute cream of mushroom soup with water; add mayonnaise. Pour soup mixture over chicken and broccoli; place cheese slices on top. Bake at 350 degrees for 20 to 25 minutes or until cheese is melted.

Pearl T. LeDaux
St. Landry Parish (Eunice)

DUCY'S BAKED CHICKEN AND YAMS

1 2½-pound broiler or fryer, cut
in quarters
Salt and pepper to taste
Fine dry breadcrumbs

2 eggs
3 tablespoons water
4 medium yams, peeled
½ cup butter, melted

Sprinkle chicken with salt and pepper. Coat with breadcrumbs. Beat eggs and water together. Dip chicken in egg mixture and breadcrumbs. Place chicken and yams in greased shallow 2-quart baking dish, baste with part of butter. Bake in oven at 350 degrees for one hour or until chicken is tender. Baste often with rest of butter. Yields: 4 servings.

Mrs. Curry Dupas (Ducy)
Avoyelles Parish (Moreauville)

CORNISH HENS CHAMPAGNE

½ cup margarine, melted
2 cups champagne or dry white
wine
3 Rock Cornish hens, halved

Salt
Pepper
1 bunch shallots, chopped

Preheat oven to 325 degrees. Combine margarine and champagne or wine; set aisde. Season hens to taste with salt and pepper. Place hens in baking pan (skin side up). Pour champagne mixture over hens. Sprinkle handful of chopped shallots on top of each hen half. Bake at 325 degrees for 1½ hours, basting every 20 minutes. Serves 6.

Mrs. Grace Graugnard
St. James Parish (St. James)

CHICKEN CASSEROLE

1 5-pound hen or broiler fryer
½ cup margarine
1 cup chopped celery
1 cup chopped green pepper
1 cup chopped onion
1 10¾-ounce can cream of
 mushroom soup

2 4-ounce jars chopped pimiento,
 drained
10 pimiento-stuffed olives, sliced
1 12-ounce package egg noodles
½ pound (8 ounces) shredded
 Cheddar cheese

Boil hen until tender. Save broth and let hen cool. Debone and dice chicken (remove skin and fat). Set aside. Melt margarine; add celery, onion, and green pepper. Cook on low heat until tender. Remove from heat. Bring chicken broth to boil; add egg noodles and cook until tender. Drain; combine noodles, chicken, sautéed vegetables, mushroom soup, pimiento, and sliced olives, mixing well. Spoon mixture into a casserole dish; top with cheese. Bake at 350 degrees until cheese melts.

Note: When boiling the hen, add salt, pepper, onion powder, garlic powder to the water.

Mrs. Don Odom (Brenda)
Claiborne Parish (Homer)

CHICKEN FRICASSE WITH DUMPLINGS

⅓ cup vegetable oil
½ cup all-purpose flour
1 medium onion, chopped
1 green pepper, chopped
 (optional)
2 stalks celery, chopped
 (optional)

1-1¼ quarts water
2 to 3-pound broiler-fryer, cut up
1 10-ounce can biscuits
Salt and pepper to taste
Hot cooked rice (optional)

In a thick cast aluminum or heavy iron pot, heat oil; add flour and stir constantly until flour-oil mixture is slightly darker than a brown grocery bag. Remove from heat; stir in chopped onion, pepper and celery, if desired, stirring until transparent. Return to heat and add water. Heat to boiling; add chicken pieces, salt, and pepper. Simmer for about one hour. Cut canned biscuits in half; place on top of meat. Cook, covered, for another 25 minutes. Serve over rice. Serves 6 to 8.

Mrs. Bernard Bordelon (Marie)
Avoyelles Parish (Moreauville)

CHICKEN FRICASSE WITH DUMPLINGS

Fricasse:

1 cup all-purpose flour
½ cup vegetable oil
1 cup chopped onions
½ cup chopped celery,
   (optional)
½ cup chopped green pepper,
   (optional)

1 2 to 3-pound hen, cut into
   serving pieces
1 quart water
Salt and pepper to taste

Make a roux by slowly browning the flour in the oil. This process must be carefully watched and stirred constantly. When roux is golden brown, add the onion, celery, and green pepper, if desired; cook, stirring constantly, until vegetables are soft. Add chicken pieces to roux mixture, stirring and cooking about 1 minute longer. Add 1 quart water and bring to a boil, stirring frequently. Continue cooking and adding water so as to render the meat tender and to give the fricassee desired consistency. (For best results, it will require several hours of slow cooking.) If dumplings are desired, add about 1 ½ cups additional water and bring to a boil. Reduce heat to simmer.

Dumplings:

2 cups all-purpose flour
1 teaspoon baking powder
Salt and pepper to taste
½ cup chopped green onion
   tops or fresh parsley

2 egg yolks
½ cup water

In small bowl combine flour, baking powder, seasoning and onion tops; mixing well. In separate bowl, beat egg yolks and add ½ cup water; add to flour mixture until a soft dough is formed. Drop dough by spoonful in simmering fricasse; cook slowly, stirring very little until dumplings are cooked. Serve on hot fluffy rice.

Robella Langlinais
Vermilion Parish (Erath)

CHICKEN BREAST MAGNIFIQUE

8 chicken breast halves
½ cup butter or margarine, melted
1 cup sliced mushrooms
2 10¾-ounce cans cream of chicken soup

Garlic powder to taste
Pinch of thyme leaves
Pinch of rosemary leaves
1 cup water to thin, as needed
⅔ cup half-and-half
Toasted almonds

Brown chicken well in butter; remove from skillet. Sauté mushrooms in butter; stir in soup, garlic, and seasonings. Return chicken breasts to the skillet. Cover; cook over low heat for 45 minutes, stirring occasionally. Add water as it thickens. Blend in half-and-half; heat slowly. Serve over white or wild rice or a combination of the two. Garnish with toasted almonds. Serves 8.

Denise Lipsey
Concordia Parish (Monterey)

RICE DRESSING

2 pounds chicken livers
1 pound pork sausage
1 cup chopped onion
½ cup chopped celery
1 bunch green onions, chopped
2 tablespoons chopped parsley

2 cloves garlic, minced
1½ cups cooked rice
½ 10¾-ounce can chicken broth, heated
2 chicken bouillon cubes
Salt, pepper, red pepper to taste

Sauté liver, sausage, onions, celery, parsley and garlic until done. Stir in cooked rice. Dissolve bouillon cubes in ½ can broth; add bouillon and seasonings to sausage mixture.

Evalena Moreland
Concordia Parish (Monterey)

SMOTHERED CHICKEN

1 3-pound broiler-fryer
Salt and pepper
½ cup all-purpose flour
½ cup vegetable oil

1 large onion, chopped
3 cloves of garlic, minced
1 small green pepper (optional)
Hot cooked rice (optional)

Cut fryer up into parts and season well with salt and pepper; coat well with flour. In large saucepan, heat oil over medium flame. Add chicken parts; brown well. Lower heat; add onion, garlic, and green pepper over chicken. Cover; let simmer for 45 minutes to 1 hour. Serve over cooked rice or mashed potatoes.

Mrs. Lester J. Durel (Iris)
Lafayette Parish (Lafayette)

LEMON CHICKEN

⅓ cup all-purpose flour
1 teaspoon salt
1 teaspoon paprika
1 2½ to 3-pound broiler-fryer,
  cut up
3 tablespoons lemon juice

3 tablespoons Crisco oil
1 chicken bouillon cube
¾ cup boiling water
¼ cup sliced green onion
2 tablespoons brown sugar
1½ teaspoons grated lemon peel

In bag, combine flour, salt, and paprika. Brush chicken with lemon juice. Add 2 pieces of chicken at a time to bag and shake well. In large skillet, brown chicken in hot oil. Dissolve bouillon cube in ¾ cup boiling water; slowly pour over chicken in skillet. Stir in onion, brown sugar, peel, and any remaining lemon juice. Cover; reduce heat. Cook chicken over low heat until tender, 40 to 45 minutes. Serves 4.

Mrs. John C. Taylor (Judy)
Ouachita Parish (Choudrant)

BAKED CHICKEN OR TURKEY AND DRESSING WITH GIBLET GRAVY

Chicken or turkey:
Salt poultry all over; place in pan with one cup water. Pour ½ cup melted margarine over chicken or turkey and cover with foil. Bake at 350 degrees for 3 to 4 hours or until tender. Uncover, and let brown for the last 30 minutes of baking.

Cornbread dressing:
1 pan cornbread
1 large onion, chopped
½ stalk celery, chopped
½ bunch green onions,
  chopped

2 to 3 eggs, beaten
5 to 6 hard-cooked eggs, chopped
2 10½-ounce cans chicken broth
Salt and pepper to taste

Break cornbread into small pieces or crumbs into a bowl; add the remaining ingredients, mixing well. Bake at 375 degrees for 20 to 30 minutes or until brown.

Giblet gravy:
Boil chicken neck and giblets with chopped onion and celery. Boil down 3 times. Chop giblets and chop a hard-cooked egg. Brown flour in a little melted shortening or bacon fat; add giblets, egg, and broth. Cook slowly; add salt and pepper to taste.

Mrs. Leroy Travis (Twink)
Ouachita Parish (Monroe)

GREEN CHILI CASSEROLE

1 2 to 3-pound chicken, cooked and deboned
½ cup chicken broth
½ cup green pepper, finely chopped
1 medium onion, finely chopped
1 Jalapeño pepper
1 teaspoon garlic salt
1 large bag tortilla chips, crushed

2 cups shredded Cheddar cheese
1 can Rotel tomatoes and green chilies
1 10¾-ounce can cream of mushroom soup
1 10¾-ounce can cream of chicken soup
1 tablespoon chili powder

Preheat oven to 350 degrees. Mix all ingredients in a 3-quart casserole dish. Bake at 350 degrees for 30 to 40 minutes.

Mrs. Donald Johnson (Brenda)
Ouachita Parish (Monroe)

KING'S RANCH CASSEROLE

1 10¾-ounce can cream of celery soup
1 10¾-ounce can cream of mushroom soup
1 10¾-ounce can cream of chicken soup
1 10¾-ounce can chicken broth

2 chicken bouillon cubes
1 dozen frozen tortillas, thawed
1 2 to 3-pound chicken, cooked and deboned
1 pound (4 cups) shredded Cheddar cheese
Chili powder

Mix all creamed soups with 1 can chicken broth or broth from chicken to equal 1 can with 2 bouillon cubes added. Cut up tortillas; layer ingredients in a 13 x 9 x 2-inch pan in this order: 6 tortillas, ½ of chicken, cheese, half of soup mixture, dash of chili powder, and top with cheese. Bake at 350 degrees for 45 minutes.

Note: You can make this the day before serving, if desired.

Mrs. Marvin Spangler (Inez)
Ouachita Parish (West Monroe)

POPPY SEED CHICKEN

12 chicken breasts, cooked,
deboned, and chopped
2 10¾-ounce cans cream of
chicken soup
3 8-ounce cartons commercial
sour cream

¼ cup sherry
Salt and pepper to taste
35 to 40 Ritz crackers, crumbled
2 tablespoons poppy seeds
6 tablespoons butter, melted

In 2-quart casserole or large baking dish, put a layer of chopped chicken. Mix soup, sour cream, sherry and season with salt and pepper. Pour over chicken. Top with cracker crumbs mixed with poppy seed. Pour melted butter over top. Bake at 350 degrees for 30 minutes. Can be made a day ahead.
Mrs. Ada Lee
West Carroll Parish (Oak Grove)

CHICKEN PIE

1 2 to 3-pound broiler-fryer,
cooked and deboned
1 to 1½ cups reserved chicken
broth
1 10¾-ounce can cream of
chicken soup

1 10¾-ounce can cream of celery
soup
½ cup margarine
4 hard-cooked eggs, sliced
Lattice pie crust
½ cup milk

Preheat oven to 400 degrees. Cover bottom of Pyrex dish with chicken broth; put a layer of chicken meat on broth. Add 1 can cream of chicken soup and 1 can cream of celery soup; dot with margarine and hard-cooked eggs. Top with lattice pie crust. Brush with ½ cup milk. Bake at 400 degrees until brown, about 25 to 30 minutes.
Mrs. John C. Taylor (Judy)
Ouachita Parish (Choudrant)

JAMBALAYA

1 4-pound chicken, cut cut-up
Vegetable oil
1 pound pork sausage
2 medium onions, chopped

1 small green pepper
1 cup chopped celery
3 cups water
2 cups uncooked long grain rice

Fry chicken in very little oil; set aside. Fry sausage in drippings; set aside. Drain oil from pot leaving very little in pot. Sauté onions, pepper, and celery until tender. Add 3 cups water; heat to boiling. Add rice and meat. Cover; cook until rice is done, about 30 minutes. Serves 8 to 10.
Mrs. Daniel Gonsoulin (Jeanette)
Iberia Parish (New Iberia)

CHICKEN RICE

1 2 to 3-pound chicken, cut up
    and seasoned
½ cup margarine, melted
1 onion, chopped
½ green pepper, chopped

¼ cup chopped celery
2 chicken bouillon cubes
2 cups water
1 cup uncooked long grain rice
1 4-ounce can mushrooms

In a 12-inch skillet, brown chicken in margarine until golden brown. Remove chicken from pan; set aside. Add onion, green pepper, and celery to pan drippings; fry until tender. Remove from heat; add bouillon cubes, water, rice, and mushrooms. Pour into a 13 x 9 x 2-inch pan lined with foil. (Cut foil long enough so that you can cover the whole mixture with foil forming a seal.) Place chicken pieces on top. Seal the mixture with foil and bake at 350 degrees for 1 hour and 15 minutes. Serves 10.

Mrs. James Graugnard, Jr.
West St. James Parish (St. James)

HEN STEW

1 5 to 6-pound hen, cut into
    pieces
1½ tablespoons Mazola corn oil
¼ cup all-purpose flour
½ cup chopped celery
1 large onion, chopped
½ cup chopped green pepper
Salt, red pepper and black
    pepper to taste

1½ quarts hot water
½ pound sliced fresh mushrooms
    or 1 4-ounce can sliced
    mushrooms, drained
½ cup chopped green onion tops
½ cup chopped fresh parsley
Hot cooked rice (optional)

Heat oil in heavy stew pot. Wash hen pieces and towel dry to prevent excessive popping. Brown chicken in hot oil; remove chicken from pot, reserving 4 to 5 tablespoons drippings in pot. Add flour to drippings to make a roux, stirring constantly until golden brown. Add chopped celery, onion, and green pepper; sauté until wilted. Return hen to pot; stir, and gradually add hot water. Bring to a boil; add salt and peppers. Cook on simmer 1½ to 2 hours; add mushrooms, green onions, and parsley. Cook until hen is tender, but not falling from bones. Taste to correct seasoning. Serve over rice.

Mrs. Claude Schexnayder, Jr. (Joyce)
West St. James Parish (St. James)

SOUTHERN STYLE CHICKEN AND YAMS

4 large yams or sweet potatoes,
    peeled and thinly sliced
1 onion, sliced
Salt and pepper
1 2 to 3-pound broiler-fryer,
    cut up

¼ cup chopped walnuts
¼ cup butter or margarine
¼ cup prepared mustard
¼ cup honey
¼ cup orange juice

Preheat oven to 375 degrees. Arrange yams and onions in 3-quart shallow baking dish; sprinkle with salt and pepper. Place chicken on top of yams; season with salt and pepper. Sprinkle with walnuts. Melt butter in a small saucepan; stir in mustard, honey, and orange juice. Spoon over chicken and yams; cover with foil. Bake at 375 degrees for 1 hour, occasionally spooning sauce over the chicken, until potatoes are almost tender. Uncover; bake 15 to 20 minutes longer or until potatoes are tender and brown.

Pam Accardo
Ouachita Parish (Monroe)

CHEESY ITALIAN SUPPER PIE

Pastry for a 2-crust pie
5 eggs
2 cups cottage cheese
1 cup grated Parmesan cheese
¼ cup chopped onion
2 tablespoons snipped parsley
½ teaspoon salt
¼ teaspoon pepper
2 cloves garlic, minced

1 teaspoon dried oregano, crushed
⅛ teaspoon salt
2 tablespoons vegetable oil
1 6-ounce can tomato paste
⅔ cup sliced ripe olives
1 8-ounce package sliced
    Mozzarella cheese
¼ cup sliced mushrooms
½ cup sliced green pepper

Prepare pastry for one 2-crust pie; roll out and line a 10-inch pie plate with half the pastry. Trim edge. Beat the eggs; stir in cottage cheese, Parmesan cheese, onion, parsley, salt and pepper. Set aside. Cook garlic, oregano, and salt in hot oil for 1 minute. Stir in tomato paste and olives. Spread half the egg mixture in pastry shell. Top with half of the sliced Mozzarella cheese, then half the tomato mixture. Place mushrooms and green pepper over cheese layer. Repeat layers. Roll out remaining pastry; place over filling. Cut slits in top and seal flute edges. Cover edges with foil; bake at 425 degrees for 20 minutes. Uncover and bake 25 to 30 minutes more. Serves 6 to 8.

Mrs. James E. Comeaux (Gloria)
Iberia Parish (New Iberia)

BRUNCH EGGS

16 slices of bread
16 slices of cooked ham
16 slices of Cheddar cheese
16 slices of thin Swiss cheese
8 beaten eggs

3 cups milk
½ teaspoon onion salt
½ teaspoon dry mustard
3 cups crushed corn flakes
¼ cup melted butter

Grease a 13 x 9 x 2-inch pan. Layer bread, meat and cheese in pan. Combine eggs, milk, salt and mustard; pour over bread-cheese layers. Place corn flakes on top; pour melted butter over all. Chill overnight. Bake, uncovered, at 375 degrees for 40 minutes. Serves 16.

Mrs. Henry Hess (Peggy)
Avoyelles Parish (Moreauville)

QUICHE LORRAINE

Pastry for 9-inch quiche pan or
   pie pan
2 eggs
2 egg yolks
1½ cups half-and-half
½ teaspoon salt

½ teaspoon ground nutmeg
Pinch of white pepper
1¼ cups shredded Swiss cheese
12 slices bacon, cooked and
   crumbled

Line a 9-inch quiche pan or pie pan with pastry and trim excess around edge of pan. Place a piece of buttered aluminum foil, buttered side down, over pastry; gently press into pastry shell. This will keep the sides of the shell from collapsing. Bake at 400 degrees for 10 minutes; remove foil. Prick shell and bake 3 to 5 minutes longer. Cool. Combine eggs, egg yolks, half-and-half and seasonings in a mixing bowl; mix until well blended. Stir in cheese. Sprinkle bacon in quiche shell; gently add custard mixture. Bake at 375 degrees for 25 minutes or until custard puffs. Serve hot. Yield: one 9-inch quiche.

Mrs. A. G. Savell
East Baton Rouge Parish (Zachary)

DEVILED EGG CASSEROLE

Deviled eggs:

10 hard-cooked eggs, peeled
½ teaspoon salt
¼ teaspoon pepper
1½ tablespoons sweet pickle
  juice

¼ cup chopped sweet pickles
1 teaspoon prepared mustard
⅓ cup mayonnaise

Slice eggs in half lengthwise, removing yolks. Combine yolks with 6 remaining ingredients and mix until smooth. Fill the egg halves with mixture; chill.

Casserole:

⅓ cup melted butter or
  margarine
1 small green pepper, chopped
½ cup chopped green onion
  tops
⅓ cup chopped celery
1 tablespoon parsley
3 tablespoons all-purpose flour
2 cups whole canned tomatoes
  and liquid

1 tablespoon sugar
1 teaspoon salt
¼ teaspoon garlic salt
¼ teaspoon pepper
3 tablespoons ketchup
1½ cups cooked long grain rice
10 deviled egg halves (using above
  recipe)
½ cup buttered soft breadcrumbs

Preheat oven to 425 degrees. Sauté green pepper, onion, celery, and parsley in melted butter until tender. Stir in flour until smooth. Add tomatoes and continue stirring over medium heat until thickened. Add sugar, salts, pepper and ketchup. Arrange rice in a 12 x 8 x 2-inch baking dish. Pour sauce over rice and top with deviled eggs. Sprinkle buttered crumbs over top; bake at 425 degrees for 10 to 15 minutes or until hot and bubbly. When done, remove from oven, garnish with additional parsley, and serve. Yield: 6 to 8 servings.

Mrs. James E. Comeaux (Gloria)
Iberia Parish (New Iberia)

BROWNED LOUISIANA RICE AND PORK CASSEROLE

4 ¾-inch thick loin pork chops
Texjoy steak seasoning
½ cup regular uncooked long
  grain rice
1 10-ounce can beef gravy
½ cup water
½ cup red cooking wine

1 teaspoon salt
Dash of pepper
2 large carrots, peeled, and cut
  1-inch thick at angle
4 medium onions, sliced in rings
1 4-ounce can chopped
  mushrooms, drained

Preheat oven to 350 degrees. Sprinkle chops with Texjoy steak seasoning; brown well on both sides. Remove meat to a 2-quart casserole. Add rice to drippings in skillet; cook till browned, stirring constantly over medium heat. Stir in gravy, water, wine, salt and pepper; cook until thickened. Arrange carrots, onion rings and mushrooms on chops; pour on gravy mixture. Bake, uncovered, at 350 degrees for 1 hour or until tender. Yield: 4 servings.

Laura L. LaHaye
St. Landry Parish (Eunice)

MEAL IN ONE PYRAMID

2 to 4 pounds pork roast
2 pounds dry pinto beans
1 tablespoon salt
1 tablespoon Tabasco sauce
1 large clove garlic or 1
  tablespoon garlic powder
Jalapeño peppers, chopped
1½ teaspoons chili powder
2 teaspoons cumin, if desired

½ teaspoon oregano
½ teaspoon red pepper (optional)
Water
Doritos
Shredded lettuce
Shredded Cheddar cheese
Chopped tomatoes
Chopped onion

Mix first 10 ingredients in a large Dutch oven; cover with water. Cook slowly, all day or night, until beans have cooked down and meat falls apart. This should take approximately 8 to 10 hours. Remove from heat; trim fat from meat. Start building pyramid by placing Doritos on plate, next put above mixture of beans and roast. Top with shredded lettuce and cheese, chopped tomatoes and onions.

Note: This is a very good mixture to freeze, if any is leftover. Simply warm and start to build pyramid as stated above. Quick and easy.

Mrs. Doug Moore (Liz)
Ouachita Parish (Monroe)

8 cups cooked cornbread
1 tart baking apple, peeled, cored and diced
1/3 cup chopped fresh parsley
2 cups breadcrumbs
2-3 tablespoons reserved sausage fat
2 1/2 cups coarsely chopped onions
1 cup butter or margarine
1 egg yolk, beaten
1/4 cup orange juice
2 teaspoons salt
1/4 teaspoon pepper
1 cup chicken or turkey broth
1 teaspoon poultry seasoning (optional)
1 1/2 cups cooked pork sausage or ground pork, drained and crumbled

In large bowl, crumble cornbread. Add diced apple, chopped parsley and breadcrumbs. Sauté onions in sausage fat until transparent. Melt butter until lukewarm; mix butter with one beaten egg yolk. Combine butter-egg mixture, orange juice, salt, pepper, broth and browned meat. Add to onions, stirring well. Pour over cornbread mixture; mix together well. More broth or stock may be added for moister dressing, if desired. Place in a two-quart casserole dish or stuff the turkey. Bake in a 350 degree oven until heated through and a golden crust forms. Serves 15.

Note: Prepare 2 packages Jalapeño cornbread mix and substitute for plain cornbread. Double recipe and freeze extra dressing for a busy day.

Mrs. Malcolm Coco (Millie)
Avoyelles Parish (Moreauville)

ZUCCHINI-HAM-CHEESE PIE WITH CRUMB TOPPING

1 large onion, thinly sliced
3 small zucchini, thinly sliced
   (about ¾ pound)
1 large clove garlic, crushed
⅓ cup olive oil or vegetable oil
   (or a mixture of both)
2 cups cooked ham, slivered
1 cup (4 ounces) shredded
   Swiss cheese
1¼ cups commercial sour
   cream

1 teaspoon dillweed
1 teaspoon salt
¼ teaspoon pepper
1 baked 10-inch pastry shell
2 tablespoons butter or margarine,
   melted
½ cup packaged dry breadcrumbs
¼ cup grated Parmesan cheese
Tomato wedges (optional)
Parsley (optional)

Sauté onion, zucchini, and garlic in oil in a large skillet, about 5 minutes, or until zucchini is crisp-tender. Remove skillet from heat; add ham, Swiss cheese, sour cream, dillweed, salt and pepper. Mix well; spoon into baked pie shell. Melt butter in a small skillet; stir in breadcrumbs and Parmesan cheese with a fork. Sprinkle breadcrumb mixture in a 2-inch band around edge of pie shell, leaving center open. Bake at 350 degrees for 35 minutes or until bubbly. Let stand 10 minutes before serving. Garnish with tomato wedges and parsley, if desired.

Mrs. James E. Comeaux (Gloria)
Iberia Parish (New Iberia)

PORK STEW

½ cup all-purpose flour
½ cup vegetable oil
1 large onion, chopped
1 green pepper, chopped

6 cups water
3 pounds pork backbone, cubed
Salt and pepper to taste

In a deep heavy pot, brown flour in oil until golden brown, stirring constantly. Add onion and pepper to roux; cook on low heat until vegetables are tender. Add water; cook on medium heat for 30 minutes. Season pork with salt and pepper; add to stew. Simmer on low heat until pork is tender.
Note: Thick pork chops may be substituted for pork backbone, if desired.
Mrs. Ronald Gonsoulin (Cheryl)
Iberia Parish (New Iberia)

PORK CHOPS PACIFICA

4 thick pork chops
Salt and pepper to taste
2 envelopes instant chicken
   broth
2 cups boiling water
1 cup uncooked long grain rice

3 green onions, sliced
1 large tomato, peeled and c͞͞ped
½ green pepper, chopped
1 teaspoon salt
Dash of paprika

Preheat oven to 350 degrees. Season pork chops to taste with salt and pepper. Brown well on both sides; put in shallow baking dish. Stir instant chicken broth into boiling water; pour over chops. Add rice, onion, tomato, and green pepper. Sprinkle with salt and paprika. Cover tightly with lid (or foil). Bake at 350 degrees for 1 hour. Makes 4 servings (1 pork chop and about ⅔ cup rice each).
Mrs. Wayne Petticrew (Betty)
Calcasieu Parish (Iowa)

PORK CHOPS À LA VIVI

4 lean pork chops, 1-inch thick
Salt
4 thin onion slices

4 thin lemon slices
¼ cup firmly packed brown sugar
¼ cup catsup

Heat oven to 350 degrees. Season pork chops well with salt; place in 13 x 9 x 2-inch pan or large baking dish. Top each pork chop with an onion slice and a lemon slice. Place one tablespoon of brown sugar and one tablespoon catsup on top. Cover; bake at 350 degrees 1 hour. Uncover; bake 30 minutes longer, basting occasionally. Serves 4.
Mrs. Vivian N. Anderson
East Feliciana Parish (Ethel)

PIGGY BANK PORK BAKE

4 ounces uncooked egg
  noodles
2 tablespoons shortening
2 cups cut up cooked pork
  chops or roast
1 10¾-ounce can condensed
  cream chicken soup,
  undiluted

1 8-ounce can whole kernel corn,
  undrained
1 2-ounce can sliced pimiento,
  undrained
1 cup shredded sharp Cheddar
  cheese
1 medium green pepper, finely
  chopped

Preheat oven to 375 degrees. Cook noodles as directed on package; drain and set aside. Melt shortening in skillet, brown meat. Drain off excess fat; stir in noodles, corn, pimiento, cheese, and green pepper. Pour into ungreased 1-quart casserole. Bake at 375 degrees, uncovered, for 45 minutes, stirring occasionally. Yields 6 servings.

Note: This is a good way to use leftover pork chops or pork roast.

Mrs. Donald Johnson (Brenda)
Ouachita Parish (Monroe)

RICE PIZZA

Crust:
3 cups cooked rice
2 eggs slightly beaten
1 cup (4 ounces) shredded
  Mozzarella cheese or

2 tablespoons grated Parmesan
  cheese

Combine rice, eggs, and cheese. Press firmly into a lightly greased 14 x 10-inch pizza pan or 2 9-inch square pans. Bake at 450 degrees for 20 minutes.

Topping:
2 8-ounce cans tomato sauce
1½ teaspoons basil leaves
½ teaspoon oregano leaves
½ teaspoon garlic salt
½ teaspoon salt

1 cup (4 ounces) shredded
  Mozzarella cheese or 2
  tablespoons grated Parmesan
  cheese

Mix first 5 ingredients; spread over crust. Top with Mozzarella or Parmesan cheese, as desired. Bake at 450 degrees for 10 minutes.

Topping variations: cooked ground beef, pepperoni, cooked pork sausage, sliced mushrooms, chopped green pepper, and salami.

Mrs. Michael Zaunbrecher (Blandina)
Avoyelles Parish (Simmesport)

SAUSAGE JAMBALAYA

¾ pound smoked link sausage,
thinly sliced
½ cup chopped green pepper
½ cup chopped onion
⅔ cup uncooked long grain rice
1 cup chicken broth

1 cup drained canned tomatoes,
chopped
½ teaspoon garlic powder
½ teaspoon pepper
1 bay leaf

Preheat oven to 350 degrees. In an ovenproof skillet, cook sausage until light brown; add onion, green pepper, and cook till tender. Stir in rice, broth, tomatoes, and seasonings; bring to a boil. Remove from heat. Place skillet in oven; bake at 350 degrees for 30 minutes or until rice is tender and liquid is absorbed. Fluff with fork, and remove bay leaf, before serving.

Mrs. Donald Johnson (Brenda)
Ouachita Parish (Monroe)

FROZEN HAM AND CHEESE SANDWICHES

8 hamburger buns
½ cup softened butter
½ cup mayonnaise
3 tablespoons Zatarains' Creole
mustard

1 tablespoon grated onion
1 tablespoon poppy seed (optional)
Swiss cheese slices
Sliced boiled ham

Spread butter, mayonnaise, mustard, onion, poppy seed on both sides of bread. Layer a generous portion of Swiss cheese and ham on each. Wrap in foil and freeze. Bake, frozen, at 350 degrees for 30 minutes. This recipe is for only 8 sandwiches.

Note: Keep a supply of these delicious sandwiches in your freezer. Everyone loves them. Make 50 at a time and you will never run out.

Mrs. Louis D. Curet (Jean)
East Baton Rouge Parish (Baton Rouge)

PORK RIB JAMBALAYA

3 pounds pork ribs, cut in
   serving pieces
Salt and pepper to taste
2 tablespoons vegetable oil or
   melted shortening

Water
1 cup chopped onions
2 cups uncooked long grain rice
4 cups water
1 cup chopped green onion tops

Brown seasoned meat in oil, adding water as necessary to cook meat thoroughly and almost tender. (Cooking time will depend on age of hog.) When water has almost completely evaporated, add onion (chopped celery or green peppers may also be added); sauté until onions are tender. Add rice and 4 cups water to meat mixture; bring to a slow boil. Add green onion; stir well. Cover; cook on low heat until rice is done, about 30 minutes.

Robella Langlinais
Vermilion Parish (Erath)

COMPANY RICE

1 pound bulk pork sausage
1 onion, thinly sliced
3 stalks celery, sliced
1 green pepper, sliced
2 packages dry chicken noodle
   soup mix

1 cup uncooked long grain rice
1 4-ounce can chopped
   mushrooms, drained
4 cups boiling water

Brown sausage; pour off fat. Mix all ingredients in large casserole. Refrigerate overnight, if desired. Bake at 350 degrees for 1 hour and 30 minutes to 2 hours. Yield: 10 servings.

Laura L. LaHaye
St. Landry Parish (Eunice)

CABBAGE WITH SAUSAGE

6 sausage links
1 quart minced cabbage

½ teaspoon pepper
Salt, if desired

Fry the sausage links until crisp and brown. Remove sausage from the frying pan and pour off all but 3 tablespoons of the fat. Put cabbage in frying pan; cook 6 minutes. Arrange cabbage on a hot dish; garnish with cooked sausage.

Note: My husband's grandmother made this often and it was a favorite of her grandchildren.

Mrs. Kerry Burns (Nancy)
Webster Parish (Minden)

Vegetables

Pirogue Makers

ARTICHOKE CASSEROLE

1 14-ounce can artichoke
hearts, undrained
1 14-ounce can French-style
green beans, undrained

1 3-ounce jar grated Romano
cheese
¾ cup olive oil
2 cups Italian-style dry breadcrumbs

Preheat oven to 375 degrees. In a large bowl combine all ingredients; mix well. Pour mixture into a 3-quart greased casserole. Bake, uncovered, at 375 degrees for 30 minutes.

Mrs. Lois Landry
Ascension Parish (Donaldsonville)

ARTICHOKE CASSEROLE

3 14-ounce cans artichoke
hearts
1 8-ounce box Italian-style dry
breadcrumbs
3 cups olive oil
1 tablespoon Worcestershire
sauce

Tabasco sauce to taste
1 3-ounce can grated Parmesan
cheese
4 cloves pressed garlic
Salt to taste
Pepper to taste

Preheat oven to 350 degrees. Drain artichokes, reserving 2 cups liquid; cut into quarters. Combine all ingredients in a large mixing bowl; mix well. Place in a large lightly greased casserole. Bake at 350 degrees for 45 minutes or until bubbly hot.

Mrs. Louis D. Curet (Jean)
East Baton Rouge Parish (Baton Rouge)

BOURBON BAKED BEANS

2 1-pound 15-ounce cans pork
and beans
1 medium onion, chopped
½ cup finely chopped green
pepper
½ cup finely chopped celery

½ cup catsup
½ cup Worcestershire sauce
½ cup firmly packed brown sugar
½ cup bourbon whiskey
Dash of red pepper
Bacon strips

Preheat oven to 350 degrees. In a large mixing bowl, combine all ingredients; mix thoroughly. Place beans in a 13 x 9 x 2-inch casserole. Cover with bacon strips, as desired. Bake at 350 degrees for 1 hour and 45 minutes.

Note: The alcohol will cook out with baking.

Alice Faye Hart
Ouachita Parish (Monroe)

BAKED BEANS FOR A CROWD

¼ pound bacon
1 6½-pound can plus 1
  26-ounce can pork and beans
  (1 gallon)
1 cup firmly packed light brown
  sugar

1 tablespoon prepared mustard
1 cup catsup
1 1⅜-ounce package Lipton dry
  onion soup mix

Preheat oven to 325 degrees. Cook bacon in a small amount of water until done. Mix beans, sugar, mustard, catsup and soup mix in a large casserole; stir in bacon. Bake at 325 degrees for 1 hour. (Do not overcook or beans will fall apart). Serves 20.
Note: This recipe can be doubled or tripled depending on the size of the crowd.

Mrs. Randall Bracy (Regina)
Tangipahoa Parish (Amite)

BROCCOLI CHEESE CASSEROLE

2 10-ounce packages frozen
  broccoli spears, thawed
1 tablespoon butter, melted
1 10¾-ounce can cream of
  mushroom soup
1 teaspoon onion salt

Pinch of garlic powder
Pepper to taste
1 4-ounce can mushrooms,
  undrained
Shredded Cheddar cheese

Preheat oven to 350 degrees. In a large mixing bowl combine butter, mushroom soup, onion salt, garlic powder, pepper and mushrooms; mix well. Add broccoli spears. Place mixture in a well-greased casserole; sprinkle cheese over top. Bake at 350 degrees for 30 to 35 minutes or until bubbly.

Anita Joiner
Tangipahoa Parish (Hammond)

BROCCOLI CASSEROLE

1 large bunch fresh broccoli
½ medium onion, chopped
2 cups cooked rice

1 10¾-ounce can cream of
  mushroom soup
¾ cup shredded Cheddar cheese

Preheat oven to 350 degrees. In a heavy saucepan boil the broccoli and chopped onions until tender. Spread cooked rice in a long casserole dish. Add grated cheese and then a layer of broccoli. Cover with cream of mushroom soup. Cook for 45 minutes.

Mrs. James Parkerson (Joyce)
Ouachita Parish (Monroe)

BROCCOLI CASSEROLE

2 10-ounce packages frozen
chopped broccoli
½ cup margarine, melted
1 bunch green onions, chopped
3 large stalks celery
1 4-ounce can sliced
mushrooms, drained

1 10¾-ounce can cream of
mushroom soup, undiluted
2 tablespoons all-purpose flour
1 8-ounce roll cheese (garlic,
smoked or Cheddar)
½ cup margarine
1½ cups cracker crumbs

Preheat oven to 350 degrees. In a medium saucepan, cook broccoli according to package directions; drain. In a large skillet, sauté ½ cup melted margarine, onion, celery, and mushrooms; cook until tender. Add soup, flour, and cheese; stir well. Combine mixture with cooked broccoli; mix well. Pour mixture into a greased glass 13 x 9 x 2-inch baking dish. In a small saucepan melt remaining ½ cup margarine; add cracker crumbs, mixing well. Top casserole with crumbs. Bake at 350 degrees for 30-45 minutes.

Mrs. Hardee Brian (Betty Jo)
East Baton Rouge Parish (Zachary)

BROCCOLI CASSEROLE

2 10-ounce packages frozen
broccoli
¼ cup minced onion
1 10¾-ounce can cream of
mushroom soup, undiluted
1 cup (4 ounces) shredded
Cheddar cheese, divided

1 clove garlic, minced
1 4-ounce can mushrooms, drained
¾ cup Italian-style dry breadcrumbs
¼ cup margarine, melted
Salt to taste
Pepper to taste
Slivered almonds

Cook broccoli according to package directions. Drain well. Preheat oven to 350 degrees. Combine broccoli, onion, soup, ⅔ cup cheese, garlic, mushrooms, ½ cup breadcrumbs, margarine, salt, and pepper; mix well. Pour broccoli mixture into a buttered casserole; sprinkle with remaining ¼ cup breadcrumbs and ⅓ cup cheese. Garnish with slivered almonds. Bake at 350 degrees for 30 minutes or until bubbly.

Note: 2 small jars process cheese spread may be used instead of shredded cheese, if desired.

Mary Moreland
Concordia Parish (Monterey)

BROCCOLI CASSEROLE (MICROWAVE)

½ cup chopped onion
3 tablespoons vegetable oil
2 10-ounce packages frozen
  chopped broccoli
6 slices process American
  cheese

1 10¾-ounce can cream of
  mushroom soup, undiluted
1½ cups breadcrumbs
½ cup melted butter

Combine onions and oil in a 1½-quart dish; microwave on HIGH for 3 minutes. Add broccoli; cover with waxed paper. Microwave on HIGH for 7 minutes, stirring once or twice. Spoon half the broccoli mixture into lightly-greased 2-quart casserole. Top with ½ the cheese and ½ of the soup. Combine breadcrumbs with butter; stir until well coated. Place ½ the crumbs over the soup; top with remaining soup, then breadcrumbs. Cover with waxed paper. Microwave on HIGH for 8 minutes, rotating dish 2 times while cooking.

Mrs. Jude Plauche (Margaret)
Avoyelles Parish (Hamburg)

BROCCOLI-CHEESE CASSEROLE

2 large onions, chopped
½ cup butter, melted
6 10-ounce packages frozen
  chopped broccoli
3 10¾-ounce cans cream of
  mushroom soup, undiluted

3 8-ounce rolls of garlic process
  cheese
2 teaspoons monosodium
  glutamate
1 8-ounce can chopped
  mushrooms, drained

Preheat oven to 300 degrees. Sauté onions in melted butter in a 10-inch skillet. Add broccoli; cook over low heat until tender. Add mushroom soup, cheese, monosodium glutamate, and mushrooms; cook on low heat, stirring until cheese melts. Pour mixture into a large greased casserole or into 2 separate dishes. Bake at 300 degrees until bubbly.

Note: I usually pour mixture into 2 casserole dishes and freeze one. Freezes very well. This dish also may be served as a hot dip with crackers and chips.

Mrs. Randall F. Bracy (Regina)
Tangipahoa Parish (Amite)

BROCCOLI RICE CASSEROLE

½ cup chopped onions
½ cup chopped celery
¼ cup margarine, melted
1 10-ounce package Bird's Eye
frozen broccoli
1 10¾-ounce can cream of
mushroom soup, undiluted

1 8-ounce jar Kraft Cheez Whiz
2 cups cooked rice
½ teaspoon salt
¼ teaspoon pepper
1 cup shredded American cheese

Preheat oven to 350 degrees. Sauté onions and celery in saucepan with melted margarine until tender; set aside. Cook broccoli according to package directions; drain well. In a large mixing bowl, combine broccoli, onion mixture, soup, Cheez Whiz, and rice. Pour into 1-quart casserole; season with salt and pepper. Sprinkle cheese on top. Bake uncovered, at 350 degrees for 30 minutes. Serves 6.

Mrs. Yvonne Ardoin
Jeff Davis Parish (Welsh)

BROCCOLI RICE

2 10-ounce packages frozen
chopped broccoli
¼ cup margarine
1 large onion, chopped
¼ cup chopped green pepper
½ cup chopped celery
1 10¾-ounce can cream of
mushroom soup, undiluted
1 10¾-ounce can cream of
chicken soup, undiluted

1 8-ounce roll Jalapeño-flavored
process cheese
3 cups cooked rice
Salt to taste
Pepper to taste
Paprika (optional)
Shredded American cheese
(optional)

Preheat oven to 350 degrees. Prepare broccoli according to package directions; drain well. Melt margarine in a 10-inch skillet; sauté onion, green pepper, and celery in melted margarine until tender. Add soups and cheese; cook over low heat, stirring constantly, until cheese melts. Stir in broccoli, rice, salt and pepper. Pour mixture into a 2-quart buttered casserole; sprinkle with paprika or shredded American cheese, if desired. Bake at 350 degrees for 25 to 30 minutes. Serves 8.

Mrs. Kathleen Zeringue
West St. James Parish (St. James)

BROCCOLI RICE

2 10-ounce packages frozen
  chopped broccoli
2 medium onions, chopped
3 tablespoons butter
1 8-ounce jar Cheez Whiz
½ teaspoon prepared mustard

1 10¾-ounce can cream of
  mushroom soup, undiluted
3 cups cooked rice
4 hard-cooked eggs, quartered
1 3-ounce can French fried onion
  rings

Preheat oven to 325 degrees. Prepare broccoli according to package instructions; drain. In a 4-quart saucepan, melt butter over low heat; add onions and sauté until tender. Add Cheez Whiz, mustard, soup, broccoli, and rice to onions; mix well. Remove from heat; stir in hard-cooked eggs. Pour mixture into a buttered 2-quart casserole; garnish with onion rings. Bake at 325 degrees for 20 minutes.

Mrs. James Graugnard, Jr.
West St. James Parish (St. James)

BROCCOLI-CAULIFLOWER CASSEROLE

2 10-ounce packages frozen
  chopped broccoli
2 10-ounce packages frozen
  cauliflower
2 tablespoons butter
1 5.33-ounce can evaporated
  milk

1 10¾-ounce can cream of chicken
  soup, undiluted
1 cup grated Parmesan cheese
1 large onion, chopped
1 cup buttered soft breadcrumbs

Preheat oven to 350 degrees. Cook the broccoli and cauliflower according to package directions. Melt butter in a saucepan; add onions and sauté until tender. Remove from heat; add milk, soup, and cheese, stirring well. Layer the cooked broccoli and cauliflower in a 2-quart buttered casserole; pour soup mixture over vegetables. Top with buttered breadcrumbs. Bake at 350 degrees until mixture is bubbly.

Note: Fresh cauliflower may be substituted for frozen cauliflower.

Mrs. Mansel S. Slaughter (Pearl)
East Baton Rouge (Baker)

GREEN BEAN CASSEROLE I

3 1-pound 4-ounce cans
French-style green beans,
drained
¼ cup chopped onions
¼ cup butter, melted
1 8-ounce jar Cheez Whiz
1 tablespoon Lea and Perrins
Worcestershire sauce

1 teaspoon salt
½ teaspoon pepper
Dash of Tabasco sauce
1 8-ounce carton commercial sour
cream
Slivered almonds

Preheat oven to 350 degrees. Sauté onions in butter until clear; remove from heat. Mix onion mixture, beans, Cheez Whiz, Worcestershire sauce, salt, pepper and Tabasco in a bowl; toss gently until well mixed. Pour into well greased casserole; top with sour cream. Sprinkle slivered almonds on top. Bake at 350 degrees for 30 minutes.

Mrs. Melba McIntosh
West Carroll Parish (Pioneer)

GREEN BEAN CASSEROLE II

2 10-ounce packages frozen cut
green beans
1 teaspoon salt
¾ cup milk
1 10¾-ounce can cream of
mushroom soup, undiluted

⅛ teaspoon pepper
2 tablespoons diced pimiento
1 3-ounce can French fried onions

Preheat oven to 350 degrees. Cook beans in salted water until crisp-tender; drain. Place beans in a lightly greased 1½-quart casserole. Combine milk, soup and pepper; mix well and pour over beans. Top with ½ can fried onions. Bake at 350 degrees for 20 minutes; garnish with remaining fried onions and pimiento. Bake 5 minutes longer. Serves 6.

Note: Frozen beans may be substituted with 2 16-ounce cans of cut green beans, drained.

Mrs. Melanie Gonsoulin
Iberia Parish (New Iberia)

GREEN BEAN CASSEROLE (MICROWAVE)

4 strips bacon
1/2 cup chopped onion
1 cup chopped celery
1/4 cup chopped green pepper
2 tablespoons bacon drippings
1 10 1/2-ounce can Rotel
   tomatoes, cut-up, drained

1/4 teaspoon salt
1/8 teaspoon pepper
1/2 pound (8 ounces) American
   cheese, shredded
2 16-ounce can green beans,
   drained

Cook bacon in microwave until crisp. Drain bacon, reserving 2 tablespoons fat. Crumble bacon; set aside. Microwave onion, celery and green pepper in 2 tablespoons reserved bacon drippings on HIGH for 4 minutes in a 4-cup measure. Stir in tomatoes, salt and pepper. Microwave on HIGH for 5 minutes. Stir in cheese. Place drained beans in casserole dish; top with sauce and crumbled bacon. Cover with waxed paper. Microwave on MEDIUM for 15 minutes, rotating dish once during cooking time. Serves 8-10.

Mrs. Sidney S. Joffrion, Jr. (Vicky)
Avoyelles Parish (Cottonport)

CARROT AND PEAS CASSEROLE

1 2½-ounce jar sliced
  mushrooms, undrained
½ pound carrots, peeled, sliced
½ pound fresh green peas
1 4-ounce can sliced water
  chestnuts, drained
½ teaspoon salt

¼ teaspoon pepper
¼ teaspoon crushed hot red pepper
1 10¾-ounce can cream of
  Cheddar cheese soup, undiluted
½ cup melted margarine, divided
Breadcrumbs

Preheat oven to 350 degrees. Combine vegetables and seasonings; stir well. Pour half of vegetable mixture into a lightly greased casserole. Top casserole with ½ cheese soup and ¼ cup margarine. Add remaining vegetable mixture, then top with remaining soup. Sprinkle with breadcrumbs; top with remaining margarine. Bake at 350 degrees for 1-1½ hours. Serves 8-10.

Note: If fresh vegetables are used, be sure they are tenderized before preparing casserole. Other vegetables may be substituted.

Mrs. C. L. Gauthier, Jr. (Narcille)
Avoyelles Parish (Moreauville)

CREAMED CAULIFLOWER

1 large head cauliflower
¼ cup butter
3 tablespoons all-purpose flour
1½ cups milk
½ teaspoon salt

¼ teaspoon pepper
¼ to ½ cup shredded Cheddar
  cheese
¼ cup soft breadcrumbs
2 tablespoons butter

Preheat oven to 350 degrees. Prepare cauliflower by washing and breaking into flowerettes. Add cauliflower to boiling salty water; boil for 10 minutes. Drain well. Place cauliflower in a 1-quart glass casserole. In a 2-quart saucepan melt the butter over low heat; add flour, stirring constantly. Gradually add milk, stirring constantly. Cook over low heat, stirring constantly, until thickened. Stir in salt, pepper and cheese. Cook until cheese is melted; pour cheese mixture over cauliflower. Sprinkle with breadcrumbs and dot with butter. Bake for 30 minutes. Serves 8-10.

Mrs. James Graugnard, Jr.
West St. James Parish (St. James)

CORN CASSEROLE

½ cup butter
1 small green pepper, chopped
1 medium onion, chopped
¼ cup all-purpose flour
1 16-ounce can tomatoes
3 16-ounce cans whole kernel
  corn, drained

2 hard-cooked eggs, chopped
2 cups cooked rice
Tabasco sauce to taste
Worcestershire sauce to taste
Shredded Cheddar cheese

Melt butter in a skillet over low heat; add green pepper and onion. Sauté green pepper and onion until tender. Add flour, stirring constantly; set aside. Mash and drain tomatoes. Combine tomatoes, corn, and sautéed vegetables; stir in chopped eggs and rice. Season to taste. Pour mixture in a casserole dish. Bake at 350 degrees until bubbly; sprinkle with cheese. Bake 3 to 5 minutes or until cheese melts. Serves 15.

Note: If frozen corn is substituted, cook before mixing.

Mrs. Randall F. Bracy (Regina)
Tangipahoa Parish (Amite)

DEVILED CORN CASSEROLE

¼ cup butter
3 tablespoons all-purpose flour
1 cup milk
1 teaspoon salt
1 teaspoon dry mustard
1 teaspoon sugar

½ teaspoon paprika
1 17-ounce can whole kernel corn, drained
2 eggs, well beaten
1 tablespoon Worcestershire sauce
¾ cup shredded Cheddar cheese

Preheat oven to 350 degrees. In a saucepan, melt butter over low heat. Add flour, stirring constantly. Cook 1 minute; gradually add milk, salt, mustard, sugar and paprika, stirring constantly. Cook until thick, stirring constantly. Remove from heat; add corn, eggs, and Worcestershire sauce. Mix well, and pour into greased 1-quart casserole. Cover with cheese; bake at 350 degrees for 30 minutes.

Mrs. U. M. Youngblood (Carrie Jo)
Caldwell Parish (Columbia)

CORN CASSEROLE

2 16½-ounce cans cream-style corn
4 eggs, beaten
1 teaspoon baking powder
¾ cup Wesson oil

¾ cup plain corn meal
Chopped jalapeño peppers (about 10)
2 teaspoons salt
1 cup shredded Cheddar cheese

Preheat oven to 350 degrees. Mix corn, eggs, baking powder, oil, corn meal, peppers and salt together. Stir in shredded cheese. Pour into a greased casserole; bake at 350 degrees for 45 minutes.

Note: You can use either 2 small cans of chili pepper or if you have jalapeño pepper in your garden use them. I use 10. This depends on how hot you like it.

Mrs. Don Odom (Brenda)
Claiborne Parish (Homer)

FRIED SNAP BEANS

½ pound sliced salt pork

2 quarts freshly snapped beans

Fry salt pork in a skillet over medium heat until light brown and crisp. Pour off excess fat. Add beans to salt pork in hot skillet, stirring constantly. Sauté beans until they turn dark green in color and start to brown. Reduce heat to low; cover and simmer until beans are tender.

Note: Good served with new Irish potatoes and crackling bread.

Claudia Ford
Catahoula Parish (Jonesville)

HOMINY AND ROTEL CASSEROLE

1 14½-ounce can hominy,
  drained
½ pound bulk sausage, (hot if
  desired)
½ cup chopped onions

⅓ cup chopped green pepper
1 10½-ounce can Rotel tomatoes
  and chilies
Shredded Cheddar cheese

Preheat oven to 400 degrees. Brown sausage, onion and green pepper in a
large skillet; drain. Combine sausage mixture, hominy, and Rotel tomatoes;
place in a greased casserole. Sprinkle cheese on top; bake at 400 degrees for
30 minutes.

Mrs. Wayne Jennings (Kaye)
Ouachita Parish (Monroe)

BAKED CORN

1 cup water
1 10-ounce package frozen
  cream-style corn
1 10-ounce package frozen
  whole kernel corn

2 tablespoons all-purpose flour
1 teaspoon salt
1 teaspoon sugar
½ cup margarine

Preheat oven to 350 degrees. In a heavy saucepan bring water to a boil. Add
corn, and cook until tender. Add flour, salt, sugar and margarine to corn,
mixing well. Pour corn into a greased baking dish. Bake at 350 degrees for 1
hour, stirring once or twice.

Mrs. Roy Anderson (Catherine)
Ouachita Parish (Monroe)

BAKED GRITS I

1 cup uncooked grits (regular
  or quick-cooking)
¼ cup butter
⅓ cup milk
3 eggs, beaten

¼ pound (4-ounces) sharp Cheddar
  cheese, shredded
¼ pound (4 ounces) Velveeta
  cheese, shredded
Salt to taste

Preheat oven to 400 degrees. Prepare grits according to package directions.
Remove from heat; add remaining ingredients, beating well. Place in a lightly
greased 1½-quart casserole. Bake at 400 degrees for 1 hour or until firm and
slightly brown. Serve at once.

Note: Good with barbecue.

JoBaya Foreman
Beauregard Parish (DeRidder)

BAKED GRITS II

1 cup uncooked grits (regular
  or quick-cooking)
3 eggs, beaten
½ cup margarine
½ pound shredded sharp
  Cheddar cheese

⅓ cup milk
Salt to taste
Dash of Tabasco sauce

Preheat oven to 325 degrees. Prepare grits according to package directions. Remove from heat; add remaining ingredients, mixing well. Pour mixture into a greased baking dish. Bake at 325 degrees for 30 minutes or until firm and browned.

Note: I sometimes use 1 8-ounce roll of process garlic cheese and 1 8-ounce roll of Jalapeño cheese in place of sharp cheese, if desired.

Mrs. Wayne Jennings (Kaye)
Ouachita Parish (Monroe)

GARLIC CHEESE GRITS

3½ cups water
1 teaspoon salt
1 cup grits
1 8-ounce roll process garlic
  cheese

2 eggs, well beaten
Milk
½ cup butter, melted

Preheat oven to 350 degrees. Bring water and salt to a boil. Stir in grits. Cook until thick, stirring frequently. Over low heat, stir in cheese until melted. Remove from heat. Beat eggs in a 1-cup measure adding enough milk to make 1 cup. Stir eggs, milk and butter into grits. Pour grits into a 13 x 9 x 2-inch baking dish. Bake at 350 degrees for 1 hour.

Note: Great with barbecue!!

Doris Querry
Madison Parish (Tallulah)

GOLDEN HOMINY

½ pound seasoned bulk pork
  sausage

1 quart yellow hominy
Salt to taste

Shape pork sausage into small bite size patties. Brown in hot skillet. Drain off excess fat. Pour hominy and liquid in with sausage patties. Simmer uncovered until all liquid is dissolved. Serve hot.

Mrs. Rose Yearke Zimmerman
Catahoula Parish (Jonesville)

EGGPLANT FRITTERS

2 medium eggplants
1 egg, well beaten
½ teaspoon salt
1 cup all-purpose flour

½ cup sugar
1 teaspoon baking powder
Dash of salt

Peel eggplants and cube; steam in a small amount of salted water. Drain eggplant; mash with a fork. Combine eggplant, egg, and salt, mix thoroughly. In a mixing bowl, combine flour, sugar, baking powder and salt. Combine eggplant mixture with flour mixture, adding enough flour to make batter hold its shape. Drop batter from spoon into hot (375 degrees) deep fat. Fry until golden brown. Drain on absorbent paper.

Mrs. Dolan P. Kleinpeter
Iberia Parish (New Iberia)

EGGPLANT CASSEROLE I

1½ cups eggplant slices
Water
1 medium onion, chopped
1 tablespoon melted margarine
⅔ cup drained cooked
   tomatoes

Salt to taste
Pepper to taste
½ cup soft breadcrumbs
⅔ cup shredded Velveeta cheese

Preheat oven to 350 degrees. Boil eggplant in a small amount of water until tender; drain well. Cook onions in a skillet with margarine until clear; add tomatoes and eggplant, salt, and pepper. Stir in breadcrumbs. Pour mixture into a pyrex baking dish; top with cheese. Cover; bake at 350 degrees for 45 minutes. Serves 4 to 6.

Mrs. Neldred Bordelon (Melba)
Avoyelles Parish (Moreauville)

EGGPLANT CASSEROLE II

1 medium eggplant
1 cup milk
2 eggs, well beaten
1 cup Cheddar cheese, grated

1 cup soft breadcrumbs
1 tablespoon margarine, melted
Salt to taste
Pepper to taste

Preheat oven to 350 degrees. Peel eggplant and cube. Cook eggplant in a small amount of water until tender; drain well. Combine eggplant with remaining ingredients in a greased 1½-quart casserole. Bake at 350 degrees for 40 minutes.

Mrs. Marvin Spangler (Inez)
Ouachita Parish (West Monroe)

EGGPLANT AND TOMATO CASSEROLE

1 medium eggplant
All-purpose flour
Vegetable oil
Salt and pepper to taste
4 medium tomatoes, peeled
    and sliced

½ cup chopped onion
2 tablespoons brown sugar
¼ cup butter
½ cup buttered breadcrumbs

Preheat oven to 325 degrees. Peel eggplant and slice into ¼-inch slices. Coat eggplant slices in flour seasoned with salt and pepper. Fry eggplant slices in oil, until browned. Drain slices thoroughly on absorbent paper. In a large casserole dish layer eggplant slices. Top with tomato slices, chopped onion, brown sugar, butter, salt and pepper to taste. Sprinkle buttered crumbs over top. Bake at 325 degrees for 1 hour or until bubbly.

Note: This recipe can't be rushed. The secret is long, slow cooking and stirring thoroughly while cooking.

Mrs. Louis D. Curet (Jean)
East Baton Rouge Parish (Baton Rouge)

SUMMER EGGPLANT

1 medium eggplant
Seasoned bread crumbs
1 large onion, sliced
1 or 2 large fresh tomatoes
1 large green pepper
Grated Parmesan cheese,
    shredded Mozzarella cheese,
    or sharp Cheddar cheese

½ cup hot water
1 4-ounce can tomato sauce
Pinch of basil leaves
Pinch of oregano leaves
1 clove garlic, minced
Salt to taste
Pepper to taste

Preheat oven to 350 degrees. Peel and slice eggplant into ½-inch slices. Let stand a few minutes. Dredge in breadcrumbs. Place eggplant in a single layer on ungreased cookie sheet. Bake at 350 degrees until tender. Layer eggplant in bottom of a 13 x 9 x 2-inch casserole; cover with layers of onions, tomatoes, peppers and cheese. Repeat layers. Combine hot water with tomato sauce, basil, oregano, garlic, salt, and pepper; pour mixture over casserole. Cover with foil. Bake at 350 degrees for 30 minutes or until bubbly.

Note: This freezes well before baking.

Mrs. Grace Graugnard
St. James Parish (St. James)

FRIED EGGPLANT

1 large eggplant
Salt
1 egg, beaten
Pepper to taste

Seasoned Italian-style dry
   breadcrumbs
Vegetable oil

Cut eggplant into ½-inch slices. Salt both sides and cover in a bowl. Allow to sit for 1 hour. Drain water and wipe salt off eggplant with paper towel. Dredge eggplant slices in beaten egg, seasoned with salt and pepper to taste, then in bread crumbs. Fry in deep fat at medium temperature until brown on both sides. Drain on paper towel.

Note: This recipe may be used for fried okra. When using okra, wash, stem and cut into 2-inch pieces. Variation of this recipe is add ½ cup evaporated milk to egg, beat thoroughly. Dredge in flour instead of bread crumbs. Cook in deep-fat.

Louisiana Farm Bureau Women's Committee

FRIED ONION RINGS

1 cup milk
1 egg, beaten
Pinch of salt
Dash of pepper

All-purpose flour
3 to 4 large onions
Vegetable oil or shortening

In a mixing bowl combine milk, egg, salt and pepper. Add enough flour to make a medium thin batter. Wash and cut onions crosswise into ¼-inch slices. Separate into rings. Dip rings, one at a time, in batter. Fry in deep, hot oil about 375 degrees. Turn each ring only once so that both sides are very brown. Yield: 8 servings.

Mrs. Kerry Burns (Nancy)
Webster Parish (Minden)

QUICK 'N GOOD BEANS

¼ pound bacon, cut up
2 medium onions, chopped
½ cup firmly packed dark
   brown sugar

1 16-ounce can pork and beans
1 teaspoon pepper
½ teaspoon salt

Fry bacon in a skillet until almost done; add onions. Cook over low heat until onions are tender. Stir in sugar and beans; season with pepper and salt. Simmer 3 to 5 minutes before serving. Serves 2 generously, or 4.

Mrs. Ronald R. Anderson
Feliciana Parish (Ethel)

MIRLITONS-STUFFED AND BAKED

4 large mirlitons
1 pound ground beef
2 to 3 tablespoons melted
  shortening
1 medium onion, minced
1 medium green pepper,
  minced
2 stalks celery, minced

1 teaspoon salt
¼ teaspoon pepper
¼ teaspoon hot red pepper
8 to 10 bread slices
1 egg, slightly beaten
½ cup milk
Margarine
Breadcrumbs (optional)

Wash and dry mirlitons. Slice mirlitons lengthwise and remove seeds; place in a saucepan an steam in 1-inch of water until tender. Remove from water. Scrape pulp into a bowl, leaving the shell for stuffing. In a separate pan, brown meat in shortening. Add seasonings to meat. Let simmer for 30 minutes or until meat is tender. Preheat oven to 350 degrees. While meat is cooking, crumble bread and soften with egg and milk. Add bread mixture to meat; stir in mirliton pulp, mixing well. If mixture looks dry add small amount of milk until right consistency is obtained. Season again, if desired. Stuff mirliton shells with mixture. Top each with a pat of margarine. Sprinkle bread crumbs over top, if desired. Bake at 350 degrees until light brown. Serves 6-8.

Note: Shrimp, crabs, or other seafood may be substituted for meat.

Mrs. C. L. Gauthier, Jr. (Narcille)
Avoyelles Parish (Moreauville)

 # BLACK-EYED PEAS

Ham bone
3 quarts water
1 pound dried black-eyed peas
1 cup chopped onion, white or
  green
1 green pepper, chopped
½ cup chopped parsley

2 bay leaves
1 teaspoon basil leaves
Salt to taste
Pepper to taste
½ to 1 pound smoked sausage, cut
  into ½-inch slices

Combine all ingredients, except the sausage, in a heavy Dutch oven. Cook for 1 hour. Brown the sausage slices in a skillet; drain well. Add sausage to beans; continue to cook until creamy. Adding a little oil helps the creaminess, if lean ham or pork is used. If extra water has to be added, it should be cold when added. Serve hot over rice.

Note: Any kind of pork may be substituted for the sausage, including ham, salt meat, pickled pork or even andouille.

Louisiana Farm Bureau Women's Committee

LOUISIANA BELL PEPPERS

4 large green peppers
1 teaspoon salt
1 pound raw, fresh shrimp,
 cleaned and deveined
½ cup butter
¼ cup chopped onion

¼ cup chopped celery
1 4-ounce can sliced mushrooms,
 drained
1 cup cooked rice
1 8-ounce can tomato sauce
Water

Slice peppers in half lengthwise and clean inside. Place the peppers in a saucepan with enough water to cover. Add salt. Cover and cook for 5 minutes. Remove peppers; drain upside down. Preheat oven to 350 degrees. Slice the shrimp in half lengthwise, reserving 8 whole shrimp for garnish. In a large skillet melt butter over low heat; add shrimp. Cook for 10 minutes over low heat. Add onion, celery and mushrooms; sauté until tender. Stir in rice and tomato sauce; remove from heat. Stuff the green peppers with shrimp mixture. Garnish each with a whole shrimp. Place peppers in a 2-quart casserole with enough water to cover the bottom of the dish. Bake at 350 degrees for 20-25 minutes. Serves 8.

Pam Accardo
Ouachita Parish (Monroe)

STUFFED BELL PEPPERS

14 white bread slices
1 6-ounce can tomato paste
2 teaspoons salt
1 teaspoon pepper
3 eggs, beaten
3 slices bacon, cut into pieces
3 slices ham, cubed

½ cup milk
½ cup green pepper seeds
½ cup chopped green pepper
2 tablespoons Crisco shortening
½ cup margarine
10 large green peppers, halved
1 cup soft breadcrumbs

Soak bread in enough water to moisten; combine bread, tomato paste, salt, pepper, eggs, bacon, ham, milk, green pepper seeds and green pepper. Mix well. In a large black skillet melt Crisco; when melted, add mixed ingredients. Cook on low heat, stirring occasionally until mixture dries somewhat. Add margarine and keep on stirring from bottom of skillet. Cook on low heat for 1 hour. Remove from heat. Preheat oven to 250 degrees. Stuff cooked mixture into halved green peppers. Sprinkle breadcrumbs over top. Place peppers in a large baking pan. Bake at 250 degrees for 50 to 60 minutes. Serves 12-16.

Note: This recipe is "The Brian Family Special" as their mother prepared these stuffed peppers every Sunday for her family of 9 children.

Mrs. Hardee Brian (Betty Jo)
East Baton Rouge Parish (Zachary)

STUFFED PEPPERS SUPREME

6 large green peppers
½ cup chopped celery
1 medium onion, chopped
2 cloves garlic, chopped
½ cup melted margarine
1½ pounds shrimp, peeled, deveined, and chopped
1 medium tomato, peeled
1 8-ounce can crabmeat, drained

½ cup chopped green onion
½ teaspoon salt
¼ teaspoon pepper or ground red pepper
1 16-ounce package long grain rice, cooked
1 egg
Pimiento strips

Clean and cut green peppers in half. In a heavy saucepan boil the peppers for 5 minutes. Drain and set aside. Preheat oven to 350 degrees. In a skillet, sauté celery, onion, and garlic in margarine until tender. Add shrimp and cook until pink. Add tomato, crabmeat, onion, salt and pepper. Cook for 10 minutes over medium heat. Add cooked rice and egg to shrimp mixture. Stuff mixture into cooked peppers. Garnish with pimiento strips. Bake at 350 degrees for 25 minutes. Serves 6.

Note: This recipe was the 1979 parish winning rice cookery contest entered in the Rice Festival in Crowley by Miss Glenda Litteral of Jennings.

Mrs. Barbara Litteral
Jeff Davis Parish (Jennings)

OKRA CASSEROLE

1 tablespoon vegetable oil
1 cup ground beef
1 medium onion, chopped
2 cups smothered okra

1 8-ounce can tomato sauce
Salt to taste
Pepper to taste
1 cup shredded Velveeta cheese

Preheat oven to 350 degrees. Heat oil in a large skillet over medium heat; add meat and onions. Cook until done; drain off excess water. Add smothered okra to meat; mix well. Add tomato sauce, salt and pepper to meat. Pour mixture into a greased 9-inch square pyrex dish. Top with cheese; bake at 350 degrees for 45 minutes. Serves 6.

Note: You may smother okra with tomatoes, frozen or fresh.

Mrs. Neldred Bordelon (Melba)
Avoyelles Parish (Moreauville)

POTATO STEW

½ cup all-purpose flour
½ cup vegetable oil, heated
1 large onion, quartered
½ medium-size green pepper

6 cups water
4 medium red potatoes, cubed
Salt and pepper to taste

In a deep heavy pot, brown flour with oil on low heat until golden brown, stirring constantly for 20 minutes. Add onion and green pepper; cook on low heat until wilted. Add water; heat to boiling. Reduce heat and simmer for 1 hour. Season cubed potatoes with salt and pepper; add potatoes to stew. Cook until potatoes are tender.

Mrs. Stanly Melancon (Della)
St. Martin Parish (St. Martinville)

POTATO CASSEROLE SUPREME

9 medium baking potatoes,
  peeled
½ cup butter
1½ teaspoons salt

¼ teaspoon pepper
⅔ cup warm milk
1½ cups shredded Cheddar cheese
1 cup heavy cream, whipped

Preheat oven to 350 degrees. Boil potatoes until they are tender; drain. In a large mixing bowl, beat potatoes with an electric mixer until fluffy. Add butter, seasonings, and milk; mix well. Place potato mixture into a buttered shallow 1½-quart casserole. Fold cheese into whipped cream; spread over potatoes. Bake at 350 degrees for 25 minutes or until golden brown. Serves 10.

Note: Casserole may be prepared ahead of time and topping added just before baking.

Mrs. Don Odom (Brenda)
Claiborne Parish (Homer)

POTATO CASSEROLE (QUICK)

10 Irish potatoes
1 medium onion, grated
1 16-ounce carton commercial
  sour cream
½ cup butter, melted

¾ pound Cheddar cheese, shredded
  and divided
1 teaspoon salt
½ teaspoon pepper

Preheat oven to 300 degrees. In a heavy saucepan boil the potatoes until done. Drain; allow to cool. Remove skins from potatoes. In a large mixing bowl grate potatoes; add onion, sour cream, butter, 2 cups cheese, salt and pepper. Pour mixture into a buttered 13 x 9 x 2-inch pyrex dish; top with remaining 1 cup cheese. Bake at 300 degrees for 30 minutes or until bubbly.

Mrs. Hardee Brian (Betty Jo)
East Baton Rouge (Zachary)

CHEESY-POTATO CASSEROLE

5 medium white potatoes
¾ cup coffee creamer
¼ cup all-purpose flour
Salt to taste
Pepper to taste
2 tablespoons dried minced
  onion

1 teaspoon dried parsley flakes
¼ cup margarine
1¼ cups evaporated milk
1 10¾-ounce can Campbell's
  Cheddar cheese soup

Preheat oven to 400 degrees. Wash and peel potatoes; dice or slice in favorite manner. Boil potatoes until partially tender; drain well. In a small mixing bowl, combine coffee creamer, flour, salt, pepper, onions, and parsley flakes. Butter an 11 x 7 x 2-inch baking dish; place one layer of potatoes in dish. Sprinkle layer of dry mixture over potatoes. Dot with margarine. Repeat procedure until all potatoes are used. Pour evaporated milk over entire dish. Dot with margarine; spoon cheese soup over top. Bake at 400 degrees for 30 minutes until bubbly. Serves 8-10.

Mrs. Bernard Bordelon (Marie)
Avoyelles Parish (Moreauville)

CRAB STUFFED POTATOES

8 medium baking potatoes
1½ cups half-and-half, heated
1 8-ounce roll process garlic
  cheese
½ cup butter
1 6½-ounce can crabmeat

2 to 3 green onions, chopped
Dash of salt
Dash of pepper
Dash of Tabasco sauce
Dash of Lea & Perrin's
  Worcestershire sauce

Preheat oven to 375 degrees. Wash and grease potatoes. Bake potatoes in oven for 45 minutes to 1 hour. Let cool slightly, then cut in half lengthwise. Hold potatoes with a hot pad while scooping out pulp. Place potato pulp in large mixing bowl; add remaining ingredients. Beat with electric mixer on low speed, scraping sides of bowl. Stuff potato shells with filling. Bake at 375 degrees for 10 to 15 minutes before serving. Serves 16.

Note: Potatoes can be wrapped and frozen. Pull out and bake until hot.

Louisiana Farm Bureau Women's Committee

STUFFED POTATOES

4 medium baking potatoes
½ cup butter
½ cup half-and-half
1 teaspoon salt
Pepper to taste

4 teaspoons grated onion
1 cup shredded sharp Cheddar
  cheese
1 6½-ounce can crabmeat, drained
½ teaspoon paprika

Preheat oven to 325 degrees. Scrub potatoes well; dry thoroughly. Place potatoes in oven; bake until able to pierce with a fork. Let cool. Cut potatoes lengthwise; scoop out potato pulp, leaving shells intact. Whip potatoes with butter, half-and-half, salt, pepper, onion and cheese. Add crabmeat; stir well. Fill potato shells with stuffing; sprinkle with paprika. Bake at 325 degrees for 15 minutes. Serves 8.

Note: These freeze very well.

Mrs. Ronald R. Anderson
East Feliciana Parish (Ethel)

HOT POTATO SALAD

6 medium potatoes
Dash of salt
Dash of paprika
⅓ cup diced celery
¼ cup vegetable oil
1 lemon, thinly sliced

¼ cup vinegar
6 slices bacon, cooked, drained,
  and crumbled
2 tablespoons chopped green
  onions or chives

Preheat oven to 350 degrees. Boil potatoes in a heavy saucepan. Peel and slice potatoes while hot. Place potatoes in a greased shallow baking dish. Add salt, paprika, and celery. In a saucepan over medium heat combine oil, lemon, and vinegar; bring to a boil. Pour oil mixture over potatoes; sprinkle bacon on top. Bake at 350 degrees until dressing is absorbed. Serve hot. Garnish with lettuce, if desired. Serves 10-12.

Mrs. Robert Thevis (Sadie)
Avoyelles Parish (Simmesport)

VEGETABLE CASSEROLE WITH MUSHROOM SAUCE

1 10-ounce package frozen
chopped cauliflower
1 10-ounce package frozen
chopped broccoli
1 10-ounce package frozen
chopped brussel sprouts
1 8-ounce can water chestnuts,
drained and sliced

1 2½-ounce jar sliced mushrooms,
drained
1 cup chopped onion
1 cup shredded Cheddar cheese
1 10¾-ounce can cream of
mushroom soup, undiluted

Preheat oven to 350 degrees. Prepare each vegetable according to package directions. Drain vegetables well; stir vegetables together. In a separate bowl, combine water chestnuts, mushrooms, onion and cheese. In a casserole dish alternate layers of vegetables with layers of cheese mixture. Pour mushroom soup over top. Bake at 350 degrees for 30 minutes. Serves 6 to 8.

Mrs. Henry Hess (Peggy)
Avoyelles Parish (Moreauville)

RICE AU GRATIN SUPREME

4 cups cooked rice
½ cup chopped onion
½ cup chopped green pepper
¼ cup chopped pimiento
1 10¾-ounce can cream of
mushroom soup, undiluted

⅓ cup salad dressing or
mayonnaise
2 cups shredded Cheddar cheese
½ cup milk
1 teaspoon salt
¼ teaspoon pepper

Preheat oven to 350 degrees. Combine rice, onions, green pepper and pimiento in a large bowl. Blend soup, salad dressing, 1 cup grated cheese, milk and seasonings in a separate bowl; stir into rice mixture. Pour rice mixture into a buttered shallow 2-quart casserole; sprinkle with remaining 1 cup cheese. Bake at 350 degrees for 25 minutes or until hot and bubbly. Serves 6.

Mrs. Dolan P. Kleinpeter
Iberia Parish (New Iberia)

FRIED RICE BALLS

1 tablespoon margarine
1 tablespoon all-purpose flour
½ cup cream, hot
½ teaspoon salt
½ cup grated Parmesan cheese
2 egg yolks, beaten

2 cups cooked rice, chilled
1 cup cubed Mozzarella cheese
¾ cup uncooked long grain rice
Kosher salt or any coarse salt
Vegetable oil

In a saucepan melt margarine over low heat; stir in flour, blending well. Gradually stir in cream and salt; cook over low heat, stirring constantly, until thickened. Stir in Parmesan cheese until well blended; remove from heat. Stir some of hot mixture into beaten egg yolks; add to remaining hot mixture, stirring constantly. Cook 2 minutes longer; remove from heat. Combine cooked rice with sauce. Place a small amount of rice mixture in palm of hand. Press a cube of Mozzarella cheese in it. Cover with a little more rice mixture and form into a ball. Continue until all ingredients are used. Put the uncooked rice and a small amount of coarse salt into a blender, a little at a time. Pulverize the rice and salt. Roll rice balls into dry rice-salt mixture; allow to dry on waxed paper for 20 minutes. Heat 2 to 3 inches of oil to 375 degrees in a heavy saucepan. Fry a few rice balls at a time until browned. Drain on absorbent paper. Serve hot. Serves 6.

Mrs. Patricia Pousson
Jeff Davis Parish (Welsh)

GREEN RICE

1 10-ounce package frozen
  chopped broccoli
3 stalks celery, chopped
½ medium onion, chopped
¼ cup margarine, melted

1 8-ounce jar Cheez Whiz
2 cups cooked rice
1 10¾-ounce can cream of celery
  soup, undiluted

Prepare broccoli according to package directions; drain well. Preheat oven to 350 degrees. Sauté celery and onions with margarine until tender. Combine Cheez Whiz, broccoli, rice and soup; add sautéed vegetables, and mix well. Place in a lightly greased casserole. Bake at 350 degrees for 30 minutes.

Note: This may be frozen and baked when needed.

Mrs. Albert Burke (Anna Lee)
Avoyelles Parish (Moreauville)

OREGANO RICE

8 stalks green onions, chopped
2 4-ounce cans mushrooms, drained
1/2 cup margarine, melted
2 cups uncooked long grain rice
2 10-ounce cans beef bouillon

2 10-ounce cans water or 1 1/2 cups water
1/2 teaspoon cayenne red pepper
2 teaspoons salt
1 teaspoon whole oregano leaves

Preheat oven to 350 degrees. In a large skillet, sauté green onions and mushrooms in margarine until tender. Remove from heat; add rice, bouillon, and water. Season with red pepper, salt and oregano. Mix well and pour into a lightly greased 1 1/2-quart casserole. Bake at 350 degrees for 1 hour. Serves 6 to 8.

Louisiana Farm Bureau Women's Committee

ONIONY RICE

1/4 cup margarine
1 1 3/8-ounce package Lipton onion soup mix

1 cup Uncle Ben's converted rice
2 1/2 cups water

Preheat oven to 350 degrees. Melt margarine in a shallow baking dish or 2-quart casserole; stir in onion soup mix. Add rice, and mix well. Stir in water. Cover; bake at 350 degrees for 1 hour or until all water is absorbed.

Note: For plain rice, omit soup mix and reduce margarine to 1 tablespoon. This recipe allows you to cook rice with a roast or some other oven prepared meat.

Reba Duncan
Madison Parish (Tallulah)

CHINESE RICE

1 1/2 cups peeled, and deveined raw shrimp
1/2 cup butter, melted
1/2 teaspoon garlic powder
1/2 teaspoon salt
1/2 teaspoon oregano leaves
1/2 teaspoon crushed red pepper
1/2 teaspoon pepper

1/2 cup chopped onions
1/2 cup chopped celery
1/2 cup chopped sweet pepper
2 1/2 to 3 cups cooked rice
1 1/2 teaspoons soy sauce
1 1/2 teaspoons Worcestershire sauce

In an electric skillet combine shrimp and seasonings in butter; cook slightly. Add other ingredients, except the rice. Allow ingredients to cook down, leaving the vegetables slightly crisp. Add rice; heat through. Serve hot. Serves 6.

Mrs. Thelma Smith
St. James Parish (St. James)

SPINACH AND ARTICHOKE CASSEROLE

2 10-ounce packages frozen
chopped spinach
1 15½-ounce can artichoke
hearts, drained and diced
½ cup butter

1 8-ounce package cream cheese,
cut into chunks
Salt to taste
Pepper to taste
Soft breadcrumbs

Preheat oven to 350 degrees. Prepare spinach according to package directions; drain well. Melt butter over low heat in a saucepan; add cream cheese, stirring until softened. Remove from heat. Add spinach and artichokes; season with salt and pepper. Pour mixture into a 1½-quart baking dish. Top with breadcrumbs, as desired. Bake at 350 degrees for 40 minutes. Serves 6 to 8.

Dottie Schoendorf
St. Tammany Parish (Folsom)

TOP "T" STOVE MAC AND CHEESE

1 6-ounce package elbow
macaroni
½ cup melted margarine
1 cup whipping cream or
evaporated milk

1½ cups diced pasteurized process
cheese
Pinch of salt
⅔ cup sugar

Cook macaroni; rinse and set aside. In a heavy cast aluminum saucepan combine margarine, cream, cheese and salt; cook over low heat, stirring often to prevent scorching. Add sugar, and continue to cook until thickened and bubbly. Add macaroni to cheese mixture; cook for a few minutes, stirring constantly. Make sure macaroni is thoroughly coated with cheese mixture. Spoon into serving platter. Serves 6-8.

Mrs. Bernard Bordelon (Marie)
Avoyelles Parish (Moreauville)

CROCK POT SOYBEANS

5 cups dried chopped soybeans
5 slices bacon, chopped
1 large onion, chopped

1 teaspoon salt
½ teaspoon black pepper

Boil soybeans in water until tender. Combine soybeans and water, bacon, onion, salt and pepper in a crock pot; cook on high heat for 1 hour. Turn to low and cook for 4 to 6 hours longer. Serves 6 to 8.

Mrs. Kathleen Watkins
Jeff Davis Parish (Iowa)

BAKED SOYBEANS

½ pound ground beef
5 cups cooked soybeans
1 large onion, chopped
¼ cup catsup
¼ cup molasses or firmly
    packed dark brown sugar

2 teaspoons salt
2 tablespoons prepared mustard
2 tablespoons Worcestershire sauce
½ teaspoon pepper
½ teaspoon cayenne red pepper
4 slices bacon

Brown ground beef in a heavy skillet. Drain meat well. Preheat oven to 300 degrees. Combine beans, onion, catsup, molasses, salt, mustard, Worcestershire sauce, pepper, cayenne pepper, and ground beef in a 13 x 9x 2-inch baking dish. Mix well. Taste and add more seasonings, if desired. Top with bacon strips; bake at 300 degrees for 1½ to 2 hours. Serves 6-8.

Mrs. Kathleen Watkins
Jeff Davis Parish (Iowa)

BASIC SOYBEAN RECIPE

1 cup dried soybeans, cleaned
    and washed
6 cups water

1-1½ teaspoons salt
½ teaspoon soda

Place beans, water, salt and soda in a large bowl. Refrigerate overnight. Place beans and water in a heavy saucepan; simmer on low heat for 4 hours. Serve hot.

Note: Cook for 1 hour in a 6-quart pressure cooker, if desired. You may use soybeans just as they come out of the farm bins, if desired.

Mrs. Kathleen Watkins
Jeff Davis Parish (Iowa)

WHITE BEANS

Water
2 pounds dry white beans
3 large onions, chopped
4 cloves garlic, chopped
1 pound salt pork, cut up

½ cup bacon fat or shortening
1 large bunch shallots, chopped
1 small bunch parsley, chopped
Salt to taste
Pepper to taste

Wash and pick over beans; place in a large pot and cover with water. Boil for 30 minutes on medium heat. Drain water from beans. Place beans in fresh water; add onions, garlic, and salt pork. Heat to boiling; reduce heat and simmer for 1 hour. When beans are tender, add shortening, shallots, parsley, salt and pepper to taste; cook over low heat until desired consistency.

Mrs. Ronald Gonsoulin
Iberia Parish (New Iberia)

YELLOW SQUASH WITH SOUR CREAM CASSEROLE

5 pounds tender yellow squash
1 large white onion, chopped
1 cup butter
¼ cup sugar

Salt and pepper to taste
1 1½-ounce can seasoned bread
crumbs
1 8-ounce carton commercial sour
cream

Chop squash and cook slowly with onion, butter, sugar, salt and pepper until squash is very tender and done. Add ¾ of bread crumbs and sour cream. Place in greased baking dish and sprinkle remaining crumbs over top. Bake at 350 degrees for about 20 minutes. Serve hot. Serves 10.

Note: Freezes well. Frozen squash may be substituted for fresh, if desired.

Mrs. Randall F. Bracy (Regina)
Tangipahoa Parish (Amite)

RED HOT SQUASH

6 medium yellow summer
squash, sliced
1 large onion, chopped
1 teaspoon salt
1 teaspoon sugar
¼ pound (4 ounces) Velveeta
cheese, cut into chunks

2 tablespoons milk
2 Jalapeño peppers, seeded and
minced
Parsley flakes
Paprika

Preheat oven to 350 degrees. Boil squash and onion in water with sugar and salt until tender; drain well in colander. Place squash into a lightly greased 1½-quart casserole. Prepare a sauce of Velveeta and milk over low heat. Pour sauce over squash. Add peppers and stir well. Top with parsley and paprika; bake at 350 degrees for 10 to 15 minutes.

Note: Green pepper can be used instead of Jalapeño peppers. It will not be red hot. This can be made ahead of time.

Mrs. Alden Horton (Susan)
Vermilion Parish (Gueydan)

SQUASH CASSEROLE I

1½ pounds summer squash	2 eggs, slightly beaten
1 medium onion, chopped	3 tablespoons margarine, melted
1 cup (4 ounces) shredded	Salt and pepper to taste
Cheddar cheese	Paprika
1 tablespoon sugar	

Preheat oven to 350 degrees. Cook squash and onion until tender in lightly salted water. Drain well. Combine all ingredients, except ½ cup cheese; stir lightly. Pour mixture into a buttered 2-quart casserole; top with remaining ½ cup cheese; sprinkle with paprika. Bake at 350 degrees for 20 to 25 minutes. Serves 6-8.

Note: Two 10-ounce packages frozen squash may be substituted for fresh, if desired. This dish freezes well.

Mrs. Leroy Travis (Twink)
Ouachita Parish (Monroe)

SQUASH CASSEROLE II

1½ pounds yellow summer squash, washed and diced	1 8-ounce carton commercial sour cream
4 small carrots, finely chopped or grated	1 10¾-ounce can cream of chicken soup, undiluted
1 medium onion, chopped	1 package Pepperidge Farm Light Bread Stuffing
1 2½-ounce jar chopped pimiento, drained	

Preheat oven to 350 degrees. Cook squash in a small amount of water until tender. Drain squash well and mash. Combine all ingredients except ⅓ of the bread stuffing; mix thoroughly. Pour mixture into a buttered 2-quart casserole; sprinkle remaining bread stuffing over top. Dot with margarine. Bake at 350 degrees for 25 minutes. Serves 8-10.

Mrs. U. M. Youngblood (Carrie Jo)
Caldwell Parish (Columbia)

SQUASH DELIGHT

1 pound yellow summer squash
½ cup margarine, melted
½ cup chopped onion
½ cup chopped green pepper
½ cup mayonnaise
1 teaspoon sugar

½ teaspoon cayenne pepper
1 egg, beaten
½ cup shredded Cheddar cheese
1 8-ounce can water chestnuts,
   drained and sliced

Preheat oven to 350 degrees. In a saucepan, boil squash and a small amount of water until tender. Drain squash well. Combine all ingredients in a bowl; stir well. Pour mixture into a greased casserole; bake at 350 degrees for 20 minutes or until bubbly hot.

Mrs. H. G. Hardee, Jr. (Sue)
Vermilion Parish (Gueydan)

SWEET POTATO CASSEROLE

Filling:
2¼ cups cooked mashed sweet
   potatoes
1½ cups sugar
¼ cup butter, melted
2 eggs

1 teaspoon baking powder
1 teaspoon vanilla extract
½ teaspoon lemon juice
¾ cup milk

Preheat oven to 375 degrees. Combine all ingredients, mixing well. Pour mixture into a greased baking dish.

Topping:
⅓ cup butter, melted
1 cup firmly packed brown
   sugar

⅓ cup all-purpose flour
1 cup chopped pecans

In a saucepan melt butter. Remove from heat and stir in brown sugar, flour and pecans. Sprinkle mixture over sweet potatoes. Bake at 375 degrees for 25 minutes. Serves 6 to 8.

Anita Joiner
Tangipahoa Parish (Hammond)

SWEET POTATO CASSEROLE

Casserole:

4 large sweet potatoes or 3
   cups mashed sweet potatoes
½ cup sugar
½ cup butter, softened

2 eggs, well beaten
1 teaspoon vanilla extract
⅓ cup milk

Boil the sweet potatoes until tender in a heavy saucepan; drain off excess water. Mash potatoes with a fork. Preheat oven to 350 degrees. Combine sugar, butter, eggs, vanilla and milk in a mixing bowl; mix well. Add mashed sweet potatoes, mixing well. Pour into a lightly greased 13 x 9 x 2-inch baking dish.

Topping:

⅓ cup butter, melted
1 cup firmly packed brown
   sugar

½ cup all-purpose flour
1 cup chopped pecans

In a small saucepan melt butter. Remove from heat and add sugar, flour and pecans. Mix well. Sprinkle mixture over casserole. Bake at 350 degrees for 25 minutes. Serves 10 to 12.

Thelma Rowland
Caldwell Parish (Columbia)

YUMMY YAMS

4 large sweet potatoes
⅔-¾ cup sugar
⅓ cup whipping cream

Pinch of salt
¼ cup margarine
Ground cinnamon, if desired

Preheat oven to 450 degrees. Peel sweet potatoes and cut into strips (like French fries). In a mixing bowl, combine sugar, cream, and salt. Place cut potatoes in a well-buttered 13 x 9 x 2-inch baking dish; pour cream mixture over potatoes. Dot with margarine; sprinkle cinnamon over top, if desired. Bake at 450 degrees for 45 minutes. Serve hot.

Note: The amount of sugar will vary according to the size of the potatoes. If desired, garnish with marshmallows or shredded Cheddar cheese.

Mrs. Bernard Bordelon (Marie)
Avoyelles Parish (Moreauville)

YAM-APPLE CRISP

1 20-ounce can Lucky Leaf
  sliced apples, drained
1 17-ounce can yams, drained
  and sliced
½ teaspoon ground nutmeg
½ teaspoon ground cinnamon

1 tablespoon lemon juice
⅓ cup butter, softened
½ cup uncooked oats
1 tablespoon all-purpose flour
½ cup firmly packed brown sugar
½ cup chopped pecans

Preheat oven to 350 degrees. Drain apples and yams. Slice yams. Layer apples and yams in a 2-quart casserole dish. Sprinkle nutmeg, cinnamon and lemon juice over yams and apples. In a small mixing bowl combine butter, oats, flour, sugar and pecans; mix well. Sprinkle sugar mixture over apples and yams. Bake uncovered at 350 degrees for 30 to 40 minutes. Serves 8.

Note: Substitute raw sugar for brown sugar, if desired.

Mrs. Ronald Gonsoulin (Cheryl)
Iberia Parish (New Iberia)

HOLIDAY SWEET POTATO

Casserole:
1 egg, beaten
1 30-ounce can sweet potatoes,
  drained
1 to 2 teaspoons ground
  cinnamon

¼ cup sugar
2 tablespoons butter, melted
¼ cup milk
Dash of salt

Preheat oven to 350 degrees. In a large mixing bowl, combine all ingredients; beat until light and fluffy. Place in an 8 x 8 x 2-inch pan.

Topping:
¼ cup butter, softened
2 tablespoons all-purpose flour

½ cup firmly packed brown sugar
½ cup chopped pecans

In a mixing bowl, cream together butter, flour, and sugar. Stir in pecans. Spread mixture evenly over top of potato mixture. Bake at 350 degrees for approximately 50 minutes. Serve hot.

Mrs. Eddie Schexnaydre (Doris)
Terrebonne Parish (Schriever)

Breads

Café Du Monde · New Orleans

OLD-TIME BUTTERMILK BISCUITS

2 cups self-rising flour
¼ teaspoon soda
¾ cup buttermilk

⅓ cup vegetable oil
Butter

In large bowl, mix flour and soda. Add milk and oil; mix until well blended. Flour hands and roll out each biscuit. Place on greased pan. Mash down each biscuit gently with fingertips. Place a dab of butter on top of each biscuit. Bake at 450 degrees for 12-15 minutes.

Beth Hart
Ouachita Parish (Monroe)

BISCUITS

2 cups self-rising flour
1 cup milk

2 heaping tablespoons Crisco
shortening

Preheat oven to 350 degrees. Sift flour into a large bowl. Make a well in the middle of the flour; pour milk and shortening into well. Gradually mix liquid with flour until a soft dough is formed. Pinch off amount of dough for a biscuit, and roll between palms until biscuit-shaped. Place biscuits in a greased Corning Ware pie plate or pan until pan is filled. Bake at 350 degrees for 20 minutes. Yield: 12 biscuits.

Note: Biscuits are better if made up and let sit at room temperature for a while before baking.

Mrs. Donald Johnson (Brenda)
Ouachita Parish (Monroe)

BUTTER BISCUITS TO FREEZE

4 cups Pioneer biscuit mix
1 heaping tablespoon sugar
1 scant tablespoon salt
½ teaspoon cream of tartar

1 teaspoon baking powder
1½ cups melted butter, cooled
1½ cups milk

In large bowl, place biscuit mix, sugar, salt, cream of tartar and baking powder. Add butter to center of mixture and pour milk around it. Mix dough thoroughly with floured hands. Roll mixture into little balls and pat into place on a cookie sheet. Freeze until hard. Place biscuits into plastic bags and return to freezer until needed. Bake at 400 degrees for 10-12 minutes. Yield: about 50 little bite-sized biscuits.

Note: You may bake before freezing, if desired.

Mrs. Martin Cancienne (Sally)
Assumption Parish (Belle Rose)

HANDY BISCUIT MIX

Basic Mix:

5 pounds all-purpose flour
2½ cups dry milk solids
¾ cup double acting baking
  powder

3 tablespoons salt
½ cup sugar
2 tablespoons cream of tartar
4 cups shortening

Combine first 6 ingredients in a large bowl; stir well. Cut in shortening until mixture resembles coarse meal. Store mix at room temperature in an airtight container.

Biscuits:

1 heaping cup handy biscuit
  mix

Water

Combine mix and enough water to form a soft dough in a medium mixing bowl; shape into a ball. Cut dough out into biscuits. Put on cookie sheet; bake at 400 degrees for 25 minutes or until browned. Yield: 5 biscuits.

Note: Combine desired amount of mix and water to make a large amount of biscuits ahead of serving time. Cut dough out, place on cookie sheets, and freeze for 3 hours. Remove from sheet and place in plastic freezer bags to store frozen. Bake at 400 degrees as directed above.

Pancakes:

½ cup milk
1 egg

¼ cup vegetable oil
1 cup handy biscuit mix

Combine first 3 ingredients in container of electric blender; blend well. Add biscuit mix; blend until smooth. Drop batter onto a lightly greased hot griddle and cook until pancakes are browned on both sides. Yield: about 5 (4-inch) pancakes.

Note: If dry milk solids are ommitted in the basic recipe, combine mix with enough milk to form a soft dough instead of water, as listed.

Mrs. Bernard Bordelon (Marie)
Avoyelles Parish (Moreauville)

ASPHODEL BREAD

5 cups Pioneer biscuit mix
¼ cup sugar
½ teaspoon salt
2 packages active dry yeast

2 cups warm milk (105° to 115°)
4 eggs
¼ teaspoon cream of tartar

Preheat oven to 350 degrees. In very large bowl, sift together biscuit mix, sugar and salt. Sprinkle dry yeast into milk to dissolve; let stand 5 minutes. Beat eggs with cream of tartar until eggs are thoroughly broken up. Combine milk and eggs, stirring well; pour into dry ingredients. Mix until well blended. This is a heavy sticky batter. Cover bowl with a damp towel or plastic wrap and let rise in a warm place (85°) until double in bulk. Punch dough down; place dough in 2 oiled loafpans, filling about halfway. Let dough rise again until doubled. Bake at 350 degrees about 40 minutes.

Note: This bread freezes quite well. Be sure to completely thaw before reheating. May have to put foil on top to keep from browning too fast.

Louisiana Farm Bureau Women's Committee

YEAST BISCUITS

2 packages active dry yeast or 2
  cakes compressed yeast
¼ cup warm water (105° to
  115°)
½ cup sugar
1 tablespoon salt

2 heaping tablespoons Crisco
  shortening
2 cups boiling water
2 eggs, well beaten
8 cups all-purpose flour
Melted butter

Preheat oven to 350 degrees. Use very warm water (105 degrees to 115 degrees fahrenheit) for dry yeast; use lukewarm water (80 degrees to 90 degrees fahrenheit) for compressed yeast. Sprinkle dry yeast or crumble cakes into water and stir until dissolved. In large bowl, mix sugar, salt, Crisco and boiling water until Crisco becomes melted. Let cool to 105° or 115°. Add dissolved yeast, eggs and 4 cups of flour. Mix well. Add remainder of flour and mix well. Put dough in an airtight container and place in refrigerator. Remove dough from container as needed. Flour hands and roll dough into biscuits. Place biscuits on greased pan. In warm place, (85°), free from drafts, let rise until double in bulk. Bake at 350 degrees until golden brown. Brush tops with melted butter.

Note: You may use self-rising flour, if desired, but omit salt.

Mrs. Emmett Moore (Lillian)
Ouachita Parish (Monroe)

HOMEMADE BREAD

2½ packages active dry yeast
2 cups warm water (105° to
  115°)
2 teaspoons salt

½ cup sugar
½ cup Wesson oil
5 cups Pillsbury bread flour

In small bowl dissolve yeast in warm water; let stand 5 minutes. In large bowl, combine salt, sugar and oil. Add dissolved yeast to mixture and stir until well blended. Add flour and mix well. If sticky, add enough flour to make a stiff dough that will not stick to bowl. Turn out on well floured surface and knead hard for 10 minutes. Put in greased bowl; turn once. Let dough rise in warm place (85°) for 1½ to 2 hours or until doubled in bulk. Punch down and let rest 5 minutes. Grease 2 iron skillets. Shape dough into rolls and place in greased skillets; cover and let rise for 1½ hours or until doubled in bulk. Bake at 400 degrees for 20 minutes.

Allen J. Brouillette
Avoyelles Parish (Marksville)

HARVEST BREAD

2 packages dry yeast
1 cup soy flour
1 cup whole wheat flour
½ cup all-purpose flour
¼ cup wheat germ
3 cups warm water (105° to
  115°
¾ cup non-fat dry milk solids

3½ cup all-purpose flour
2 tablespoons sugar
1 tablespoon brown sugar
3 teaspoons salt
2 tablespoons shortening, melted in
  water
Additional all-purpose flour

Preheat oven to 375 degrees. In large bowl, combine yeast, soy flour, whole wheat flour, all-purpose flour, and wheat germ. Add warm water and non-fat dry milk. Beat with electric mixer for 2 minutes at medium speed, scraping bowl occasionally. Add 3½ cups flour, sugars, salt and shortening, changing from mixer to hand mixing when dough becomes stiff. Add enough more additional flour to make dough pliable, if necessary. Turn out on floured cloth and knead for 8 to 10 minutes. Place dough in a greased bowl and cover. Let rise until doubled. Punch dough down; cover and let rest for 15 minutes. Shape dough into loaves or rolls. Let rise until doubled about 30 to 40 minutes. Bake loaves at 375 degrees for about 1 hour; bake rolls at 400 degrees for 12 to 15 minutes longer. Remove from pans and cool on wire rack. Yield: 2 large loaves or 4 to 5 dozen rolls.

Note: This recipe won the National 4-H honor from Louisiana and was submitted by Suzanne Robichaux.

Mrs. Patsy Granger
Jeff Davis Parish (Jennings)

HOMEMADE BREAD

1½ cups warm water (105° to 115°)
1 package active dry yeast
3 tablespoons sugar

1 teaspoon salt
4 cups all-purpose flour
2 tablespoons butter

In large bowl combine water, yeast, sugar and salt; stir until yeast is dissolved. Add 3 cups flour, one cup at a time, stirring constantly (Dough will be sticky). Add remaining 1 cup flour; turn out and knead until dough is smooth and no longer sticky. Let rise in warm place until dough is doubled in bulk. Punch dough down, and place dough in loafpan or shape rolls the size of small apples and place in a 9-inch round pan. Cover and let rise until doubled in bulk. Bake at 350 degrees for approximately 35 minutes or until browned. Immediately after removing from oven, rub butter on top of hot bread. Butter will melt as you rub.

Note: This recipe has been handed down 3 generations. I've been making this since I was 12 years old.

Mrs. John Boudreaux (Diana)
Vermilion Parish (Abbeville)

HOT MAMA'S BREAD

2 packages dry yeast
1½ cups warm water (105° to 115°)
¾ teaspoon salt

¼ cup vegetable oil
3 tablespoons sugar
4 cups all-purpose flour
½ cup melted margarine

In a glass or stainless steel bowl, sprinkle yeast in very warm water; let stand for about 3 to 4 minutes. Add salt, oil and sugar; mix well. Add 3 cups flour and mix until smooth and elastic. Add remainder of flour, mixing until dough becomes one big ball. Set dough in warm place (85°) to rise for about 1 to 1½ hours or until doubled in bulk. Punch dough down and knead on a floured surface for about 2-3 minutes, working well. Cut dough into 2-inch balls and place in well greased baking pan to rise for about 1 hour. Bake at 400 or 425 degrees about 30 minutes or until golden brown. Brush top of rolls with margarine. Yield: 18-20 rolls.

Note: To make rolls with smooth crust, after "2-inch balls" are cut, roll around the palm of hand and pinch bottom. Place in oiled baking pan. Always brush oil or margarine on top of rolls when cut and placed to rise.

Mrs. Bernard Bordelon (Marie)
Avoyelles Parish (Moreauville)

BREAD (PULL-APART LOAVES)

5½ to 6½ cups all-purpose
  flour
3 tablespoons sugar
2 teaspoons salt
1 package Fleischmann's active
  dry yeast

1½ cups water
½ cup milk
3 tablespoons margarine or butter,
  melted

In large bowl or mixer with dough hook, combine 2 cups flour, sugar, salt and yeast. Combine water, milk and margarine in saucepan. Cook over low heat until liquids become very warm (120 degree to 130 degrees Fahrenheit). (Margarine does not need to melt.) Gradually add liquid mixture to flour mixture, beating constantly. Beat for 2 minutes on medium speed, scraping bowl occasionally. Add ¾ cup flour. Beat at high speed for 2 minutes, scraping bowl occasionally. Stir in enough additional flour to make a stiff dough. Turn dough out onto a lightly floured board. Knead until smooth and elastic (about 8 to 10 minutes). Put dough in greased bowl, turn once. Cover and let rise until doubled in bulk in warm place (85°), free from drafts, about 1 hour. Punch dough down; divide dough in half. Cover and let rest on board 15 minutes. Roll ½ of dough out into a 12 x 8-inch rectangle. Brush with melted margarine. Cut rectangle into 4 equal strips, 8-inches long. Stack 4 strips; cut stack into 4 2-inch pieces. Place pieces on edge in greased 8½ x 4½ x 2½-inch loafpan so that pieces form one long row down length of pan. Repeat procedure in second pan with other half of dough. Cover and let rise until doubled about 1 hour. Bake at 400 degrees about 30 minutes or until done. Remove from pans and cool on wire racks. Serve warm or cold.

Mrs. James E. Comeaux (Gloria)
Iberia Parish (New Iberia)

POTATO BREAD

3 eggs
½ cup sugar
½ to ⅔ cup cooked, mashed
  potatoes
2 cakes compressed yeast

½ cup warm water (80° to 90°)
1 cup warm milk
6 to 7 cups all-purpose flour
2 teaspoons salt
½ cup margarine, melted

In large bowl, beat eggs and sugar until well blended. Add potatoes. Dissolve compressed yeast in lukewarm water; let stand 5 minutes. Add yeast to potato mixture. Add warm milk, flour and salt; mix well. Let rise until doubled. Punch down, pinch off pieces the size of rolls and dip into melted margarine. Place rolls in greased pans. Let rise until doubled. Bake at 350 degrees for 35 minutes. Pour margarine over sides and top of baked rolls.

Mrs. C. L. Gauthier, Jr. (Narcille)
Avoyelles Parish (Moreauville)

HOMEMADE BREAD (SWEET DOUGH)

1½ cups lukewarm milk (80° to 90°)
½ cup sugar
2 teaspoons salt
2 packages dry yeast

½ cup water (105° to 115°)
2 eggs, slightly beaten
½ cup shortening
7 to 7½ cups sifted all-purpose flour

In large bowl, mix milk, sugar, and salt. Dissolve yeast in warm water; let stand for 5 minutes. Add yeast mixture to the milk mixture. Stir in eggs, until blended. Add flour, mixing by spoon and then by hand until dough does not stick to side of bowl. Turn out onto lightly floured board and knead until dough is smooth and elastic. Put dough in greased bowl and turn once. Cover with damp cloth and let rise in warm area (85°) until doubled, about 1½ to 2 hours. Punch down, turn dough over and let rise again, about 30 to 45 minutes. Punch dough down; shape into desired sized rolls. Place rolls in greased baking dish. Cover with cloth and let rise for 15 to 30 minutes. Depending on size of rolls, bake at 425 degrees for 12 to 20 minutes. Yield: 2 loaves.

Mrs. Weston Monceaux, Jr. (Naomi)
Allen Parish (Oberlin)

CINNAMON ROLLS

4¼ cups all-purpose flour
⅓ cup sugar
1 teaspoon salt
2 packages Fleischmann's active dry yeast
¾ cup milk
½ cup water

½ cup margarine
½ cup all-purpose flour
2 eggs
3 tablespoons margarine, melted
1 cup sugar
1 tablespoon ground cinnamon

In large bowl, combine flour, sugar, salt and yeast; set aside. Heat milk, water and margarine to 120-130 degrees Fahrenheit. Add to dry ingredients and beat for 2 minutes at medium speed of electric mixer, scraping bowl occasionally. Add flour and eggs. Beat at high speed for 2 minutes. Add enough additional flour to make a stiff dough. Cover tightly. Refrigerate for 2 hours or as long as 2 days. Turn dough onto floured board. Roll dough into three 12 x 9-inch rectangles; brush with melted margarine. Combine sugar and cinnamon; sprinkle mixture over dough. Roll rectangles up from short end. Seal seams. Cut each roll into 1-inch slices. Place 9 slices into greased 8-inch round pan. Repeat procedure until all slices are used up. Cover and let rise until doubled about 45 minutes. Bake at 375 degrees for 20-25 minutes or until done. Remove rolls from pans. Cool on wire racks. Yield: approximately 24 rolls.

Note: If desired, frost with powdered sugar frosting.

Mrs. Alvin Klein (Margie)
Allen Parish (Oberlin)

FRENCH DONUTS

1 package active dry yeast
½ cup warm water (105° to 115°)
1 cup milk
¼ cup shortening
½ cup sugar

1 teaspoon salt
1 cup boiling water
2 eggs, beaten
7½ cups all-purpose flour
Fat or oil for deep fat frying
Powdered sugar

In small bowl dissolve dry yeast in warm water; let stand 5 minutes. In saucepan boil milk then let cool to lukewarm. In bowl, combine shortening, sugar, salt, and boiling water; stir well. Let mixture cool. In large bowl mix dissolved yeast, cooled milk and the shortening mixture. Add eggs and flour; mix until well blended. Roll dough out thin and cut into strips. Heat fat or oil to 375 or 400 degrees in deep fat fryer or kettle; drop strips into the hot fat. Turn strips as they rise to surface. Fry until golden brown. Coat with powdered sugar.

Mrs. S. L. Ford, Sr.
Catahoula Parish (Jonesville)

POTATO DOUGHNUTS

2 cups cooked mashed Irish potatoes
2 cups sugar
3 tablespoons shortening
1 cup milk
4 eggs

¼ teaspoon salt
½ teaspoon freshly grated nutmeg
5 to 6 cups all-purpose flour
5 teaspoons baking powder
Fat or oil for deep fat frying
Powdered sugar

In large bowl mix potatoes, sugar, shortening, milk, eggs, salt, nutmeg, flour and baking powder. Add enough more flour to make dough stiff. Roll dough out on a floured surface and cut with floured doughnut cutter. Heat fat or oil to 350 degrees in deep fat fryer or kettle. Drop doughnuts into hot fat; turn doughnuts as they rise to surface and fry until golden brown. Drain and sprinkle powdered sugar over doughnuts or shake in bag with powdered sugar, while hot.

Note: Dough may be refrigerated and used when needed.

Mrs. Ray Marcotte (Mickey)
Avoyelles Parish (Mansura)

Hint: Hush puppies are toothsome morsels from Louisiana hunters. When they sat around their camp fish-fries, their hunting dogs would whine for the good smelling food. The men tossed leftover corn patties to them saying, "Hush, puppies". Satisfied, the dogs hushed.

Louisiana Farm Bureau Women's Committee

MARDI GRAS DOUGHNUTS

1 cup scalded milk
2 tablespoons butter or
   margarine
1 tablespoon sugar
1 tablespoon brown sugar
1 package dry yeast

3 cups all-purpose flour
1 teaspoon salt
½ teaspoon ground nutmeg
1 egg
Fat or oil for deep fat frying
Powdered sugar

In large bowl stir milk, butter and sugar together until butter is melted; cool to lukewarm (105° to 115°). Add yeast to cooled mixture; stir to dissolve. Gradually add 1½ cups flour, salt and nutmeg to make a batter. Add egg and beat until well blended. Add remainder of flour, blending well. Cover and let rise until doubled in bulk. Turn out on a floured board and knead gently. Roll out dough to ¾-inch thickness. Cut dough into diamond shapes; place on greased baking sheets. Cover and let rise for ½ to 1 hour. Heat fat or oil to 385 degrees in deep fat fryer or kettle. Drop doughnuts into hot fat; turn as they rise to surface, and fry until browned. Drain doughnuts, and dust with powdered sugar.

Mrs. B. Lemoine, Jr. (Grace)
Avoyelles Parish (Hamburg)

SPOON BREAD

2 cups milk
1 cup corn meal
3 tablespoons butter

½ teaspoon salt
4 eggs, separated

Heat milk until scalding; stir in meal slowly. Add butter, then remove from heat. Add salt and beaten egg yolks. Mix well. Beat egg whites until stiff. Fold into corn meal mixture. Bake in buttered dish at 350 degrees until brown.

JoAnn Irvine
Beauregard Parish (DeRidder)

CORN BREAD

1 cup corn meal
1 cup Pioneer biscuit mix
½ teaspoon salt
1 teaspoon soda

¼ cup vegetable oil
2 eggs
1½ cups buttermilk

Preheat oven to 425 degrees. In large bowl mix corn meal, biscuit mix, salt, soda, and oil. Add eggs, one at a time, beating well. Add buttermilk; mix well. Pour batter into greased pan and bake at 425 degrees for 25 minutes.

Anita Joiner
Tangipahoa Parish (Hammond)

LOUISIANA CORN BREAD

1 cup plain corn meal	1 cup buttermilk
¼ teaspoon soda	1 egg
½ teaspoon salt	⅓ to ½ cup water
1 tablespoon baking powder	Oil

In medium bowl mix corn meal, soda, salt, and baking powder until well blended. Add buttermilk and egg; mix well. This will be a thick batter. Gradually add water to make it a little soupy. Cover bottom of a number 6 black skillet with oil or grease and put in a 500 degree oven. Remove from oven when oil is hot and pour batter in skillet. Bake at 500 degrees for 20 minutes or until golden brown.

Note: You may leave skillet in oven while you make corn bread until it becomes hot. This is my Mother's corn bread recipe and to me it is the best corn bread I have ever eaten. It took me a while to learn the skillet had to be real hot.

Mrs. Don Odom (Brenda)
Claiborne Parish (Homer)

HOT WATER CORN BREAD

1 cup corn meal	1 teaspoon salt
¼ cup all-purpose flour	2 tablespoons vegetable oil
2 teaspoons baking powder	Boiling water

Preheat oven to 425 degrees. In large bowl sift corn meal, flour, baking powder and salt. Add oil and stir. Add enough boiling water to mixture to make a firm dough. Coat an iron skillet with oil. Heat skillet in oven until hot. Place dough in skillet and turn once to cover with oil. Bake at 425 degrees for 1 hour and 30 minutes. Bread will be hard and crusty. Serves 5.

Lavone G. Pruitt
Webster Parish (Minden)

COUNTRY CORN STICKS

1 cup self-rising flour	2 eggs, beaten
½ teaspoon soda	1 cup buttermilk
1 tablespoon sugar	3 tablespoons butter, melted
¾ cup yellow corn meal	

In large mixing bowl combine flour, soda, sugar, and corn meal. Add remaining ingredients; beat together until well blended. Pour batter in greased heated corn stick or muffin pans (fill pans until ⅔ full). Bake at 425 degrees for 20 to 25 minutes. Yield: 18 sticks or 24 muffins.

Alice Faye Hart
Ouachita Parish (Monroe)

JALAPEÑO CORN BREAD

2 8½-ounce boxes Jiffy corn
  bread mix
12-18 slices process American
  cheese, chopped
1 medium onion, chopped
3 to 4 bottled jalapeño peppers,
  chopped or 3 fresh jalapeño
  peppers, chopped
2 tablespoons bottled jalapeño
  pepper juice
½ teaspoon minced garlic
3 eggs
½ cup vegetable oil
1 teaspoon salt
½ cup milk
1 16-ounce can whole kernel corn,
  drained

In large bowl mix Jiffy corn bread mix, cheese, onion, peppers, juice, and garlic. Add eggs one at a time, beating well after each addition. Add oil, salt, milk and corn; mix together well. Pour batter in a slightly greased 9-inch square pan or pyrex dish and bake at 375 degrees for 45 minutes or until golden brown. Serves approximately 12.

Mrs. Gladys L. Dupuis
Lafayette Parish (Carencro)

MEXICAN CORN BREAD NUMBER II

2 cups yellow corn meal
¼ cup all-purpose flour
2 teaspoons baking powder
1 teaspoon soda
2 tablespoons sugar
1½ cups buttermilk
3 slices fried bacon, crumbled

Bacon drippings
½ cup chopped onion
4 jalapeño peppers, seeded and chopped
1 16½-ounce can cream-style corn
1 pound Cheddar or process American cheese, shredded

In large bowl combine all ingredients; mix well. Pour mixture into 13 x 9 x 2-inch baking pan. Bake at 450 degrees for about 40 minutes. Serves 10 or 12 generous portions.

Mrs. Wayne Zaunbrecher (Linda)
Vermilion Parish (Gueydan)

HUSH PUPPIES I

1½ cups yellow corn meal
½ cup all-purpose flour
2 teaspoons baking powder
1 teaspoon salt
2 tablespoons sugar
¾ cup milk

1 egg, beaten
1 tablespoon jalapeño peppers, chopped
4 or 5 green onions, chopped
Fat or oil for deep fat frying

In large bowl combine corn meal, flour, baking powder, salt, and sugar. Add milk, egg, peppers and onions; stir until blended. Batter will be stiff. Heat fat or

HUSH PUPPIES III

2 cups yellow corn meal
2 tablespoons all-purpose flour
1/4 cup onions, finely chopped
2 teaspoons salt
Generous amount of freshly
    ground black pepper

Boiling water
1/4 cup milk
1 egg, slightly beaten
2 teaspoons baking powder
Fat or oil to deep fat fry

In large bowl mix corn meal, flour, onion, salt, and pepper until well blended. Add enough water to make a thick mush. Add milk, egg, and baking powder to mush and mix thoroughly. Heat fat or oil to 375 degrees in deep fat fryer or kettle. Drop batter by spoonfuls and fry until golden brown all over.

Note: These are excellent with fish and fried shellfish. You may like a small amount of sugar in the recipe.

Louisiana Farm Bureau Women's Committee

GERMAN PANCAKES

1/3 cup all-purpose flour
1/2 cup evaporated milk
1/4 teaspoon salt
4 extra large eggs, or 5 medium
    eggs

4 tablespoons butter or
    margarine
Powdered sugar

Preheat oven to 425 degrees. In large bowl, combine flour, evaporated milk, and salt; mix until well blended. Using a wire whisk, add eggs one at a time, beating after each addition. In a 10-inch ovenproof skillet melt butter. Pour batter into skillet; bake at 425 degrees for 15 minutes or until puffed and golden brown. Pancake will be puffed up into billowy, irregular mounds. Sprinkle with powdered sugar. Serve at once. Serves 4 to 6.

Note: Serve with fresh strawberries or apples with orange sauce (recipe below).

Apples with Orange Sauce:
1 16-ounce can of sliced apples
1/2 cup powdered sugar

2 tablespoons orange juice or
    orange-flavored liqueur

In saucepan, combine all ingredients; cook for a few minutes until mixture thickens. Serve over German Pancakes.

Mrs. Thelma Smith
St. James Parish (St. James)

FAVORITE PANCAKES

1 ¼ cups sifted all-purpose flour
1 tablespoon baking powder
½ teaspoon salt
1 tablespoon sugar

1 egg, beaten
1 cup milk
2 tablespoons salad oil

In large bowl sift together flour, baking powder, salt and sugar; set aside. In bowl combine egg, milk and oil; add to flour mixture and stir until moist. Pour batter onto lightly greased hot griddle or skillet. Yield: 12 dollar-sized pancakes.

Note: A little less or a little more milk may be needed depending on how you like them.

Mrs. Donald Johnson (Brenda)
Ouachita Parish (Monroe)

PANCAKES

2 tablespoons vegetable oil
1 egg
1 cup milk
1 cup all-purpose flour

2 tablespoons baking powder
6 tablespoons sugar
½ teaspoon salt
1 tablespoon milk

In large bowl, mix together oil, egg, and 1 cup milk until well blended; set aside. In bowl sift together flour, baking powder, sugar, and salt. Add flour mixture to milk mixture; blend well. Stir in 1 tablespoon milk. Pour batter on lightly oiled hot griddle and fry until done. Yield: about 8 pancakes.

Mrs. Neldred Bordelon (Melba)
Avoyelles Parish (Moreauville)

BREAD STICKS

2 cups butter or margarine
1 clove pressed garlic or garlic
   powder

Red pepper to taste
2 packages hot dog buns
Dry parsley flakes

Preheat oven to 250 degrees. In saucepan melt butter over low heat; add garlic and red pepper. Remove from heat. Cut each bun into 6 strips. Place buns closely together in a jelly-roll pan. Brush buns generously with melted butter mixture. Sprinkle parsley flakes over top. Bake at 250 degrees for 45 minutes or until very dry and slightly browned.

Note: Will keep for weeks if stored in an airtight container.

Mrs. Charles Waguespack (Lisa)
Ascension Parish (Donaldsonville)

BANANA HOT CAKES

1½ cups self-rising flour
3 tablespoons sugar
1 egg, beaten
¾ cup milk

3 tablespoons melted shortening
1 large or 2 small bananas, sliced
Powdered sugar

In large bowl, mix flour and sugar together. Add egg, milk, and shortening until well blended. If batter is too thick for your liking, add enough more milk for desired consistency. Fold in bananas. Pour batter on hot greased griddle or frying pan. Be sure that each hot cake has 3 or 4 slices of banana. Turn, and cook other side until browned. Sift or sprinkle powdered sugar over.

Note: Amount of powdered sugar varies with individual taste. These take a little longer to get done than regular hot cakes.

Mrs. B. F. Lemoine, Jr. (Grace)
Avoyelles Parish (Hamburg)

WILLIAMSBURG SWEET POTATO MUFFINS

1¼ cups sugar
1¼ cups cooked, mashed
   sweet potatoes
½ cup butter, softened
2 large eggs at room
   temperature
1½ cups all-purpose flour
2 teaspoons baking powder

1 teaspoon ground cinnamon
¼ teaspoon ground nutmeg
¼ teaspoon salt
1 cup milk
½ cup chopped raisins
¼ cup chopped pecans
2 tablespoons sugar
¼ teaspoon cinnamon

Preheat oven to 400 degrees. In large bowl beat sugar, sweet potatoes, and butter until smooth. Add eggs, one at a time, and blend well. Sift together flour, baking powder, cinnamon, nutmeg and salt; add flour mixture alternately with milk to sweet potato mixture, stirring just to blend. Do not overmix. Fold in raisins and pecans. Thoroughly grease 24 muffin cups, then spoon in batter. Mix sugar and cinnamon together in a small bowl; sprinkle over filled muffin cups. Bake at 400 degrees for 25-30 minutes or until muffins are done. Serve warm. Yield: 24 muffins.

Note: May be easily frozen and reheated.

Mrs. Louis D. Curet
E. Baton Rouge Parish (Baton Route)

219

BANANA FRUIT BREAD

½ cup butter or margarine,
    softened
1 cup sugar
2 eggs
3 mashed ripe bananas
½ cup quartered maraschino
    cherries

1¾ cups all-purpose flour
1 teaspoon soda
¼ cup chopped nuts
¼ cup chocolate chips

Preheat oven to 350 degrees. In large bowl, cream butter and sugar. Add eggs, one at a time, and beat until light. Stir in bananas and cherries. Sift flour and soda together; mix into batter. Stir in nuts and chocolate chips. Pour batter into well-greased loafpan. Bake at 350 degrees for approximately 40 minutes. Bread will be done when inserted toothpick comes out clean.

Note: Mrs. Louis Curet omits cherries, nuts and chocolate chips.

Mrs. Eddie Schexnaydre (Doris)
Terrebonne Parish (Schriever)

STRAWBERRY BREAD

3 cups all-purpose flour
2 cups sugar
1 teaspoon ground cinnamon
1 teaspoon salt
1 teaspoon soda

4 eggs
1¼ cups Wesson oil
1 cup chopped pecans
2 10-ounce packages frozen
    strawberries, thawed

Preheat oven to 350 degrees. In large mixing bowl, sift together flour, sugar, cinnamon, salt, and baking soda. Set aside. In small bowl, beat eggs and Wesson oil. Add pecans and strawberries. Add strawberry mixture to dry ingredients. Grease and flour two 9 x 5 x 3-inch loafpans; pour mixture in loafpans and bake at 350 degrees for 1 hour. (Bake 45 to 50 minutes for smaller pans.) Yield: 2 large loaves or 4 small loaves.

Mrs. John B. McIntosh (Melba)
W. Carroll Parish (Pioneer)

PERSIMMON BREAD

2 eggs
¾ cup sugar
½ cup vegetable oil
1 teaspoon soda
1 cup persimmon pulp

1½ cups sifted all-purpose flour
1 teaspoon ground cinnamon
½ teaspoon salt
½ cup chopped pecans or walnuts
½ cup raisins (optional)

Preheat oven to 325 degrees. In large bowl, mix eggs, sugar and oil. In small bowl mix soda with persimmon pulp; add to sugar mixture. Combine flour, cinnamon and salt; add chopped nuts and raisins. Fold dry ingredients into persimmon mixture. Pour batter into oiled 9 x 4 x 3-inch loafpan. Bake at 325 degrees for 1 hour and 15 minutes.

Mrs. Leonard Gauthier (Motsy)
Avoyelles Parish (Moreauville)

FRENCH BREAD

1 loaf French bread
¼ cup margarine, softened
½ cup mayonnaise

6 green onions, chopped
1 clove garlic, minced
1 cup shredded mozzarella cheese

Split bread lengthwise. In bowl, mix margarine and mayonnaise until well blended; stir in onion and garlic. Spread mixture evenly on bread. Sprinkle

NUTTY BUNS

1 10-ounce can biscuits
½ cup margarine
½ cup sugar

1½ teaspoons ground cinnamon
½ cup finely chopped pecans

Cut biscuits in halves or thirds as desired. Dip biscuits in mayonnaise. In bowl, combine sugar, cinnamon and pecans. Roll biscuits in mixture. Grease muffin tin and put 2 or 3 biscuit pieces in each muffin cup. Bake at 375 degree oven for 12 to 15 minutes. Yield: 10 nutty rolls.

Note: Drizzle with powdered sugar glaze, if desired.

Glaze:
½ cup powdered sugar

Boiling water

Mix powdered sugar and enough water to make a thin paste. Drizzle over baked nutty buns.

Mrs. Bernard Bordelon (Marie)
Avoyelles Parish (Moreauville)

Desserts

Shrimp Boat - "The Spirit of Morgan City"

LAYERED BLUEBERRY DELIGHT

14 whole graham crackers
1 6-ounce package Jello vanilla
  instant pudding and pie filling
1 cup thawed non-dairy whipped
  topping

1 21-ounce can blueberry pie filling
  or 1 recipe Blueberry Glaze

Line 9-inch square pan with whole graham crackers, breaking crackers, if necessary. Prepare pudding mix as directed on package for pudding. Let pudding stand 5 minutes; then blend in whipped topping. Spread half the pudding mixture over the crackers. Add another layer of crackers; top with remaining pudding mixture and remaining crackers. Spread pie filling or glaze over top layer of crackers. Chill 3 hours. Makes 9 servings.

Blueberry Glaze:
1 cup fresh blueberries
1 cup water
¾ cup sugar

3 tablespoons cornstarch
2 tablespoons lemon juice

Combine 1 cup blueberries and 1 cup water; heat just to boiling point. Reduce heat and simmer 2 minutes. Strain, reserving juice (about 1½ cups). Set berries aside. Combine ¾ cup sugar and 3 tablespoons cornstarch in a saucepan. Gradually stir in juice. Cook over low heat, stirring constantly, until thick and clear. Remove from heat; add 2 tablespoons lemon juice. Pour over berries.

Note: This is also good poured in a pastry shell, chilled, and topped with whipped cream.

Mrs. John C. Taylor (Judy)
Ouachita Parish (Choudrant)

BLUEBERRY SUPREME

½ cup margarine, melted
1 cup all-purpose flour
1 cup chopped pecans
1 8-ounce package cream
  cheese

1 cup powdered sugar
1½ cups thawed Cool Whip
1 16-ounce can blueberries

Bottom layer: Combine margarine, flour and nuts. Put on the bottom of 13 x 9-inch pan. Bake at 350 degrees for 20 minutes. Cool.
Middle Layer: Soften cream cheese; add sugar and Cool Whip. Spread on flour and nut layer.
Top layer: Add can of blueberries. Chill before serving.

Mrs. Henry Hess (Peggy)
Avoyelles Parish (Moreauville)

NEW ORLEANS CUSTARD

3 eggs
1 cup sugar

1 quart milk
1 teaspoon vanilla extract

Variations:
1½ cups cooked rice
4 slices toasted bread,
  crumbled

1 medium apple, finely chopped
½ cup raisins
½ cup chopped pecans

Beat eggs and sugar well; stir in milk and vanilla. At this time you may add any or a combination of the above variations. Pour into a 2-quart pyrex bowl. Place bowl in a pan of water. Bake at 325 degrees until a knife blade inserted comes out clean.

Note: It is important that you keep water in the pan; it keeps the custard from drying out.

Mrs. Allen Bares (Lynn)
Vermilion Parish (Erath)

FLOATING ISLAND CUSTARD

6 cups milk
1 cup sugar
2 tablespoons cornstarch
6 eggs, separated

2 teaspoons vanilla extract
½ teaspoon salt
6 tablespoons sugar

Cook milk in large pot until warm. Beat sugar, salt, egg yolks, and cornstarch together; gradually add to milk, stirring constantly. Cook on medium heat, stirring constantly, until thickened. Remove from heat and pour into large bowl. Beat egg whites until stiff; gradually add 6 tablespoons sugar, beating constantly. Drop egg white mixture by spoonfuls into a pan of cold water (about 1-inch of water in pan), and bake for 20 minutes at 350 degrees. Spoon "islands" over custard; refrigerate.

Note: This custard may be served over angel food or pound cake.

Mrs. Mary Ann Graugnard
West St. James Parish (St. James)

BREAD PUDDING I

Pudding:

8 to 12 slices stale bread
Butter as needed
1 20-ounce can sliced peaches
 or fruit cocktail, undrained
4 eggs, separated

1 cup sugar
1 teaspoon vanilla extract
¼ teaspoon salt
3 cups scalded milk
¼ cup sugar

Toast bread, and butter each slice generously. Butter baking dish. Place 4 or 6 slices on bottom of pan, depending on size of pan. Pour 2 cans of peaches over bread. Place another layer of bread over peaches. Beat egg yolks, 1 cup sugar, vanilla, and salt together with a fork. Gradually add scalded milk and pour mixture over bread. Mash and stir ingredients in pan about gently with a fork. Place baking dish in a pan of hot water; bake at 350 degrees for 30 to 35 minutes. Beat egg whites with ¼ cup sugar until stiff; spread on top of pudding, making decorative peaks while spreading. Bake 5 to 10 minutes longer or until brown. Serve with rum sauce.

Rum Sauce:

½ cup sugar
2 tablespoons butter

½ cup water
Rum

Cook sugar, butter, and water till dissolved. Add rum to taste. Serve hot over warm bread pudding. Whiskey or brandy may be used instead of rum, if desired.

Louisiana Farm Bureau Women's Committee

BREAD PUDDING II

1 cup sugar
3 eggs
4 cups milk
1 jigger dark rum
2 tablespoons butter or
 margarine, softened

½ loaf stale French bread, torn in
 pieces and softened
1 cup raisins or dates (optional)

Beat sugar and eggs until creamy; add milk, rum, and butter. Mix well. Pour into pyrex dish with bread. Add raisins or dates, if desired. Set pyrex dish in pan of water; bake at 350 degrees for 45 minutes to 1 hour, until set.

Mrs. Ray Marcotte (Mickey)
Avoyelles Parish (Mansura)

BUTTERSCOTCH PUDDING

1 cup firmly packed brown
  sugar
5 tablespoons all-purpose flour
Few grains of salt

1½ cups milk
2 egg yolks
2 tablespoons butter
Meringue

Mix brown sugar, flour, and salt in a medium saucepan. Gradually add milk; mix well. Beat egg yolks; add to milk mixture. Cook over hot water, stirring constantly, until thickened. Add butter. Pour into custard cups. Swirl meringue on filling. Bake at 325 degrees, for 20 minutes. If desired, omit meringue and garnish with whipped cream.

Mrs. S. L. Ford, Sr.
Catahoula Parish (Jonesville)

PARADISE PUDDING

1 can apple or cherry pie filling
1 20-ounce can crushed
  pineapple
½ can flaked coconut

1 18½-ounce package cake mix
1 cup chopped pecans
½ can flaked coconut
1 cup margarine, melted

Put ingredients in 13 x 9-inch dish in order in which they are listed. Bake at 350 degrees for 1 hour.

Rosalie C. Melancon
St. Martin Parish (St. Martinville)

STRAWBERRY VANILLA PUDDING

5 cups (6 ounces) cubed angel
  food cake
1 3-ounce package instant
  vanilla pudding mix
1 cup cold milk

1 3-ounce package strawberry
  flavored gelatin
1½ cups boiling water
1 pint vanilla ice cream, softened
2 pints fresh strawberries, sliced

Place angel food cake cubes in bottom of a pan. Prepare vanilla pudding according to package directions (using 1 cup milk); let cool. Mix gelatin and hot water; cool. Combine pudding mixture and vanilla ice cream. Place on top of angel food cake cubes in pan. Combine strawberry gelatin and fresh strawberries and pour on top of pudding mixture. Be sure gelatin mix is thin enough to trickle down through pudding and ice cream mixture.

Mary Jo Harrell
Ouachita Parish (West Monroe)

CHIFFON CHEESECAKE (NO BAKE RECIPE)

1 3-ounce package lemon Jello
1 cup boiling water
¼ cup lemon juice
1 cup sugar
1 8-ounce package cream
  cheese

1 13-ounce can evaporated milk
1½ cups graham cracker crumbs
⅜ cup sugar or 6 tablespoons
  sugar
¼ cup margarine

In a small bowl, dissolve Jello in boiling water; set aside. Cream the lemon juice, sugar, and cream cheese until smooth. Combine Jello mixture and creamed mixture together; let cool. Pour evaporated milk into a large bowl and chill for several hours. When milk is chilled, whip until stiff with electric mixer. Fold whipped milk into cheese mixture. Mix cracker crumbs, sugar and melted margarine; press on bottom and sides of a 12 x 9 x 2-inch baking dish. Pour cheesecake filling into dish; chill for 3 hours.

Mrs. Wilson B. Viator, Sr. (Frances)
Iberia Parish (Jeanerette)

FOUR LAYER DELIGHT

Crust:
1 cup all-purpose flour
1 cup grated pecans

¾ cup firmly packed brown sugar
½ cup butter, softened

Combine all ingredients; press into the bottom of a 12 x 9 x 2-inch pan. Bake at 350 degrees for 20 minutes. Let cool.

Filling:
1 8-ounce carton Cool Whip,
  thawed
1 8-ounce package cream
  cheese, softened
1¾ cups unsifted powdered
  sugar, sifted

1 3¾-ounce package Jello
  chocolate instant pudding
1 4-ounce carton Cool Whip,
  thawed

Combine 8-ounce carton Cool Whip, cream cheese, and powdered sugar in a large mixing bowl; mix well. Spread over cooled crust. Prepare chocolate pudding according to package directions; spread over cream cheese layer in pan. Top with remaining carton of Cool Whip. Chill until serving time.

Note: Strawberry, blueberry, or pistachio pudding mix may be substituted for chocolate, if desired.

Mrs. Rick Caldwell (Jeanie)
Ouachita Parish (West Monroe)

SNOWBALL CAKE

2 envelopes unflavored gelatin
1 cup boiling water
1 cup sugar
1 20-ounce can crushed
  pineapple, drained
Juice of one lemon

3 envelopes whipped topping mix,
  divided
1 10¾-ounce angel food cake, torn
  into bite-size pieces
1 3½-ounce can flaked coconut

Sprinkle gelatin over boiling water; stir until gelatin dissolves. Add sugar, pineapple, and lemon juice; stir well, and refrigerate until slightly thickened. Prepare 2 envelopes whipped topping mix according to package directions; stir into gelatin mixture. Place a layer of cake pieces in a 2½-quart mold or dish; top with a layer of gelatin mixture. Alternate layers of cake and gelatin until all is used. Refrigerate until set. Prepare remaining whipped topping mix according to package directions. Unmold cake on a serving platter; frost with whipped topping and sprinkle with coconut. Yield: 10 servings.

Mrs. Helin McCauley (Lou)
Allen Parish (Oberlin)

CONGEALED STRAWBERRY SHORTCAKE

1 3-ounce package strawberry
  Jello
1½ cups boiling water
1 tablespoon sugar
Pinch of salt

1 10-ounce package frozen
  strawberries
1 4½-ounce carton Cool Whip,
  thawed
½ prepared angel food cake

Dissolve Jello in boiling water, add sugar and salt. When Jello is completely dissolved, add frozen strawberries. Cool until partly congealed; fold in Cool Whip. Break cake into small pieces. Spoon half of Jello mixture in bottom of a 9-inch square dish. Top with cake. Cover with remaining Jello mixture. Congeal until ready to serve.

Mary Jane Rye
West Carroll Parish (Pioneer)

ICE CREAM

6 eggs
2⅓ cups sugar
3 large cans Pet milk

2 tablespoons vanilla extract
4 cups milk, approximately
Pinch of salt

Beat eggs until light. Add sugar gradually, beating until thick. Add salt, Pet milk and vanilla; stir well. Add enough milk to fill ice cream cannister to full line. Chill mixture in cannister; freeze in ice cream freezer until hardened. Yield: 1 gallon.

Mrs. Charles Staples (Bobbie)
Ouachita Parish (Calhoun)

HOMEMADE ICE CREAM

5 eggs, beaten well
2 cups sugar
2 tablespoons vanilla extract
3 6-ounce cans Pet milk or 99
   percent fat-free Pet milk

2 quarts milk or 2 percent fat-free
milk

Mix all ingredients together; chill several hours before starting. Freeze in an electric ice cream freezer (It takes approximately 25 minutes). The ice cream will have a delicious and very firm flavor, if left to stand in freezer after hardened. Pack freezer with ice and salt for one hour. Yield: 1 gallon.

Note: This recipe is still very good if fat-free products are used.

Mrs. Doug Moore (Liz)
Ouachita Parish (Monroe)

NO COOK HOMEMADE ICE CREAM

2 10-ounce cans sweetened
   condensed milk
2 large cans Pet evaporated
   milk
1 quart milk

½ cup sugar
½ teaspoon salt
1 teaspoon vanilla extract
Mashed banana, cherries, or
   pineapple, (optional)

Mix condensed milk, evaporated milk, whole milk, sugar, salt, and vanilla; add fruit of your choice; chill. Freeze in ice cream freezer until hardened.

Mrs. Martin Cancienne (Sally)
Assumption Parish (Belle Rose)

LIME SHERBERT

1 3-ounce package of lime Jello
1 cup boiling water
1½ cups sugar
Juice of 2 lemons

Rind of 2 lemons, grated
1 quart milk
1 cup whipping cream

In large bowl, mix lime Jello and boiling water; stir until dissolved. Add sugar; stir until dissolved. Add lemon juice and grated lemon rind; let cool. When cool, add milk and stir well until thoroughly mixed. Freeze mixture in ice trays or shallow container. Beat frozen mixture; add whipping cream and continue beating. Freeze.

Mrs. Mark Swafford
Natchitoches Parish (Natchitoches)

EASY LEMON ICE CREAM

2 cups whipping cream or
  half-and-half
1 cup sugar

1 tablespoon fresh grated lemon
  rind
⅓ cup fresh lemon juice

In large bowl, combine cream and sugar until dissolved. Blend in rind and juice. Freeze until firm, about 4 hours.

Mrs. Louis D. Curet
East Baton Rouge Parish (Baton Rouge)

ICE TREATS (POPSICLES)

1 3-ounce package Jello
1 small package Kool-Aid
1 cup sugar

2 cups boiling water
2 cups cold water

Dissolve Jello and Kool-Aid in boiling water. Add sugar, then cold water. Beat well; freeze in popsicle holders. Makes 14 popsicles.

Mrs. R. Ernest Girouard, Jr.
Vermilion Parish (Kaplan)

 # PEACHES AND CREAM

2 tablespoons margarine,
  melted
¾ cup all-purpose flour
1 large package vanilla pudding
  mix
1 egg

1 16-ounce can sliced peaches,
  drained and juice reserved
¾ cup milk
1 8-ounce package cream cheese,
  softened
½ cup sugar

Pour margarine in a 13 x 9 x 2-inch baking dish. Mix flour, dry pudding mix, egg, peach juice, and milk. Pour in pan. Carefully place peaches in mixture. Beat cream cheese and sugar until creamy; spread over peaches. Bake at 350 degrees for 45 minutes.

Wenonah Lafferty
Caldwell Parish (Columbia)

FUDGE ICE CREAM DESSERT

1 pound package chocolate
  wafers, crushed
⅔ cup melted butter
4 squares (4 ounces)
  unsweetened chocolate
1 cup sugar

2 tablespoons butter
1⅓ cups evaporated milk
½ gallon vanilla ice cream, softened
1 large carton Cool Whip, thawed
½ cup chopped pecans

Combine cookies and add ⅔ cup melted butter; mix well and press on bottom of a 13 x 9 x 2-inch pan. Chill. Melt chocolate over low heat; stir in sugar and 2 tablespoons butter, and evaporated milk, slowly. Cook, stirring constantly, until thickened. Chill. Spread ice cream over chilled chocolate crust; spread chocolate mixture on top. Freeze. When frozen, spread on Cool Whip and top with pecans. Freeze until set.

Mrs. A. G. Savell
East Baton Rouge Parish (Zachary)

FRENCH CHOCOLATE MOUSSE

6 egg whites, at room
  temperature
7 ounces (¾ cup plus 2
  tablespoons) sugar

½ cup Hershey's cocoa

Beat egg whites until very stiff. Using a wooden spoon with circular movement, gradually add sugar and cocoa. Chill. Eat the same day, as whites will weep if kept longer. Serves 5 to 6 persons.

Mrs. Louis D. Curet
East Baton Rouge Parish (Baton Rouge)

BETH'S DUMP DESSERT

1 15½-ounce can crushed
  pineapple
1 21-ounce can cherry pie filling
1 18½-ounce box Duncan
  Hines yellow cake mix

¾ cup margarine
1 7-ounce can flaked coconut
1 cup chopped pecans

Spread pineapple in bottom of 13 x 9 x 2-inch dish. Put cherry filling on top of this. Sprinkle dry cake mix over filling. Melt margarine and pour over this. Put layer of coconut. Cover with chopped pecans. Bake at 350 degrees for 45 minutes.

Note: Do not use whipped margarine in this recipe.
Beth Hart
Ouachita Parish (Monroe)

CHOCOLATE DREAM

1 cup all-purpose flour
½ cup margarine, softened
1 cup chopped pecans
1 cup powdered sugar
1 8-ounce package cream cheese, softened
1 cup thawed Cool Whip

1 small package instant chocolate pudding
1 small package instant vanilla pudding
2 cups milk
1 cup thawed Cool Whip
Grated chocoate or M-and-M candies

Mix together the flour, margarine, and pecans. Press in the bottom of a 13 x 9 x 2-inch pan and bake 20 minutes at 350 degrees. Let cool. Mix the sugar, cream cheese and 1 cup of Cool Whip; spread it over crust. Mix the dry pudding mixes and the milk (do not follow directions on the pudding box). Spread this mixture on top of the previous layer in the pan. Top with a layer of Cool Whip. May sprinkle with grated chocolate or M-and-M candy pieces, if desired. Chill. Serves 12 to 15.

Beth Logan
Caddo Parish (Gilliam)

PINEAPPLE GELATIN

1 package lime Jello
1½ cups boiling water
12 large marshmallows
½ cup pineapple juice
1 cup crushed pineapple

2 cups nuts
1 8-ounce package cream cheese, softened
1 tablespoon mayonnaise
1 cup whipped cream

Dissolve one package of Lime Jello in boiling water with marshmallows. Add pineapple juice. Put in refrigerator until it begins to set. Combine cream cheese and add mayonnaise; add cheese mixture, crushed pineapple, and nuts to chilled mixture. Fold in whipped cream. Chill until congealed. Serves about 12 persons.

Mrs. Henry Hess (Peggy)
Avoyelles Parish (Moreauville)

FRUIT PIZZA

1 can cherry pie filling
1 large can crushed pineapple,
  undrained
1 18½-ounce package yellow
  cake mix

1 cup chopped pecans
½ cup plus 3 tablespoons
  margarine, melted

Preheat oven to 325 degrees. Grease 13 x 9 x 12-inch pan; set aside. Spread pie filling over bottom of pan; top with pineapple, including juice. Sprinkle dry cake mix over pineapple; top with pecans. Pour butter over cake mix layer. Bake at 325 degrees about 1 hour and 15 minutes or until golden brown. Serve hot with vanilla ice cream, if desired.

Mrs. Ronald R. Anderson
East Feliciana Parish (Ethel)

STRAWBERRY SURPRISE

First layer:
1 cup crushed vanilla wafers
1 cup chopped pecans

½ cup margarine, melted

Mix all ingredients; pack in 11 x 14-inch baking dish.

Second layer:
3 eggs
1 cup sugar

1 8-ounce package cream cheese,
  softened

Mix well; pour over first layer. Bake at 325 degrees for 35 to 40 minutes.

Third layer:
1 8-ounce carton commercial
  sour cream

ten and bake 10 minutes

FRESH APPLE CAKE

3 eggs
1½ cups Wesson oil
3 cups sugar
3 cups all-purpose flour
1 teaspoon soda
1 teaspoon baking powder
1 teaspoon salt
1 teaspoon cinnamon

1 teaspoon ground nutmeg
2 teaspoons vanilla extract
1 cup chopped nuts
3 cups chopped apples
1 cup chopped dates, coconut or
    drained, chopped fig preserves
    (optional)

Beat eggs, adding one at a time; add oil and sugar, creaming well. Sift flour with remaining dry ingredients; add to egg mixture. Stir in vanilla, pecans, apples and dates. Place in a greased and floured loafpan; bake at 325 degrees for 1 to 1½ hours or until done.

Note: Spoon batter into a greased tube pan and bake at 350 degrees for 45 minutes.

Mrs. C. L. Gauthier, Jr. (Narcille)
Avoyelles Parish (Moreauville)

FRESH APPLE CAKE I

1 cup vegetable oil
2 cups sugar
4 cups chopped Delicious
    apples (do not peel)
2 eggs
3 cups all-purpose flour
2 teaspoons soda

1 teaspoon salt
1½ teaspoons ground cinnamon
½ teaspoon ground allspice
1 teaspoon vanilla extract
1 cup nuts
1 cup raisins

Preheat oven to 325 degrees. Pour cooking oil over sugar and apples. Let soak for 1 hour. Beat 2 eggs lightly; add to sugar, apple and oil mixture. Add flour, soda, salt, cinnamon, allspice and vanilla. Mix well. Add nuts and raisins. Pour into a greased 10-inch tube pan. Bake at 325 degrees for 1 hour and 15 minutes. A delicious cake, very moist.

Lavon G. Pruitt
Webster Parish (Minden)

FRESH APPLE CAKE II

3 cups self-rising flour
3 cups sugar
3 eggs
1 cup Crisco oil

½ teaspoon baking soda
1 teaspoon ground cinnamon
1 teaspoon vanilla extract
4 medium green apples, diced

Preheat oven to 350 degrees. Combine ingredients in large bowl. (This dough is very stiff and it is best to work the apples in by hand.) Turn into a greased and floured 11 x 13-inch pan. Bake at 350 degrees for 1 hour.

Icing:

¼ cup margarine, softened
1 8-ounce package cream
  cheese, softened

1½ cups powdered sugar
1 teaspoon vanilla extract
2 to 3 tablespoons milk

Cream margarine and cream cheese; beat in sugar and vanilla. Add milk to make spreadable. Spread on hot apple cake.

Wynnde Farmer
Beauregard Parish (Dry Creek)

OATMEAL CAKE

1¼ cups boiling water
½ cup margarine
1 cup uncooked oats
1 cup firmly packed light brown
  sugar

1 cup sugar
1¼ cups plain flour
1 teaspoon soda
1½ teaspoons ground cinnamon
2 eggs

Preheat oven to 350 degrees. Combine boiling water, oleo, oatmeal, and set aside for 20 minutes. In another bowl mix brown sugar, white sugar, flour, soda and cinnamon. Combine both bowls of ingredients and add 2 beaten eggs. Mix thoroughly. Pour into a 9 x 13 inch greased dish and bake for 35 minutes at 350 degrees.

Topping:

½ cup margarine
¾ cup sugar
¼ cup sweetened condensed
  milk

1 teaspoon vanilla extract
1 cup chopped pecans

In a saucepan, combine margarine, sugar, condensed milk and vanilla. Bring to a boil, stirring constantly over low heat. Do not overcook. Add chopped pecans. Have topping ready when cake comes out of oven. Spread topping evenly over cake and place it under the broiler and brown, watching carefully.

Mrs. Gilbert Mills (Lejeune)
East Baton Rouge Parish (Zachary)

BANANA SPLIT CAKE I

2 cups graham cracker crumbs
1½ cups margarine, melted and divided
2 cups powdered sugar
2 eggs
4 bananas
1 8¼-ounce can crushed pineapple, drained

½ cup chopped pecans
½ small jar cherries, drained and chopped
1 small container Cool Whip, thawed

Make crust with graham cracker crumbs and ½ cup melted margarine; press in a pie plate. Mix 2 cups powdered sugar, remaining 1 cup melted margarine and 2 eggs. Pour these ingredients over crust. Slice 4 bananas over top of sugar layer. Spoon crushed pineapple over bananas. Add Cool Whip on top of crushed pineapple. Sprinkle ½ cup pecans and chopped cherries on top of pecans. A colorful and delicious dessert!

Mrs. Sam Womack
East Baton Rouge Parish (Zachary)

BANANA SPLIT CAKE II

1½ cups margarine, softened and divided
2 cups graham cracker crumbs
¼ cup sugar
¼ teaspoon ground cinnamon
2 eggs
2 cups sifted powdered sugar
1 teaspoon vanilla extract

1 20-ounce can crushed pineapple, drained
4 bananas
Juice of 1 lemon
1 8-ounce container Cool Whip, thawed
½ cup chopped pecans
Chopped maraschino cherries

Combine ½ cup margarine, 2 cups graham cracker crumbs, sugar, and cinnamon; mix well. Pat firmly in bottom of a 13 x 9 x 2-inch pan. Cream 1 cup margarine well; add eggs, one at a time, beating after each. Add sugar, a little at a time; add vanilla. Beat on high for 15 minutes with mixer. *(Very important).* Spoon sugar mixture on crust. Place pineapple on top of filling; slice 4 bananas and dip in lemon juice. Layer bananas on top of pineapple layer. Cover with Cool Whip. Garnish with chopped nuts and cherries. Chill. Yield: 8 to 10 servings.

Mrs. Donald Johnson (Brenda)
Ouachita Parish (Monroe)

BANANA SPLIT CAKE III

2 eggs
1 cup butter or margarine,
  softened
2 cups powdered sugar
2 9-inch graham cracker crusts
2 or 3 bananas

1 16-ounce can crushed pineapple,
  drained
1½ cups chopped pecans
1 cup chopped cherries
2 cups thawed Cool Whip

Beat eggs, butter, and powdered sugar for 10 minutes. Pour half of mixture into each crust. Add sliced bananas in layers on top. Add crushed pineapple. Mix pecans, cherries and Cool Whip; spoon onto top of pineapple layer. Chill. Yield: 2 (9-inch) pies.

Mrs. Henry Hess (Peggy)
Avoyelles Parish (Moreauville)

BANANA SPLIT CAKE IV

1 cup margarine, divided
2½ cups powdered sugar
2 cups graham crackers
2 egg whites
1 8¼-ounce can crushed
  pineapple

4 ripe bananas
1 8-ounce container Cool Whip,
  thawed
1 cup chopped pecans
½ cup chopped maraschino
  cherries

First layer: Melt ½ cup margarine in a 2-quart pot; add ½ cup powdered sugar and all of graham crackers. Mix together and press into bottom of a 13 x 9 x 2-inch pan.
Second layer: In a small mixing bowl, beat egg whites, ½ cup margarine, and remaining 2 cups powdered sugar for 10 minutes. Spoon over crust layer in pan.
Third layer: Drain 1 can of crushed pineapple and spoon over sugar layer.
Fourth layer: Slice bananas (crosswise) over top of pineapple.
Fifth layer: Spread Cool Whip over bananas, and sprinkle with chopped pecans and chopped cherries.
Refrigerate at least one hour until ready to serve.

Mrs. James Graugnard, Jr.
West St. James Parish (St. James)

RUM POUND CAKE I

1 cup margarine, softened
½ cup shortening
3 cups sugar
5 eggs
3 cups all-purpose flour

½ teaspoon salt
1 teaspoon baking powder
1 cup milk
1 teaspoon rum flavoring
1 teaspoon almond flavoring

Preheat oven to 325 degrees. Cream margarine and shortening in large bowl. Add the sugar, one tablespoon at a time, beating constantly. Add eggs, one at a time, beating well. Sift the flour, salt, and baking powder together. Add flour mixture and milk alternately to creamed mixture ending with the flour. Add the extracts; mix well. Place in a greased and floured 10-inch tube pan; bake at 325 degrees for 1 hour and 25 minutes.

Mrs. James Parkerson (Joyce)
Ouachita Parish (Monroe)

RUM POUND CAKE II

1 cup margarine
½ cup Crisco shortening
3 cups sugar
5 eggs
3 cups cake flour

½ teaspoon salt
1 teaspoon baking powder
1 cup milk
1 teaspoon rum extract
1 teaspoon coconut extract

Cream margarine and Crisco until light and fluffy; add sugar, a spoonful at a time, beating constantly. Add eggs, one at a time, beating well. Sift flour, salt, and baking powder together; add alternately with milk to creamed mixture, beginning and ending with flour. Add extracts last. Place in a 10-inch tube pan; bake at 325 degrees for about 1½ hours. Remove from pan and glaze while the cake is hot.

Glaze:
1 cup sugar
½ cup water

1 teaspoon almond extract

Combine all ingredients in a saucepan; bring to a full boil. Remove from heat, and add almond extract. Let glaze cool. As soon as the cake is done, remove it from pan and brush on the glaze.

Note: Be sure to follow the directions in adding the sugar. This recipe was published in our church cookbook, submitted by my pastor, Reverand James R. Shepherd. Needless to say, this exceptionally good cake is enjoyed by our congregation quite often at church suppers. Also he bakes this for our shut-ins.

Mrs. Doug Moore (Liz)
Ouachita Parish (Monroe)

CINNAMON-TOPPED SOUR CREAM POUND CAKE

1 cup butter, softened	1 8-ounce carton commercial sour
2 cups sugar	cream
2 eggs	1 teaspoon vanilla extract
2 cups all-purpose flour	1/2 cup chopped pecans
1 teaspoon baking powder	1/2 teaspoon ground cinnamon
1/2 teaspoon salt	2 teaspoons sugar

Combine butter and sugar with an electric mixer until light and fluffy. Add eggs, one at a time, beating 30 seconds after each addition. Combine flour, baking powder, and salt; stir 1/3 of the flour mixture into creamed mixture; stir until blended. Add 1/2 carton sour cream to creamed mixture; stir until blended. Repeat procedure, ending with dry ingredients. Stir in vanilla extract. Pour 1/3 of the batter into a greased bundt pan. Combine pecans, cinnamon, and 2 teaspoons sugar; sprinkle 1/3 of mixture over batter in bundt pan. Pour 1/3 of the batter over topping; sprinkle another 1/3 of cinnamon mixture over batter. Pour remaining batter into pan; sprinkle remaining nut mixture over batter. Bake at 350 degrees for 55 to 60 minutes. Cool 1 hour in pan; invert.

Note: This cake leaves a delicious aroma in your kitchen.

Mrs. Richard Hebert (Marca)
Evangeline Parish (Ville Platte)

PECAN POUND CAKE

2 cups butter (do not use	3 cups all-purpose flour
margarine)	1 ounce lemon flavoring
2 cups sugar	1 ounce vanilla flavoring
6 eggs	Pinch of salt
1 pound chopped pecans	

You can use either a large bundt pan or two loafpans. Put butter in all divisions of bundt pan or pour cooking oil in bottom of loafpans and set in cold oven. Cream butter and sugar thoroughly. In another mixing bowl put six eggs and beat together until foamy. Gradually pour into sugar and butter mixture. Mix flour and pecans together in a small bowl; stir to mix well. Add flour and nuts alternately with extracts to creamed mixture. Add salt. While mixing batter, turn oven to 250 degrees and let butter be melting in pans. Pour batter into hot pan and set back in oven. If you use a bundt pan, bake for three hours; if you use loafpans, bake for 1 1/2 hours. Let cool, or if you like, while still warm, pour a few drops of wine over the cake and let it get cold before wrapping in foil and freezing. When ready to use, take out the night before and let thaw.

Note: I give these at Christmas to special friends.

Mrs. Don Odom (Brenda)
Claiborne Parish (Homer)

POUND CAKE

1 cup butter
½ pound Crisco shortening
3 cups sugar

9 eggs
3 cups all-purpose flour
1 teaspoon vanilla extract

Preheat oven to 350 degrees. Cream margarine and Crisco until light; add sugar, mixing well. Add eggs, one at a time, beating after each addition. Sift flour 3 times; gradually add to creamed mixture. Beat well. Add vanilla. Pour into a greased 10-inch tube pan. Bake at 350 degrees for 1 hour.

Mrs. Emmett Moore (Lillian)
Ouachita Parish (Monroe)

DOE'S GATEAU SIROP

1½ cups sugar
1 cup vegetable oil
1 cup Steens syrup
2 teaspoons soda
1 cup boiling water

½ teaspoon ground cinnamon
1 teaspoon ground ginger
½ teaspoon ground nutmeg
2½ cups all-purpose flour
2 eggs, well beaten

In large bowl, combine sugar, oil, and syrup; stir well. Add soda to boiling water. Add water combination to creamed mixture; mix well. To above mixture, add cinnamon, ginger, nutmeg and flour; beat until thoroughly mixed. Fold in eggs; bake at 350 degrees in a well greased 10 x 8-inch pan for 40 minutes.

Mrs. Jackie Theriot (Sue)
St. Martin Parish (St. Martinville)

soda water; beat thoroughly. Add eggs, 1 at a time, beating after each addition. Gradually stir flour into batter. Blend in fruits and nuts. Pour into greased tube pan and bake at 275 degrees for about 1½ hours. Remove from pan to cool, but leave paper on cake until used.

Mrs. Marie Perque
St. James Parish (Vacherie)

FRESH COCONUT CAKE

1 18½-ounce package butter
cake mix

Prepare cake mix according to package instructions.

Filling:

2 7-ounce packages frozen
fresh coconut, thawed
2 cups sugar

1 8-ounce carton commercial sour
cream
1 4-ounce package Cool Whip,
thawed

Mix in a large bowl, coconut, sugar, and sour cream. After baking cake, split each layer in half, making four layers. Spread the mixture between layers of the cake. Add the Cool Whip to the remaining filling and seal the outside of the cake with it. Let the cake set in the refrigerator for 3 days before cutting.

Note: It is hard to let it set three days without eating it so you will need to prepare it ahead of time.

Pam Accardo
Ouachita Parish (Monroe)

OLD TIME COCONUT CAKE

1 cup butter
2 cups sugar
4 eggs
3 cups all-purpose flour

1 cup milk
1 teaspoon baking powder
1 teaspoon vanilla

Cream butter and sugar in a large mixing bowl. Add eggs, one at a time, beating well after each. Sift flour and baking powder together. Add to creamed mixture alternately with milk, beginning and ending with flour. Stir in vanilla. Bake in 2 layer pans in 350 degree oven. When cool, put filling between the two layers. The center filling should be as thick as the layer.

Filling:
1 fresh grated coconut
Juice of 2 lemons
2 tablespoons cornstarch

2 cups sugar
1 cup boiling water

Mix above ingredients in a saucepan. Cook over medium heat until thick. Let cool; spread between cake layers. Ice cake with white icing. I use 7-minute icing with a little lemon juice.

Note: This cake keeps well and gets better with age.

Mrs. Earl Duhe
Caldwell Parish (Columbia)

COCONUT POUND CAKE

1 cup softened butter or
  margarine
⅔ cup shortening
3 cups sugar
5 eggs

3 cups all-purpose flour
1 teaspoon baking powder
1 cup milk
1 teaspoon vanilla extract
1 3-ounce can flaked coconut

Preheat oven to 300 degrees. Cream butter and shortening with sugar; beat in eggs, one at a time. Add flour and baking powder alternately with the milk. Add vanilla and coconut. Pour into a greased and floured tube pan or bundt pan. Bake at 300 degrees for two hours. Let cool in pan 5 or 10 minutes before inverting onto plate.

Note: This cake makes a good crust while baking. It can be prepared with an electric mixer or by hand.

Karen Dill
Red River Parish (Westdale)

COCONUT CAKE

½ cup hot water
1 3-ounce package lemon Jello
1 18½-ounce yellow Duncan
 Hines cake mix
⅔ cup Wesson oil
4 eggs

¼ cup orange juice
1 teaspoon butter flavoring
1 teaspoon vanilla extract
1½ cups sugar
½ to ⅔ cup sugar

Combine water and Jello, stirring well until dissolved; let cool. Mix all ingredients except sugar and water. Pour batter into 3 greased and floured 9-inch cake pans. Bake according to cake package directions. Mix sugar and water and put between layers of cake. Frost cake with 2 boxes Betty Crocker Fluffy White Frosting.

Annie R. Cooper
Caldwell Parish (Columbia)

COCONUT CAKE

1 cup butter or margarine,
 softened
2 cups sugar
3 cups all-purpose flour

4 eggs
1 tablespoon baking powder
1 cup milk
1 teaspoon vanilla extract

In a medium mixing bowl, cream butter and sugar. Add eggs; mix well. Combine dry ingredients; add dry ingredients, and milk, alternately to creamed mixture. Add vanilla. Fill 3 greased and floured 9-inch cake pans. Bake at 350 degrees for 45 minutes. Let layers cool.

Coconut Filling:
1 7-ounce can flaked coconut
1 cup milk
¾ cup sugar

1 tablespoon butter or margarine
1 tablespoon cornstarch

Cook the above ingredients, except cornstarch, in a medium saucepan until mixture comes to a hard boil. Then add 1 tablespoon cornstarch; cook until thickened. Cool; spread between cake layers. Frost cake with seven-minute frosting.

Eveline Smith
Beauregard Parish (DeRidder)

FUDGE RIBBON CAKE

Cake:

1 cup sugar	½ teaspoon salt
¾ cup butter	2 cups cake flour
2 eggs, well beaten	½ cup milk
⅛ teaspoon soda	1 teaspoon vanilla extract

Cream butter and sugar until light. Add eggs; mix thoroughly. Add soda and salt. Add flour, alternately with milk, to creamed mixture. Add vanilla and mix well. Pour batter into 2 greased and floured cake pans. Swirl Fudge Ribbon on top of batter, swirling with a knife. Bake at 375 degrees for 30 minutes or until cake springs back to touch Top with fudge icing or top slices with whipped cream.

Fudge Ribbon:

1 cup sugar	1 egg, well beaten
¾ cup cocoa	1 cup milk

Combine sugar and cocoa in the top of a double boiler; add well beaten egg. Stirring constantly, add milk, and cook in double boiler until thick. Let mixture cool.

Note: This is an old recipe of Essie Harrigill Zimmerman submitted by her daughter.

Mrs. S. L. Ford, Sr.
Catahoula Parish (Jonesville)

TUNNEL OF FUDGE CAKE

1½ cups butter, at room temperature	2 cups sifted all-purpose flour
6 eggs	2 cups chopped walnuts or pecans
1½ cups sugar	1 package Pillsbury Fudge Frosting Mix

Preheat oven to 350 degrees. Cream butter; add 1 egg at a time, beating well. Add sugar; cream on high speed until fluffy. Stir in flour; add nuts and mix well. Pour into greased and floured 10-inch bundt pan. Bake at 350 degrees for 60 minutes. Cool 2 hours before removing from pan. (Don't cheat—it's very moist).

Note: This is a chocolate lover's delight!

Donna Bolton Jenkins
East Baton Rouge Parish (Baton Rouge)

TWENTY MINUTE CHOCOLATE CAKE

½ cup margarine
¼ cup cocoa
1 cup water
2 cups all-purpose flour
2 cups sugar
½ cup buttermilk

2 eggs
1 teaspoon soda
½ teaspoon salt
1 teaspoon ground cinnamon
1 teaspoon vanilla extract

Preheat oven to 400 degrees. Grease and flour 15 x 10-inch sheet cake pan; set aside. Combine margarine, cocoa, and water in saucepan. Bring to boil; remove from heat. Sift flour and sugar into large bowl. Add chocolate mixture and beat at medium speed until blended. Continue beating while adding buttermilk, eggs, soda, salt, cinnamon, and vanilla. Pour into prepared pan and bake at 400 degrees for 20 minutes. (Cake may not appear to be done, but it is.) Remove from oven; let cake remain in pan and frost while hot.

Icing:
1 pound box powdered sugar,
  sifted
½ cup margarine, melted
¼ cup cocoa

6 tablespoons milk
1 cup chopped pecans
1 teaspoon vanilla extract

Combine sugar, margarine, cocoa and milk in a mixing bowl; mix well. Stir in vanilla and pecans. Spread on cake while hot. (I melt cocoa and margarine on stove and combine the rest.) Delicious! Cool cake before cutting.

Mrs. Fernand Falgoust (Joan)
St. James Parish (St. James)

DEVIL'S FOOD CAKE

1 cup sugar
½ cup cocoa
1 tablespoon all-purpose flour
1 egg, beaten
1 cup milk
½ cup butter

1 cup sugar
2 eggs
1 teaspoon soda
½ cup buttermilk
2 cups all-purpose flour
1 teaspoon vanilla extract

Boil first 5 ingredients until thick over low heat; let cool. Add remaining ingredients and mix well. Pour into three 8-inch cake pans; bake at 350 degrees until done for 40 minutes.

Annie R. Cooper
Caldwell Parish (Columbia)

CHOCOLATE TORTE

Crust:
1 cup vanilla wafer crumbs
¼ cup chopped almonds

3 tablespoons butter, melted

Mix ingredients together; pack into an angel food cake pan. Freeze.

Filling:
1 package vanilla pudding
1 cup milk
½ teaspoon almond extract

½ cup whipping cream, whipped
½ gallon chocolate ice cream,
softened

Beat pudding and milk for 1 minute. Fold in extract and whipped cream. Spoon a thin layer of softened ice cream over frozen crust. Top with ½ of pudding. Repeat layers with remaining ice cream and pudding until ingredients are used—end layering with ice cream. Freeze 6 hours. Serve as you would slice a cake. A cool summer treat!

Mrs. Martin Cancienne (Sally)
Assumption Parish (Belle Rose)

CHOCOLATE CAKE SUPREME

1 18½-ounce box Duncan
Hines yellow butter cake mix
4 eggs
½ cup Crisco oil

¼ cup sugar
¼ cup water
1 cup commercial sour cream

Combine all ingredients in a large mixing bowl. Mix well at medium speed on mixer; beat on high speed for two minutes. Pour into three 9-inch cake pans. Bake at 375 degrees for 25 minutes.

Frosting:
½ cup butter or margarine
⅓ cup cocoa
¼ teaspoon salt

⅔ cup evaporated milk
2 cups sugar
2 teaspoons vanilla extract

Melt butter slowly in heavy saucepan; add remining ingredients, except vanilla. Stir and mix well. Boil for three minutes over medium heat. Add vanilla. Set aside to cool. While warm beat to spreading consistency. Do not overbeat. Spread on cooled cake (Hardens on cake).

Helen Morland
Concordia Parish (Monterey)

Cakes and Frostings

GERMAN CHOCOLATE CAKE

Cake:

2 cups sugar
1 cup shortening
4 egg yolks
¼ pound (4-ounces) German
   sweet chocolate
½ cup boiling water

2½ cups all-purpose flour
1 teaspoon soda
1 cup buttermilk
1 teaspoon vanilla extract
Pinch of salt
4 egg whites, stiffly beaten

Preheat oven to 350 degrees. Cream sugar and shortening until fluffy. Add egg yolks, one at a time. Melt chocolate in boiling water; add to creamed mixture. Combine flour and soda; add flour mixture alternately with buttermilk to creamed mixture. Add vanilla and salt. Fold in beaten egg whites. Pour into three 9-inch cake pans. Bake at 350 degrees for 30 minutes.

Icing:

1½ cups sugar
1½ cups evaporated milk
¾ cup butter
4 egg yolks, beaten

2 cups flaked coconut
1 cup chopped pecans
2 teaspoons vanilla extract

Cook sugar, milk, butter, and egg yolks in a double boiler over low heat until thickened stirring constantly. Remove from heat; add coconut, pecans, and vanilla. Pour between layers and on top of cake.

Mrs. Donald Johnson (Brenda)
Ouachita Parish (Monroe)

MILKY WAY CAKE

8 Milky Way candy bars
1 cup margarine
2 cups sugar
4 eggs
2½ cups all-purpose flour

½ teaspoon soda
½ teaspoon salt
1 cup buttermilk
1 cup chopped pecans or 1 cup
   grated coconut

Melt candy bars and 2 tablespoons margarine on low heat. Set aside. Cream sugar and ½ cup plus 6 tablespoons margarine; add eggs, one at a time, beating well after each egg. Sift flour, soda and salt; add to creamed mixture. Add buttermilk. Fold in candy mixture, nuts or coconut. Pour batter in tube pan; bake at 350 degrees for 1½ to 2 hours.

Note: If you like, you can use a cream glaze on top.

Mrs. Perry Fisher (Bert)
Ouachita Parish (Monroe)

"THE CAKE"

½ cup butter, softened
1 18½-ounce box Duncan
  Hines yellow cake mix
1 tablespoon water
1 egg

1 8-ounce package Philadelphia
  cream cheese, softened
3 eggs, at room temperature
1 16-ounce box powdered sugar
1½ teaspoons vanilla extract

Cream butter; add cake mix, water, and egg. Beat well in electric mixer. Press dough into a 13 x 9 x 2-inch pyrex baking dish. Beat cream cheese until light; beat in eggs, one egg at a time, beating well after each addition. Add powdered sugar; beat well. Add vanilla. Pour mixture over pressed dough. Bake at 350 degrees about 45 minutes or until browned. Cool completely and cut into squares. Delicious!

Grace Graugnard
St. James Parish (St. James)

PINK LEMONADE CAKE

1 18½-ounce box yellow cake
  mix
1 quart vanilla ice cream
6 drops red food coloring
1 6-ounce can frozen pink
  lemonade concentrate,

1 cup whipping cream
2 tablespoons sugar
Decorative rosebud candy mints
  (optional)

PINEAPPLE SOUR CREAM CAKE

1 18½-ounce box butter cake
  mix
1 can crushed pineapple
½ cup sugar

⅓ cup cornstarch
2 tablespoons lemon juice
2 8-ounce cartons sour cream

Bake cake according to package directions, putting batter in 3 pans. Cool. Cook pineapple, sugar, cornstarch and lemon juice for about 7 minutes or until thick. Let cool. Stir in sour cream, and spread mixture in between layers and on top of cake.

Mrs. Wilmer Juneau (Joycie)
Avoyelles Parish (Bordelonville)

CREME DE MENTHE CAKE

1 18½-ounce package deluxe
  white cake mix
4 large eggs
1 3½-ounce package vanilla
  pudding mix
½ cup orange juice

½ cup vegetable oil
¼ cup water
¼ cup green creme de menthe
  liqueur
¼ teaspoon vanilla extract
1 5½-ounce can chocolate syrup

Preheat oven to 350 degrees. Grease and flour 10-inch bundt or tube pan. Combine all ingredients except chocolate syrup, in a large mixing bowl; beat about 4 minutes. Remove ⅓ of batter to a separate bowl; add chocolate syrup to the ⅓ portion, and pour into prepared pan. Pour remaining batter over chocolate layer (do not mix). Bake at 350 degrees for 35 to 45 minutes or until done. Cool in pan.

Glaze:
1 cup powdered sugar

2 tablespoons creme de menthe or
  milk and green food color

Combine ingredients to form a glaze; spoon over cake.

Mrs. Clark Van Sickle (Virginia)
East Baton Rouge Parish (Baton Rouge)

STRAWBERRY CAKE

1 18½-ounce box yellow cake
  mix
¾ cup Wesson oil
¾ cup frozen sliced
  strawberries, thawed

½ cup strawberry juice
½ cup flaked coconut
4 eggs
1 box strawberry Jello
¾ cup chopped pecans

Mix all ingredients, except pecans, in a large bowl; mix well. Add pecans. Pour batter into a greased 12 x 9 x 2-inch dish. Bake at 350 degrees for 45 minutes. Let cool.

Strawberry Icing:
1 1-pound box powdered sugar
½ cup margarine, softened
⅓ cup frozen sliced
  strawberries, thawed

½ cup flaked coconut
½ cup chopped pecans

Combine all ingredients; mix until spreading consistency. Frost cooled cake.

Mrs. Sam Womack (Tops)
East Baton Rouge Parish (Zachary)

STRAWBERRY DELIGHT CAKE

1 18½-ounce box Duncan
Hines yellow cake mix
1 8-ounce package Philadelphia
cream cheese, softened

1 8-ounce container Cool Whip,
thawed
1 16-ounce frozen strawberries in
syrup, thawed

Prepare cake mix according to package directions. Allow cake to cool and split layers in half. Beat cream cheese; add Cool Whip. Drain half of the syrup from strawberries; add strawberries and ½ syrup to cheese mixture. Beat well. Frost each layer and top cake with a heavy frosting. Refrigerate. Improves second day.

Grace Graugnard
St. James Parish (St. James)

SWEETHEART CREAM CAKE

1 cup buttermilk
1 teaspoon soda
5 eggs, separated
½ cup margarine, softened
½ cup Crisco shortening
2 cups sugar

2 cups flour
1 teaspoon vanilla extract
1 cup chopped pecans
1 3½-ounce can Angel Flake
coconut

Preheat oven to 350 degrees. In small bowl, combine buttermilk and soda; set aside. Beat egg whites until stiff; set aside. Cream margarine, Crisco, and sugar until light and fluffy. Add egg yolks, and beat well. Add buttermilk to creamed mixture alternately with flour. Stir in vanilla; fold in egg whites. Gently stir in nuts and coconut. Spoon into three 9-inch greased and floured pans; bake at 350 degrees for 25 to 30 minutes. Let cool completely; and frost.

Icing:
1 8-ounce package cream
cheese, softened
½ cup margarine, softened

1 16-ounce package powdered
sugar
1 teaspoon vanilla extract

Beat together cream cheese and margarine until light and fluffy; add sugar, and beat until smooth. Add vanilla; mix well. Frost cake between layers, keeping plenty for top and sides. Sprinkle ground pecans between layers and on cake top, if desired. Yield: one 3-layer cake.

Mrs. Grace Graugnard
West St. James Parish (St. James)

SOUTHERN SPICY GINGERBREAD (OLD TIME RECIPE)

¾ cup sugar
¾ cup cane syrup
¾ cup melted shortening
2 eggs, well beaten
2½ cups all-purpose flour
2 teaspoons ground ginger

1½ teaspoons ground cinnamon
½ teaspoon ground cloves
½ teaspoon ground nutmeg
½ teaspoon baking powder
2 teaspoons soda
1 cup boiling water

Mix sugar, syrup and melted shortening in a large mixing bowl. Add eggs, beating well. Add dry ingredients which have been sifted and mixed. Then add hot water. Pour into 12 x 9 x 2-inch greased pan; bake at 350 degrees for 30 minutes. Good without icing, but a lemon, butter, powdered sugar icing is good on it.

Mrs. B. F. Lemoine, Jr. (Grace)
Avoyelles Parish (Hamburg)

RED VELVET CAKE I

2½ cups all-purpose flour
1 teaspoon cocoa
1 teaspoon soda
1 teaspoon salt
1½ cups oil
1½ cups sugar

2 eggs
1 cup buttermilk
1 teaspoon vanilla extract
1 teaspoon vinegar
1 2-ounce bottle red food coloring

Preheat oven to 350 degrees. Sift together flour, cocoa, soda, and salt. Mix oil, sugar, and eggs in a large mixing bowl; add dry ingredients, then buttermilk, vanilla, vinegar, and food coloring. Mix well. Grease and flour four 8-inch pans or three 9-inch pans; pour batter into pans. Bake at 350 degrees for 25 minutes. Let cool; frost. Yield: one layer cake.

Frosting:
1 8-ounce package cream
  cheese, softened
½ cup margarine, softened

1 cup chopped nuts
1 16-ounce box powdered sugar,
  unsifted

Cream together cheese and margarine; add sugar and nuts, beating well. Spread frosting over cake.

Mrs. Donald Johnson (Brenda)
Ouachita Parish (Monroe)

RED VELVET CAKE II

1½ cups sugar
½ cup shortening
2 eggs
2 cups all-purpose flour
1 teaspoon salt
1 tablespoon cocoa

1 cup buttermilk (or 1 cup milk
  plus 1 teaspoon vinegar)
1 teaspoon vanilla extract
1 2-ounce jar red food coloring
1 teaspoon baking soda
1 tablespoon vinegar

Cream sugar and shortening. Add eggs; beat well. Sift flour, salt and cocoa together; add alternately with buttermilk to creamed mixture; add vanilla and red food coloring, mixing well. Combine soda and vinegar; fold into batter. (Do not beat the batter.) Pour batter into greased and floured 13 x 9 x 2-inch pan; bake at 350 degrees for 30 minutes. Let cool; frost. Yield: one cake.

Frosting:
1 cup milk
¼ teaspoon salt
¼ cup all-purpose flour
1 cup sugar

1 cup butter (not margarine)
1 teaspoon vanilla extract
Flaked coconut (optional)

Combine milk, salt, and flour in a saucepan; boil until thickened. Cover and chill. Combine sugar, butter, and vanilla; beat until fluffy. Add chilled mixture and continue beating until very fluffy. Spread on cake and sprinkle with coconut, if desired.

Mrs. Charles Klein (Elizabeth)
Allen Parish (Oberlin)

YOLANDE'S WHITE FRUITCAKE

2 cups margarine or butter,
  softened
2 cups sugar
6 eggs

3 pounds mixed candied fruits
1 pound chopped pecans
4 cups all-purpose flour
1 2-ounce bottle lemon extract

In large mixer bowl, cream margarine and sugar until light. Add eggs, one at a time, mixing well after each. In separate bowl, mix fruits, nuts, and ½ cup flour. Add lemon extract to creamed mixture; mix well. Add flour to creamed mixture, mixing thoroughly. Add fruit-nut mixture to creamed mixture. Pour into two greased and floured 10-inch tube pans. Bake at 325 degrees for 2 hours or until done. Test by inserting a toothpick into cake; if it comes out clean, the cake is done. Let cool; then wrap in foil or place in a tin container. Whiskey may be put on the cake and aged, if desired. Yield: one 10-inch cake.

Mrs. Jackie Theriot (Sue)
St. Martin Parish (St. Martinville)

TEN-POUND FRUITCAKE

4½ cups all-purpose flour
1 pound chopped pecans
1 pound mixed candied fruit
1 teaspoon ground allspice
1 teaspoon ground mace
2 teaspoons ground cinnamon
2 cups margarine, softened
1 16-ounce box brown sugar
1 pint fig preserves

1 cup blackberry jelly
10 eggs
½ cup milk
½ cup dry cooking sherry
Additional candied cherries
Pecan halves
Blanched almonds

Combine flour with fruit, nuts, and spices; stir well, and set 1 cup mixture aside. Cream margarine and sugar until light and fluffy in a large mixing bowl. Add preserves and jelly; mix well. Add eggs, one at a time, beating well after each addition. Add flour mixture to creamed mixture, alternately with milk and sherry; mix well. Add remaining 1 cup flour-nut mixture; mix well. Pack batter into foil-lined 9 x 5 x 3-inch loafpans. Garnish the tops of each loaf with candied cherries, pecan halves, and almonds. Place a pan of hot water on bottom shelf of oven. Bake at 275 degrees for 2 hours or until firm to touch. Let cool; remove from pans.

Mrs. Gilbert McCroskey (Granny)
Iberia Parish (New Iberia)

MOM'S FRUITCAKE—MERE' TEEYA

½ teaspoon soda
⅓ cup water or pineapple juice
1 cup sugar
1 cup shortening
3 eggs
3 cups all-purpose flour
1 cup dark syrup
1 teaspoon ground cinnamon
½ teaspoon ground cloves
½ teaspoon ground allspice
¼ teaspoon ground nutmeg

⅓ quart ground pecans
⅔ quart coarsely chopped pecans
⅔ quart seedless raisins
1 cup grated grapefruit ring
2 cups pear preserves
3 cups mushmelon preserves
⅓ quart fig preserves, chopped
⅓ quart can red pineapple, chopped
1 16-ounce jar maraschino cherries,
   drained and chopped

Dissolve soda in ⅓ cup water or juice; set aside. Combine sugar and shortening; add eggs and beat well. Add remaining ingredients and mix well. Bake at 275 degrees until done, about 1½ hours. Yield: six 1-pound cakes.

Note: This recipe has been in the family for 70 years. The time had to be decided by the second generation, as the first baked them in wood stoves.

Mrs. Herman Waguespack (Jerry)
St. James Parish (Vacherie)

ICE BOX FRUITCAKE

1 box plus 1 pack graham
  crackers, crushed
1½ cups chopped pecans or
  English walnuts
1 cup raisins (more or less as
  desired)
1 14-ounce can Angel Flake
  coconut

1 pound candied pineapple,
  chopped
1 pound candied cherries, chopped
1 cup sugar
1 cup undiluted canned milk
1 10-ounce pack marshmallows

In very large container, mix first six ingredients. In top of double boiler combine sugar, milk and marshmallows; cook until marshmallows are melted. Pour melted mixture over dry ingredients; mix thoroughly. Pack in containers and refrigerate. Bake at 300° for 2 hours or until done.

Note: Other fruits and nuts may be added to taste, if desired. Better when aged.

Mrs. Garland Broussard (Diane)
St. Martin Parish (St. Martinville)

NUT CAKE

1 cup butter, softened
2 cups sugar
6 eggs
4 cups all-purpose flour
1 teaspoon baking powder
½ cup molasses
¼ cup whiskey
1 15-ounce box seedless raisins

1 quart chopped pecans
1 small bottle maraschino cherries,
  drained and chopped
2 8-ounce packages pitted dates
1 teaspoon ground cinnamon
1 teaspoon ground nutmeg
1 teaspoon ground allspice
¼ cup all-purpose flour

In large bowl, mix butter and sugar until light. Add eggs and 4 cups flour alternately with baking powder until thoroughly mixed. Add molasses and whiskey to batter; mix until the liquids blend with batter. In a separate bowl, combine raisins, pecans, cinnamon, nutmeg, allspice, cherries, dates and remaining ¼ cup flour. Combine batter and fruit mixture until thoroughly mixed. Grease and flour a 10-inch tube pan. Pour cake batter into tube pan; bake at 250 degrees for 2 hours or until a toothpick comes out of cake clean.

Note: This recipe belonged to Mrs. Lena Jordan.

Mrs. Mark Swafford
Natchitoches Parish (Natchitoches)

ITALIAN CREME CAKE

½ cup margarine
½ cup shortening
2 cups sugar
6 egg yolks
2 cups all-purpose flour
1 teaspoon soda

1 cup buttermilk
1 teaspoon vanilla extract
1 3½-ounce can flaked coconut
1 cup chopped nuts
6 egg whites, stiffly beaten

Cream margarine and shortening until fluffy; add sugar and beat until smooth. Add egg yolks; beat well. Sift flour and soda together; add to creamed mixture alternately with buttermilk. Stir in vanilla, coconut and nuts. Fold in stiffly beaten egg whites. Bake in 3 well greased and floured 9-inch cake pans at 350 degrees for 25 minutes or until cake is done.

Frosting:
1 8-ounce package cream
   cheese, softened
¼ cup margarine, softened

1 pound box powdered sugar
1 teaspoon vanilla extract
1 cup chopped pecans

Beat cream cheese and margarine until smooth; add sugar and mix well. Add vanilla; fold in pecans. Spread frosting between layers of cake, on sides, and over top. Store in refrigerator. Makes 20 servings.

Sandra Sotile
Ascension Parish (Donaldsonville)

MOIST PINEAPPLE CAKE

2 cups all-purpose flour
1½ cups sugar
Dash salt
2 teaspoons soda

2 eggs
1 teaspoon vanilla extract
½ cup Wesson oil
1 10-ounce can crushed pineapple

Combine dry ingredients; add other remaining ingredients and mix well. Bake 45 minutes at 325 degrees in a greased oblong pan.

Icing:
½ cup margarine
1 cup sugar
½ cup Pet evaporated milk

½ cup chopped nuts
1 cup coconut

Melt margarine; add sugar and milk. Cook 2 minutes. Add nuts and coconut. Pour over hot cake.

Mrs. Roy Anderson (Catherine)
Ouachita Parish (Monroe)

PINA COLADA CAKE

1 18½-ounce package white
   cake mix
4 eggs
½ cup water
⅓ cup dark rum (80 proof)

¼ cup Wesson oil
1 3-ounce package coconut cream
   or vanilla instant pudding
1 cup flaked coconut (only if vanilla
   pudding is used)

Blend all ingredients, except coconut in large mixer bowl. Beat 4 minutes at medium speed. Pour into 2 greased and floured 9-inch layer pans. Bake at 350 degrees for 25 to 30 minutes or until cake springs back when lightly pressed. Cool in pan 15 minutes, remove and cool on rack.

Note: When using vanilla pudding, increase water to ¾ cup and add 1 cup flaked coconut to batter.

Frosting:
1 8-ounce can crushed
   pineapple (in juice)
1 3-ounce package coconut
   cream or vanilla instant
   pudding

⅓ cup dark rum (80 proof)
1 9-ounce container frozen whipped
   topping, thawed
Flaked coconut, if desired

Combine all ingredients except whipped topping and coconut in a bowl. Beat until well blended. Fold in thawed whipped topping. Fill and frost cake; sprinkle with coconut. Chill. Refrigerate any leftover cake.

Mrs. Robert Thevis (Sadie)
Avoyelles Parish (Simmesport)

HAWAIIAN CAKE

1 18½-ounce box yellow cake
   mix
1 6-ounce box instant vanilla
   pudding
1 cup milk
1 8-ounce package cream
   cheese, softened

1 9-ounce Cool Whip
1 20-ounce can crushed pineapple
½ cup chopped maraschino
   cherries
½ cup flaked coconut
½ cup chopped nuts

Prepare cake mix as directed on box; bake in a greased and floured jelly-roll pan at 250 degrees for 15 minutes or until done. Let cool. Mix vanilla pudding with 1 cup cold milk. Beat cream cheese into pudding mix. Fold Cool Whip into pudding mixture; spread on cooled cake. Drain crushed pineapple, and place on top of pudding layer. Sprinkle with cherries, coconut, and nuts. Keep cake refrigerated until ready to serve.

Mrs. Sam Womack
East Baton Rouge Parish (Zachary)

BROWN SUGAR CAKE

1 1-pound package brown
  sugar
4 eggs

1½ cups self-rising flour
1 teaspoon vanilla extract
1 cup chopped pecans

Preheat oven to 350 degrees. Mix sugar, eggs, flour, and vanilla well by hand. Add nuts. Place in a greased 13 x 9 x 2-inch pan. Bake at 350 degrees for 35 to 40 minutes. Top with icing; serve in pan.

Icing:
1 16-ounce package powdered
  sugar
2 3-ounce packages cream
  cheese, softened

½ cup butter, softened

Mix sugar, cheese, and butter well. Spread on cooled cake.

Mrs. Donald Johnson (Brenda)
Ouachita Parish (Monroe)

CAJUN CAKE

2 cups all-purpose flour
2 eggs
1 15-ounce can crushed
  pineapple

1½ cups sugar
1½ teaspoons soda
Pinch of salt

Mix all ingredients together and beat by hand for 1 minute. Place in greased 14 x 11-inch pan. Bake at 300 degrees for 40 minutes. Spread with topping while hot.

Topping:
½ cup margarine
1 5.33 ounce can evaporated
  milk
1 cup sugar

1 teaspoon vanilla extract
1 cup chopped pecans
1 cup flaked coconut

Mix margarine, milk, and sugar in a saucepan; heat to boiling. Boil for 5 minutes. Add vanilla, nuts, and coconut; spread on hot cake. Let cake cool; cut into squares to serve.

Mrs. Wilmer Juneau (Joycie)
Avoyelles Parish (Bordelonville)

✳ CARROT CAKE

1½ cups Wesson oil *1 C OIL*
2 cups sugar *½ C APPLE SAUCE*
4 eggs
2 cups all-purpose flour *1 C WW*
2 teaspoons baking powder
2 teaspoons ground cinnamon

1 teaspoon salt
2 teaspoons soda
3 cups carrots, grated
½ teaspoon vanilla extract
1 cup chopped pecans

Cream oil and sugar in a large bowl. Add eggs one at a time, beating well after each addition. Sift dry ingredients; stir in carrots. Add flour mixture, vanilla, and pecans to creamed mixture. Pour batter into three 9-inch pans or two 12-inch pans. Bake at 375 degrees for 45 minutes to 1 hour.

Topping:
¾ cup margarine, softened
1 8-ounce package cream
   cheese

1 16-ounce box powdered sugar

Beat all ingredients well. Spread over cake. Sprinkle with pecans, if desired.

Note: Add a little vanilla and orange juice for an unusual and different taste to the topping.

Mrs. Rick Caldwell (Jeanie)   *Mrs. Louis Curet (Jean)*
Ouachita Parish (West Monroe)   *East Baton Rouge Parish (Baton Rouge)*

PERSIMMON CAKE

½ cup shortening or margarine
2 cups sugar
1 egg
1¾ cups sifted cake flour
1 teaspoon soda
¼ teaspoon salt

1 teaspoon ground cinnamon
1 teaspoon ground cloves
1 cup raisins
1 cup pecans
1 cup persimmon pulp

Cream shortening and sugar until light. Add egg; beat one minute on medium speed of mixer. Sift flour, soda, salt, cinnamon and cloves; stir in raisins and pecans. Add persimmon pulp to creamed mixture, alternately with dry ingredients, beating well after each addition. Pour in a greased and floured 9-inch square pan. Bake at 350 degrees for 35 to 40 minutes.

Mrs. Michael Zaunbrecher (Blandins)
Avoyelles Parish (Simmesport)

BLUEBERRY CHEESECAKE

Filling:

1 cup whipping cream
1 8-ounce package Philadelphia
  cream cheese, softened
1 tablespoon Pet milk

⅔ cup powdered sugar
1 teaspoon almond extract
½ can blueberry pie filling

Whip cream and set aside. Beat cream cheese with milk until smooth; add sugar and almond extract. Beat until fluffy, then fold into whipped cream. Add to graham cracker pie shell. Top with ½ can blueberry pie filling. Chill well.

Crust:

1 box graham crackers—use
  1½ packets
1 tablespoon sugar

1 teaspoon ground cinnamon
1 tablespoon butter, melted

Crush graham crackers; add sugar, cinnamon, and melted butter. Press into pie pan and bake at 325 degrees for 10 minutes; cool.

Mrs. Arthur Lemann (Camille)
Ascension Parish (Donaldsonville)

BLUEBERRY CAKE

1 cup margarine, softened
2 cups sugar
3 eggs
3 cups all-purpose flour
1½ teaspoons baking powder
⅛ teaspoon salt

¼ teaspoon mace
2 cups fresh, canned or frozen
  blueberries
2 teaspoons sugar
½ cup milk

Preheat oven to 350 degrees. Cream margarine and sugar; add eggs, one at a time, beating well. Combine flour, baking powder, salt, and mace. Coat berries with 2 teaspoons sugar and 2 tablespoons flour mixture; set aside. Add flour mixture to creamed mixture, alternately with milk. Fold berry mixture into batter. Pour batter into greased and floured tube pan. Bake at 350 degrees for 70 to 80 minutes.

Mrs. H. E. Baird (Tena)
Ouachita Parish (Monroe)

HOMEMADE CAKE

Cake:

2½ cups plain flour
2 teaspoons baking powder
½ cup butter or ½ cup Crisco
  shortening

2½ cups sugar
1 cup milk
3 eggs

Preheat oven to 325 degrees. Sift flour and baking powder. Cream butter and sugar; add flour mixture, milk, and eggs. Mix well. Reserve 3 tablespoons batter for filling. Place batter in thin layers in four 8-inch pans. Bake at 325 degrees for 25 to 30 minutes.

Filling:

2 cups sugar
2½ cups milk

3 tablespoons cake batter

Mix sugar and milk; cook over low heat until warmed. Add batter, and cook until thickened. Place between layers and on top of cake.

Mrs. Emmett Moore (Lillian)
Ouachita Parish (Monroe)

JEWISH COFFEE CAKE

1 cup butter
2 cups sugar
2 eggs, well beaten
1 13-ounce can Pet evaporated
  milk

3 cups all-purpose flour, sifted
2 teaspoons baking powder
1 teaspoon vanilla extract

Cream butter and sugar; add eggs, beating well. Combine dry ingredients; add to creamed mixture alternately with milk. Mix well. Add vanilla. Pour batter in 10-inch bundt pan or 2 small loaf pans. Bake at 350 degrees for 1 hour.

Note: I make this cake and freeze it to be given to friends for house warmings, hospital stays, visits to senior citizens and so forth.

Mrs. Richard Hebert (Marca)
Evangeline Parish (Ville Platte)

BIG BOY SATIN WEDDING CAKE

1 cup shortening
2½ cups sugar
4 cups sifted cake flour
5 teaspoons baking powder

Pinch of salt
1½ cups milk
2 teaspoons almond extract
6 egg whites, beaten stiff

Preheat oven to 350 degrees. Cream shortening and sugar until light. Combine dry ingredients; add to creamed mixture alternately with milk. Add flavoring. Blend well. Fold in egg whites. Spoon batter into greased loafpans or layer pans. Bake at 350 degrees for 30 to 35 minutes or until golden brown.

Mrs. Herman Waguespack (Jerry)
St. James Parish (Vacherie)

SUNSHINE CAKE I

7 egg whites (at room
   temperature)
1¼ cups sugar
5 egg yolks

1 tablespoon lemon or vanilla
   extract
1 cup all-purpose flour
1 teaspoon cream of tartar

Beat egg whites until stiff and dry; gradually add sugar and continue beating. Beat yolks until thick and lemon-colored; add to beaten whites. Add extract. Cut and fold in flour sifted with cream of tartar. Spoon batter into an angel food cake pan. Bake at 325 degrees for 50 minutes. Let cool.

Mrs. Eddie Schexnaydre (Doris)
Terrebonne Parish (Schriever)

SUNSHINE CAKE II

6 eggs, separated
¼ teaspoon salt
1 cup sugar

1 teaspoon vanilla extract
1 cup flour, sifted
1 teaspoon cream of tartar

Separate eggs. Beat whites until stiff; add salt, then beat in ½ cup sugar. Beat egg yolks until thick and light colored; add remaining sugar, then vanilla. Fold egg yolks into egg white mixture. Sift flour and cream of tartar; fold into combined egg mixture. Spoon batter into 10-inch ungreased angel food cake pan. Bake at 325 degrees for 45 minutes. Let cool. Serve with fresh fruit slices.

Mrs. Peter Curra (Susan)
Waldo Parish (Thorndike)

SEVEN-UP CAKE

1 cup margarine	3 cups flour
½ cup shortening	¾ cup 7-Up soft drink
3 cups sugar	1 teaspoon vanilla extract
5 eggs	1 teaspoon lemon juice

Put margarine, shortening, and sugar into a large mixer bowl; beat until sugar is blended. Add eggs, one at a time, beating after each addition. Alternately add flour and 7-Up, beginning and ending with flour. Add vanilla and lemon juice; mix well. Place in greased cake pans. Bake at 350 degrees for 1 hour and 20 minutes.

Mrs. Roy Anderson (Catherine)
Ouachita Parish (Monroe)

SPICED SWEET POTATO CAKE

2 cups sugar	1 teaspoon ground cinnamon
4 eggs	½ teaspoon salt
1 cup corn oil	2 teaspoons baking powder
2 cups cooked and mashed	1 teaspoon baking soda
sweet potatoes	1 cup chopped nuts
2 cups all-purpose flour	

Cream sugar, eggs, and oil until light; add potatoes, mixing until smooth. Stir in dry ingredients. Add nuts. Pour batter in greased and floured cake pans. Bake at 325 degrees for 40 minutes. Yield: one cake.

Mrs. Weston Monceaux, Sr. (Vergie)
Allen Parish (Oberlin)

RUBY'S PLAIN CAKE

½ to ¾ cup shortening	3 egg yolks or 2 whole eggs
1½ cups sugar	1 cup milk
2½ cups all-purpose flour	1½ teaspoons vanilla extract
1 teaspoon baking powder	

Preheat oven to 350 degrees. Cream shortening and sugar until light. Sift flour and baking powder; add to creamed mixture. Add eggs, one at a time, beating well after each egg is added. Add milk and vanilla; mix well. Place in 8 or 9-inch pans. Bake at 350 degrees for 30 minutes.

Mrs. Emmett Moore (Lillian)
Ouachita Parish (Monroe)

DUMP CAKE

1 15½-ounce can crushed
   pineapple
1 21-ounce can cherry pie filling

1 18½-ounce box Duncan Hines
   yellow cake mix
¾ cup margarine

Preheat oven to 350 degrees. Spread pineapple in bottom of 13 x 9 x 2-inch pan; top with cherry filling. Sprinkle dry cake mix over filling; melt butter and pour over cake mix. Bake at 350 degrees for 40 minutes.

Note: This recipe was given to me by my aunt, Mrs. B. R. Alpha.

Mrs. Donald Johnson (Brenda)
Ouachita Parish (Monroe)

PLAIN BUNDT CAKE

1 18½-ounce box Duncan
   Hines yellow cake mix
1 3¾-ounce box vanilla instant
   pudding mix

¾ cup Wesson oil
¾ cup water
4 eggs

Mix all ingredients thoroughly; pour in a greased and floured bundt pan. Bake at 350 degrees for 45 minutes or until done. Yield: one cake.

Note: Grease bundt pan well even if it is Teflon coated.

Mrs. Allen Weeks (Cindy)
Ouachita Parish (West Monroe)

VANILLA WAFER CAKE

1 cup margarine, softened
2 cups sugar
6 eggs
1 12-ounce package vanilla
   wafers, crushed

½ cup milk
1 7-ounce package flaked coconut
1 cup chopped pecans

Preheat oven to 350 degrees. In a large bowl, cream the margarine and sugar with electric mixer. Add eggs, one at a time, beating well after each addition. Add vanilla wafers alternately with milk to creamed mixture. Add coconut and pecans. Place butter in a greased 10-inch bundt cake pan. Bake at 350 degrees for one hour. Let cool.

Pam Accardo
Ouachita Parish (Monroe)

CARAMEL FROSTING

1 18½-ounce box yellow or
  white cake mix
1 cup sugar (to be browned)
1 cup sugar

½ cup margarine
1 13-ounce can evaporated milk
Pinch salt
1 tablespoon vanilla extract

Prepare cake mix according to package directions; bake, and let cool. In a heavy skillet brown 1 cup sugar until light rusty color, stirring constantly over low heat. In a heavy saucepan, place all other ingredients. Cook over medium heat, stirring constantly. Let mixture boil until your browned sugar is ready. Add browned sugar to the milk mixture; stir well. Cook over medium heat until firm, soft ball stage (234°) is reached. Beat mixture well, while pricking cake layers. Add filling a layer at a time. Use remaining filling to cover or frost cake.

Mrs. Bernard Bordelon (Marie)
Avoyelles Parish (Moreauville)

COCONUT PECAN FROSTING

½ cup butter
1 cup sugar
3 egg yolks, well beaten
1 cup evaporated milk

1 teaspoon vanilla extract
1 cup ground pecans
1 cup flaked coconut

Melt butter in the top of a double boiler. Stir in sugar, and mix well. Add egg yolks and beat well. Add milk and vanilla; cook until thick, stirring constantly. Remove from heat, and let cool. Add ground pecans and coconut. Frost your favorite layer cake as desired.

Mrs. Emmett Moore (Lillian)
Ouachita Parish (Monroe)

CHOCOLATE FUDGE OR CAKE FILLING

3 cups sugar
3 tablespoons cocoa
2 tablespoons Mrs.
  Butterworth's Syrup
2 tablespoons butter or
  margarine

1 13-ounce can Carnation
  evaporated milk
1 teaspoon vanilla extract
Pinch of salt

Cook all ingredients in heavy iron skillet over low heat, stirring constantly. Let come to a boil; cook ten minutes. Let cool to lukewarm; whip until creamy.

Frances Holland
Concordia Parish (Monterey)

DEVIL'S FOOD CAKE ICING

1 pound box powdered sugar
8 teaspoons cocoa
½ cup margarine or butter

5 tablespoons black coffee
1 tablespoon vanilla extract

Mix all ingredients well. Spread on your favorite Devil's Food cake.

Annie R. Cooper
Caldwell Parish (Columbia)

SEVEN MINUTE FROSTING

1½ cups sugar
2 egg whites
⅓ cup water

2 teaspoons light corn syrup
Dash of salt
1 teaspoon vanilla extract

Combine first 5 ingredients in the top of a double boiler; beat 1 minute or until well combined with an electric mixer. Place pan over boiling water; add vanilla, and beat until frosting is of spreading consistency. Yield: 4½ cups.

Evelina Smith
Beauregard Parish (DeRidder)

LEMON FILLING

2 cups sugar
6 egg yolks, beaten
1 cup melted butter

Grated rind of 1 lemon
Juice of 3 lemons
Pinch of salt

Combine first 5 ingredients in a small saucepan; cook over low heat, stirring constantly, until thickened. Add salt; remove from heat. Yield: 3 cups.

Josie Vance Cross
Concordia Parish (Monterey)

EASY CARAMEL FUDGE

2 cups sugar
1 cup firmly packed light brown
  sugar
¼ cup light corn syrup

⅔ cup evaporated milk
1 tablespoon butter
1 teaspoon almond or vanilla extract

Combine first 4 ingredients in a heavy medium saucepan; cook over medium heat, stirring constantly, until mixture reaches soft ball stage (234°). Remove from heat; add butter and flavoring, as desired. Cool about 20 minutes or until lukewarm. Beat until mixture thickens and loses its gloss. Pour into a buttered pan. Let stand until firm. Yield: about 3 dozen.

Laurie Ann Hart
Ouachita Parish (Monroe)

GOLD BRICK CANDY

4½ cups sugar
1 large can evaporated milk
3 6-ounce packages chocolate
   chips

1 7-ounce jar marshmallow creme
1 cup margarine
3 to 4 cups chopped pecans

Combine sugar and milk in a medium saucepan; cook over low heat until mixture reaches boiling point. Remove from heat; stir in remaining ingredients until all are dissolved. Pour into a buttered pan; let stand until firm. Cut into squares to serve. Yield: 3 to 4 dozen.
Mrs. Henry Hess (Peggy)
Avoyelles Parish (Moreauville)

CHOCOLATE BALLS

1½ packages (12 squares)
   Baker's semisweet chocolate
½ cup butter
1 14-ounce can sweetened
   condensed milk

1 heaping teaspoon ground
   cinnamon
Candy decors

Melt chocolate and butter in the top of a double boiler. Add milk, stirring well. Heat until smooth. Remove from heat; add cinnamon. Chill 18 to 24 hours or until mixture is very hard.

Roll mixture into balls; cover with candy decors. Chill. Yield: 3 dozen.

Note: Chocolate balls will soften considerably at room temperature.
Mrs. Louis D. Curet
E. Baton Rouge Parish (Baton Rouge)

CHOCOLATE TURTLES

1 6-ounce package chocolate
   chips
1 3½-ounce jar marshmallow
   creme

1 cup pecan halves
2¼ cups sugar
6½ ounces evaporated milk
¼ cup margarine

Combine marshmallow creme, chocolate chips, and pecans in a large bowl; stir gently to combine (do not mix). Combine sugar, milk, and margarine in a medium saucepan; cook over low heat, stirring constantly, until mixture reaches boiling point. Boil 7½ minutes; remove from heat. Pour hot mixture over chocolate chip mixture; mix well. Drop by heaping teaspoonfuls onto waxed paper. Let stand until firm. Yield: 55 pieces.
Mrs. Allen Weeks (Cindy)
Ouachita Parish (West Monroe)

MARTHA WASHINGTON CHOCOLATE BALLS

½ cup margarine, softened
2 16-ounce packages powdered
  sugar
1 14-ounce can sweetened
  condensed milk

2 cups finely chopped pecans
1 teaspoon vanilla extract
1 8-ounce package Baker's
  semi-sweet chocolate
½ bar paraffin

Cream margarine until fluffy in a small mixing bowl; gradually add sugar and milk, alternately, beating constantly. Add nuts and vanilla; chill until firm. Shape cooled mixture into 1-inch balls. Melt chocolate and paraffin in the top of a double boiler; dip balls into chocolate mixture, using a toothpick. Place on waxed paper; let cool. Yield: about 4 dozen.

Mrs. Donald Johnson (Brenda)
Ouachita Parish (Monroe)

CARAMELS

1 cup butter or margarine
2 cups sugar
2 cups light corn syrup
2 14-ounce cans sweetened
  condensed milk

½ cup sifted all-purpose flour
1 teaspoon vanilla extract
2 cups chopped pecans

Melt butter in a medium saucepan over low heat; add sugar and corn syrup. Heat to boiling; boil 5 minutes over medium heat, stirring constantly. Add 1½ cans milk; stir well.

Combine flour and remaining ½ can milk; stir well to blend. Add to sugar mixture, stirring constantly. Cook over medium heat until mixture reaches firm ball stage (240°). Remove from heat; stir in vanilla and nuts. Pour into a buttered 13 x 9 x 2-inch pan; let stand 24 hours. Cut into 1-inch squares with a buttered knife; wrap squares in waxed paper. Yield: 5 dozen.

Mrs. Danile Gonsoulin (Jeanette)
Iberia Parish (New Iberia)

CHOW-MEIN CANDY

1 can prepared milk chocolate
  frosting
½ cup canned chow-mein
  noodles

½ cup miniature marshmallows
½ cup chopped pecans
1 teaspoon vanilla extract

Combine all ingredients, stirring well. Drop by tablespoonfuls onto waxed paper; let stand until firm. Yield: 2 dozen.

Mrs. Ronald Scioneaux (Hazel)
St. James Parish (Vacherie)

DATE NUT CANDY

1 12-ounce package vanilla
  wafers, crushed
1 14-ounce can sweetened
  condensed milk

1 8-ounce package pitted dates,
  chopped
1 cup chopped pecans
Powdered sugar

Combine first 4 ingredients in a large bowl; mix well with hands. Shape dough into small logs; roll each log into powdered sugar. Wrap logs in waxed paper; chill until firm. Slice and serve. Yield: 3 to 4 logs.

Note: This candy is great for parties.

Pam Accardo
Ouachita Parish (Monroe)

DATE LOAF CANDY

2 cups sugar
⅔ cup milk

2 cups chopped dates
2 cups chopped pecans

Combine sugar and milk in a medium saucepan; cook over medium heat until mixture boils. Add dates; cook over medium heat until mixture reaches soft ball stage (234°). Remove from heat; add nuts. Roll date mixture onto a damp dish towel to form a log. Let cool; cut into slices. Yield: 1 log.

Jackie Hymel
St. James Parish (Convent)

DATE LOAF CANDY

1 pound package graham
  crackers
2 8-ounce packages chopped
  dates
4 cups chopped pecans
2 cups miniature marshmallows

1 4-ounce jar maraschino cherries,
  chopped and juice reserved
1 14-ounce can sweetened
  condensed milk
Powdered sugar

Prepare crumbs from graham crackers; set aside. Combine dates, pecans, marshmallows, cherries and juice in a large bowl; add graham cracker crumbs and mix well. Mix for 5 minutes; divide into 4 portions. Shape each portion into a 10-inch log. Roll each log in powdered sugar. Wrap each log in waxed paper; chill. To serve, remove waxed paper and slice. Yield: 4 10-inch logs.

Mrs. Lester J. Durel (Iris)
Lafayette Parish (Lafayette)

BROWN CANDY

6 cups sugar
2 cups milk
¼ teaspoon soda

½ cup margarine
1 teaspoon vanilla extract
4 cups broken pecans

Place 2 cups sugar in a heavy 10-inch skillet; cook over low heat, stirring constantly with a wooden spoon, until sugar melts and is light brown.
Meanwhile, combine remaining 4 cups sugar and milk in a heavy Dutch oven; cook over low heat until mixture has small bubbles around edges of pan. Pour hot sugar syrup into milk mixture, stirring constantly. Cook over medium heat, stirring constantly, until mixture reaches the firm ball stage (242°).
Remove from heat; add soda, stirring well as it foams. Add margarine, stirring until melted. Add vanilla, beating until candy begins to thicken and loses its gloss. Gently stir in pecans. Pour candy into a greased or buttered pan. Let cool; cut into squares. Yield: 6 pounds.
Mrs. Helin McCauley (Lou)
Allen Parish (Oberlin)

DIVINITY CANDY

2¾ cups sugar
¾ cup light Karo syrup
¾ cup water
1 tablespoon vinegar

2 egg whites, stiffly beaten
1 cup chopped nuts
1 teaspoon vanilla extract

Combine sugar, syrup, and water in a medium saucepan; cook over medium heat until mixture reaches soft ball stage (235°). Add vinegar, and continue to cook until mixture reaches hard ball stage (250°). Slowly pour hot mixture into beaten egg whites, beating constantly. Beat until mixture is thick and will drop from a spoon. Stir in nuts and vanilla. Drop candy by teaspoonfuls onto waxed paper or a lightly buttered cookie sheet. Cool; store in airtight container. Yield: about 2 dozen pieces.
Mrs. Wista White
Ouachita Parish (Monroe)

NATCHEZ PRALINES

2½ cups sugar
1½ cups firmly packed brown
    sugar
1 cup light corn syrup

1 cup evaporated milk
3 tablespoons butter
2 cups pecan halves

Combine first 5 ingredients in a medium saucepan; cook over medium heat until mixture reaches soft ball stage (234°). Add pecans, stirring well. Drop candy into shapes onto waxed paper or greased cookie sheets.
Mrs. S. L. Ford, Sr.
Catahoula Parish (Jonesville)

NOT-TOO-SWEET PRALINES

1 6-ounce package regular
  vanilla pudding mix
1 cup sugar
½ cup firmly packed brown
  sugar

½ cup milk
1 tablespoon margarine
1½ cups chopped pecans

Combine first 5 ingredients in a medium saucepan; cook over medium heat until mixture reaches soft ball stage (234°). Add pecans; beat with a spoon until mixture begins to thicken and loses its gloss. Drop by tablespoonfuls onto waxed paper; let stand until firm. Store in an airtight container. Yield: about 2 dozen.

Mrs. Doug Moore (Liz)
Ouachita Parish (Monroe)

COCONUT PRALINES

3 cups sugar
2½ cups coconut meat, grated
1 cup coconut milk or milk

¼ cup butter
½ teaspoon almond extract

Combine first 3 ingredients in a 3 to 4-quart Dutch oven; cook over medium heat until mixture forms a soft ball stage (234°). Remove from heat; add butter and flavoring. Beat until mixture becomes thick and loses its gloss (about 5 to 10 minutes). Drop candy by tablespoonfuls onto waxed paper or greased cookie sheets. Let stand until firm. Yield: 3 dozen.

Mrs. James Graugnard, Jr.
West St. James Parish (St. James)

LOUISIANA PRALINES-MICROWAVE

2 cups sugar
2 cups pecan halves
¾ cup buttermilk

2 tablespoons butter
⅛ teaspoon salt
1 teaspoon soda

Combine first 5 ingredients in a 4-quart glass casserole; Microwave on HIGH for 12 minutes, stirring every 4 minutes. Add soda, stirring well as it foams. Microwave on HIGH 1 minute longer; beat mixture until thickened and loses its gloss (about 1 minute). Drop candy by teaspoonfuls onto waxed paper; let stand until firm.

Note: You may need to adjust cooking time with your microwave oven. Soft failures are just as delicious to eat as firm pralines.
Mrs. Jude Plauché (Margaret)
Avoyelles Parish (Hamburg)

PEANUT BUTTER CANDY

2 cups peanut butter
2 cups margarine, softened
2 16-ounce packages powdered
  sugar

1 teaspoon vanilla extract
1 12-ounce package chocolate
  chips
½ bar paraffin

Combine peanut butter and margarine in a large mixing bowl; gradually add powdered sugar and mix well. Add vanilla. Shape dough into 1-inch balls. Melt chocolate chips and paraffin in the top of a double boiler; using a toothpick, dip each ball of candy into chocolate mixture. Place on waxed paper; cool. Yield: about 4 dozen.
Mrs. Perry Fisher (Bert)
Ouachita Parish (Monroe)

PEANUT BRITTLE

2 cups sugar
1 cup light corn syrup
½ cup boiling water

4 cups raw peanuts
1 tablespoon soda

Combine sugar, syrup and water in a heavy 2-quart Dutch oven; cook over medium heat until mixture spins a thread (230° to 234°). Add peanuts, cook to soft crack stage (about 290°), stirring constantly. Remove from heat; add soda, stirring well. Pour onto greased marble slab or cookie sheet. Cool; break into pieces. Yield: about 1½ pounds.

Note: Be very careful not to burn yourself or your counter top as this candy gets very hot.
Mrs. Patrick J. Quinn (Mary Kathryn)
Concordia Parish (Monterey)

NEVER FAIL DIVINITY

2 egg whites
⅛ teaspoon salt
3 cups sugar
⅔ cup water

½ cup Karo syrup
1 teaspoon vanilla extract
1 cup chopped pecans

Combine egg whites and salt in a small mixing bowl; beat with electric mixer until stiff peaks form. Set aside. Combine sugar, water, and syrup in a saucepan; cook over medium heat until mixture reaches the hard ball stage (262°). Pour syrup mixture into egg whites, beating while pouring. Add vanilla, and continue to beat until thickened. Stir in nuts. Drop by tablespoonfuls onto waxed paper. Cool; store in airtight container. Yield: about 2 dozen pieces.
Mrs. Donald Johnson (Brenda)
Ouachita Parish (Monroe)

CATHEDRAL ROLL

1 14-ounce package milk
  chocolate silver bells
½ cup butter or margarine

1 cup chopped pecans
1 10½-ounce package miniature
  marshmallows

Melt chocolate and butter over low heat; cool. Add nuts and marshmallows to chocolate mixture. Shape into a roll 1½ to 2 inches in diameter on foil. Freeze 2 hours.

When thoroughly chilled, slice roll into ½-inch slices. Yield: 3 dozen cookies.

Grace Graugnard
St. James Parish (St. James)

CHOCOLATE BUTTERSWEETS

½ cup butter, softened
½ cup sifted powdered sugar
¼ teaspoon salt

1 teaspoon vanilla extract
1¼ cups all-purpose flour

Cream butter in a large mixing bowl; gradually add sugar, salt and vanilla, beating well. Add flour; blend well. Shape dough by teaspoonfuls into balls. Place dough on ungreased cookie sheets; make a deep indentation in the center of each cookie. Bake at 350 degrees for 12 to 15 minutes or until lightly browned. Yield: 3 dozen.

Creamy Nut Filling:
1 3-ounce package cream
  cheese, softened
1 cup sifted powdered sugar
2 tablespoons all-purpose flour

1 teaspoon vanilla extract
½ cup chopped walnuts
½ cup flaked coconut

Beat cream cheese until fluffy in a small mixing bowl; add sugar, flour, and vanilla; mix well. Stir in nuts and coconut. Fill cookies with filling while still warm.

Chocolate Frosting:
½ cup semi-sweet chocolate
  chips
2 tablespoons butter

2 tablespoons water
½ cup sifted powdered sugar

Melt chocolate chips, butter, and water over low heat, stirring occasionally. Add sugar; beat until smooth. Frost thoroughly cooled cookies.

Mrs. Melba McIntosh
W. Carroll Parish (Pioneer)

ANGEL SUPREME

2¼ cups miniature
  marshmallows
1 10-ounce can crushed
  pineapple, undrained
1 8-ounce bottle maraschino
  cherries, undrained

1 envelope unflavored gelatin
1 cup milk, divided
2 cups heavy cream, whipped or 1
  envelope Dream Whip, prepared
1 10-inch Angel Food cake
Strawberry slices (optional)

Combine first 3 ingredients in a large bowl; cover and let soak overnight. Combine gelatin and ½ cup milk; let stand 5 minutes. Meanwhile, heat remaining ½ cup milk until warm; add to softened gelatin, stirring until dissolved. Chill gelatin mixture until slightly thickened. Stir gelatin mixture into fruit; fold in whipped cream. Tear cake into bite-size pieces; top with fruit mixture. Top with strawberry slices, if desired. Yield: 8 servings.

Note: 1 cup crushed strawberries (fresh or frozen) may be substituted for cherries, if desired. Also, 1 8-ounce carton Cool Whip, thawed, may be substituted for whipped cream, if desired.

Mrs. Doug Moore (Liz)
Ouachita Parish (Monroe)

CHEWY BROWNIES

1 cup margarine
¼ cup breakfast cocoa mix
4 eggs
2 cups sugar

1 cup all-purpose flour
1 teaspoon vanilla extract
Pinch of salt
1 cup chopped nuts, divided

Combine margarine and cocoa mix in a small saucepan; cook over low heat until margarine is melted. Remove from heat; set aside to cool. Combine eggs and sugar in a large mixing bowl; beat until creamy. Add flour, vanilla and salt; mix well. Add ½ cup nuts and cooled chocolate mixture to batter; mix well. Pour batter into a well greased and floured 15 x 10 x 1-inch pan. Bake at 350 degrees for 35 to 40 minutes or until done. Top with glaze; sprinkle with remaining ½ cup nuts. Let cool before cutting into squares. Yield: 36 brownies.

Glaze:
1 cup sifted powdered sugar
¼ cup cocoa
Pinch of salt

½ teaspoon vanilla extract
Boiling water

Combine sugar, cocoa and salt in a small bowl; add vanilla and enough boiling water to make a thin paste. Spread on hot brownies; top with ½ cup nuts.
Mrs. Bernard Bordelon (Marie)
Avoyelles Parish (Moreauville)

CHEESECAKE SQUARES

2 cups all-purpose flour
⅔ cup firmly packed brown
  sugar
⅔ cup melted margarine
1 8-ounce package cream
  cheese, softened

1 8-ounce carton commercial sour
  cream
1 egg, beaten
¼ cup sugar
½ teaspoon vanilla extract

Combine flour and brown sugar in a large bowl; stir well. Add margarine; mix until crumbly. Press mixture into an ungreased 13 x 9 x 2-inch baking pan; bake at 350 degrees for 15 minutes. Let cool. Combine remaining ingredients in a large mixing bowl; mix at medium speed of electric mixer until smooth. Pour over baked crust layer. Bake at 350 degrees for 30 minutes. Let cool; chill, and cut into squares.

Mrs. Donald Johnson (Brenda)
Ouachita Parish (Monroe)

COCONUT BROWNIES

2 eggs
2 cups firmly packed dark
  brown sugar
½ cup plus 2 tablespoons
  vegetable oil

1 cup self-rising flour
1 teaspoon vanilla extract
1 cup chopped pecans
1 small can Angel Flake coconut

Combine eggs, sugar, and oil in a large mixing bowl; mix well. Add remaining ingredients; mix well. Pour batter into a well greased and floured 13 x 9 x 2-inch pan. Bake at 350 degrees for 30 to 35 minutes or until done. Let cool; cut into squares. Yield: about 2 dozen.

Mrs. James Graugnard, Jr.
West St. James Parish (St. James)

MAGIC COOKIE BARS

1½ cups corn flakes crumbs
3 tablespoons sugar
½ cup melted margarine
1 6-ounce package semi-sweet
  chocolate morsels

1 3½-ounce can flaked coconut
1 cup chopped walnuts or pecans
1 14-ounce can sweetened
  condensed milk

Combine crumbs, sugar, and margarine in a bowl; mix well. Press into a 13 x 9 x 2-inch pan; sprinkle with chocolate morsels. Top with coconut, then nuts; pour milk over nuts. Bake at 350 degrees for 25 minutes or until lightly browned around the edges. Cool; cut into 2 x 1-inch bars. Yield: 54 bars.

Donna Bolton Jenkins
East Baton Rouge Parish (Baton Rouge)

GRAHAM CRACKER BARS

1 1-pound package graham
  crackers
1 cup sugar
½ cup margarine

½ cup milk
1 egg, beaten
1 small can flaked coconut
1 cup chopped nuts

Crush enough graham crackers to yield 1 cup crumbs; set crumbs aside. Place a layer of graham crackers in the bottom of a 13 x 9 x 2-inch pan. Combine sugar, margarine, milk, and egg in a saucepan; cook over low heat until mixture comes to a boil. Remove from heat; stir in coconut, nuts, and 1 cup graham cracker crumbs. Spread cooked mixture over graham cracker layer in pan; top with another layer of graham crackers.

Icing:
½ cup margarine, melted
2 tablespoons evaporated milk
2 cups sifted powdered sugar

1 teaspoon vanilla extract
¼ cup chopped nuts

Combine margarine and milk in a small saucepan; heat to boiling. Remove from heat; add sugar and vanilla. Mix well. Stir in nuts. Spread over graham cracker layer in pan. Chill well before cutting into squares or bars. Keep refrigerated. Yield: 2 dozen bars.
Mrs. Donald Johnson (Brenda)
Ouachita Parish (Monroe)

LEMON BARS

Crust:
2 cups all-purpose flour
1 cup melted butter

1 cup sifted powdered sugar
¼ teaspoon salt

Combine all ingredients in a medium bowl; blend well. Press mixture into a 14 x 10-inch pan. Bake at 325 degrees for 20 minutes or until done.

Filling:
2 cups sugar
¼ cup all-purpose flour
¼ cup lemon juice

4 eggs, slightly beaten
Grated rind of 1 lemon
Powdered sugar

Combine all ingredients except powdered sugar in a medium bowl; mix well. Pour over baked crust; bake at 325 degrees for 25 additional minutes. Cool thoroughly. Sprinkle with powdered sugar, and cut into small squares. Keep refrigerated. Yield: 10 servings.

Mrs. R. Ernest Girouard, Jr.
Vermilion Parish (Kaplan)

GAYE'S CHOCOLATE COVERED PEANUT BUTTER BALLS

1 cup melted margarine
2 cups smooth peanut butter
1 16-ounce box powdered
  sugar

¼ bar paraffin
1 12-ounce package chocolate
  chips

Combine margarine, peanut butter and powdered sugar in a large bowl; mix well. Shape dough into 1-inch balls (additional powdered sugar may be added if mixture is sticky); set aside. Melt paraffin and chocolate chips in the top of a double boiler. Using a toothpick, dip each peanut butter ball into chocolate mixture; place on waxed paper to dry. Yield: about 9 dozen.

Note: Dough balls may be chilled before dipping in chocolate, if desired.
Gaye Kennedy
Claiborne Parish (Bernice)

WEDDING DATE BALLS

½ cup butter
1 cup sugar
1 8-ounce package chopped
  dates

1 egg, beaten
2 cups Rice Krispies cereal
1 cup chopped pecans
1 cup flaked coconut

Combine butter, sugar, dates, and egg in a medium saucepan; cook over medium heat, stirring occasionally, for 8 to 10 minutes or until thickened. Remove from heat; add cereal and pecans. Let cool slightly. Shape mixture into balls; roll in coconut. Yield: about 1 dozen.
Mrs. Louis D. Curet
East Baton Rouge Parish (Baton Rouge)

CHOCOLATE CHIP OATMEAL COOKIES

2 cups rolled oats, uncooked
2 cups all-purpose flour
1 teaspoon soda
½ teaspoon salt
½ teaspoon baking powder
1 cup shortening

¾ cup sugar
¾ cup firmly packed brown sugar
2 eggs
1 teaspoon vanilla extract
1 6-ounce package chocolate chips

Combine first 5 ingredients in a medium bowl; set aside. Combine shortening, sugar, and eggs, in a large mixing bowl; cream well. Add flour mixture; mix well. Stir in chocolate chips. Drop dough by spoonfuls onto a lightly greased cookie sheet. Bake at 375 degrees for 10 to 15 minutes or until light brown. Yield: about 5 dozen.
Shirley Wood
West Carroll Parish (Pioneer)

CHOCOLATE CHIP COOKIES

1¼ cups all-purpose flour
½ teaspoon soda
¼ teaspoon salt
1 cup sugar
½ cup margarine, softened

1 teaspoon vanilla extract
1 egg
2 cups Rice Krispies cereal
1 6-ounce package chocolate chips

Sift together flour, soda, and salt; set aside. Cream sugar and margarine until light and fluffy in a large mixing bowl; add vanilla and egg, mixing well. Add flour mixture; mix well. Stir in remaining ingredients. Drop dough by spoonfuls onto lightly greased cookie sheets. Bake at 350 degrees for 12 minutes. Cool on wire racks. Yield: about 5 dozen.

Mrs. Lorraine Watkins
Jeff Davis Parish (Welsh)

CHRISTMAS COOKIES

3½ cups all-purpose flour
2 teaspoons baking powder
1 teaspoon soda
½ teaspoon salt
1 cup sugar

¼ cup shortening
¼ cup softened butter
½ cup evaporated milk
1 egg, well beaten
1 teaspoon vanilla extract

Sift together flour, baking powder, soda, and salt; set aside. Cream sugar shortening, and butter in a large mixing bowl. Add milk, egg, and vanilla; mix well. Add flour mixture; mix well. Turn dough out onto a lightly floured surface; roll out to ⅛-inch thickness. Cut dough as desired, and place on a lightly greased cookie sheet. Bake at 375 degrees for 20 minutes. Let cool on wire racks. Yield: 3 to 4 dozen.

Variation:
Filling:
½ cup sugar
1 tablespoon all-purpose flour
1 cup chopped raisins

½ cup chopped nuts
Water

Combine sugar and flour in a small saucepan; add raisins, nuts, and enough water to form a paste. Cook over low heat, stirring constantly, until thickened. Cool thoroughly. Spread on ½ of rolled out dough; top with remaining half of rolled dough. Cut as desired. Bake as directed above.

Mrs. Herman Waguespack (Jerry)
St. James Parish (Vacherie)

DELICIOUS BUTTER COOKIES

2 cups butter, softened
2 cups sugar
2 teaspoons ground cinnamon
1 teaspoon vanilla extract

2 egg yolks
4 cups all-purpose flour
1 cup chopped pecans
2 egg whites, slightly beaten

Combine first 4 ingredients in a large mixing bowl; beat until creamy. Add egg yolks, beat well. Add flour, a small amount at a time, blending well after each addition. Spread dough very thin onto 3 large greased cookie sheets; press or pat nuts into dough. Brush dough with egg whites. Bake at 350 degrees for 15 minutes or until light brown. Remove from oven; immediately cut into small squares. Let cool on cookie sheets; store in an airtight container. Yield: 5 dozen.

Mrs. Louis D. Curet
East Baton Rouge Parish (Baton Rouge)

LIZZERS

2 pounds candied cherries,
  chopped
2 pounds candied pineapple,
  chopped
1 pound dark raisins
1 pound golden raisins
6 cups pecans, broken
All-purpose flour
4 to 6 cups all-purpose flour
1 tablespoon soda

1 teaspoon ground cinnamon
1 teaspoon ground allspice
1 teaspoon ground nutmeg
1 teaspoon ground cloves
1½ cups firmly packed dark brown
  sugar
½ cup butter, softened
4 eggs
1 cup bourbon whiskey
3 tablespoons milk

Combine first 5 ingredients in a large bowl; dredge fruit with enough flour to coat; set aside. Combine remaining dry ingredients; set aside. Cream butter and sugar until fluffy in a large mixing bowl; add eggs, one at a time, beating well after each addition. Add bourbon, milk, and dry ingredients, mixing well. Add fruit mixture to batter; mix well with hands. Drop dough by teaspoonfuls onto greased cookie sheets. Bake at 275 degrees for 12 minutes or until lightly browned. Yield: about 6 dozen.

Annie R. Cooper
Caldwell Parish (Columbia)

OLD FASHIONED TEA CAKES

1 cup sugar	2 teaspoons baking powder
½ cup butter, softened	¼ teaspoon salt
2 eggs, beaten	1 tablespoon milk (optional)
2¼ cups all-purpose flour	½ teaspoon vanilla extract

Cream sugar and butter until light and fluffy in a large mixing bowl; add eggs, mixing well. Combine dry ingredients; add to creamed mixture, mixing well. Add vanilla and milk, if dough is too dry. Chill dough 1 hour. Roll dough out to ⅛-inch thickness on a floured surface; cut as desired. Place dough on ungreased cookie sheets; bake at 375 degrees for 13 to 15 minutes or until lightly browned. Yield: 3 to 4 dozen cookies.

Velma Chappell
Ouachita Parish (Monroe)

T-CAKES

1 cup shortening	1 teaspoon vanilla extract
2 cups sugar	4 cups self-rising flour
3 eggs	

Cream shortening in a large bowl; add sugar, mixing well. Add eggs and vanilla; mix well. Stir in flour. Turn dough out onto a lightly floured surface; knead gently. Roll dough out to ¼-inch thickness; cut with a 2-inch biscuit cutter. Place dough on lightly greased cookie sheets; bake at 350 degrees for 10 minutes or until lightly browned.

Mrs. Jack Bairnsfather
Concordia Parish (Monterey)

GRANNY'S TEA CAKES

1 cup sugar	3¼ cups self-rising flour
1 cup shortening	2 teaspoons vanilla extract
2 eggs	

Combine sugar and shortening in a large mixing bowl; cream well. Add eggs, beat well by hand. Add flour and vanilla; mix well (dough will be stiff). Drop dough onto greased cookie sheets about 1-inch apart. Bake at 325 degrees until lightly browned. Yield: about 3½ dozen.

Mrs. Emmett Moore (Lillian)
Ouachita Parish (Monroe)

SNOWBALLS

Filling:

1 cup butter or margarine,
softened
1 cup sugar
2 egg yolks, beaten

1 cup drained crushed pineapple
1 cup chopped pecans
2 egg whites, stiffly beaten

Cream butter and sugar until fluffy in a large mixing bowl; add egg yolks, mixing well. Add pineapple and nuts, stirring well. Gently fold beaten egg whites into pineapple mixture; set aside.

Other ingredients:

1½-pound box Sunshine
butter cookies
1 12-ounce carton Cool Whip,
thawed

1 3½-ounce can flaked coconut

Place several cookies on an ungreased cookie sheet; top each cookie with a heaping teaspoonful of filling. Place a layer of cookies on top of filling; repeat with filling and cookies until all ingredients are used. Freeze. Frost each cookie stack with Cool Whip; sprinkle each stack with coconut. Freeze until serving time.

Mrs. Norbert Meyr (Evelyn)
Perry County (Altenburg, Missouri)

GINGERBREAD COOKIES

½ cup butter
¼ cup boiling water
½ cup firmly packed brown
sugar
½ cup dark molasses
3 cups all-purpose flour

1 teaspoon baking powder
1 teaspoon salt
1½ teaspoons ground ginger
½ teaspoon freshly grated nutmeg
½ teaspoon ground cloves

Combine butter and water in a large mixing bowl, stirring well. Add sugar and molasses; mix well. Sift together remaining ingredients; add to molasses mixture. Mix well. Shape dough into a ball; chill overnight. Roll dough out to ⅛-inch thickness on a lightly floured surface; cut into desired shapes with cookie cutters. Place on greased cookie sheet (or cookie sheet lined with parchment paper). Bake at 350 degrees for 10 minutes or until lightly browned. Decorate cookies with colored icing, if desired. Yield: about 2 dozen.

Mrs. James Henderson (Elise)
West St. James Parish (St. James)

SUGAR COOKIES

1 cup butter, softened
¾ cup sugar
1 egg
2½ cups sifted all-purpose flour

½ teaspoon baking powder
⅛ teaspoon salt
1 teaspoon vanilla extract

Beat butter until creamy in a large mixing bowl; gradually add sugar and egg, beating constantly. Sift together flour, baking powder, and salt three times. Add flour mixture and vanilla to creamed mixture; mix well. Roll dough out to ⅛-inch thickness on a floured surface; cut into oblong shapes, as desired. Place dough on greased cookie sheets; bake at 400 degrees for 10 to 12 minutes or until lightly browned. Yield: about 3 dozen cookies.
Mrs. Eddie Schexnaydre (Doris)
Terrebonne Parish (Schriever)

MAMA'S SUGAR COOKIES

1 cup shortening
2 cups sugar
2 eggs
½ cup milk

2 teaspoons vanilla extract
4 cups all-purpose flour
1 teaspoon soda
1 teaspoon salt

Cream shortening; add sugar and mix until light and fluffy. Add eggs; mix well. Add milk and vanilla to creamed mixture, mixing well. Combine remaining ingredients, stirring well. Add dry ingredients to creamed mixture, mixing well. Drop dough by teaspoonsfulls onto a floured surface; form dough into small balls. Place dough balls onto lightly greased cookie sheets; bake at 400 degrees for 8 minutes or until lightly browned. Yield: about 4 dozen.
Mrs. John R. Denison
Calcasieu Parish (Iowa)

OATMEAL COOKIES

2 cups sugar
1 cup shortening
2 eggs
3 tablespoons milk

2 cups self-rising flour
1 teaspoon ground nutmeg
3 cups regular oats, uncooked
1½ cups raisins (optional)

Cream sugar and shortening until fluffy in a large mixing bowl; add eggs, mixing well. Add milk; blend well. Stir in flour and nutmeg until well combined. Add oats and raisins, if desired; mix well. Drop dough by teaspoonfuls onto lightly greased cookie sheets. Bake at 325 degrees for 10 minutes or until done. Yield: about 6 dozen.
Mrs. Emmett Moore (Lillian)
Ouachita Parish (Monroe)

OATMEAL COOKIES

1 cup sugar
1 cup firmly packed brown
  sugar
1 cup vegetable oil
2 eggs, well beaten
1 teaspoon vanilla extract

1½ cups all-purpose flour
1 teaspoon soda
1 teaspoon salt
3 cups regular oats, uncooked
1 cup chopped nuts (optional)

Combine sugar and oil in a large mixing bowl; beat until creamy. Add eggs and vanilla; mix well. Combine dry ingredients; add to batter, mixing well. Stir in oats and nuts, if desired. Drop dough by teaspoonfuls onto lightly greased cookie sheets. Bake at 350 degrees for 8 to 10 minutes or until lightly browned. Yield: about 3 dozen cookies.
Mrs. Yvonne Waguespack
Terrebonne Parish (Gray)

LACE COOKIES

2 cups sugar
2 cups rolled oats, uncooked
1 heaping tablespoon
  all-purpose flour

½ teaspoon salt
1 cup hot melted butter
2 eggs, beaten
1 teaspoon vanilla extract

Combine first 4 ingredients in a large bowl; add butter, stirring until sugar is dissolved. Add eggs, and vanilla; mix well. Drop dough by ½ teaspoonfuls onto a foil-lined cookie sheet. Bake at 325 degrees for 10 to 15 minutes or until lightly browned. Allow to cool on foil; remove, and serve.
Diane Lemann
Ascension Parish (Donaldsonville)

MOLASSES COOKIES

1 cup sugar
1 cup shortening
1 cup molasses
1 tablespoon plus 1 teaspoon
  soda
2 teaspoon ground ginger

2 teaspoons ground cinnamon
½ teaspoon ground cloves
½ teaspoon ground nutmeg
1 cup buttermilk
4 to 6 cups all-purpose flour

Cream sugar and shortening until fluffy in a large mixing bowl; add molasses, mixing well. Combine soda, ginger, cloves, and nutmeg; add to sugar mixture alternately with buttermilk. Mix well. Add enough flour to make a soft dough. Roll dough out to ⅛-inch thickness on a floured surface; cut as desired. Place on lightly greased cookie sheets. Bake at 350 degrees for 8 to 10 minutes or until lightly browned. Yield: about 6 dozen cookies.
Mrs. Earl Duhe
Caldwell Parish (Columbia)

MOLASSES COOKIES

1 cup sugar
⅔ cup shortening
1 egg
¼ cup molasses
2 cups all-purpose flour

2 teaspoons soda
1 teaspoon ground cinnamon
½ teaspoon salt
½ teaspoon ground ginger
Sugar

Cream sugar and shortening until fluffy in a large mixing bowl; add egg, beating well. Gradually add molasses, mixing well. Combine remaining ingredients, except additional sugar; add to sugar mixture, mixing well. Chill until dough can be easily rolled into 1-inch balls. Roll each ball in sugar; place on lightly greased cookie sheets. Bake at 350 degrees for 10 to 12 minutes or until lightly browned. Yield: about 5 dozen.

Note: Do not substitute syrup for molasses.

Mrs. Debra Harmon
Claiborne Parish (Athens)

TRIPLET COOKIES

1 cup sugar
1 cup firmly packed brown
  sugar
1 cup shortening

2 eggs
2½ cups all-purpose flour
1 teaspoon soda
1 teaspoon salt

Cream sugar and shortening in a large mixing bowl until light and fluffy. Add eggs; mix well. Combine remaining ingredients; add to creamed mixture, mixing well. Divide dough into 3 portions. Drop one portion of dough onto lightly greased cookie sheets; bake at 350 degrees for 15 to 18 minutes or until lightly browned.

Variations:
1. Add ½ cup chopped drained maraschino cherries, ½ cup flaked coconut, and ¼ teaspoon almond extract to one portion of dough. Drop dough by teaspoonfuls onto lightly greased cookie sheets; bake as directed above.
2. Add ½ cup chopped dates and ½ cup chopped nuts to one portion of dough; Drop and bake as directed above.
3. Add ⅓ cup melted chocolate morsels; add to one portion of dough. Shape dough into 1-inch balls; roll in ½ cup powdered sugar. Bake as directed above.

Mrs. Jackie Theriot
St. Martin Parish (St. Martinville)

SOUR CREAM FRUIT COOKIES

1 cup butter, softened
1 16-ounce package light brown
  sugar
2 eggs, at room temperature
½ cup buttermilk
3½ cups sifted cake flour
1 teaspoon salt

½ teaspoon soda
2 cups chopped dates
2 cups chopped mixed candied fruit
1 cup chopped pecans
1 tablespoon plus 1 teaspoon
  bourbon whiskey

Cream butter and sugar until light and fluffy in a large mixing bowl; add eggs, one at a time, beating well after each addition. Stir in buttermilk. Combine flour, salt, and soda; add to creamed mixture, mixing well. Stir in remaining ingredients; chill overnight. Drop dough by heaping teaspoonfuls onto lightly greased cookie sheets. Bake at 400 degrees for 8 to 10 minutes or until lightly browned. Cool on wire racks. Yield: 4 dozen.

Mrs. Eugene Graugnard
West St. James Parish (St. James)

SKILLET COOKIES

½ cup margarine
1 cup sugar
1 cup chopped dates
1 egg, well beaten

2 cups Rice Krispies cereal
1 cup pecans, chopped
1 teaspoon vanilla extract
½ cup sifted powdered sugar

Melt margarine in a skillet; add sugar, dates, and egg. Cook over medium heat, stirring constantly, for 5 minutes. Remove from heat; add cereal, pecans, and vanilla. Shape dough into a long roll 1 to 1½-inches in diameter. Sprinkle roll with powdered sugar. Wrap in waxed paper; chill. Cut into slices to serve. Yield: 1 roll.

Note: Dough may be shaped into 1-inch balls and rolled in flaked coconut, if desired.

Mrs. Lorraine Watkins
Jeff Davis Parish (Welsh)

PEANUT BUTTER PATTIES

1 16-ounce package powdered
  sugar
1 18-ounce jar smooth peanut
  butter

1 cup margarine, softened
1 12-ounce package milk chocolate
  chips
¼ bar paraffin

Combine first 3 ingredients in a large bowl; knead well. Shape dough into patties that are 2-inches wide and ¼-inch thick. Chill for several hours. Melt chocolate and paraffin in the top of a double boiler. Using a fork or a toothpick, dip each pattie in chocolate mixture; place on waxed paper. Let stand until firm.

Pecan Patties:

1 16-ounce package powdered
  sugar
1 cup margarine, softened

1 cup ground pecans
1 teaspoon vanilla or almond
  extract

Combine all ingredients in a large bowl; shape, chill and dip as above.

Mint Patties:

1 16-ounce package powdered
  sugar
1 cup ground pecans
½ cup margarine, softened

1 teaspoon peppermint or
  spearmint extract
Pink food coloring or green food
  coloring

Combine all ingredients in a large bowl, using pink food coloring if peppermint extract is used, and green if spearmint extract is used. Shape, chill, and dip as above.

Mrs. Bernard Bordelon (Marie)
Avoyelles Parish (Moreauville)

PECAN CHEWIES

4 eggs
¼ cup butter
1 pound dark brown sugar
1½ cups all-purpose flour

1¼ teaspoons baking powder
Pinch of salt
2 or 3 cups chopped nuts

Beat eggs well; add butter and sugar. Place egg mixture in top of a double boiler; cook until well dissolved. Set aside. Add remaining ingredients to cooked mixture. Pour into 2 8-inch square pans; bake at 350 degrees for 25 to 35 minutes until done. Do not frost. These freeze well.
Annie R. Cooper
Caldwell Parish (Columbia)

ENGLISH APPLE PIE

Filling:
4 large baking apples, peeled
1 cup sugar
1 teaspoon ground cinnamon

Dice apples; place in a buttered baking dish. Combine sugar and cinnamon; sprinkle over apples.

Crust:
½ cup margarine, softened
½ cup firmly packed brown
  sugar
1 cup all-purpose flour
3 tablespoons water
1 teaspoon ground cinnamon

Cream margarine and sugar until fluffy; add remaining ingredients, mixing well, (batter will be very stiff). Spread batter over apples; bake at 350 degrees for 1 hour or until golden brown. Yield: 6 servings.

Mrs. Roy Martin Anderson (Linda Sue)
Ouachita Parish (Monroe)

APPLE CRUMB PIE

4 cups peeled, sliced apples
¼ cup orange juice
1 cup sugar
¾ cup sifted all-purpose flour
½ teaspoon ground cinnamon
Dash of salt
½ cup butter, softened
Whipped cream or ice cream
  (optional)

Place apples in a buttered 9-inch pie plate; pour orange juice over apples. Combine dry ingredients; cut in butter until mixture resembles crumbs. Sprinkle crumb mixture over apples. Bake at 375 degrees for 45 minutes or until apples are tender and top is crisp. Serve warm with whipped cream or ice cream, if desired. Yield: 6 servings.

Note: Substitute one 18-ounce can pre-sliced apples, drained, for fresh sliced apples, if desired.

Mrs. Gary Bordelon (Melanie)
Avoyelles Parish (Moreauville)

QUICK BLACKBERRY COBBLER

1 8-ounce can sliced pineapple, undrained
2 cups fresh blackberries or 1 16-ounce can blackberries, drained
¾ cup sugar

1 9-ounce package yellow cake mix
¼ cup margarine
½ cup milk
1 8-ounce carton Cool Whip, thawed

Drain pineapple, reserving juice. Cut pineapple into bite-size pieces. Place pineapple and berries in the bottom of a 11 x 9 x 1-inch glass baking dish; top with sugar. Pour pineapple juice over fruit. Sprinkle dry cake mix over fruit mixture; dot with margarine. Pour milk over dry mix; mix with a fork until mix is moist. Bake at 325 degrees for 40 minutes. Serve with Cool Whip, if desired.

Note: Half of one 18.5-ounce package yellow cake mix may be substituted for small package of cake mix, if desired.

Mrs. Harvey Core
St. Tammany Parish (Folsom)

OLD FASHIONED BLUEBERRY COBBLER

4 cups fresh blueberries
1½ cups sugar
2 cups water

Your favorite pastry recipe
¼ cup margarine
Sugar

Combine blueberries, sugar, and water in a saucepan; heat to boiling. Boil 2 minutes; remove from heat and set aside. Roll out half of your favorite pastry to fit the bottom of a deep baking dish. Place half of berry mixture over pastry; top with margarine. Roll remaining pastry out to ⅛-inch thickness; cut into strips. Place half of pastry strips over berry layer; top with remaining berries and juice. Dot with additional margarine. Top with remaining pastry strips. Dot with margarine. Sprinkle with sugar, as desired. Bake at 350 degrees for 45 minutes or until lightly browned. Yield: 6 to 8 servings.

Note: Taste berries after they have been boiled; add more sugar, if desired.

Mrs. H. E. Baird (Tena)
Ouachita Parish (Monroe)

PEACH CRISP

Filling:
2 cups fresh sliced peaches

Place peaches in the bottom of an 8-inch square pan.

Crust:
¾ cup sugar
¼ cup butter or margarine,
   softened
1 cup all-purpose flour

1 teaspoon baking powder
½ teaspoon salt
½ cup milk

Cream sugar and butter until light in a small mixing bowl. Combine dry ingredients in a bowl; add to creamed mixture alternately with milk, mixing well between additions. Spoon batter over peaches.

Topping:
1 cup sugar
1 tablespoon cornstarch
¼ teaspoon ground nutmeg

1 cup boiling water
Whipped cream or ice cream
   (optional)

Sift together dry ingredients; sprinkle over batter in pan. Pour water over all. Bake at 350 degrees for 1 hour or until lightly browned. Serve warm with whipped cream or ice cream, if desired. Yield: 6 servings.

Mrs. J. C. Taylor (Judy)
Ouachita Parish (Choudrant)

PEACH COBBLER

1 cup all-purpose flour
1 cup sugar
1⅓ cups milk
1 20-ounce can sliced peaches,
   undrained

½ cup melted margarine
1 teaspoon vanilla extract

Combine all ingredients; mix well. Pour into a lightly greased casserole. Bake at 350 degrees for 45 minutes or 1 hour or until lightly browned. Yield: 4 servings.

Mrs. Roy Martin Anderson (Linda Sue)
Ouachita Parish (Monroe)

Pies

EASY LEMON PIE

1 8-ounce container Cool Whip, thawed
1 6-ounce can frozen lemonade, thawed
1 14-ounce can sweetened condensed milk
1 9-inch baked pie shell

In large mixing bowl, combine Cool Whip, lemonade, and condensed milk; pour into prepared pie shell. Chill for 1 hour before serving. Yield: one 9-inch pie.

Anita Joiner
Tangipahoa Parish (Hammond)

STRAWBERRY PIE

1 9-inch baked pie shell
¾ cup sugar
1 cup plus 2 tablespoons water
Pinch of salt
3 tablespoons cornstarch
½ teaspoon red food coloring
1 tablespoon lemon juice
1 pint sliced fresh strawberries
Whipped cream (optional)

Combine sugar, water, salt, and cornstarch in a saucepan; cook over medium heat until thick. Add food coloring and lemon juice. Let cool. Add strawberries. Pour into baked pie shell. Chill. Top with whipped cream, if desired. Yield: one 9-inch pie.

Mrs. Donald Johnson (Brenda)
Ouachita Parish (Monroe)

STRAWBERRY CHIFFON PIE

1 14-ounce can sweetened condensed milk
¼ cup lemon juice
1 small carton Cool Whip, thawed
1 pint sliced strawberries
1 9-inch graham cracker crust or vanilla wafer crust

Combine condensed milk and lemon juice in large mixing bowl. Stir in Cool Whip, until mixed thoroughly. Fold in strawberries and mix well. Pour mixture into graham cracker crust. Chill at least ½ hour before serving. Yield: 8 servings.

Note: Any fresh fruit or canned drained fruit may be substituted for fresh strawberries.

Charlotte Harris
Washington Parish (Angie)

FRESH STRAWBERRY PIE

1½ to 2 pints fresh
  strawberries, washed and
  hulled
1 cup water
1 cup sugar
1 tablespoon light Karo syrup

2 tablespoons cornstarch
3 tablespoons strawberry Jello
1 8-inch baked pie shell
Whipped cream or thawed Cool
  Whip

Combine water, sugar, syrup and cornstarch in a saucepan; cook over low heat until thick. Add Jello, stirring to dissolve. Allow mixture to cool; pour ½ cooled mixture into baked pie shell, add strawberries and pour in remaining cooled mixture. Top with whipped cream or Cool Whip. Refrigerate for 1 hour before serving. Yield: one 8-inch pie.

Connie Granger
Beauregard Parish (DeRidder)

BLACKBERRY COBBLER

1 egg
¼ cup sugar
⅓ cup milk
3 tablespoons shortening
1 cup all-purpose flour

2 teaspoons baking powder
½ teaspoon salt
1 quart fresh blackberries
1 cup sugar
1 teaspoon ground cinnamon

Beat egg until well mixed in a small mixing bowl. Add ¼ cup sugar, milk, and shortening to egg; mix well. Sift together flour, baking powder, and salt; add to milk mixture, mixing well. Place blackberries in the bottom of a 14 x 10-inch pan; top with 1 cup sugar and cinnamon. Cover with batter; bake at 375 degrees for 35 to 40 minutes. Serve warm or cold. Yield: 6 servings.

Mrs. R. Ernest Girouard, Jr.
Vermilion Parish (Kaplan)

QUICK AND EASY PEACH COBBLER

3 tablespoons melted butter
2 cups Pioneer biscuit mix
1 cup sugar

1 20-ounce can sliced peaches,
  undrained

Place butter in a 3-quart casserole. Combine remaining ingredients, mixing well. Spoon into buttered casserole. Cover; bake at 350 degrees for 35 to 40 minutes or until top is golden brown. Yield: 4 to 6 servings.

Carol Bonnecaze
East Baton Rouge Parish (Baton Rouge)

SWEET CRUST DEWBERRY COBBLER

Crust:

1 cup sugar
½ cup butter or margarine,
  softened
1 egg
1 teaspoon vanilla extract

⅓ cup commercial sour cream
¼ teaspoon soda
¼ teaspoon salt
2 cups sifted all-purpose flour
Additional all-purpose flour

Cream sugar and butter until light and fluffy in a medium mixing bowl; add egg and vanilla, mixing well. Combine sour cream, soda, and salt; add to creamed mixture alternately with 2 cups flour, mixing well. Using a spoon, spread ⅔ of dough into the bottom of a 13 x 9 x 2-inch pan. Sprinkle 1 to 2 tablespoons flour over dough in pan; pat smooth with hands.

Filling:

6 heaping cups fresh dewberries
2 cups sugar

2 tablespoons all-purpose flour

Combine all ingredients; mix well. Pour into prepared crust. Drop remaining crust dough by tablespoonfuls into additional flour; pat dough with flour into thin pieces. Place dough pieces over berry layer, sealing dough at edges. Bake at 350 degrees for 35 to 40 minutes or until golden brown. Yield: 8 servings.

Note: Strawberries, blackberries or any other fruit may be substituted, if desired. Add ½ teaspoon vinegar or lemon juice to rich milk and use instead of sour cream, if desired.

Mrs. Dan Hoffpauir (Edith)
Calcasieu Parish (Lake Charles)

EASY FRUIT PIE

¼ cup lemon juice concentrate
1 14-ounce can sweetened
  condensed milk
1 cup drained crushed
  pineapple

1 8-ounce carton Cool Whip,
  thawed
1 teaspoon vanilla extract
2 9-inch graham cracker pie crusts

In a large mixing bowl, combine lemon juice and condensed milk, mixing well. Fold in pineapple, Cool Whip and vanilla. Pour mixture into prepared graham cracker crusts. Chill. Yield: 2 pies.

Note: Other fruit may be substituted or combined; also nuts may be added.

Mrs. Maxwell Desselle (Margaret)
Avoyelles Parish (Moreauville)

PEACH-A-BERRY COBBLER

Filling:

2 to 3 cups sliced fresh
  Louisiana peaches
Sugar
¼ cup firmly packed brown
  sugar

1 tablespoon cornstarch
½ cup cold water
1 tablespoon margarine
1 tablespoon lemon juice
1 cup fresh blueberries

Sprinkle peaches with sugar, as desired; set aside. Combine brown sugar, cornstarch, and water in a small saucepan; cook over medium heat, stirring occasionally, until mixture is thickened. Remove from heat; add margarine, lemon juice, sugared peaches, and blueberries. Pour fruit mixture into a 8½ x 1¾-inch ovenware cake dish.

Topping:

1 cup all-purpose flour
½ cup sugar
1½ teaspoons baking powder
½ teaspoon salt
½ cup milk

¼ cup margarine, softened
2 tablespoons sugar
¼ teaspoon ground nutmeg
Whipped cream or ice cream
  (optional)

Sift together first 4 ingredients in a medium bowl; add milk and margarine. Beat with an electric mixer until smooth. Pour over fruit mixture. Combine remaining 2 tablespoons sugar and nutmeg; sprinkle over topping. Bake at 350 degrees for 30 minutes or until lightly browned. Serve warm with whipped cream or ice cream, as desired. Yield: 6 servings.

Mrs. John C. Taylor (Judy)
Ouachita Parish (Choudrant)

COCONUT PIE

2 cups milk
¾ cup sugar
½ cup Bisquick mix
4 eggs

¼ cup margarine or butter
1½ teaspoons vanilla extract
½ cup freshly grated coconut

Preheat oven to 350 degrees. Combine milk, sugar, Bisquick mix, eggs, margarine and vanilla extract in a blender. Thoroughly blend for 3 minutes. Pour into 9-inch pie plate and sprinkle grated coconut on top. Let stand for 5 minutes. Bake at 350 degrees for 40 minutes or until golden brown.

Mrs. Yvonne Waguespack
Terrebonne Parish (Gray)

CRUSTY COCONUT PIE

½ cup milk
1¼ cups flaked coconut
¼ cup margarine or butter
1 cup sugar

3 eggs
1 teaspoon vanilla extract
1 9-inch unbaked pie shell

Preheat oven to 350 degrees. Pour milk over coconut and set aside. Cream together margarine and sugar until light and fluffy. Add eggs, and beat mixture well. Add coconut mixture and vanilla extract if desired. Pour into unbaked 9-inch pie shell. Bake at 350 degrees for 30 minutes or until pie is golden brown and firm.

Marie Harper
Tangipahoa Parish (Hammond)

CREAMY COCONUT PIE

¾ cup sugar
3 tablespoons cornstarch
Dash of salt
2 cups milk
3 egg yolks, well beaten

¾ teaspoon vanilla extract
¼ teaspoon almond extract
1 9-inch baked pie shell
2 3½-ounce cans flaked coconut

In heavy saucepan, combine sugar, cornstarch and salt. Gradually stir in milk until smooth. Over medium heat, bring mixture to a boil, stirring occasionally. Cook for 1 minute or until thick and shiny. Quickly stir some of the hot mixture into egg yolks. Add egg mixture to hot mixture, mixing well. Cook over low heat for 3 minutes, stirring constantly. Remove from heat. Stir in extracts. Pour into a small bowl. Cover with waxed paper and chill for 1 hour. Pour chilled filling into baked pie shell. Sprinkle with half of flaked coconut. Top with whipped cream. Sprinkle other half of coconut on top. Serve at once; or refrigerate for 1 hour.

Topping:
1 cup chilled whipping cream
2 tablespoons powdered sugar

In chilled mixing bowl, beat cream and powdered sugar until firm. Cover and refrigerate.

Note: 2 cups freshly grated coconut may be substituted for canned, if desired.

Mrs. Jude Plauché (Margaret)
Avoyelles Parish (Hamburg)

COCONUT PIE

Filling:

⅓ cup flour
1 cup sugar
2 cups milk
3 egg yolks
Dash of salt

1 teaspoon vanilla extract
2 tablespoons butter
½ cup flaked coconut
1 9-inch baked pie shell

In a large saucepan over low heat, combine flour and sugar. Stir in ½ cup milk and one egg yolk at a time, mixing thoroughly. Add the rest of the milk, and dash of salt. Cook until mixture thickens. Add vanilla extract, butter and coconut. Pour into 9-inch baked pie shell. Set aside and allow to cool while preparing topping.

Topping:

3 egg whites
½ cup sugar

1 teaspoon vanilla extract
Additional flaked coconut (optional)

In a glass mixing bowl, beat the egg whites until stiff, while adding the sugar and vanilla. Spread over pie filling; sprinkle with additional coconut, if desired. Place under broiler unit until brown.

Mrs. Donald Johnson (Brenda)
Ouachita Parish (Monroe)

DELICIOUS CUSTARD PIE FILLING

2 tablespoons margarine or
  butter
¼ cup cream cornstarch
¾ cup sugar

½ teaspoon salt
2 cups milk
2 egg yolks, slightly beaten
1 teaspoon vanilla extract

In a heavy saucepan over low heat melt margarine; blend in cornstarch, sugar and salt. Gradually add the milk, stirring constantly. Over medium heat, bring to a boil stirring constantly. Boil for 1 minute or until thick and creamy. Quickly stir some of the hot mixture into the egg yolks; add to remaining hot mixture, stirring well, making sure all ingredients are well combined. Allow to cook for 2 minutes. Remove from heat; add vanilla; stir well. This makes 2 cups of pudding or filling for 1 9-inch baked pie shell.

Mrs. Yvonne Waguespack
Terrebonne Parish (Gray)

CUSTARD PIE

3 eggs
¼ cup sugar
¼ teaspoon salt
2¼ cups milk

2 teaspoons vanilla extract
Ground nutmeg
1 9-inch unbaked pie shell

Preheat oven to 425 degrees. In a mixing bowl, beat the eggs thoroughly. Add sugar, salt, milk, and vanilla, stirring well. Pour into unbaked pie shell. Sprinkle nutmeg on top. Bake at 425 degrees for 40 minutes or until inserted knife comes out clean.

Mrs. Arlie Newman Harrigille
Grandmother of Mrs. S. L. Ford, Sr.
Concordia Parish (Monterey)

LEMON CHESS PIE

1 cup sugar
4 eggs
Juice of 2 lemons

½ cup melted margarine
1 9-inch unbaked pie shell

Preheat oven to 350 degrees. Combine sugar, eggs, and lemon juice; mix well. Pour margarine into mixture and stir until dissolved. Pour into unbaked pie shell. Bake at 350 degrees for 45 minutes to 1 hour.

Mrs. Hardee Brian
East Baton Rouge Parish (Zachary)

CHESS PIE

2 cups sugar
1 tablespoon all-purpose flour
1 tablespoon waterground or
    regular white corn meal
4 eggs

¼ cup milk
¼ cup melted butter
¼ cup lemon juice
1 teaspoon finely grated lemon rind
1 9-inch unbaked pie shell

Preheat oven to 350 degrees. In a large bowl, stir together the sugar, flour, and corn meal. Add eggs, milk, butter, and lemon juice; beat well. Add lemon rind; mixing well. Pour into 9-inch pastry shell. Bake at 350 degrees for 50 to 60 minutes, or until knife comes out clean. Serves 6 to 8.

Note: Bake on rack just below the center until top is very brown.

Pam Accardo
Ouachita Parish (Monroe)

CHOCOLATE PIE

Filling:
¾ cup sugar
6 tablespoons flour
6 tablespoons cocoa
½ teaspoon salt
2½ cups milk

3 beaten egg yolks
2 tablespoons butter
1 teaspoon vanilla extract
1 9-inch baked pie shell

Combine sugar, flour, cocoa, and salt in a saucepan. Gradually stir in milk; cook over medium heat, stirring constantly until thick. Pour a small amount of hot mixture into beaten egg yolks, stirring well. Return to hot mixture; stir well and cook 2 minutes longer. Remove from heat; add butter and vanilla, mixing well. Pour into 9-inch baked pie shell. Set aside while preparing meringue.

Meringue:
3 egg whites
⅓ cup sugar

½ teaspoon vanilla extract

In mixing bowl, beat egg whites on high speed of electric mixer, gradually adding sugar and vanilla. Beat until mixture holds firm peaks. Spread meringue over pie. Bake at 350 degrees for 12 to 15 minutes or until browned.

Shirley Wood
West Carroll Parish (Pioneer)

CHOCOLATE PIE

⅓ cup all-purpose flour
1⅓ cups sugar
⅓ cup cocoa
3 eggs, well beaten
1 cup milk

1 teaspoon vanilla extract
4 tablespoons margarine or butter
1 10-inch baked pie shell
Whipped cream (optional)

Combine flour, sugar, and cocoa in a saucepan. Gradually stir in the milk and cook over low heat until thickened. Stir in beaten eggs; cook until thick. Remove from heat. Add margarine and vanilla extract. Pour into 10-inch baked pie shell. Refrigerate. Before serving, garnish with whipped cream, if desired. Yield: one 10-inch pie.

Betty Bairnsfather
Concordia Parish (Monterey)

CHOCOLATE CHESS PIE

2 to 3 tablespoons cocoa
1½ cups sugar
½ cup melted margarine
2 eggs, well beaten

1 teaspoon vanilla extract
1 5.33-ounce can Pet evaporated
  milk
1 9-inch unbaked pie shell

Preheat oven to 350 degrees. Mix cocoa, sugar, and margarine. Add eggs, milk and vanilla, mixing thoroughly. Pour into unbaked pie shell and bake at 350 degrees for 1 hour.

Marie Harper
Tangipahoa Parish (Hammond)

CHOCOLATE PIE

Filling:
1⅓ cups sugar
3 tablespoons cocoa
Dash of salt
3 tablespoons cornstarch
2 cups milk

1 teaspoon margarine, melted
3 egg yolks, well beaten
1 teaspoon vanilla extract
1 9-inch baked pie shell

In heavy saucepan, mix sugar, cocoa, salt, and cornstarch; stir in milk and margarine. Cook over medium heat, stirring constantly until thickened. Add 3 egg yolks to ¼ cup hot mixture; mix well. Add to remaining hot chocolate mixture. Cook over medium heat until it begins to thicken, 2 to 3 minutes. Remove from heat. Add vanilla; pour into baked pie shell. Set aside to cool.

Meringue:
3 egg whites
½ cup sugar

1 teaspoon vanilla extract

In large mixing bowl, beat egg whites until stiff. Gradually add sugar and vanilla, beating constantly. Egg whites should hold firm peaks. Spread over pie and bake at 350 degrees for 12 to 15 minutes or until browned. Yield: one 9-inch pie.

Mrs. Donald Johnson (Brenda)
Ouachita Parish (Monroe)

BUTTERMILK PIE

1 9-inch unbaked pie shell	3 eggs
½ cup softened margarine	1 cup buttermilk
1½ cups sugar	1 teaspoon vanilla extract
3 well-rounded tablespoons all-purpose flour	Dash of ground nutmeg

Preheat oven to 350 degrees. In a mixing bowl, cream the margarine and sugar until light and fluffy. Add flour and eggs, beating well. Stir in buttermilk. Add vanilla; mix well. Pour into unbaked 9-inch pie shell. Sprinkle with nutmeg. Bake at 350 degrees for 45 to 50 minutes or until firm in the center. Allow to cool before serving.

Mrs. Albert Burke (Anna Lee)
Avoyelles Parish (Moreauville)

BUTTERMILK PIE

1 cup margarine, softened	¼ cup lemon juice
3 cups sugar	½ teaspoon ground nutmeg
6 eggs	1 teaspoon vanilla extract
6 tablespoons all-purpose flour	2 9-inch unbaked pie shells
2 cups buttermilk	

Preheat oven to 350 degrees. In a large mixing bowl, cream the margarine and sugar until light and fluffy. Add eggs; beat well. Add remaining ingredients in order listed above. Don't beat mixture much after adding the buttermilk. Pour into 2 unbaked 9-inch pie shells. Bake at 350 degrees for 30 minutes or until firm in the center. Yields two 9-inch pies.

Note: This is an old, old recipe. I got it from a friend's grandmother.
Mrs. B. F. Lemoine, Jr. (Grace)
Avoyelles Parish (Hamburg)

OLD-FASHIONED BUTTERMILK PIE

½ cup softened margarine or butter	¼ cup all-purpose flour
2 cups sugar	1 cup buttermilk
3 eggs	Dash of ground nutmeg
	1 10-inch unbaked pie shell

Preheat oven to 350 degrees. In a mixing bowl, combine the margarine and sugar, creaming well. Add flour and eggs, beating until light and fluffy for about 2 minutes. Fold in buttermilk and nutmeg. Pour into unbaked 10-inch pie shell. Bake at 350 degrees for 50 minutes. Allow to cool at room temperature. Yield: one 10-inch pie.

Thelma Rowland
Caldwell Parish (Columbia)

DONNA'S DELIGHT...A PIE TO PLEASE ALL TASTES!!

1 14-ounce can sweetened
condensed milk
¼ cup lemon juice
1 3-ounce can flaked coconut
1 cup chopped pecans
1 10-ounce can crushed
pineapple, drained

1 8-ounce carton Cool Whip,
thawed
1 9-inch graham cracker crust or
prepared crust

In a large mixing bowl, combine condensed milk and lemon juice. Add coconut, pecans, and pineapple. Fold in Cool Whip. Spread into crumb or prepared crust. Chill.
Note: This is my husband's favorite dessert. It is simple and delicious!!
Mrs. Ronald R. Anderson
East Feliciana Parish (Ethel)

IMPOSSIBLE PIE

2 cups milk
4 eggs
½ cup sugar
2 teaspoons vanilla extract

1 cup flaked coconut
½ cup cubed margarine or butter
½ cup Bisquick mix

Preheat oven to 350 degrees. Grease a 9-inch pie pan and set aside. In a blender, combine milk, eggs, sugar, vanilla, coconut, margarine and Bisquick mix. Cover and blend for 1 minute. This process may also be done in a food processor. Pour batter into greased pie pan. Bake at 350 degrees for 35 to 40 minutes or until a knife inserted in center comes out clean. Serves 8.
Mrs. Wayne Petticrew (Betty)
Calcasieu Parish (Iowa)

MILLIONAIRE PIE

4 cups sifted powdered sugar
1 cup butter
3 eggs
½ teaspoon salt
½ teaspoon vanilla extract

1 9-inch baked pie shell
3 cups whipping cream
2 cups drained crushed pineapple
(1 20-ounce can, drained)
1 cup chopped pecans

Cream together powdered sugar and butter. Add eggs, salt and vanilla, mixing well until light and fluffy. Spread over baked 9-inch crust and chill. Whip cream until stiff; blend in crushed pineapple and pecans. Spoon mixture over chilled layer. Chill until serving time. Yield: one 9-inch pie.
Mrs. Louis D. Curet
East Baton Rouge Parish (Baton Rouge)

MILLIONAIRE PIE

1 10-ounce can Eagle Brand
  sweetened condensed milk
1 10-ounce can crushed
  pineapple, drained
1 16-ounce can peach slices,
  drained

¼ cup lemon juice
1 8-ounce container frozen Cool
  Whip, thawed
2 9-inch graham cracker crusts

Combine all ingredients in a large mixing bowl, mixing well. Pour into graham cracker crusts. Refrigerate before serving. Yields: two 9-inch pies.

Note: Do not substitute another brand of condensed milk or topping as it simply does not taste as good.

Mrs. Doug Moore (Liz)
Ouachita Parish (Monroe)

Reba Duncan
Madison Parish (Tallulah)

THREE LAYER PIE

Bottom Layer:
1 cup all-purpose flour
½ cup margarine, melted

1 cup chopped pecans

Preheat oven to 350 degrees. Mix flour, margarine, and nuts together; pat into a 13 x 9 x 2-inch pan. Bake at 350 degrees for 20 minutes. Allow crust to cool.

Second Layer:
1 cup sifted powdered sugar
1 8-ounce package cream
  cheese, softened

1½ cups thawed Cool Whip

Cream sugar and cream cheese; fold in Cool Whip. Spread over cooled crust.

Third Layer:
1 3-ounce package instant
  vanilla pudding mix
1 3-ounce package instant
  chocolate pudding mix

Additional thawed Cool Whip

Prepare puddings separately, according to package directions. Spread chocolate pudding over cream cheese layer. Spread vanilla pudding over chocolate layer. Top with additional Cool Whip. Refrigerate overnight.

Helen Moreland
Concordia Parish (Monterey)

PECAN PIE

1 cup sugar
½ cup firmly packed light
  brown sugar
¼ cup all-purpose flour
2 eggs

2 tablespoons corn syrup
1 teaspoon vanilla extract
½ cup melted margarine or butter
1 cup finely chopped pecans
1 9-inch unbaked pie shell

Preheat oven to 350 degrees. In large mixing bowl, combine all ingredients, except pecans, mixing well. If mixture is lumpy, use electric mixer to combine all ingredients well. Stir in pecans. Pour mixture into unbaked 9-inch pie shell. Bake at 350 degrees for 45-50 minutes or until done.

Mrs. Hardee Brian
East Baton Rouge Parish (Zachary)

PECAN PIE FILLING

1 egg, well beaten
½ cup firmly packed dark
  brown sugar
¾ cup sugar
1 tablespoon melted butter

1 teaspoon vanilla extract
⅛ teaspoon salt
1 cup chopped pecans
1 9-inch unbaked pie shell

Preheat oven to 350 degrees. Mix all ingredients together in large mixing bowl. Pour into unbaked pie shell; bake at 350 degrees for 25 minutes. Allow to cool for 5 minutes and serve with pointed knife.

Pat Cain
St. Landry Parish (Opelousas)

PECAN PIE

1 cup sugar
½ cup margarine or butter,
  softened
1 cup white Karo syrup

2 eggs
Dash of salt
1 cup chopped pecans
1 9-inch unbaked pie shell

Preheat oven to 300 degrees. Cream butter and sugar until light and fluffy. Add remaining ingredients, in order given; mix well. Pour into unbaked pie shell. Bake at 300 degrees for about 1 hour or more. Test for doneness by shaking pie plate (Middle of pie should shake a little). Don't overbake. Yield: one 9-inch pie.

Note: You may like to bake it at 275 degrees and a little longer time. It is yummy!!

Mrs. B. F. Lemoine, Jr. (Grace)
Avoyelles Parish (Hamburg)

BLACK RIVER PECAN PIE

1 cup pecan halves
1 9-inch unbaked pie shell
3 eggs
½ cup light corn syrup

1 tablespoon melted butter
½ teaspoon vanilla extract
1 cup sugar
1 tablespoon all-purpose flour

Preheat oven to 350 degrees. Arrange pecan halves in unbaked pie shell. In large mixing bowl, beat the 3 eggs well. Add corn syrup, butter, and vanilla; mix well. In a small bowl, combine sugar and flour; add to egg mixture and pour over nuts. Let stand until nuts rise to the top of the mixture. Bake at 350 degrees for 30 to 40 minutes or until golden brown.

Note: This is one of the favorite pies in the Black River Area because we have the small native pecans.

Mrs. S. L. Ford, Sr.
Catahoula Parish (Jonesville)

PECAN PIE

3 eggs
1 cup firmly packed brown
  sugar
1 tablespoon melted butter
1 cup light corn syrup
1 cup chopped pecans

1 teaspoon vanilla extract
¼ teaspoon salt
1 teaspoon almond extract
  (optional)
1 9-inch unbaked pie shell

Preheat oven to 350 degrees. Beat eggs well in a large mixing bowl. Add other ingredients in order given; mix well. Pour mixture into unbaked pie shell. Bake at 350 degrees for 45 minutes until crust is done and filling is set. Yield: 1 pie.

Note: Mrs. Cindy Weeks, Ouachita Parish omits salt and almond flavoring. She uses white sugar instead of brown sugar.

Addie H. Beach
Ouachita Parish (Monroe)

PEACH YOGURT PIE

2 8-ounce cartons peach yogurt
1 4-ounce carton Cool Whip, thawed
1 9-inch graham cracker crust

1 3-ounce package peach-flavored gelatin
1 cup sliced fresh peaches (more, if desired)

Stir yogurt and Cool Whip together; pour into graham cracker crust. Chill. Prepare gelatin according to package directions, using slightly less water as directed. Chill gelatin until slightly thickened; fold in peach slices. Spoon gelatin mixture over chilled filling. Garnish with additional sliced peaches, if desired. Chill until top is set. Yield: one 9-inch pie.

Mrs. John C. Taylor (Judy)
Ouachita Parish (Choudrant)

CREOLE PRALINES

2 cups sugar
1 cup firmly packed dark or light brown sugar
1 stick butter

1 cup milk
2 tablespoons Karo syrup
4 cups pecan halves

In a 3-quart saucepan, combine all ingredients except the pecans. Bring to a boil over medium heat. Cook for 20 minutes, stirring occasionally. Add pecans, and cook the mixture until the liquid forms a soft ball when a little is dropped into cold water (234°). Stir well. Drop by spoonfuls onto waxed paper. You may place a few sheets of newspaper beneath the waxed paper, if desired.

Allen J. Ellender

PUMPKIN EGG NOG PIE

½ cup firmly packed brown sugar
½ cup sugar
½ teaspoon salt
½ teaspoon cinnamon
½ teaspoon ground ginger

½ teaspoon ground nutmeg
1 cup commercial egg nog
3 eggs
1 cup canned mashed pumpkin
1 tablespoon cornstarch
1 9-inch unbaked pie shell

Preheat oven to 350 degrees. In large mixing bowl, combine all ingredients, until well blended. Pour into unbaked pie shell. Bake at 350 degrees for 45 minutes or until knife inserted in center of pie comes out clean. Yield: one 9-inch pie.

Reba Duncan
Madison Parish (Tallulah)

GRASSHOPPER PIE

Crust:

1½ cups chocolate wafer crumbs

¼ cup butter, melted

In a medium size bowl, mix the cookie crumbs and melted butter. Press mixture into a 9-inch pie plate. Reserve ¼ cup crumb mixture for garnishing top of pie.

Filling:

24 medium size marshmallows
⅓ cup milk
¼ cup Crème de Cacao

2 tablespoons Crème de Menthe
1 cup whipped cream

In a heavy saucepan, melt the marshmallows with milk over low heat. Allow to cool. Stir in liqueurs. Fold in whipped cream. Gently pour into the prepared crust. Garnish with reserved cookie crumbs. Refrigerate 1 hour before serving.

Mrs. Allen Bares (Lynn)
Vermilion Parish (Erath)

OUT OF THIS WORLD PIE

1 9-inch unbaked pie shell
2 large eggs
½ cup all-purpose flour
1 cup sugar
1 teaspoon vanilla extract

½ cup melted butter
1 cup chopped pecans
1 cup semi-sweet chocolate chips
Whipped cream (optional)

Preheat oven to 325 degrees. Beat eggs until thick and lemon-colored in a medium mixing bowl. Add flour and sugar; continue beating 2 minutes. Add vanilla, butter, pecans and chocolate chips. Pour into pie shell; bake at 325 degrees for 60 minutes. Serve warm or at room temperature. Garnish with whipped cream, if desired.

Note: Do not put pie in refrigerator until after serving. When cold the texture changes. Before serving any leftover pie, take it out of the refrigerator and put it in a warm oven (200 degrees) and then cool at room temperature.

Mrs. Louis D. Curet
East Baton Rouge Parish (Baton Rouge)

FROZEN STRAWBERRY RICE PIE

½ cup whipping cream, whipped
1 8-ounce package cream cheese, softened
½ cup sugar
1½ cups frozen strawberries, drained and sliced

1½ tablespoons unflavored gelatin
¼ cup strawberry juice, heated
1 cup cold cooked rice
1 9-inch baked pie shell

In a large mixing bowl, beat cream cheese and sugar until fluffy. Add drained strawberries. Dissolve gelatin in heated strawberry juice; let stand. Combine with cream cheese mixture. Stir in cooked rice; fold in whipped cream. Pour into baked pie shell. Chill and serve. Serves 6.

Mrs. Loretta Treme
Jeff Davis Parish (Elton)

SWEET POTATO PIE

3 separated eggs
1 cup sugar, divided
1 cup cooked mashed sweet potatoes
1 teaspoon ground cinnamon
1 teaspoon ground pumpkin pie spice

½ teaspoon ground nutmeg
½ cup milk
1 tablespoon unflavored gelatin
¼ cup cold water
1 baked 9-inch pastry shell

Beat egg yolks until thick and lemon colored in top of a double boiler. Add ½ cup sugar, sweet potatoes, spices and milk. Soften gelatin in ¼ cup cold water. Cook potato mixture in top of double boiler, stirring constantly, until thick. When thick, stir in softened gelatin until dissolved. Let cool 10 minutes. Beat egg whites until stiff, adding remaining ½ cup sugar. Fold egg whites into cooled potato mixture. Pour into baked pie shell. Chill 2 hours. Yield: one 9-inch pie.

Edwina Harper
West Carroll Parish (Oak Grove)

PUDDING PIE

½ cup melted margarine
1 cup all-purpose flour
1 cup chopped pecans
1 8-ounce package cream
cheese, softened
1 cup thawed Cool Whip
1 cup sifted powdered sugar

1 baked 9-inch pie shell
1 6-ounce box instant chocolate
pudding mix
1 6-ounce box instant vanilla
pudding mix
Cool Whip, thawed

Preheat oven to 350 degrees. Mix margarine, flour, and pecans together; press mixture into a 12 x 9 x 2-inch pan. Bake at 350 degrees for about 7 minutes, until slightly brown. Allow crust to cool. Mix cream cheese, 1 cup Cool Whip, and powdered sugar until well combined; spread over baked crust. Mix instant chocolate pudding according to package directions, omitting ¼ cup milk; spread over first layer. Mix vanilla pudding according to package directions, omitting ¼ cup milk; spread over chocolate layer. Top with desired amount of Cool Whip; chill before serving. Yield: one 9-inch pie.

Mrs. Maxwell Desselle (Margaret)
Avoyelles Parish (Moreauville)

TANG PIE

1 14-ounce can sweetened
condensed milk
1 8-ounce carton commercial
sour cream
¼ cup Tang instant breakfast
drink
1 9-ounce carton Cool Whip,
thawed

1 10-inch graham cracker crust
Mandarin oranges and banana slices
(optional)
Additional thawed Cool Whip
(optional)

Combine milk and sour cream; mix well. Stir in Tang (This will congeal rather quickly). Fold in Cool Whip. Add fruit, if desired. Pour into graham cracker crust. Refrigerate overnight. Garnish with additional Cool Whip, if desired.

Note: This makes a lovely salad with sliced bananas; just cut into squares to serve.

Dorothy Neill
Madison Parish (Tallulah)

CREAM CHEESE PIE SHELLS

1 3-ounce package cream
  cheese, softened
½ cup butter, softened

1 cup plus 1 teaspoon sifted
  all-purpose flour

Combine cream cheese and butter, mixing until smooth; add flour, mixing well. Chill 1 hour. Shape dough into 1-inch balls; place each in a well-greased miniature muffin cup, shaping into a shell. Bake at 350 degrees for 25 minutes. Allow to cool before filling. Yield: about 2 dozen.

Pat Cain
St. Landry Parish (Opelousas)

MERINGUE I

2 egg whites, at room
  temperature

¼ teaspoon salt
6 tablespoons sugar

Beat egg whites until stiff, but not dry; gradually add salt, beating constantly. Add sugar, beating constantly until sugar is dissolved. Swirl over pie filling, sealing edges well. Bake at 325 degrees for 20 minutes or until lightly browned. Cool slowly. Yield: enough to cover a 8 or 9-inch pie.

Note: Use 3 egg whites, ½ teaspoon salt, and 9 tablespoons sugar to cover a 10-inch pie.

Mrs. S. L. Ford (Claudia)
Catahoula Parish (Jonesville)

NEVER FAIL PASTRY

2¾ cups all-purpose flour
1½ teaspoons salt
1 cup shortening

1 egg
Cold water

Combine flour and salt in a medium bowl; cut in shortening until mixture resembles crumbs. Beat egg in a measuring cup; add enough cold water to make ½ cup. Add egg mixture to dough, stirring well with a fork. Shape dough into a ball; wrap in waxed paper and chill. Yield: enough for 2 to 3 9-inch pies.

Pat Cain
St. Landry Parish (Opelousas)

PIE DOUGH MIX

7 cups sifted all-purpose flour   1 tablespoon plus 1 teaspoon salt
2 cups shortening   Water

Combine first 3 ingredients in a large mixing bowl; mix on low speed of electric mixer until well combined. Place dough in a covered container; store in the refrigerator for up to 1 month. To use, measure 1 cup mix for each 9-inch pie shell desired. Sprinkle enough water over 1 cup mix to moisten (about 2 to 4 tablespoons water); roll dough out onto a lightly floured surface, as desired. Yield: enough for nine 9-inch pastry shells.

Mrs. B. F. Lemoine, Jr. (Grace)
Avoyelles Parish (Hamburg)

PIE CRUST

1 cup all-purpose flour   ½ cup butter, softened
¼ cup firmly packed brown   ½ cup chopped pecans
  sugar

Combine flour and sugar; cut in butter until mixture resembles coarse crumbs. Stir in pecans. Press mixture firmly into a 9-inch pie pan. Bake at 400 degrees for 15 minutes or until golden brown. While pastry is hot, break up pie shell and press evenly into pie pan once again, if desired. Yield: one 9-inch pie shell.

Edwina Harper
West Carroll Parish (Oak Grove)

SOY PIE CRUST

1⅓ cups all-purpose flour   1 teaspoon salt
⅔ cup soy flour   5 tablespoons shortening
1 teaspoon sugar   3 to 4 tablespoons cold water

Combine dry ingredients; cut in shortening. Add enough water to moisten dough, mixing well with a fork. Shape dough into a ball; roll dough out on a floured surface. Place in pie plate and bake at 350 degrees for 12 to 15 minutes or until lightly browned. Yield: enough for two 9 or 10-inch pie plates.

Sara Schexnayder
Pointe Coupe Parish (Ventress)

Pickles
and Preserves

Natchez

HOW TO PRESERVE A HUSBAND

First, use care and get one not too young, but tender and a healthy growth. Make your selection carefully and let it be final, otherwise they will not keep. Do not pickle or put in hot water, this makes them sour. Like wine they sweeten with age. Prepare as follows: Sweeten with smiles according to variety. The sour bitter kind are improved by a pinch of common sense. Spice with patience. Wrap well in a mantle of charity. Preserve over a good fire of steady devotion. Serve with peaches and cream.

Note: The poorest varieties may be improved by this process and keep for years in any climate.

Marie Harper
Tangipahoa Parish (Hammond)

PRESERVED CHILDREN

1 large field	Pinch of brook
6 children	Pebbles
2-3 small dogs	Flowers

Take 1 large field, half a dozen children, dogs and a pinch of brook, and some pebbles. Mix the children and dogs well. Put them on the field, stirring constantly. Pour the brook over the pebbles; sprinkle the field with flowers. Spread over all a deep blue sky and bake in the sun. When brown, set aside to cool in the bathtub.

Louisiana Farm Bureau Women's Committee

SWEET PICKLES

Cucumbers (as many as you desire)	2 quarts vinegar
	8 cups sugar
1 cup lime	2 tablespoons salt
1 gallon water	2 tablespoons pickling spices

Slice cucumbers in round slices. Place them in a large container and soak for 24 hours with 1 cup lime to 1 gallon of water. Rinse and then soak for 2 hours in ice water. Pour off liquid. Put vinegar, sugar, salt, and pickling spices over the cucumbers; let set overnight. The next day place on medium heat and bring to a boil. Let set for 30 minutes and then pour into sterilized jars. Seal.

Pam Accardo
Ouachita Parish (Monroe)

AUNT ETTA'S STRING BEANS (CANNING)

½ gallon water
1 cup distilled vinegar
½ cup sugar

1 gallon snapped beans
4 quart jars

In a large pot, combine water, vinegar, and sugar; bring to a rolling boil. Add snapped beans and boil for 3 minutes. Have jars and tops hot. Place beans in quart jars and pour liquid over them. Secure tight tops and rings on jars. Set on cabinet and allow to cool. This is all there is to do! When you are ready to cook these pour off the liquid and cook in cold fresh water. Add seasonings as you usually do. Another method of cooking is to pour the entire contents of the jar into a pot and cook as you normally do, adding your favorite seasonings.

Note: I cook mine in the liquid it was in because of the vinegar taste (it's not a strong vinegar taste). This recipe is my husband's aunt, Mrs. W. A. Adams, mother-in-law of former Governor of Louisiana, Jimmie Davis and the aunt of Louisiana Commissioner of Agriculture, Bob Odom.

Mrs. Don Odom (Brenda)
Claiborne Parish (Homer)

BREAD AND BUTTER PICKLES

Base:
1 gallon sliced cucumbers
8 small onions, sliced

½ cup salt
1 quart water

Mix the above ingredients together. Place in the refrigerator for 3 hours or overnight. Drain and set aside. Prepare the syrup.

Syrup:
5 cups sugar
5 cups vinegar
1½ teaspoons turmeric

½ teaspoon whole cloves
1 teaspoon celery seed
2 tablespoons mustard seed

Mix all syrup ingredients together in a heavy, large saucepan. Add cucumbers and onions; barely scald over low heat. Pour into prepared pint jars. Seal. Makes 8-10 pints.

Mrs. Doug Moore (Liz)
Ouachita Parish (Monroe)

GREEN TOMATO RELISH

2 quarts chopped green
   tomatoes
2 medium chopped onions

2 quarts water
½ cup salt

Combine chopped tomatoes, onions, water and salt in a crock. Allow to soak for 3 hours. Drain and rinse in cold water.

Seasoning:
1½ cups white vinegar
½ cup boiling water
2 cups sugar
1½ teaspoons celery seed

1 tablespoon mustard seed
½ teaspoon turmeric
½ teaspoon ground cinnamon
¼ teaspoon dry mustard

In a heavy saucepan, combine seasoning ingredients in given order; bring to a boil. Boil for 3 minutes. Add tomatoes and onions. Simmer, uncovered, for 10 minutes. Pack in 4 to 5 sterile pint jars and seal.

Mrs. Marvin Spangler (Inez)
Ouachita Parish (West Monroe)

HOT DILL PICKLES

1 cup plain salt
1 quart vinegar
2 quarts water
1 gallon sliced or whole
   cucumbers

2 teaspoons turmeric
2 cloves garlic
1 teaspoon dill seed
3 hot peppers

In a large saucepan, combine salt, vinegar and water; bring to a boil. Set aside. Place turmeric, garlic, dill seed and hot peppers in empty jars. Pack cucumbers on top of ingredients already placed in jars. Pour hot liquid mixture into jars. Seal with heated lids.

Note: This is an old family recipe, and those who do not like homemade pickles will find this quite a treat. Frances Kelly, my sister gave this recipe to me.

Mrs. Doug Moore (Liz)
Ouachita Parish (Monroe)

315

OLD FASHIONED PICKLED OKRA

4 pounds small, tender okra
10 pods red or green hot
  peppers
10 cloves garlic

8 cups pure vinegar
1 cup water
¾ cup plain salt

Wash okra leaving short stems on pods. Pack in hot clean jars. Place one pepper pod and one clove of garlic in each jar. Heat vinegar, water and salt in heavy saucepan to boiling. If desired, other seasonings such as celery or mustard seed may be added to the vinegar mixture. Pour hot vinegar mixture over okra. Seal. Let stand for 8 weeks before using. Makes 10 pints.

Note: We love the delicious crisp taste.

Mrs. Wayne Zaunbrecher (Linda)
Vermilion Parish (Gueydan)

INDOOR SUNSHINE PEACH PRESERVES

3 tablespoons strained lemon
  juice
2 pounds peeled, pitted, and
  sliced peaches

3 cups sugar

In a wide 2½-quart saucepan, pour the lemon juice. Slice the peeled peaches right into the pan. Turn the peach slices over to coat them with the juice. Gradually add the sugar and toss gently with a wooden spoon. If they prove to be very juicy, allow to stand 10-15 minutes for syrup to form; if not, they may need to stand an hour or more. When most of the sugar has become syrup, bring the mixture to a boil quickly over high heat, stirring to prevent sticking. Boil rapidly for 10 minutes or until the sugar has melted and the fruit is tender. Pour at once into a shallow pan or baking dish to a depth of ¾ to 1-inch. Bake at 170 degrees for about 6 hours. While in oven, stir occasionally. When the syrup is thick and the fruit is opaque, take pans from the oven and allow to cool. Spoon preserves into hot, sterilized 8-ounce jelly glasses leaving ⅛ inch head space. Cover immediately with paraffin. Let the preserves mellow before using. Makes 3½ cups. Label and store.

Note: In the event you have to go out during the cooking period, turn off the oven, leave the preserves inside and reset the oven when you return.

Mrs. John C. Taylor
Ouachita Parish (Choudrant)

FIG PRESERVES

Fresh figs   Soda
Sugar   Lemon slices

Use two part figs to one part sugar. Let figs soak in soda water for 10 minutes. Then wash in cold water. Put into container to be cooked. Add sugar, lift gently for sugar to sift through figs. Let set 30-40 minutes. Start on very low heat until sugar melts. After figs have started cooking, add 3-4 slices of lemon to figs. Let cook until syrup is thick as you want it. To test, spoon a little of the syrup in a saucer. Seal in sterilized jars.

Mrs. Ada Lee
West Carroll Parish (Oak Grove)

STRAWBERRY FIG JAM

6 cups ripe figs   1 package unsweetened strawberry
4 cups sugar   soft drink mix
4 boxes strawberry gelatin

Wash figs and remove stems. Pass figs through a blender. Pour into medium size saucepan the figs, sugar, gelatin and soft drink mix. Cook on medium heat for 35 minutes, stirring constantly. Pour mixture into sterilized jars. Makes 3 to 4 pints.

Mrs. Bernard Bordelon (Marie)
Avoyelles Parish (Moreauville)

STRAWBERRY FIG PRESERVES

3 cups cooked, mashed figs   1 6-ounce package strawberry Jello
3 cups sugar

In a heavy saucepan, combine all ingredients. Over medium heat, let come to a boil. Cook for 3 minutes or until thick.

Note: Any flavor Jello may be used.

Mrs. Rick Caldwell (Jeanie)
Ouachita Parish (West Monroe)

OUT OF THIS WORLD STRAWBERRY JAM (MICROWAVE)

1 quart fresh strawberries   4 tablespoons powdered pectin
3½ cups sugar

Wash, stem and drain the strawberries. Crush strawberries into 2½-quart bowl. Stir in sugar and pectin. Cook in microwave for 3 minutes. Stir. Cook 2 minutes. Stir. Cook 2 minutes. Stir. Cook 1 minute and test for doneness. (It will fall from the spoon in thick streams). Pour mixture into glass jars and seal with paraffin. Makes five 9-ounce glass jars.

Bobby Ann Lee
Madison Parish (Tallulah)

PEAR RELISH

35 medium pears   2 tablespoons dry mustard
4 large onions   2 tablespoons turmeric
8 green peppers   1 to 2 red peppers
4 cups sugar   2 pints vinegar
¼ cup salt

Grind the pears, onions and peppers; drain off some of the juice. Add sugar, salt, mustard, turmeric and vinegar; cook slowly over low heat for 45 minutes. Seal in sterilized jars. Makes about 4 quarts.

Juanita Storey
Madison Parish (Tallulah)

PEAR MINCEMEAT (OLD)

7 pounds fresh Bartlett or   1 tablespoon ground cinnamon
   pineapple pears   1 tablespoon ground allspice
1 pound raisins   1 tablespoon ground nutmeg
2 cups sugar   1 tablespoon ground cloves
1 cup vinegar

Select ripe, sound pears. Wash thoroughly. Core and quarter the pears. Grind pears and raisins. Place ground mixture in a heavy saucepan; add sugar, vinegar and spices. Bring to a slow boil over low heat. Cook until mixture is thick. For canning, simmer for 30 minutes. This recipe is good for canning and freezing.

Note: We have learned to make the most of what has been handed down by the Ford Family.

Mrs. May Ford
Concordia Parish (Monterey)

PICKLED SQUASH

8 cups sliced squash
2 cups diced onions
3 green peppers, dried
Salt
2 cups white vinegar

½ teaspoon dry mustard
2 teaspoons celery seed
2 teaspoons mustard seed
2½ cups sugar

In a heavy saucepan, layer squash, onions and green peppers. Sprinkle with salt and let stand for 1 hour. Drain off excess liquid. In a small saucepan, combine remaining ingredients; pour this mixture over the vegetables in saucepan. Bring to a boil. Remove from heat and spoon into jars. Yield: about 4 pints.

Charlotte Harris
Washington Parish (Angie)

PEPPER JELLY

¼ cup ground red peppers
¾ cup ground green peppers
6½ cups sugar
1½ cups apple cider vinegar
1 6-ounce bottle of Certo liquid
    pectin

Red or green food coloring
1 8-ounce package Philadelphia
    cream cheese (optional)

Prepare bell peppers by cutting and removing seeds. Your hands may begin to burn so you will probably want to wear rubber gloves. Grind the peppers, saving the juice. In a large saucepan, boil the peppers, sugar and vinegar for 10 minutes. Let set for 5 minutes. Add Certo and desired food coloring. Store in glass jars.

Note: Usually green food coloring is used for green peppers and red food coloring for red hot peppers. This is excellent with hot or cold meats or just crackers. This may also be served with Philadelphia cream cheese, if desired.

TABASCO JELLY

3 cups sugar
1 cup water
⅓ cup lemon juice
4 to 6 tablespoons Tabasco
    Sauce

⅓ cup plus 1 tablespoon liquid
    pectin
Red food coloring, if desired

In a heavy saucepan, combine the sugar, water, lemon juice and Tabasco sauce, bringing to a boil over medium heat. Add liquid pectin. Allow to come to a boil; boil for 1 minute. Add food coloring, if desired (The food coloring helps make a prettier jelly). Pour into sterilized jars.

Mrs. Eddie Schexnaydre (Doris)
Terrebonne Parish (Schriever)

Special Friends

Houmas House

BREAD AND BUTTER PICKLES

8 pounds medium cucumbers
2 cups pickling lime
2 gallons water
½ gallon vinegar
5 pounds sugar

1 tablespoon salt
1 teaspoon pickling spices
1 teaspoon celery seed
1 teaspoon whole cloves

On the first day, wash and slice cucumbers about ¼-inch thick. Place in stainless steel pot or earthenware crock. Add lime and water. Soak in refrigerator overnight, stirring occasionally.

On the second day, rinse cucumbers well. Soak in clear water for 3 hours. Rinse well and place cucumbers in a container. Mix solution of vinegar, sugar and salt. Pour over cucumbers. Tie spices in a cloth bag and drop into container. Soak in solution overnight in refrigerator.

On the third day, remove pickles from refrigerator. Boil for 45 minutes. Pack in sterile jars and seal.

Note: I always add ¼ teaspoon green food coloring while pickles are boiling. These are delicious crisp pickles.

Mrs. S. T. Moore, Jr.
South Hill, Virginia

BROWNIES

Brownies:
½ cup butter, softened
1 cup sugar
4 eggs

1 cup plus 2 tablespoons flour
1 16-ounce can Hershey chocolate
syrup

Preheat oven to 350 degrees. Cream butter and sugar until light fluffy. Add eggs one at a time, beating well after each addition. Add flour; mix thoroughly. Add syrup. Pour into a greased and floured 13 x 9 x 2-inch pan; bake at 350 degrees for 30 minutes.

Frosting:
6 tablespoons butter, softened
2½ cups powdered sugar
6 tablespoons cocoa

6 tablespoons strong hot coffee
1 teaspoon vanilla extract

Cream butter until soft. Sift together powdered sugar and cocoa. Add to butter alternately with hot coffee; mix thoroughly. Add more sugar, if needed to make it spreading consistency. Add vanilla extract. Spread on brownies. Cut as desired.

Mrs. Lovell Rousseau
Phoenix, Arizona

BROWNIES

1 cup Crisco	2¼ cups sifted all-purpose flour
3 cups sugar	1½ teaspoons baking powder
6 eggs	1½ cups chopped pecans
3 tablespoons cocoa	Pinch of salt
1 tablespoon vanilla extract	

Preheat oven to 350 degrees. Cream Crisco, 1 cup sugar, cocoa, vanilla, and salt in a large mixing bowl until light. Add 2 eggs, beating well. Continue beating until all remaining sugar and eggs are added, alternating each. Sift flour once; measure, and sift again with baking powder. Add flour to creamed mixture, mixing well. Add chopped pecans, mixing thoroughly. Spread mixture in a greased 15 x 11 x 2-inch baking pan lined with wax paper. Bake at 350 degrees for 55 minutes. Allow to cool for 10 minutes. Turn over on waxed paper over kitchen towel. Cut into squares. Yields 50 to 60 brownies.

Mrs. James Graugnard, Sr.
West St. James Parish (St. James)

BUSTER BARS

Crust:

1 pound Oreo cookies	½ gallon vanilla ice cream
½ cup melted margarine	1½ cups Spanish peanuts

Place Oreo cookies in a plastic bag and crush with rolling pin. Mix crushed cookies and margarine; press into the bottom of a 13 x 9 x 2-inch pan. Slice ice cream and place over the crust. Sprinkle with peanuts. Put in freezer while preparing the sauce.

Sauce:

2 cups powdered sugar	½ cup butter
1½ cups evaporated milk	1 teaspoon vanilla extract
⅔ cup chocolate chips	

In a heavy saucepan over medium heat, combine the sugar, milk, chocolate chips and butter. Bring to a boil. Boil for 8 minutes, stirring constantly. Remove from heat, add vanilla. Allow to cool. Spread sauce over ice cream layer. Freeze until serving time.

Mrs. Richard Kleinjan
Bruce, South Dakota

C.D.Q. (CAN DO QUICK) CINNAMON ROLLS

Dough:

2 packages active dry yeast
½ cup warm water (105 to 115
  degrees)
1¼ cups buttermilk
2 eggs
5½ cups Gold Medal
  all-purpose flour

½ cup butter or margarine,
  softened
½ cup sugar
2 teaspoons baking powder
2 teaspoons salt

In a large mixing bowl, dissolve yeast in water; let stand 5 minutes. Add buttermilk, eggs, 2½ cups flour, butter, sugar, baking powder and salt. Blend 30 seconds on low speed. Scrape down sides and bottom of bowl. Beat 2 minutes on medium speed. Stir in remaining flour. Dough should remain soft and slightly sticky. Knead dough on lightly floured board for 5 minutes. Divide dough in half. Roll ½ of dough into a 12 x 7-inch rectangle. Preheat oven to 375 degrees. Grease round pan.

Filling:

¼ cup sugar
1 teaspoon ground cinnamon

Softened butter or margarine

Mix sugar and cinnamon together thoroughly. Spread butter over dough; sprinkle cinnamon-sugar mixture on top. Roll up, beginning at wide side. Seal edges well. Cut into 12 slices. Place slices in greased 9-inch round pan, leaving a small space between each slice. Cover and let rise for 1 hour. Bake at 375 degrees for 25 minutes. Remove from pan. Top with icing, if desired. Repeat with other half of dough, or freeze until needed. Yield: 2 dozen.

Mrs. Url Goller
New Bavaria, Ohio

CRANBERRY SALAD

½ pound fresh cranberries
⅛ teaspoon soda
1 pint water
⅛ teaspoon salt
1 cup sugar
1 3-ounce box strawberry Jello

15 large marshmallows, cut in
  pieces
1 cup diced apples
1 cup diced celery
½ cup chopped nuts

In heavy saucepan over medium heat, combine cranberries, water and salt; bring to a boil. Add soda. Boil for 10 minutes. Remove from heat. Stir in sugar and Jello until thoroughly dissolved. Add chopped marshmallows, stirring well. Allow to cool. Add apples, celery, and nuts. Pour mixture into an 8-inch square pan. Refrigerate until firm. Serve on lettuce leaf.

Mrs. Wallace Hirschfeld (Edna)
New Bremen, Ohio

EASY CHEESE CAKE

Crust:

20 graham crackers, crushed or
  1¼ cups crumbs

2 tablespoons sugar
6 tablespoons melted butter

In a mixing bowl, combine all ingredients with a fork; press firmly on bottom and side of a 9-inch square baking pan. Set aside.

Filling:

2 8-ounce packages cream
  cheese, softened
2 eggs
2 teaspoons vanilla extract

2 tablespoons melted butter
½ cup sugar
½ cup commercial sour cream

In large mixing bowl, beat cream cheese until fluffy. Add eggs, one at a time, beating well. Add remaining ingredients; mix thoroughly. Pour into graham cracker crust. Bake at 350 degrees for 30 to 40 minutes. Chill. Serve with crushed strawberries or other fruit if desired.

Marilyn R. Campbell
Salem, New Hampshire

LIMA BEANS AND SHRIMP

½ cup corn oil
½ cup all-purpose flour
1 cup cleaned and deveined
  shrimp
½ cup chopped onions
½ cup green onions
2 cloves garlic, minced
¼ cup chopped green pepper
¼ cup chopped celery

½ cup peeled, diced tomatoes
2 8-ounce packages frozen baby
  lima beans, thawed
⅛ cup chopped fresh parsley
3 cups hot water
1 pat butter or margarine
1 teaspoon salt
¼ teaspoon red pepper
Hot cooked rice

In a 4-quart pan prepare roux with oil and flour until golden brown. Add shrimp and all chopped ingredients. Cook for 10 minutes. Add beans; cook 10 minutes longer. Add hot water, butter, and seasonings; cover and cook for 45 minutes, stirring occasionally. Remove from heat. Serve over rice, if desired. Serves 6-8.

Mrs. James Graugnard, Sr., wife of Louisiana Farm Bureau President
West St. James Parish (St. James)

DOUBLE DELIGHT CRANBERRY PIE

1 10-inch unbaked pie shell	1 cup pecan halves
1 16-ounce can Ocean Spray jellied cranberry sauce	

Preheat oven to 450 degrees. Stir cranberry sauce with a fork to soften; add nuts. Spread over bottom of pie shell. Bake at 350 degrees for 15 minutes. Remove from oven and cool. Reduce heat to 350 degrees.

2 3-ounce packages cream cheese, softened	2 eggs
¼ cup sugar	½ teaspoon lemon extract

In mixing bowl, beat cream cheese until fluffy using an electric mixer on medium speed. Add sugar gradually, mixing well. Beat in eggs and lemon extract. Pour over cranberry layer. Bake for 20 minutes or until custard layer is firm. Remove from oven; allow to cool. Chill. This process may be done early in the morning or a day ahead of time, if desired.

1 tablespoon unflavored gelatin	1 cup Ocean Spray
¼ cup cold water	Cranberry-Orange relish
1 16-ounce carton commercial sour cream	3 tablespoons honey or light corn syrup

Soften gelatin in cold water in the top of double boiler; let stand 5 minutes. Heat over hot water until dissolved; remove from heat. Blend sour cream, relish, and honey; stir into dissolved gelatin. Chill for 40 to 45 minutes or until mixture nearly holds its shape. Heap on top of chilled pie and return to refrigerator until serving time.

Note: This recipe is a family holiday favorite and won first prize for our oldest daughter in the 1977 Massachusetts Cranberry Festival, "Make it Better with Cranberries" contest. We are particularly fond of it because it lets us enjoy cranberries even after our supply of fresh and fresh-frozen cranberries are gone.

Jean O. Gibbs
Carver, Massachusetts

FRUITCAKE

4 ounces candied red cherries
4 ounces candied green cherries
8 ounces candied pineapple
1 8-ounce package pitted dates
1 cup white raisins
4 cups chopped pecans

3 cups self-rising flour
4 large eggs
1½ cups sugar
1 cup Wesson oil
1 cup pineapple juice
2 teaspoons ground cinnamon

Preheat oven to 275 degrees. Grease 10-inch tube pan; set aside. Chop fruit; combine with nuts in large bowl. Add 1 cup flour. Using your hands mix flour, nuts and fruit until all is covered. Set aside. Beat eggs, sugar, and oil, thoroughly. Add remaining 2 cups flour, cinnamon, and pineapple juice, alternately. Pour batter over fruit mixture; mix thoroughly. Pour into prepared tube pan. Bake at 275 degrees for 2½ hours or until done.

Mrs. Goodwin L. Myrick (Deanie)
Montgomery, Alabama

RICE SALAD

1 box curried rice
1 box wild and long grain rice
6 hard-cooked eggs, chopped
½ cup chopped celery

½ cup chopped onion
½ cup sweet pickle relish
Mayonnaise or salad dressing to
    taste

Prepare rice according to package directions. Allow to cool. In a large bowl, mix eggs, celery, onion and pickle thoroughly. Stir in rice using a large fork to mix lightly. Add desired amount of mayonnaise or salad dressing to moisten.

Note: I find that a little pickle juice improves the flavor along with a little salt and pepper.

Mrs. Hugh M. Arant, wife of Mississippi Farm Bureau President
Ruleville, Mississippi

HOT DISH

1 pound ground beef
1 pound ground pork
2 small onions, chopped
1 cup chopped celery
2 cans cream-style corn

1 can mixed peas and carrots
2 cans chicken with rice soup
1 7-ounce package ring macaroni,
    cooked and drained
1 teaspoon salt

Preheat oven to 350 degrees. In a large skillet over medium heat, brown the first 4 ingredients. Add remaining ingredients and simmer on low for 5 to 7 minutes. Place in large dish and bake at 350 degrees for 1½ hours.

Mrs. Earl Prigge (Laureen)
Goodhue, Minnesota

JAPANESE FRUIT PIE

1 9-inch unbaked pie shell
2 eggs, separated
1 cup sugar
¾ stick melted butter or
   margarine

½ cup flaked coconut
½ cup raisins
½ cup chopped pecans

Preheat oven to 300 degrees. In mixing bowl, combine egg yolks, sugar, and melted butter; mix well. Add coconut, raisins and pecans, mixing well. Beat egg whites until stiff. Fold into fruit mixture. Pour into unbaked pie shell. Bake at 300 degrees for 1 hour. Yield: one 9-inch pie.

Mrs. Bob Nash (Betty)
The Rock, Georgia

STRAWBERRY DESSERT

Crust:
½ cup firmly packed brown
   sugar

½ cup margarine
1½ cups crushed pretzels

Preheat oven to 275 degrees. In large mixing bowl, combine brown sugar, margarine and crushed pretzels. Pat into a 13 x 9 x 2-inch pan. Bake at 275 degrees for 7 minutes. Allow to cool.

Layer 1:
1 8-ounce package cream
   cheese, softened

¾ cup sugar
1 cup thawed Cool Whip

In large bowl, cream together cream cheese, sugar and Cool Whip. Spread over cooled pretzel layer.

Layer 2:
1 6-ounce package strawberry
   Jello
2 10-ounce packages frozen
   strawberries

2 cups boiling water

In a medium saucepan, dissolve the strawberry Jello in boiling water. Add frozen strawberries, mixing well. Remove from heat. Let set until it starts to gel. Spread over cream cheese layer. Refrigerate until set. Serves 12.

Agnes Ekstrum
Kimball, South Dakota

ORANGE CHARLOTTE

1 tablespoon unflavored gelatin
¼ cup cold water
½ cup boiling water
1 cup sugar
1 cup fresh orange juice

2 tablespoons lemon juice
2 egg whites
1 cup whipping cream, whipped
Orange slices

In a mixing bowl, dissolve gelatin in cold water; let stand 5 minutes. Add boiling water, sugar, orange juice, and lemon juice. Stir until sugar is dissolved. Let set in refrigerator until it has the consistency of egg whites. It is important that the mixture sets long enough to be softly set, but not too firm. If not it will settle on the bottom. Beat egg whites until stiff enough to hold peaks. Fold egg whites into gelatin mixture until well blended. Chill several hours; top with whipped cream. Garnish with orange slices. Serves 8.

Note: Frozen orange juice concentrate may be used, if desired. Dilute juice with only ⅔ the amount listed.

Mrs. Henry L. Parr (Mittie)
Newberry, South Carolina

PECAN CREAM PIE

Filling:
2 cups sugar
⅔ cup water
¼ cup butter
5 egg yolks

2 tablespoons all-purpose flour
1 cup evaporated milk
1 teaspoon vanilla extract
1½ cups chopped pecans
2 9-inch baked pie shells

In a heavy saucepan, over medium heat, combine sugar, water, and butter. Cook until mixture comes to a boil; remove from heat. Allow to cool. In a mixing bowl, combine flour, milk, and beaten egg yolks; mix well. Add to cooled mixture. Cook over medium heat until thickened. Add vanilla and pecans. Pour mixture into baked pie shells. Set aside while preparing meringue.

Meringue:
5 egg whites
¼ cup salt

½ cup sugar

In a large mixing bowl beat egg whites and salt until foamy; add sugar and beat until stiff and holds peaks. Spread meringue over pies. Bake at 350 for 7 to 12 minutes or until browned. Servings will be according to size cut.

Mrs. Glenn Barrick (Betty), Kentucky Farm Bureau Women's Committee Chairman
Glasgow, Kentucky

PINEAPPLE-RAISIN DROP COOKIES

1 cup shortening
2 cups firmly packed brown
  sugar
1 teaspoon vanilla extract
2 eggs, well beaten
1 cup seedless raisins, or
  chopped dates

1 cup drained crushed pineapple
4 cups sifted all-purpose flour
2 teaspoons baking powder
2 teaspoons baking soda
1 teaspoon salt
½ cup chopped nuts (optional)

Preheat oven to 375 degrees. Grease cookie sheet and set aside. In a large mixing bowl, cream shortening and sugar until light and fluffy. Add vanilla, eggs, raisins and pineapple, mixing thoroughly. Sift in dry ingredients, mixing thoroughly. Add chopped nuts, if desired. Drop by teaspoonfuls on prepared cookie sheet about 1½ inches apart. Bake at 375 degrees for 10 to 15 minutes. Yields 6 dozen cookies.

Mrs. Fanny St. Clair
Buckannon, West Virginia

PINEAPPLE SHEET CAKE (EASY)

Cake:
1 20-ounce can crushed
  pineapple, undrained
½ cup melted butter
2 cups all-purpose flour
2 cups sugar

1 teaspoon soda
½ teaspoon salt
2 eggs
½ cup commercial sour cream

Preheat oven to 375 degrees. Combine all ingredients; beat well with wooden spoon. Pour into a greased 15 x 10 x 1-inch baking prepared pan. Bake at 375 degrees for 25 minutes.

Icing:
½ cup melted butter
⅓ cup milk
1 16-ounce box powdered
  sugar

1 teaspoon vanilla extract
½ cup chopped pecans

Combine all ingredients in a large bowl; mix well. Pour immediately over hot cake. Allow to cool. Yield: one cake.

Mrs. Vivian Lott, Michigan State Farm Bureau Women's Committee Chairman
Mason, Michigan

HAM YAM LOAF

3 eggs
½ cup milk
½ cup crushed soda crackers
1 teaspoon prepared mustard
1 pound ground ham
1 pound ground pork sausage

½ cup chopped onion
1 18-ounce can sweet potatoes,
   drained and mashed
½ cup orange marmalade
½ teaspoon salt
⅛ teaspoon ground cloves

Preheat oven to 350 degrees. In large mixing bowl, beat 2 eggs and milk; add crackers and mustard. Add meats and onions; mix well. Put half of mixture in a 9-inch square baking pan. Combine sweet potatoes, 1 egg, marmalade, salt and cloves; spread over meat layer. Top with remaining meat mixture. Cover with foil. Bake at 350 degrees for 1 hour. Uncover and bake for 30 more minutes. Serves 8.

Charlotte Mohr
Eldridge, Iowa

SWEET POTATO CASSEROLE

Filling:

3 cups mashed, cooked sweet
   potatoes'
1 cup sugar
½ cup milk

⅓ cup butter
2 eggs, beaten
1 teaspoon vanilla extract

Preheat oven to 350 degrees. Mix all ingredients in a large mixing bowl. Spread mixture in a shallow baking dish.

Topping:

1 cup flaked coconut
1 cup chopped pecans
1 cup firmly packed brown
   sugar

⅓ cup all-purpose flour
⅓ cup melted butter

Mix all ingredients in mixing bowl; sprinkle over sweet potatoes. Bake at 350 degrees for 20 minutes or until brown.

Note: This casserole is delicious and is very popular with family and friends.

Mrs. Donald LeFlis, Florida Farm Bureau Women's Committee Chairman
Osteen, Florida

SPECIAL K SNAX

1 cup light Karo syrup
1 cup sugar

1 cup creamy peanut butter
6 cups Special K cereal

Combine Karo and sugar in large saucepan; cook over medium heat, stirring constantly, until sugar dissolves. Continue to cook until mixture begins to boil hard. Remove from heat. Stir in peanut butter until smooth. Add Special K cereal 1 cup at a time, mixing well. Drop by spoonful on waxed paper. Allow to cool. Store in airtight container.

Note: I use Special K cereal because it is a rice cereal and is not as big as flakes. We think it is a very nutritious snack food.

Mrs. Nicky Hargrove, wife of Arkansas Farm Bureau President
Stuttgart, Arkansas

STRAWBERRY PRETZEL DESSERT

Crust:
2½ cups coarsely crushed
   pretzels

¾ cup melted butter or margarine
¼ cup sugar

Preheat oven to 325 degrees. Mix pretzels, butter, and sugar; pat into a 13 x 9 x 2-inch glass baking dish. Bake at 325 degrees for 15 minutes. Watch carefully during the last few minutes of baking to prevent scorching. Allow crust to cool.

Filling:
1 8-ounce package cream
   cheese, softened
½ cup powdered sugar
1 teaspoon vanilla extract

1 4½-ounce container Cool Whip,
   thawed
2 cups miniature marshmallows

Beat cream cheese, sugar, and vanilla until light and fluffy. Fold in Cool Whip and marshmallows. Spread over cooled crust.

Topping:
1 6-ounce package strawberry
   Jello
2½ cups boiling water

1 10-ounce package frozen
   strawberries

In a large mixing bowl, dissolve Jello in boiling water. Add frozen strawberries and stir until thawed. When strawberry mixture begins to thicken, pour over filling layer. Chill for several hours. Serve with Cool Whip and a large strawberry on top. Serves 12 to 15.

Note: Fresh strawberries may be used instead of frozen strawberries.

Mrs. Wendell Gangwish (Treva), wife of Nebraska Farm Bureau President
Wood River, Nebraska

TOMATO ASPIC SALAD

1 3-ounce package strawberry
    Jello
2 cups tomato juice
1 tablespoon lemon juice or
    vinegar

1 tablespoon prepared horseradish
1 tablespoon finely chopped onion
1 heaping tablespoon pickle relish
½ cup finely chopped celery
½ cup chopped black olives

In medium saucepan, combine tomato juice and Jello. Cook over medium heat, stirring constantly, to dissolve the Jello. Cool until partially set. Add lemon juice, horseradish, onion, relish, celery and olives, mixing well. Pour into an oiled 8-inch square mold. Place in refrigerator to set. Serve on endive or lettuce leaves.

Mrs. Lillian Maberry
Hilger, Montana

TOMATO SOUP SALAD

1 10¾-ounce can tomato soup
1 3-ounce package lemon Jello
1 cup Miracle Whip salad
    dressing

1 cup grated raw carrots
1 cup diced celery
1½ cups chopped green olives
1 cup small curd cottage cheese

In a saucepan, heat tomato soup over medium heat to boiling point. Add Jello and stir to dissolve. Add salad dressing and blend well. Set aside to cool until it starts to thicken. Add carrots, celery, olives and cottage cheese; mix thoroughly. Pour into an oiled salad mold. Refrigerate. Serves 8.

Note: This is a very good salad to serve with meat. It can be frozen also for a short period of time.

Bernita Sramek
McDonald, Kansas

COMPANY SALAD

1 3-ounce package lemon Jello
1 cup boiling water
1 small jar cream pimento
    cheese
2 large carrots, grated

2 large stalks celery, chopped
1 teaspoon grated onion or dried
    onion flakes
⅔ cup Tang salad dressing
1 small can crushed pineapple

Dissolve Jello in boiling water in a heavy saucepan over medium heat. Add cream pimento cheese to Jello mixture; stir well. Add remaining ingredients, mixing thoroughly. Pour into a 9-inch square salad mold. Chill until set.

Mrs. Cordelia Boleneus
Davenport, Washington

WISCONSIN BEEF COOK-OUT

¼ cup Crisco oil
1 tablespoon fresh ground
  pepper
2 teaspoons salt
2 teaspoons paprika

Pinch of rosemary
1 clove garlic, mashed
3 pounds (½ to ¾-inch thick)
  round steak

In a mixing bowl, combine first 6 ingredients; pour over round steak. Let marinate for 24 hours. Cook on charcoal grill approximately 3 minutes on each side.

Note: This recipe was used for our statewide beef promotion in June, 1980. We had a one day cook-out in 150 grocery stores to kick off the July beef promotion.

Mary Jane Nelson
Wisconsin Farm Bureau Women's Committee Chairman
Holmen, Wisconsin

ALLEN J. ELLENDER
"Chef Supreme"

The late Senator Allen J. Ellender of Louisiana served as President Pro Tem of the Senate and as its highest ranking member. He is also a chef of renown. Presidents and their First Ladies were guests of honor at the Senator's famous gumbo luncheons in Washington.

Now you can share the recipes taught to Senator Ellender by his mother when he was still a boy in Terrebonne Parish. After you've tried them, you will see why his power and influence in Washington kept the kettle boiling for Louisiana!

CHICKEN WITH SAUCE PIQUANTE

Basic sauce recipe below
1 8-ounce can tomato sauce
2 6-ounce cans tomato paste

2 2½-3 pound chickens, cut into
  pieces
Hot cooked rice

Prepare basic sauce.

Cook tomato sauce and paste with basic sauce very thoroughly. Add chicken pieces and cook until tender. To make sauce of proper consistency to suit the taste, add water as needed during last stages of cooking. It should be the consistency of a stew. Serve with rice or spaghetti. Serves 12 to 16.

Note: If a thicker sauce is preferred, make roux with 2 to 4 tablespoons flour instead of 1 tablespoon used in Basic Sauce recipe.

Allen J. Ellender

BASIC SAUCE

5 tablespoons fat (vegetable oil or smoked bacon fat)
1 rounded tablespoon all-purpose flour
2 pounds onions, finely chopped
3 stalks celery, finely chopped
1 medium green pepper, chopped

1 lemon
3 cloves garlic
Dash of Worcestershire sauce
Dash of Tabasco
Dash of thyme leaves
Dash of McCormick Season-All
2 bay leaves
Salt to taste

Heat fat in a large skillet until hot; add flour, and brown. Stir constantly to make scorchy-tasting roux. Add onions; fry slowly until well-browned and reduced to pulp. Grate rind of lemon and set aside; remove and discard white membrane from lemon. Chop pulp of lemon and set aside with grated rind. Add the remaining ingredients at one time, and continue to cook slowly for at least 30 to 45 minutes.

Allen J. Ellender

GUMBO

Basic sauce (recipe above)
2½ pounds fresh okra
2 tablespoons fat
3 pounds peeled shrimp tails

1 pound crabmeat
1 pint oysters
Chopped parsley
Chopped green onion tops

Prepare basic sauce.

Cut okra into small pieces. Cook in a small pot with fat over low heat, stirring often to prevent scorching or browning. Add to basic sauce and continue to cook for 20 minutes. Add shrimp, crabmeat and oysters; cook for 10 minutes. Add water to make the sauce of a soupy consistency; heat to boiling and cook for 20 minutes. About 10 minutes before serving, add 1 handful each of parsley and onion top. Serve over rice in soup plates. Serves 12-16.

Note: To make sauce of proper consistency to suit your taste, add water as needed during last stages of cooking, this should be of the consistency of a thick soup.

Allen J. Ellender

JAMBALAYA

Basic sauce (recipe above)
½ 8-ounce can tomato sauce
3 pints oysters

3 cups uncooked long-grain rice
1 handful chopped green onion tops
1 handful chopped parsley

Prepare basic sauce; add tomato sauce and cook thoroughly. Add oysters and cook for about 10 minutes after it starts to boil. Add rice, onion and parsley. Add enough water to make sure you have 2 cups liquid in the pot for each cup of rice. Stir and mix thoroughly until mixture comes to a boil. Cover tightly; reduce heat to simmer. Cook for 25 minutes (Do not remove lid). Test rice to be sure it is done thoroughly at the end of the 25 minute cooking period. Serves 12 to 16.

Note: To make sauce of proper consistency to suit the taste, add water as needed during last stages of cooking. This should be of the consistency of a stew.

Allen J. Ellender

COURTBOUILLON

Basic sauce (recipe above)
6 pounds Channel Bass or Red
  Snapper, cut into pieces

1 8-ounce can tomato sauce
2 3-ounce cans tomato paste
Hot cooked rice

Prepare basic sauce. Add tomato sauce and paste; cook thoroughly. Add fish, and cook slowly until done. Stir very gently as not to break up fish pieces. To make sauce of proper consistency to suit the taste, add water as needed during last stages of cooking—this should be of the consistency of a stew. Serve with rice. Serves 12 to 16.

Allen J. Ellender

OYSTER STEW

2½ tablespoons fresh bacon fat
1 pound onions, chopped
2 pints fresh oysters, undrained

3 cups hot milk
Chopped parsley
Chopped green onion tops

In a 3-quart saucepan, heat fat over medium heat. Add chopped onions; sauté onions until clear, but not brown. Add oysters with liquid and cook until oysters curl. Stir in parsley and onion. Gradually pour in hot milk, stirring well. Serve immediately.

Allen J. Ellender

ROAST DUCK

1 wild duck, cleaned
Salt
Pepper
1 stalk celery, cut into pieces
Apple slices
1 small onion, quartered
2 to 3 garlic cloves, cut into
  slivers
Peanut, vegetable, coconut oil,
  or bacon fat
1 small to medium onion, finely
  chopped

1 clove garlic, minced
1 stalk celery, finely chopped
¼ green pepper, finely chopped
1 bay leaf
Dash of ground thyme
Tabasco sauce to taste
Worcestershire sauce to taste
Salt to taste
Pepper to taste
Canned or fresh mushrooms
  (optional)
Hot cooked rice

Sprinkle inside cavity of duck with salt and pepper, as desired. Stuff cavity with celery pieces, apple slices, and onion quarters; truss, if desired. Make several slits in breast of duck and insert garlic slivers into each one. Sprinkle salt and pepper on duck, as desired. Smear outside of duck liberally with oil. Set aside.

Combine chopped onion, garlic, celery, green pepper, seasonings and a small amount of water in a large Dutch oven. Place duck on a roasting rack and position in Dutch oven over seasoned water mixture. Cover; heat to boiling. Reduce heat and simmer for 1½ hours or until duck is tender. Add more water during cooking, if necessary. Remove duck on rack, then remove the pulp on the bottom of Dutch oven. Brown duck in remaining gravy. Removed pulp and mushrooms may be returned to gravy, if desired. Continue cooking on stovetop or bake at 325 degrees until warmed. Serve duck over hot cooked rice.

Allen J. Ellender

SHRIMP CREOLE

Basic Sauce (recipe above)
2 6-ounce cans tomato paste

3 pounds peeled shrimp
Hot cooked rice

Prepare basic sauce in large heavy saucepan; add tomato paste and cook thoroughly. Add shrimp and continue to cook for 15 to 20 minutes, stirring occasionally. Serve with rice. Serves 12 to 16.

Note: To make sauce of proper consistency to suit the taste, add water as needed during last stages of cooking. This should be a consistency of a stew.

Allen J. Ellender

Helpful Hints

Louisiana Superdome

HAPPY HOME RECIPE

4 cups love	3 spoons of hope
2 cups loyalty	2 spoons of tenderness
4 cups forgiveness	4 quarts of faith
1 cup friendship	1 barrel of laughter

Take love and loyalty; mix thoroughly with faith. Blend with tenderness, kindness, and understanding. Add friendship and hope. Sprinkle abundantly with laughter. Bake with sunshine. Serve generous helpings daily.

Marie Harper
Tangipahoa Parish (Hammond)

COOKERY TERMS FOUND IN COOKBOOKS
AND ON MENUS
(Terms you should know)

1. *À la king:* Food prepared in a rich cream sauce.

2. *À la mode:* For desserts it means "with ice cream."

3. *Amandine:* With almonds.

4. *Andouille:* A French creole smoked sausage made of large chunks of ground pork highly seasoned; used mainly in gumbo and jambalaya.

5. *Antipasto:* Assortment of Italian appetizers, such as sardines, anchovies, peppery sausage, canned pimento, tuna fish and etc.

6. *Aspic:* Clear, savory jelly used in molds to garnish cold dishes; made with gelatin or from meat bones and etc.

7. *Au gratin:* French term meaning a creamed dish with broiler-browned or oven-browned topping of buttered crumbs or crumbs and cheese.

8. *Bisque:* Thick cream soup. Also frozen cream dessert.

9. *Boudin:* A rice dressing made with pork and stuffed into sausage casing.

10. *Bouillon:* A clear, strained soup of stock made from beef, veal, or fowl cooked with seasonings and vegetables.

11. *Canapé:* An appetizer.

12. *Chaudin or Ponce:* Hog stomach stuffed with tasty pork mixture and baked.

13. *Cochon de lait:* (Roast suckling pig) is the main attraction at large community or entertaining gatherings accompanied by appetite whetting dishes.

14. *Courtboullion (koo-boo-yon):* Fish stew served over rice.

15. *Crackling:* The crisp pork rind that remains after the skin has been rendered for lard.

16. *Creole:* Food prepared in a style characterized by the use of rice, okra, tomatoes, peppers, and high seasonings.

17. *Crêpes:* Thin French pancakes.

18. *Cush-cush:* Corn meal mush.

19. *Etoufée:* Anything smothered in its own juices; such as shrimp, crawfish, okra and etc.

20. *Filé:* Dried ground sassafras leaves used as thickening agent for Cajun gumbo.

21. *Fricasse:* A dish made by cutting a fowl or rabbit or other small animal into pieces and adding to a strong thick sauce.

22. *Grillades (gree-yads):* A spicy combination of beef or veal round cut into small squares, cooked in a rich dark gravy and served over rice or with grits.

23. *Gumbo:* A soup thickened with okra pods, filé or roux, and usually containing a variety of vegetables with meat such as chicken or seafoods.

24. *Hors D'Oeuvres:* French appetizers.

25. *Jambalaya:* Rice cooked with ham, sausage, chicken or oysters and usually tomatoes and seasoned with herbs.

26. *Mousse:* Frozen dessert of heavy cream mixture. Also gelatin mixture of finely ground fish, ham, chicken, and etc., combined with cream and chilled, or served hot.

27. *Pain perdu:* Lost bread, French toast.

28. *Parfait:* Rich, frozen dessert served in tall glass with long-handled spoon.

29. *Po Boy:* A huge sandwich of French bread, consisting of various cold cuts and anything available in kitchen.

30. *Roux:* Mixture of butter or oil (when making gumbo use only oil) cooked to smooth paste. Cook until brown. May be cooked to a light brown or very dark brown depending on what recipe it is being used in.

31. *Une sauce picante:* A thick, sharp-flavored sauce made with roux and tomatoes, highly seasoned with herbs and peppers, simmered for hours.

COOK'S VOCABULARY

BASTE: Moisten food, while it is cooking, by spooning on liquid.

BLEND: Combine two or more ingredients with spoon or mixer.

BOIL: Cook food in boiling water, in which bubbles constantly rise to surface and break. At sea level, water boils at 212 degrees F. Once liquid boils, lower heat just high enough to keep liquid boiling. Slow boiling is just as effective as rapid boiling.

BRUSH WITH: Use pastry brush or crumpled wax paper to cover food lightly with melted fat, salad oil, cream, beaten egg white, etc.

CARAMELIZE: In large skillet, over medium heat, melt granulated sugar, stirring constantly, until sugar becomes a golden-brown syrup. Superfine sugar caramelizes in less time.

CHILL: Place in refrigerator or other cold place until cold.

CHOP: Using knife, chopper, or chopping bowl with knife, cut up food as recipe directs. If nuts, spread on wooden board. Hold tip of long sharp knife close to surface of board; then move knife handle up, down and around, in semicircle, so blade contacts uncut nuts. Or use nut chopper, blender, or roll lightly with rolling pin.

COAT: Using shaker-top can or sifter, sprinkle with flour, sugar, etc., until coated. Or roll in flour, sugar, etc., until coated. Or shake with flour, etc., in paper bag until coated.

FOLD IN (BEATEN EGG WHITES, WHIPPED CREAM, ETC.): Heap on top of mixture. Pass wire whip, rubber spatula, or spoon down through mixture and across bottom; bring up some of mixture; place on top of egg whites (or cream), then repeat until egg whites (or cream) are evenly combined with mixture.

GREASE: Rub lightly with butter, margarine, shortening or salad oil.

GRIND: Put through food (meat) grinder.

KNEAD: With floured hands, flatten dough very slightly by pressing it firmly; shape into round, flat ball. Pick up edge of dough at point farthest away from you; fold over edge nearest you. With heels of hands, press down, 3 or 4 times. Turn dough one quarter of the way around; repeat folding, pushing, and turning until dough looks full and rounded, smooth, satiny, and tightly stretched—about 8 to 10 minutes. Dough should no longer be sticky.

MARINATE: Let stand in liquid, for indicated time.

PREHEAT: Turn on oven; heat to desired baking temperature before putting in food. Preheat broiler 10 minutes, or as manufacturer directs.

344

PURÉE: Press through fine sieve or food mill.

SAUTÉ: Cook in small amount of hot fat or salad oil in skillet.

SCALD: Heat to just under boiling point (e.g., heat milk in top of double boiler over simmering water until tiny bubbles gather at sides).

SCALLOP: Bake in layers with sauce. If desired, top with crumbs.

SCORE: With knife, make shallow slits or gashes.

SEAR: Brown surface quickly over high heat, as in hot skillet.

SEASON: Add, or sprinkle with salt (or onion, celery, garlic, or seasoned salt), monosodium glutamate, or pepper to taste.

SIFT: Put dry ingredients through flour sifter or fine sieve.

SIMMER: Cook just below boiling point—about 185 degrees F. at sea level.

SLIVER: Cut or split into long, thin pieces.

STEEP: Let stand in hot liquid.

THICKEN: Measure liquid to be thickened. For each cupful, mix 1½ tablespoons flour with 3 tablespoons water until smooth; stir into hot liquid, cook until thickened.

UNMOLD: Moisten both chilled serving plate and surface of molded gelatin with wet fingers. Dip small pointed knife in warm water and use to loosen gelatin around edge of mold. Then quickly dip mold, just to rim, in warm water; remove and shake mold gently to loosen gelatin. Cover with inverted serving plate, then invert plate and mold together. Lift off mold carefully. Repeat, if necessary.

WHIP: Beat rapidly, usually with electric mixer or hand beater, to incorporate air and increase volume.

HELPFUL HINTS

* Candles placed in refrigerator or freezer 24 hours before using will burn slower and not drip as easily.

* Club soda is especially good for removing wine stains on carpet.

* A light film of mayonnaise will often remove a white ring on furniture.

* A vanilla bean in a pint of brandy makes an excellent vanilla extract and a nice gift.

* Centerpiece: instead of flowers use artichokes. Spread open to the "choke" and use as candleholder. Use group of three at dining room table, or one on a small table.

345

* To avoid the tedious task of cleaning brushes while painting, wrap brush in foil and freeze! When ready to begin again, it will defrost in a very short time. This way only one brush-cleaning session is necessary: at the end of the job.

* Add slice of lemon to dinner water; gives it a great taste.

* A small amount of nutmeg added to flour you dredge liver with makes it a delicious dish.

* To rid a room of smoke, put 4 teaspoons soda in 1 quart water in a windex bottle and spray around room.

* If you are having guests who smoke, place several lighted candles around the room. For some reason they help clear the air.

* Club soda is a marvelous rug cleaner. Apply to fresh spill (after boiling) or to old stain (even pet stains) liberally. Then blot with large towel.

* A small paint brush is great for dusting figurines, TV., stereo, and perfume bottles.

* When warming bread, place a damp tea towel over bread to keep it soft.

* After stewing a chicken, freeze stock in either ice cube trays or muffin tins. After it's frozen, remove to a freezer bag and you can defrost 1 or as many as needed for seasoning at a later date.

* To keep from "crying" while slicing onion, run onion under cold water as you slice.

* To remove salt from "too salty" soup, slice a raw potato, boil in soup, then remove.

* When you are out of powdered sugar and just need a little, put several tablespoons granulated sugar in blender and run on high speed for a minute.

* Save the styrofoam forms on which many meats are packaged in supermarkets. They make handy "plates" for candies, cookies and such to be given as gifts. Especially nice since the plate needn't be returned. Just cover goodies with plastic wrap and tie with a ribbon.

* A little amonia takes the sting out of insect bites.

* Mineral oil removes chewing gum from hair.

* Combine one part clorox to 5 to 7 parts water in empty detergent (plastic) bottles for easy cleaning of tubs or shower.

*To whiten synthetic knits: dissolve 1 cup dishwashing detergent in one gallon hot water. Add ¼ cup clorox. Let cool. Soak garment one hour or longer. Rinse as usual. Add one cup white vinegar to last rinse water.

* When cooking cabbage, break a stalk of celery and cook with it. Remove celery before serving. There will be no odor.

* To perk up droopy celery, put it in a glass of cold water with a slice of raw potato in the bottom. Refrigerate for several hours.

* Sour dressing (available in dairy cases of grocery stores) may be substituted for sour cream in cooking. This is a way to elegant, economical eating. This is also low in calories.

* To ripen an avocado, bury it overnight in corn meal.

* Ice ring for punch bowls: 10-12 cherries or strawberries, mint leaves, Mandarin orange sections, etc. (colors to complement color of punch). Place fruit in ring mold. Add a little water—just enough to cover. Freeze. Fill mold with water. Freeze. At serving time, run under water briefly to loosen from mold. Place in punch bowl.

* A ½ slice of bacon wrapped around a Waverly or Club cracker and baked in a 350 degree oven until crisp is a delicious hors d'oeuvre. Be sure to drain on a paper towel.

* If Perma press clothes are wrinkled when removed from dryer—put them back in with damp towel and turn on for 8-10 minutes. Wrinkles will be gone!

* To prevent discoloration when making jellies, preserves, or relishes, always use enameled or stainless steel cooking utensils.

* Potatoes soaked in salt water for 20 minutes before baking will bake more rapidly.

* For an eye-catching salad, dip edge of Lettuce leaf in paprika.

* To bring out flavor of fresh fruit ice creams, add the juice of one lemon to sweetened fruit.

* When stirring pudding or pie filling, to prevent sticking, use an egg-turner or spatula. It scraps a wider area than a spoon.

* Need a rack for a small or odd shaped pan—use ribs of celery or onion sliced about ½ inch thick under meats.

* In a hurry? Use coarse grater for boiled eggs, pickles, onions, etc. instead of chopping fine.

* To remove grease from soup, gumbo, or gravy, pass a piece of paper towel across the surface. Keep doing this until you have removed as much grease as you desire.

* If you are rushed for time, make your biscuit dough ahead of time and place in an airtight container and refrigerate until ready to roll out and cut and bake. Biscuit dough (in a ball) will keep two or three days in a covered container.

* Hair spray will take out ink stains.

* If you break your lettuce instead of cutting it for salad it will not turn brown on the edges.

* To make white clothes whiter, use dishwashing detergent—Cascade to wash with.

HELPFUL HINTS FOR CHILDREN

* To make play dough: 2 cups flour, 1 cup salt, 2 tablespoons cooking oil, 2 cups water, 4 teaspoons cream of tartar, food coloring if desired. Mix in pan, heat over medium heat until mixture leaves sides of pan. Store in plastic bag or covered container.

* Let children decorate old coffee cans with old flower catalogues for stuffing with brownies and cookies at Christmas.

* To make bubble stuff: measure ½ cup liquid dishwashing detergent and place in a quart jar or glass container; add 2 cups cold water in another cup and add to the detergent. Mix well with spoon or spatula. Add food color. Every so often pass utensil to mix well. More detergent may be added if desired. Makes 2½ cups—enough to keep 2 or 3 children busy.

* To make Creative Clay: Mix 1 cup cornstarch, 2 cups baking soda, 1¼ cups cold water and food coloring in a saucepan until well blended. Cook over medium heat for four minutes. Stir constantly until mixture thickens to moist mashed potato stage. Knead as you would dough. Keep in plastic bag.
Note: Small pieces children can create can be dried overnight. Larger pieces take longer. Poster paint may be substituted. Children can sculpt objects, make pencil holders, jewelry or ornaments. Dip in clear shellac after painting or spray with clear plastic. Clear nail polish may also be brushed on.

* To make Finger Paint: Mix 1½ cups laundry starch with a little cold water to form a creamy paste. Add 1 quart boiling water, cook until mixture becomes transparent. Add ½ cup Talcum (optional) for a smoother paint. Let mixture cool a bit. Stir in 1½ cups soap flakes. Let cool. Store in screw top jars. Add poster paint as needed.
Note: Oil cloth makes a good surface for finger painting. Can be washed and reused. Shelf lining also is excellent.

SUBSTITUTIONS AND EQUIVALENTS FOR GOOD COOKS

Even the best of cooks occasionally runs out of an ingredient she needs and is unable to stop what she is doing to go to the store. At times like those, sometimes another ingredient or combination of ingredients can be used. Here is a list of substitutions and equivalents that yield satisfactory results in most cases.

INGREDIENT CALLED FOR:	*SUBSTITUTION:*
1 C. self-rising flour	1 C. all-purpose flour plus 1 tsp. baking powder & ½ tsp. salt
1 C. cake flour	1 C. all-purpose flour minus 2 Tbsp.
1 tsp. baking powder	½ tsp. cream of tartar + ¼ tsp. soda
1 Tbsp. cornstarch	2 Tbsp. all-purpose flour
1 Tbsp. tapioca	1½ Tbsp. all-purpose flour
1 whole egg	2 egg yolks + 1 Tbsp. water
1 C. commercial sour cream	1 Tbsp. lemon juice + evaporated milk to equal 1 C.; or 3 Tbsp. butter + ⅞ C. sour milk
1 C. yogurt	1 C. buttermilk or sour cream
1 C. sour milk or buttermilk	1 Tbsp. vinegar or lemon juice + sweet milk to equal 1 C.
1 C. honey	1¼ C. sugar + ¼ C. liquid
1 oz. unsweetened chocolate	3 Tbsp. cocoa + 1 Tbsp. butter or margarine
1 clove gresh garlic	1 tsp. garlic salt or ⅛ tsp. garlic powder
1 tsp. onion powder	2 tsp. minced onion
1 Tbsp. fresh herbs	1 tsp. ground or crushed dry herbs
1 lb. fresh mushrooms	6 oz. canned mushrooms

To make 1 cup fine crumbs:
    24 saltine crackers
    4 slices bread
    14 squares graham crackers
    22 vanilla wafers

Can Sizes:
#2 vacuum = 1¼ cups or 12 ounces
#2 = 2½ cups or 20 ounces
#2½ = 3½ cups or 28 ounces
#3 cylinder = 5¼ cups or 36 ounces

INGREDIENT CALLED FOR:	EQUIVALENT:
1 lb. all-purpose flour	4 cups
1 lb. granulated sugar	2 cups
1 lb. powdered sugar	3½ cups
1 lb. brown sugar	2¼ cups firmly packed
1 C. uncooked long grain rice	3 to 4 cups cooked rice
1 C. (4 oz.) uncooked macaroni	2¼ cups cooked macaroni
4 oz. uncooked noodles	2 cups cooked noodles
7 oz. uncooked spaghetti	4 cups cooked spaghetti
1 C. soft breadcrumbs	2 slices fresh bread
1 C. egg whites	Whites of 6 or 7 lg. eggs
1 C. egg yolks	Yolks of 11 or 12 lg. eggs
1 C. whipping cream	2 cups whipped cream
1 C. shredded cheese	4 oz. cheese
1 lemon	2 to 4 Tbsp. lemon juice and 1 tsp. grated rind
1 orange	6 to 8 Tbsp. lemon juice and 1 Tbsp. grated rind
1 lb. shelled pecans or walnuts	4 cups chopped pecans or walnuts
1 stick butter	½ cup butter
¼ lb. nuts (shelled)	1 cup, chopped

CRUMBS:

Saltine Crackers 7 coarsely crumbled	1 cup
Graham Crackers 9 coarsely crumbled	1 cup
Small Vanilla Wafers 20 coarsely crumbled	1 cup
a pinch	as much as can be taken between tip of finger and thumb (usually ⅓ of ½ of a teaspoon)

EQUIVALENT CHART

3 tsp. = 1 Tbsp.	2 pt. = 1 qt.
2 Tbsp. = ⅛ C.	1 qt. = 4 c.
4 Tbsp. = ¼ C.	2 C. = 1 pt.
8 Tbsp. = ½ C.	2 C. sugar = 1 lb.
16 Tbsp. = 1 C.	⅝ C. = ½ C. + 2 Tbsp.
5 Tbsp. + 1 tsp. = ⅓ C.	⅞ C. = ¾ C. + 2 Tbsp.
12 Tbsp. = ¾ C.	3½ C. powdered sugar = 1 lb.
4 oz. = ½ C.	2⅔ C. brown sugar = 1 lb.
8 oz. = 1 C.	4 C. sifted flour = 1 lb.
16 oz. = 1 lb.	1 lb. butter = 2 C. or 4 sticks
1 oz. = 2 Tbsp. fat or liquid	A Few Grains = Less than ⅛ tsp.
2 C. fat = 1 lb.	Speck = Less than ⅛ tsp.

QUANTITIES TO
SERVE 100 PEOPLE

COFFEE	—3 lbs.
LOAF SUGAR	—3 lbs.
CREAM	—3 quarts
WHIPPING CREAM	—4 pts.
MILK	—6 gallons
FRUIT COCKTAIL	—2½ gallons
FRUIT JUICE	—4 #10 cans (26 lbs.)
TOMATO JUICE	—4 #10 cans (26 lbs.)
SOUP	—5 gallons
OYSTERS	—18 quarts
WEINERS	—25 lbs.
MEAT LOAF	—24 lbs.
HAM	—40 lbs.
BEEF	—40 lbs.
ROAST PORK	—40 lbs.
HAMBURGER	—30 to 36 lbs.
CHICKEN FOR CHICKEN PIE	—40 lbs.
POTATOES	—35 lbs.
SCALLOPED POTATOES	—5 gallons
VEGETABLES	—4 #10 cans (26 lbs.)
BAKED BEANS	—5 gallons
BEETS	—30 lbs.
CAULIFLOWER	—18 lbs.
CABBAGE FOR SLAW	—20 lbs.
CARROTS	—33 lbs.
BREAD	—10 loaves
ROLLS	—200
BUTTER	—3 lbs.
POTATO SALAD	—12 quarts
FRUIT SALAD	—20 quarts
VEGETABLE SALAD	—20 quarts
LETTUCE	—20 heads
SALAD DRESSING	—3 quarts
PIES	—18
CAKES	—8
ICE CREAM	—4 gallons
CHEESE	—3 lbs.
OLIVES	—1¾ lbs.
PICKLES	—2 quarts
NUTS	—3 lbs. sorted

To serve 50 people, divide by 2
To serve 25 people, divide by 4

INDEX

355

358

INDEX TO ADDENDUM

CHAUSSONS AU CHAMPIGNONS
(Mushrooms Pastries)

¼ cup butter (no substitute)
2 cups chopped fresh mushrooms
    (Southern gourmet—grown
    and packed in
    Folsom, Louisiana)
⅔ cup ground cooked ham

1 ½ tablespoons minced green
    onions
Salt and freshly ground pepper to
    taste
Nutmeg-Butter Pastry (See recipe
    below)

Heat butter and sauté mushrooms until golden. Remove from heat; stir in ham. Add green onions and seasonings until well mixed. Place heaping teaspoonful of the mixture into center of pastry circle. Fold over and pinch edges together firmly to seal. Place on lightly greased baking sheet; prick pastries with fork and bake at 425 degrees for about 12 minutes until golden brown. Serve warm. Yield: 6 servings or if you want to pass them at a party make them smaller (biscuit cutter size) and will serve approximately 32.

Nutmeg-Butter Pastry:
2 cups all-purpose flour
1 cup butter (soft)
¼ teaspoon salt

⅛ teaspoon ground nutmeg
¼ cup water (or less)

Put flour, butter, salt and nutmeg into large bowl. Cut in butter with pastry blender until mixture resembles small peas. Gradually add water until dough holds together. Roll out on floured surface to ⅛ inch thickness. Cut into 18 circles (about 5 inches in diameter). I use a biscuit cutter. This is very rich but good!

Mrs. John McIntosh (Melba)
West Carroll Parish (Pioneer)

CANDIED CARROTS

1 ½ pounds fresh carrots
1 tablespoon butter or margarine
½ cup orange marmalade

1 tablespoon lemon juice
⅛ teaspoon mace

Melt butter in large skillet. Stir in orange marmalade, lemon juice, and mace. Add boiled carrots and cook over low heat turning several times until carrots are glazed and heated.

Mrs. Thomas Scott
Lafourche Parish (Raceland)

LIME GELATIN SALAD

1 3-ounce package lime gelatin   1 cup boiling water
1 8-ounce package cream cheese

Blend the above and put in bowl. Place in freezer until chilled.

1 quart frozen prepared whipped   1 can crushed pineapple, drained
   topping   1 cup chopped pecans
1 can fruit cocktail, drained

Fold whipped topping into chilled gelatin mixture along with pineapple, fruit cocktail and nuts. Refrigerate overnigiht.

Mrs. Avert Guidry (Carolyn)
Vermilion Parish (Gueydan)

CRABMEAT CASSEROLE

1 cup chopped onions   2 tablespoons flour
½ cup chopped celery   1 pound crabmeat
¼ cup butter or margarine   Salt and pepper to taste
¼ cup evaporated milk   10 to 12 round buttery crackers

Melt butter, add onions and celery. Cook over low heat until transparent. Add 2 tablespoons flour and mix well. Add milk and seasonings, mix well. Add crabmeat. Pour into buttered dish. Crumble crackers over crabmeat. Bake at 350 degrees for 20 minutes.

Mrs. Thomas Scott
Lafourche Parish (Raceland)

CABBAGE AND GROUND MEAT CASSEROLE

1 pound ground beef
1 cup chopped onions
2 tablespoons cooked rice

1 small can tomato soup
1 small can water
2 cups raw cabbage

Brown onions and ground meat. Add 2 tablespoons cooked rice. Add can of tomato soup. Put this cooked mixture over the cabbage which has lined the bottom of a loaf pan. Prick holes and add the water. Bake at 350 degrees for 20 minutes.

Mrs. Thomas Scott
Lafourche Parish (Raceland)

CHEESEBURGER CASSEROLE

1 pound ground beef
½ stalk celery
½ small onion
¼ medium green pepper
½ teaspoon salt

¼ teaspoon pepper
1 8-ounce can tomato sauce
1 slice of cheese per person,
    cut into strips
1 biscuit per person

Cook meat in skillet until lightly browned, stirring constantly. Place in colander and drain well. Return to skillet and add remaining ingredients except cheese and biscuits. Cook the above mixture for 15 minutes. Pour meat mixture into greased casserole dish, top with cheese strips and cover with biscuits. Bake uncovered at 350 degrees for 20 minutes or until bottom of biscuits are cooked.

Alison Zaunbrecher
Vermilion Parish (Gueydan)

GERMAN FRUIT COFFEE CAKE

¾ cup soft margarine
2 cups sugar
4 eggs
1 teaspoon soda
1 cup buttermilk
3 cups flour
½ teaspoon allspice

½ teaspoon cinnamon
½ teaspoon nutmeg
1 10-ounce jar cherry preserves
1 10-ounce jar apricot preserves
1 10-ounce jar pineapple preserves
1 cup chopped pecans
½ teaspoon vanilla

Cream margarine and sugar. Add eggs and beat well. Mix soda with dry ingredients and add alternately with dry ingredients. Fold in preserves. Add pecans and vanilla. Bake in a greased and floured angel food or bundt pan at 325 degrees for 1½ hours. Cool 15 minutes before removing from pan. 10 to 12 servings.

Great for that special Christmas morning breakfast!

Mrs. John McIntosh (Melba)
West Carroll Parish (Pioneer)

ALMOND BUTTER COOKIE

1 cup butter (no substitute)
⅔ cup granulated sugar
2¼ cups all-purpose flour
1 cup coarsely ground blanched
  almonds
Pinch salt

¼ teaspoon vanilla
½ teaspoon almond extract
Blanched whole almonds or almond
  slices
Powdered sugar

Cream butter and granulated sugar thoroughly in large bowl of electric mixer. Blend in flour, ground almonds, salt and flavorings. Chill for about 2 hours. Form into balls about the size of a quarter, place about 2 inches apart on greased cookie sheet, press down with a fork (dipping fork in flour frequently to prevent sticking). Press first in one direction, then in the other to make a checkerboard effect. Insert an almond firmly on top of each cookie. Bake at 350 degrees for 12 to 15 minutes—only until lightly golden. Remove cookies and immediately sift powdered sugar lightly over tops. Freezes beautifully. Yield: about 5 dozen.

Mrs. John McIntosh (Melba)
West Carroll Parish (Pioneer)

COOKIE BOURBON ICE CREAM

30 chocolate sandwich cookies
(crumbled)
½ gallon vanilla ice cream
½ cup bourbon

Large container of frozen prepared
whipped topping, thawed
Chocolate syrup
½ cup chopped pecans

Put layer of cookies, layer of ice cream (to which bourbon has been added), and a layer of whipped topping. Repeat all layers and dribble syrup over top adding chopped pecans. Freeze. *This dessert can be kept for serving unexpected guests.*

Mrs. F. J. Falgoust (Joan)
West St. James Parish (St. James)

CHOCOLATE ICE CREAM

1 can condensed milk
1 large can evaporated milk
2 eggs

1 quart milk
1 small can chocolate syrup

Beat eggs slightly. Then add condensed milk and beat. Add evaporated milk, milk and chocolate syrup. Cook until it thickens. Cool and then freeze.

Mrs. Thomas Scott
Lafourche Paris (Raceland)

SOUR CREAM (No Cook) HOMEMADE ICE CREAM

2 cans condensed milk	1 quart homogenized milk
2 8-ounce cartons sour cream	1 teaspoon vanilla

Mix above ingredients and add fruit of your choice. Suggestions: 1 quart straw-berries—blended; 1 pint strawberries with 2 or 3 bananas; 4-6 fresh peaches; 1 quart fresh-blended figs; 1 quart fresh-blended blackberries. (Fresh fruit should be sweetened to taste—about ½ cup.) Canned fruit such as crushed pineapple can be used with juice and no sugar added. For chocolate ice cream, add 12 ounces of chocolate syrup.

Mrs. F. J. Falgoust (Joan)
West St. James Parish (St. James)

VANILLA ICE CREAM

3 eggs	3 cups cream
1 cup sugar	3 teaspoons vanilla
2 cups milk	½ teaspoon salt

Beat eggs well. Add sugar gradually. Then add milk. Cook in double boiler until thick. Cool. Add salt and vanilla. Then add the cream. Freeze.

Mrs. Thomas Scott
Lafourche Parish (Raceland)

LOU'S PECAN BARS

2 sticks margarine, melted
½ cup powdered sugar

Touch of salt
2 cups flour

Pat the above ingredients in pan and bake 20 minutes at 350 degrees.

4 eggs (beat with fork)
2 cups sugar
¼ cup white corn syrup

1 cup pecans
1 teaspoon vanilla

Pour on top of crust and bake for 25 minutes at 350 degrees.

Mrs. Avert Guidry (Carolyn)
Vermilion Parish (Gueydan)

CHESS PIE

1¼ cups sugar
6 tablespoons butter
6 egg yolks

3 tablespoons cream
1 teaspoon vanilla extract
9-inch unbaked pie shell

Cream sugar and butter. Add egg yolks, beaten to a lemon color. Stir in the cream and vanilla. Pour into the pie shell and bake at 350 degrees for 10 minutes, then at 275 degrees for about 45 minutes. Mix this pie by *hand* not with an electric mixer.

Mrs. John McIntosh (Melba)
West Carroll Parish (Pioneer)

CHOCOLATE ALMOND BAR PIE

5 small chocolate almond bars
½ cup homogenized milk
16 large marshmallows

1 8 or 9-inch prepared pie crust
½ pint whipping cream or 8 ounces
frozen prepared whipped topping

Heat chocolate bars, milk, and marshmallows, stirring until well mixed. Allow to cool in pie shell and add whipped cream or whipped topping and freeze. Serves 7-8.

Mrs. F. J. Falgoust (Joan)
West St. James Parish (St. James)

CHOCOLATE ALMOND PIE

1 8-ounce chocolate bar with
    almonds
⅓ to ½ cup brandy

1 16-ounce container frozen
    prepared whipped topping
2 9-inch prepared pie shells

Melt chocolate bar. Add brandy until about the consistency of mayonnaise. Cool slightly. Add whipped topping and mix thoroughly. Pour into baked pie shell and refrigerate. Freeze. if desired, one 10-inch pie shell can be used—this makes a high pie that serves 10. Each of the two 9-inch pies serves 6 to 8.

Note: Any favorite liqueur can be substituted for the brandy. Crème de menthe and kahlua are both excellent.

Mrs. Fernand Falgoust (Joan)
West St. James Parish (St. James)

MARINATED CATFISH

6 5-ounce catfish fillets
1/2 cup Italian salad dressing
2 tablespoons margarine, butter
   or cooking oil
1 teaspoon Creole or Cajun
   seasoning

1/2 teaspoon lemon pepper
1/4 teaspoon garlic powder
1/4 teaspoon onion powder

Place catfish in a shallow pan; pour enough salad dressing to cover fillets at least halfway. Cover and marinate in refrigerator for 2 to 3 hours, turning at least once.

Place fillets in heated skillet. Cover and reduce heat to 225°F. Cook for 30 to 45 minutes or until fish flakes easily with a fork. (OR: Coat a 12-inch skillet with margarine, butter or oil. Heat over medium-low heat. Place seasoned fillets in skillet. Cook, covered, about 15 minutes or until fish flakes easily with a fork.)

Mrs. Huey Priest (Libby)
Franklin Parish (Wisner)

CATFISH DIP

2 8-ounce packages cream cheese
1 8-ounce package cheese spread
1/2 cup sliced green onion tops
1/2 cup snipped parsley
1 tablespoon lemon juice
2 teaspoons Worcestershire sauce
1/8 teaspoon garlic powder
1/8 teaspoon ground red pepper

Dash paprika
1 pound catfish fillets, cooked
   and flaked
1 4 1/2-ounce can shrimp, drained
   and chopped
1 6-ounce can crabmeat, drained,
   flaked and cartilage removed
Fresh vegetable dippers

Combine cream cheese and cheese spread in a mixer bowl or food processor; mix well. Add green onion, parsley, lemon juice, Worcestershire sauce, garlic powder, red pepper and paprika; mix well. Stir in catfish, shrimp, and crabmeat. Serve chilled with desired crackers or dippers. Makes about 5 cups.

Mrs. Huey Priest (Libby)
Franklin Parish (Wisner)

HONG KONG GATOR

1 pound white (tail) alligator meat, cubed
1/2 cup cider vinegar
1 14-ounce can chunk pineapple
1 8-ounce can water chestnuts
2 8-ounce cans mandarin oranges
2 large sweet peppers, cut in 1-inch squares

2 large onions, sliced
1/4 cup brown sugar
Water as needed
Salt
White or ground red pepper
Hot, cooked rice

Mix meat with vinegar; set aside. Drain pineapple, water chestnuts, and oranges; add juices to meat mix. Marinate for 24-36 hours.

Place meat and marinade in heavy sauce pan and bring to a boil. Lower heat and add water chestnuts and onions. Cook for 20-45 minutes, or until meat is almost tender. Add sugar and all remaining ingredients; stir carefully with wooden spoon so as not to break up fruit. Cook for 5 to 8 minutes longer, watching that pepper doesn't get too soft and lose color. Season as desired with salt and pepper.

Serve over hot rice.

Chicken, pork, beef or shrimp may be substituted for alligator meat. Cooking time will vary with meat used.

This recipe was a Grand Champion Winner in the Gator Gourmet Cooking Contest held annually in conjunction with the International Alligator Festival in Franklin, Louisiana.

Mrs. Antoine Luke (Margie)
St. Mary Parish (Franklin)

RED EYE STEW

2 pounds boneless alligator meat
(4 pounds if on bone)
Water to cover meat
1 large carrot, scraped
1 large potato, peeled
1 bay leaf
1 tablespoon hot sauce
3/4 cup oil
3/4 cup flour
1 12-ounce can stewed tomatoes
2 large onions, chopped
3 ribs celery, chopped
1 sweet pepper, chopped
1 8-ounce can sliced mushrooms

1/2 cup sliced or chopped
black olives
3/4 cup green, stuffed or
salad-style olives
1 tablespoon salt
1 tablespoon hot sauce
1 cup sherry or good red wine
1 lemon, sliced and seeded
1/4-1/2 cup chopped green
onion tops
1 tablespoon dry or 1/4 cup
chopped, fresh parsley
Hot cooked rice; allow 1/2 to 3/4
cup per person

Place alligator meat in water with carrot, potato, bay leaf and hot sauce. Bring to boil; simmer for 30 to 40 minutes. Meanwhile make gravy.

Make a roux by cooking flour in oil until a little darker than caramel. Add tomatoes being careful as it will spatter. Stir and add onions, celery, bell pepper, mushrooms, olives, salt, pepper sauce and wine. Add enough water to make thin gravy.

Remove meat from water and add to gravy; discard water in which the meat was boiled. Get stew very hot, almost boiling, and reduce heat. Simmer for 2 to 3 hours, stirring often to prevent sticking. Use no cover or a very light cover so that gravy can cook down. Meat should be tender and gravy thickened to your liking.

Add lemon, green onion and parsley during last 20 minutes of cooking. Check seasoning; it should be just hot enough to bring tears to your eyes (that's where this stew got it's name!)

Serve over hot rice.

Beef, pork, chicken, fish or game may be used. Use pre-boiling for game meats only. Cooking time will vary with meat used.

This recipe was a First Place winner in the Gator Gourmet Cooking Contest held annually in conjunction with the International Alligator Festival in Franklin, Louisiana.

Mrs. Antoine Luke (Margie)
St. Mary Parish (Franklin)

PEACH HONEY CRISP

6 cups fresh sliced peaches
3/4 cup light honey
2 tablespoons cornstarch
1 (18 1/2-ounce) box yellow cake
   mix

3/4 cup margarine
Pecan pieces (optional)

In a medium size sauce pan, mix peaches, honey and cornstarch well and heat on stove until mixture thickens a bit. Pour peach mixture in a 9 x 13 baking pan, pour dry cake mix over peaches. Melt margarine and evenly spoon over cake mix. Top with chopped pecans if desired. Bake at 350 degrees for 50 to 60 minutes or until top is golden brown. Top with Cool whip or ice cream for an added treat. For planning ahead, after peach mixture has been heated on stove, cool mixture and put in container and freeze until needed. Peaches are preserved by honey and will not darken.

Mrs. Dolores A. Walker
Bossier Parish (Bossier City)

ORANGE GLAZED CARROTS (MICROWAVE)

1/2 cup orange juice
3 teaspoons butter or margarine,
   melted
1/4 teaspoon salt
2 teaspoons cornstarch
3 tablespoons honey

1/2 teaspoon grated lemon peel
   (optional)
Dash nutmeg
1 pound carrots, sliced 1/2 inch
   thick

In a two quart casserole, combine orange juice, honey, butter, lemon peel, salt and nutmeg. Stir in cornstarch; mix until well blended. Stir in carrots. Cover with lid. Cook in microwave at HIGH 7 to 8 1/2 minutes; stir once. To complete, stir, let stand covered 3 minutes before serving. Yield: 4 servings.

Mrs. Dolores A. Walker
Bossier Parish (Bossier City)

HAWAIIAN RABBIT

1 rabbit, deboned and cubed
2 tablespoons butter or margarine
1 medium onion, sliced
1/2 cup diced green pepper
3/4 cup pineapple juice
1/4 cup water
1/4 cup vinegar

1/4 cup brown sugar
3/4 teaspoon salt
1 can (1 lb., 4 oz.) pineapple
  chunks
1 tablespoon soy sauce
2 1/2 tablespoons cornstarch
1/4 cup water

Place diced rabbit in slow cooker. Add butter or margarine, onion, green pepper, pineapple juice, water, vinegar, brown sugar and salt. Cover and cook on low 5 to 7 hours. Turn control to high, add pineapple chunks, and soy sauce. Mix cornstarch with 1/4 cup water, add to cooker. Cook until thickened, stirring often.

Mrs. Jeanette Caughlin
Washington Parish (Mt. Hermon)

RABBIT DELIGHT

1 young rabbit, cut into serving
  pieces
2 tablespoons shortening
1 cup beef broth
1/4 cup lemon juice
3/4 cup orange juice

2 green peppers, chopped
1/2 cup mushrooms, chopped
1 tablespoon chopped parsley
1/8 teaspoon ginger
Salt and pepper

Brown pieces of rabbit in hot fat. Add all other ingredients. Cover and cook slowly until tender, 45 minutes to 1 hour, at 300°F.

Option: Thicken liquid in pan with 2 teaspoons cornstarch dissolved in 1/4 cup water and spoon over the rabbit for a glaze.

Mrs. Jeanette Caughlin
Washington Parish (Mt. Hermon)

WHITE BEANS AND SHRIMP

1 pound white beans
1 ham hock
1 large onion, chopped
1 clove garlic, chopped

1 rib celery, chopped
1 teaspoon sugar
Salt and pepper to taste

Wash beans. Put all ingredients in heavy pot. Cover with water and cook approximately 3 hours over low heat.

2 pounds medium shrimp, peeled
2 tablespoons creole seasoning

½ cup butter or margarine

Mix shrimp and creole seasoning. Melt butter in large black skillet. Add shrimp and sauté until done.

Spoon cooked beans over rice and top with shrimp for a unique but delicious dish.

Mrs. Ronald R. (Vivian) Anderson
Wife of Louisiana Farm Bureau President
East Feliciana (Ethel)

BAKED RED SNAPPER

1 large red snapper (5-7 pounds)
½ cup flour
Salt and pepper to taste
6 tablespoons butter
½ cup chopped onion
1½ cups chopped celery
¼ cup chopped green pepper
1 16-ounce can tomatoes
1 small can tomato sauce
2 tablespoons catsup

1 teaspoon chili powder
½ lemon, finely sliced
2 bay leaves
1 clove of garlic, minced
1 teaspoon salt
1 tablespoon sugar
1 tablespoon Worcestershire sauce
Dash of red pepper
Lemon slices—parsley

Dredge fish inside and out with flour, salt, and pepper. Place it in baking dish. Melt butter in saucepan. Sauté onion, celery, green pepper until tender. Mash the tomatoes and mix with tomato sauce, catsup, chili powder, lemon slices, bay leaves, garlic salt, sugar, red pepper, and Worcestershire sauce; add to sautéed ingredients. Pour the sauce over and around fish. Bake in 350 degree oven for about 45 minutes. Baste frequently with sauce. Garnish with parsley and lemon slices. Serves 6-8.

Mrs. Ronald R. Anderson (Vivian)
East Feliciana (Ethel)